Business Information
Desk Reference

Business Information Desk Reference

Where to Find Answers to Business Questions

Melvyn N. Freed, Ph.D.
Virgil P. Diodato, Ph.D.

David A. Rouse, M.L.S.
Contributor

Macmillan Publishing Company
NEW YORK

Collier Macmillan Canada
TORONTO

Maxwell Macmillan International
NEW YORK   OXFORD   SINGAPORE   SYDNEY

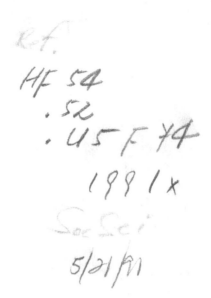

Macmillan Publishing Company
A Division of Macmillan, Inc.
866 Third Avenue, New York, N. Y. 10022

Collier Macmillan Canada, Inc.
1200 Eglinton Avenue East, Suite 200
Don Mills, Ontario M3C 3N1

Library of Congress Catalog Card Number: 90-38996

Printed in the United States of America

printing number
1 2 3 4 5 6 7 8 9 10

Library of Congress Cataloging in Publication Data

Freed, Melvyn N.
    Business information desk reference / Melvyn N. Freed, Virgil P.
Diodato ; David A. Rouse, contributor.
    p. cm.
Includes index.
ISBN 0-02-910651-6
1. Business—Information services—United States—Directories.
2. Information storage and retrieval systems—Business—Handbooks, manuals, etc. 3. Business—Databases—Databases—Directories. 4. Reference books—Business—Bibliograpy—Handbooks, manuals, etc. 5. Government publications—United States—Handbooks, manuals, etc. I. Diodato, Virgil P.
II. Rouse, David A. III. Title.
HF54.52.U5F74 1990
016.33—dc20   90-38996
                                                                                    CIP

Dedicated to the memory of
Arthur W. McHarris
gentleman, entrepreneur, friend

Contents

Foreword

In the ever-changing world of business the name of the game is problem solving, and whether the problem be one of crisis or opportunity, personal or strategic, there will always exist a need for accurate and timely information. It is here, in the information-gathering stage, that the quality and quantity of business solutions and outcomes will initially be decided!

The authors have written a new classic. *Business Information Desk Reference* will surely become *the* business source for information retrieval. This book will quickly find its way "up front" at the aspiring, self-employed, and corporate leadership levels . It contains information referral intended for everyone, anywhere, who is involved at any level in the practice or study of business. This includes the decision-maker and those impacted by the decision. Researchers, business students, and scholars will find it indispensable because of its content, format, and comprehensiveness.

Encompassed within *Business Information Desk Reference* are print materials (books, newspapers, magazines, directories, government documents, statistical digests, handbooks, loose-leaf materials, and others), online databases, federal agencies, and private organizations. It is a guide to approximately one thousand information sources. It highlights major features using a unique question-and-answer format; that is, each question focuses on a different feature of an information resource. This great detail makes the book valuable to the busy businessperson who is searching for answers to questions. The reader can quickly look up the question and learn where to find the answer. This is the encyclopedia of the twenty-first century.

Of course, all business publications could not be profiled in this first edition. As future editions are written, the authors plan to expand the coverage. If a reader cannot find his/her question, Section B offers the Mini-Guide to Printed Materials, which orients the researcher to the right *type* of information source (e.g., directories, newsletters, yearbooks). Other sections lead the reader to one or more specific titles. Almost five-hundred print sources and about four-hundred online databases are profiled. The remaining sources are federal agencies and private organizations.

The timing and publication of *Business Information Desk Reference* are both appropriate and appreciated. With the compounding demand and need for business information, the reader will now have at hand the encyclopedia of tomorrow, today!

Professor Daniel J. Yovich
Purdue University Calumet

Acknowledgments

The authors would be remiss if they did not recognize the valuable contribution that was made by others to this publishing endeavor. We express gratitude to our families—to Janet Freed and Louise Diodato, our respective wives, and to Edward Freed and David Freed. It was their sacrifices that made this book possible. A special note of appreciation is given to Patricia Higgins, Richard Wolff, Patricia Van Melle, and John Kelsey for their exceptional services as professional librarians. Acknowledgment is made of the valuable manuscript reading that was made by Dean Robert Milam, University of Wisconsin, Oshkosh, and Bernard Ostrowsky, stockbroker.

To our contributor, David A. Rouse, and to the author of the foreword, Daniel J. Yovich, we are indeed grateful. Their works add special significance to this book.

We also express our appreciation for the cooperation that was received from the various publishers who provided materials for our review. Their help greatly enhanced the comprehensiveness of this book. Finally, and not least, we publicly express our gratitude to Lloyd Chilton, Executive Editor, Reference Division, Macmillan Publishing Company, for his guidance, patience, and expertise.

M.N.F.
V.P.D.

INTRODUCTION

Here is the businessperson's guide to finding information needed to gain or maintain the competitive edge and for surviving in the world of corporate takeovers, insider trading, foreign competition, environmental controls, legal technicalities, and the myriad of other conditions with which the entrepreneur must contend. Shelves are full of reference and nonreference books that serve the business community; nevertheless, the typical businessperson is not familiar with many of their titles nor their contents. *Business Information Desk Reference* is a tool for directing the businessperson to one or more sources where answers may be found to questions in more than two dozen business areas. It is indispensable in the quest for information, especially for people whose time is limited and expensive.

Designed for experienced business professionals, beginners, and students, this is a ready-reference handbook for finding business information in printed materials, online databases, government agencies, and business organizations. It is not a traditional annotated bibliography. The number of information sources available is voluminous; consequently, a book of this nature is essential. It should be used as a beginning source for the research process.

Business Information Desk Reference presents commonly recognized titles along with lesser-known ones that may be of equal value in a given search. Due to the diversity of library collections and their varying degrees of completeness, the authors have often informed the reader of multiple titles to enhance the probability of finding the answer to the business question.

Power is knowing where and how to acquire information. Those who know are those who are prepared to act. Oftentimes the difference between winners and losers is simply possessing the strategic facts at the right time. With the advent of the information explosion, there is not only more information available but the sources for containing it have also increased. The research act has become more sophisticated and complicated. Section A offers guidelines for operating in the information environment. It provides suggestions on how to organize for the search process. Section B offers further assistance with this task.

Until now, it has been difficult to ascertain the specific and detailed contents of printed reference materials without actually examining them. For books, the researcher has had to consult the publication itself, unlike journal articles on a subject that can be identified by using one of the journal-indexing services, such as the *Business Periodicals Index*, or a parallel CD-ROM or online service. Knowing the title or general subject of a publication is insufficient because it does not disclose whether a specific item of information has been included. Subject card catalogs and annotated bibliographies are of limited value. *Business Information Desk Reference* seeks to alleviate this situation by disclosing significant features of the titles cited—through the series of questions and answers in Section C. Each question highlights an important feature of the information source. In many cases several sources with the same feature have been cited. For example:

WHERE SHOULD I GO TO FIND...	*TRY*
how to determine the amount of capital needed to start a business and sources for borrowing it?	*How to Organize and Operate A Small Business* [D-79] *How to Set Up Your Own Small Business* [D-290]

Supplementing this feature-question format is a brief description of each information source and the address and telephone number of the publisher.

A similar question-and-answer system has been used for online computer databases in Section E. As with books, the number of online databases is very large; consequently, the databases cited in Sections E and F should be considered a place to commence one's search. Both print and electronic data sources are important for one's research. Although there is much emphasis on the latter in this computer age, printed materials remain an important medium for storing and communicating business information. Even when there is an electronic version of a printed publication, the two are not always identical in content.

Finally, in Sections G and H, *Business Information Desk Reference* focuses on federal agencies and business and trade organizations. Important statistics and other information can be obtained from these agencies and organizations. The researcher of business information should not neglect contacting these agencies and organizations for up-to-date data or unpublished information. Brief profiles of these agencies and organizations have been included to assist with identifying the proper place to contact.

The citing of any single information source should not be interpreted as being an endorsement; a citation is intended only to direct the reader's attention to its existence and to the kind of information contained within it. Furthermore, the accuracy of the content of each title is the responsibility of the author(s) of that publication. Thus there is no expressed nor implied warranty as to the accuracy or completeness of any materials cited herein. Nevertheless, the authors of *Business Information Desk Reference* have endeavored to be diligent in the pursuit of their responsibilities as they worked with the publications of others.

The latest edition of each publication was profiled when conducting research for this book; however, due to the time required for the total process of researching, writing, and publishing, newer editions may have been released subsequent to the preparation of any single profile. This was beyond the authors' control.

With the understanding that timely information may be the key to the successful consummation of a business transaction, *Business Information Desk Reference* becomes an important instrument and "partner" in the business process. Whether the proper information sources are books, journals, newsletters, directories, newspapers, government documents, online databases, government agencies, or business organizations, the user of this book will find an entry point for examining these sources of business information. Knowing where to find information is the first step in acquiring it.

A

Guidelines for Finding and Evaluating Business Information

Asking the Right Question

Regardless of the quality of the information sources that are available or the professional assistance that awaits the researcher, the essential first step in a search for business information is knowing exactly what is needed. "Tell me something about Company X" is indefinite and defies a meaningful response. Specifically, what information is wanted? A precisely structured question—a definite goal—is required in order to commence a successful search.

The working question should be no broader than what is actually needed. A violation of this principle could, in the search of a computer database, result in identifying one thousand references of which only one or two may contain the facts that are being sought. When forming the question, consider the time-tested standards of what, where, when, and how?

An inquiry approached as "I'm interested in a career as a photographer" will utilize different resources than the question "I'm looking for advertising agencies that might have summer internships for student photographers." Know what you want and say what you mean! Productive research depends on clarity of purpose and clarity of communication.

A question may be stated too broadly or too narrowly. A request for a directory of all organizations in the United States when interest is in a small New York-based sports promotion agency may not produce fruitful results, or, if it does, the search process may be inefficient and take more time than was necessary. A question that is too narrowly defined may also cause one to overlook important information in a related area.

A too broadly phrased question will elicit much data of which a major portion probably will be irrelevant. Furthermore, this kind of inquiry often results in the fringe of the needed information, bypassing the "real meat." Decide on the proper breadth of the probe and then set the target. It is better to ask, "How

3

do the laws of Japan address the depreciation of capital assets?" than to ask "What are the tax laws of Japan?" Know whether the search is for information at the division level, company level, industry level, or at the national economy level. The specificity of the question will determine the information source to be used.

Finally, a question should be structured in a way that an answer will be possible if the data are available. At first this is not always feasible. As the literature is searched, sometimes the question must be refocused to fit the available data, unless one is in a position to conduct primary (original) research. For example, it may not be possible to find the consumption level of boxed chocolate candy by black residents of New York City or the percentage of women who shampoo while showering. A trade journal may be found that discusses the preferences for candy brands of various ethnic groups or a trade association may have information on the total sales of women's shampoos. It may not always be possible to find statistics in the exact form that is wanted, but a knowledge of multiple sources, as frequently disclosed in this book, will enhance one's opportunity for finding the information desired.

Where to Look: Those "Secret Places"

We live in the Information Age, where knowledge has become a strategic resource and information is a valued commodity. The explosion of information has been accompanied by a proliferation of the sources of information. The researcher must know how to select from among books, magazines, CD-ROMs, online databases, newspapers, directories, mass-communication media, and organization records (when available). The type of source determines what is being offered, its timeliness, and its relevance. Information does not exist in a vacuum; instead, it is defined by the source and oriented by time. It is dynamic and subject to change. This reality imposes the responsibility of knowing precisely what is wanted and where to obtain it.

The researcher of business and economic information is served by statistical abstracts, directories, yearbooks, handbooks, encyclopedias, newsletters, newspapers, government documents, statistical digests, computer databases, and other sources. Where should one begin? The initial focus of this text will be on printed materials, and computer databases will be discussed later.

To determine what kind of source to use, first decide if the search is for information about a person, a company, an industry, a region, the national economy, socioeconomic data, or a topic that transcends these categories, such as a legal issue. Second, what is the subject of the search? For example, if information is needed about a company, is it the address? types of products being manufactured? or name of the CEO? Third, is the search for a succinct fact or an in-depth description, analysis, or explanation? Answers to these questions will direct the researcher to the type of information source to be used.

If you are looking for a CEO's name and address, a company's products, or a brief profile of a corporation, a directory will be appropriate. If you need information on the performance of stocks, bonds, and commodities, a newspaper or a specialized investment report will suit your purpose. A search for national business and economic statistics may be satisfied by examining a statistical abstract, a decennial census document, or one of the specialized handbooks. A tax-related search could be conducted by using one of the recognized and respected loose-leaf tax guide services. Information about a person should start with a biographical dictionary (Who's Who). The important point is that the nature and extent of the targeted information will determine the type of material to be used. Be parsimonious! Overkill wastes time and yields data that will not be needed. Don't use an extensive treatise if a directory will provide the answer. By identifying the category (person, company, industry, or demography, for instance), subject, and amount of information needed, the search can commence on the most efficient track.

Overviews can be found in abstracts, digests, almanacs, yearbooks, directories, handbooks, encyclopedias, newspapers, and journals. In-depth treatment will be found in special reports, books devoted to a selected topic, and sometimes in government documents. The completeness of coverage depends on the purpose of the individual publication.

Recognizing the geographical parameters of the information being sought will help with identifying the proper source. Many cities have directories, and there are state yearbooks, regional directories, national statistical abstracts, and intergovernmental statistical digests. Sometimes a geographic-specific source will contain more detailed data.

When targeting a specific industry, it may be beneficial to use industry-specific trade journals, newspapers, and newsletters. These types of sources often contain more detailed and diversified information on an industry than more general sources. Trade publications sometimes may be the only source for certain industry information.

Indexes are indispensable tools for quickly locating information in journals and magazines. Simply look up the subject in one of the periodical indexes and you will be introduced to those articles that have been published on it, identifying the title of the journal, volume number, date, and page. Each indexing service usually covers several hundred journals and magazines. Some indexing services utilize both print and computer media.

When selecting an information source, be aware of its operating features. For example, know its publication schedule. Don't turn to a weekly newspaper for current daily stock quotations. Don't seek a publication that ceased publication years ago unless historical data are wanted. Don't pursue objective data from a lobbying group's publication. Know what you are working with. Be familiar with alternative sources of information so that you will not be stymied if a library does not subscribe to your first choice.

A major center of information is the library; however, there are different kinds of libraries, each distinguished by a purpose that prescribes the nature of its collection and the extent of its services. General community libraries serve the particular interests and needs of their communities. Some communities are large, with complex and diversified business and industrial economies. Libraries in these areas probably will collect publications that reflect and relate to these economies. Some communities are small, rural, and do not have extensive professional services. Their libraries will have a different orientation and collection.

Research libraries, such as those at major universities, offer materials that support the areas of academic pursuit that have been embraced by the institution with which they are affiliated. Located here are many primary source documents, professional journals, and unpublished papers. Research libraries have specialized collections.

Important to the business researcher are the specialized libraries. These libraries may concentrate on tax matters, accounting, insurance, labor relations, economics, or any of numerous other subjects. Many are housed in private corporations (such as insurance companies or public accounting firms), associations, or they may be independent organizations. This type of library is important because of the in-depth approach to its chosen field.

State libraries are important for documents endemic to a particular state, and for locating elusive and highly specialized statistics for that state. Economic statistics for a given region within a state may be found in this type of library.

Many public and private libraries have been designated "Federal Depository Libraries," which means they have an agreement with the U.S. Superintendent of Documents to receive and collect U.S. government publications issued in selected fields. Each library is free to decide if it wants to participate in this program and, if it does, for which fields it will accept government documents. Thus information published by a federal department or agency may be found in the appropriate Federal Depository Library. A library is not simply "a library." The businessperson needing information should identify the proper library for his/her purpose. The reference librarian at a library should be able to assist with this task.

Computer databases have become an important data source. Sections E and F address online databases; however, introductory information will be given here.

Today's emphasis on computers may make it seem that this is the only reliable and valid source of information. A more balanced view is that this modern technology has contributed an important new dimension to data storage and retrieval and that it is one of the research tools that can be used, depending on the research situation. Online searching can save time and legwork; it is also advantageous in situations such as when (1) searching for a new word, phrase, or concept (e.g., "just-in-time inventory systems" and "greenmail"); (2) the researcher has an incomplete citation, such as only a title or author's last name; (3) up-to-the-minute information is required; (4) there is an investigation of obscure or unfamiliar topics, such as long-tailed insurance companies; (5) the search is for very specific information, such as the number of shopping cart injuries or the effect of the Tylenol poisoning incident on candy sales; or (6) one chooses to use combinations of criteria, such as unions, productivity, public sector, and marketing, to select the targeted information.

There are times when online searching is not the most efficient approach. These include instances when (1) how-to information is desired, which may more directly and comprehensively be provided by books, associations, or government documents; (2) a highly specialized list is required, the cost of which is prohibitive; (3) the hard copy equivalent is readily available; (4) there is doubt that the descriptors that must be used for the search will be able to distinguish clearly and call up what is needed (e.g., a search concerning the use of computers in marketing may produce information on the marketing of computers instead of their use in the marketing process, or a search on towing icebergs to utilize the water to create energy may produce articles on the energy costs of raising iceberg lettuce); and (5) the inquiry is nebulous, such as "What is the best company to work for?" Be careful when using high tech! It has its place. Know how to get the most benefit from it.

In conclusion, sources of information are varied. To maximize the benefits of each requires an understanding of its special purpose, limitations, and unique characteristics. When these sources are considered in combination, the researcher will have a greater chance of securing the information that he/she needs.

Evaluating Information: Traps to Avoid

In research, getting is not always having. There are many possible pitfalls when searching for business facts. One may not always fully know what is in hand, as illustrated above. This risk applies to all data sources.

The business researcher should establish the authenticity of the information and its accuracy. There should be no assumed cloak of acceptability simply because the data appeared in published form. Accept only after verifying. Know the reliability and validity of what you have.

The validity of a source of information depends on the purpose for which it was written and the purpose for which it is being sought. Compatibility of these goals is essential. When working with an information source, look for a statement of its purpose, and check who wrote it and who was the publisher. Try to establish the qualifications of the author. If bias was the writer's motivation, this will skew the direction of the work. Information about medical malpractice may vary depending on whether it comes from the American Medical Association, the American Bar Association, the Insurance Information Institute, or a consumer advocacy group. It is helpful to read the preface and introduction and to look over the footnotes. These may explain what criteria, operating definitions, and analytical methods were used for selecting the data that appear in the publication. Such knowledge will divulge the prejudice that may exist and allow the reader to decide if the reported data are acceptable for his/her purpose.

The inconsistency between reports on a given topic frequently may be attributed to different operating criteria and definitions. Statistical reports from a company, a trade association, a regulatory agency, or a consumer advocacy group may involve different criteria, different operating definitions, and different analytical methods.

Be aware of the publication date. If data for 1990 are wanted yet the publication was written in 1989, obviously a different source should be consulted. Recognize that some publications require several years to compile and publish; consequently, the information may not be the most current. Finally, the date of publication does not always reflect the date of various bits and pieces of information contained within the publication. Much demographic data are derived from the decennial census; however, the publication of these raw data usually takes several years. Comparative international data are often out of date.

Does the publication provide periodic supplementary updating? When working with statistical data, the factor of time is critical.

Statistical data per se are not absolutely pure and objective. Again, the criteria for selecting and analyzing statistics "colors" the outcome. How were the data collected? Was the sample random and representative? What was its size? Was the proper analytical procedure and tool used with the data? Were differences between groups due to chance, bias, or meaningful cause?

When reading statistical reports on the same subject in different publications, the reader should be sensitive to subtle and important variations. Are the data for individual companies or for the industry? Are the data in one report representative of companies of a certain size (how defined?) while in another publication another size has been used? Does a table headed "Percent of Teenagers in the Workforce" indicate how much of the workforce is composed of teenagers, or does it report what percentage of teenagers are currently employed?

Be knowledgeable of the nature of the data with which you are working. Given the Consumer Price Index for Chicago and New York, it would seem that one could compare differences between how much it costs to live in these two cities. Understand that this index measures increases in cost, not *actual* costs; consequently, it cannot be used to compare cities except on the rate of inflation. Know the meaning of your statistical data and the proper use of it!

Some business and economic research reports will arrive at conclusions regarding cause and effect. This is an area that requires another caveat for the business researcher. There are numerous potential traps for errors in logic. Be alert to the writer whose conclusions go beyond the findings that have been supported by the data. If an economic phenomenon exists in one region and the sample was representative of only that region, the conclusions cannot properly be extended to the nation. Furthermore, the concurrence of two events does not by itself indicate which event was the cause and which was the effect. Other evidence is required to determine the role of each event.

Economic life is complex. There are many interacting forces at work. This reality makes it essential to recognize that multiple causes may underlie an event. Be cautious of oversimplified explanations and a willingness on the part of writers to accept readily available simple answers. The simple answer may be an incomplete one, or sweeping generalizations can masquerade for the real cause or answer.

The foregoing are some of the guidelines to follow when searching the literature for business and economic information. Adherence to them will minimize errors and, perhaps, expensive unwanted consequences. In summary, caveats for the business researcher include being aware of

- the purpose of the report
- operating criteria and definitions
- bias
- the time frame of statistical data
- the author's qualifications
- the publisher and/or sponsor of the study

- procedural errors in the collection and analysis of the data
- oversimplification and generalization of conclusions
- findings that are not supported by the data
- faulty reasoning concerning cause and effect

Avoid these traps and you will be better prepared for your next business meeting and that Big Deal!

Portions of this section were derived from David Rouse, "Is This Search Necessary? On-Line Data Bases, Reference Sources, and Referrals," *The Reference Librarian*, no. 21 (1988): 45–56. Published by and with permission of The Haworth Press, Inc., 10 Alice Street, Binghamton, NY 13904.

B

Linking the Research Question to the Business Information Source: The Mini-Guide to Printed Materials

One of the initial questions that business researchers often ask is, "What type of material should I examine to find my answer?" There are many different types of printed sources, and the one to be used depends on the nature of the research question. One must know in what direction to go before a specific publication can be identified. If the right type of publication is a journal, then one of the indexing services should be targeted first. If it is a directory, then a different approach is required. This section focuses on printed materials; however, the reader also should be aware of information sources in other media. (See Sections E, F, G, and H.)

Section B functions as a coordinator for the many different kinds of printed sources of information. It is a complement to Sections C and D, because these two sections direct the reader to specific titles whereas Section B guides the reader to types of research materials. It builds on the guidelines that are found in Section A. The Mini-Guide is useful when your business question cannot be found in Section C and a different approach is needed to find the information.

Generally there are common characteristics of format and content among materials of a specific type, but differences do exist. Even so, the authors offer the following broad-stroke guidance to business-information sources. The Mini-Guide is a tool that will help decide where to start, and thus shorten the distance and time to your answer. Begin by locating the appropriate category for your business question in Column 1, and then proceed to Column 2 for the suggested types of printed material that you should consult.

THE MINI-GUIDE

See Sections C and D for specific titles.

QUESTIONS CONCERNING...	*TYPES OF PRINTED SOURCES*
the identification and location of articles or reports on a selected subject that appear in journals; magazines; publications of federal/state government agencies, private organizations, international groups, and trade organizations; and in newspapers.	indexes
the summary of an article.	abstracting publications
identification of books, periodicals, directories, loose-leaf materials, government documents, online data sources, audio-visual materials, special research reports, or statistics sources.	bibliographies
identifying the names and descriptive information about newsletters and newspapers.	special directories concerning newsletters and newspapers
names, addresses, and telephone numbers of associations and organizations.	a directory that specializes on these kinds of groups
the names, addresses, and telephone numbers of banks and thrift institutions.	a banker's directory or one of the S&L directories
a company's name, address, telephone number, parent or subsidiary companies, and other brief descriptive information.	one of the business directories
names, addresses, and telephone numbers of consultants.	a specialized directory of consultants
the names, addresses, and telephone numbers of news-media organizations in a region.	specialized directories for television, radio, newspapers, and magazines
names, addresses, and telephone/telex/fax/cable numbers of foreign government officials.	directories published by governments or independent publishers

QUESTIONS CONCERNING...	*TYPES OF PRINTED SOURCES*
names, addresses, and telephone numbers of U.S. and state government officials.	U.S. and state government directories
listings and descriptions of federal and state departments and agencies, including addresses and telephone numbers.	specialized directories from government and private publishers
finding either a fax or a toll-free ("800") number.	a fax or "800" directory or a business directory
the meaning of terms and phrases unique to a field.	a specialized dictionary for the field
the identification or meaning of an abbreviation, acronym, or initial.	a general dictionary or one of the acronym and abbreviation dictionaries
biographical profiles of leaders of commerce and industry.	biographical dictionaries (Who's Who)
where to find a published biography.	a biographical index
a compendium of information on a field or industry.	a handbook on the field or industry
statistical data and norms for an industry.	indexes, abstracts, handbooks, statistical digests, almanacs, yearbooks, census reports, and trade-association reports
developments, trends, and news events about an industry.	trade journals, newsletters, trade-association reports, magazines, and newspapers
a description, summary, or evaluation of a year's activities or conditions in a country, industry, economy, or other sector.	an almanac, yearbook, or statistical digest
annual update of information in a reference source.	a yearbook or a revised edition of the publication
national and regional business and industry developments, company news, corporate personnel changes, investment news, legislative actions, administrative decisions, and judicial rulings concerning the business community.	national and metropolitan newspapers and business magazines. (Note: For other types of sources for separate information items in this list, see Section C.)

QUESTIONS CONCERNING...	*TYPES OF PRINTED SOURCES*
current and historical economic statistics regarding the national economy and individual industries.	U.S. government documents and nongovernment statistical digests
descriptive data for the U.S. population and major industry groups, including the retail trade, wholesale trade, service industry, and construction industry.	almanacs, yearbooks, statistical digests, and U.S. government documents
statistical and other descriptive information on stocks, bonds, and other investments.	handbooks, digests, specialized encyclopedias, newspapers, and newsletters
formulas for business operations, financial transactions, and investments.	handbooks, encyclopedias, and other books on this subject
principles and methodologies followed in business and economic forecasting.	handbooks, journals, and other books on this subject
providers of special services in an industry.	an industry directory
suppliers of products.	a general or special industry directory and trade journals
venture capital sources.	directories of venture capitalists
advertising rates and terms for newspapers, magazines, radio, television, and other media.	special advertising directories
marketing data.	specialized advertising directories, statistical digests, U.S. government documents, trade journals, and special reports and reference publications
a brief overview of a subject.	a general or specialized encyclopedia or a handbook
a collection of articles on a subject that express the opinions and views of experts in a field.	a topical book that is a collection of readings, sometimes titled a "handbook"
a summary of federal tax regulations and rules.	tax handbooks and government documents

QUESTIONS CONCERNING...	*TYPES OF PRINTED SOURCES*
recent developments in federal and/or state laws, regulations, and decisions concerning matters of taxes, labor, securities, and insurance.	loose-leaf services, government documents, metropolitan newspapers, and journals
updates of the laws and regulations governing business transactions in foreign nations.	loose-leaf services and industry trade journals and newspapers
U.S. patent and trademark classifications, regulations, procedures, and fees.	U.S. Patent and Trademark Office publications and topical books by private authors
an overview of occupational information.	specialized encyclopedias, occupational handbooks and dictionaries, and U.S. government documents

C

Where Should I Go to Find Information in Printed Sources?

Printed materials remain a valuable source of information even in this computer age. This section addresses books, journals, newsletters, and other sources of information that appear in print form. The purpose is to provide a master guide (not a master index) to the contents of those items that appear herein.

Referenced in this section are both popular publications and some that, although not widely known, offer valuable assistance in the pursuit of answers to business questions. To facilitate finding information contained within these sources, a question-and-answer approach has been used in which various principal features of available printed material have been identified by use of a separate question to highlight each feature. At the top of the left column of each page is the stem, "Where Should I Go to Find...," of the succeeding questions, each of which describes a specific feature. The right column, labeled "Try," provides some of the titles that contain the information prompted by the feature-question. This format enables the reader to learn about the contents of these publications, and consequently know where to find the information. Several feature-questions may describe a single source.

The feature-questions have been classified, first, under broad subject areas and, second, under more specific topics. To assist the reader, the feature-questions oftentimes have been placed in more than one category; that is, the question appears wherever the researcher may logically search. This approach will enhance one's ability to locate the information source vis-à-vis the traditional single-entry classification.

The authors recognize that no library can shelve every publication in the field of business; for this reason, multiple titles have often been cited in the event that any single one is not available to the researcher. Furthermore, since similar publications still have their individual uniqueness, the listing of several titles expands one's choices and resources.

Following each title in Section C is a bracketed item entry number. This will aid the reader in locating the title in Section D, where an expanded description will be found. This includes the full bibliographic citation and a more comprehensive description of the contents. The reader can find the name of the publisher in Section D and then, if necessary, refer to Appendix II for the publisher's address and telephone number.

The item entry number has several components; namely, the section letter and the title number. Thus D-1 means Section D, title number 1. Following is a sample feature-question.

SAMPLE

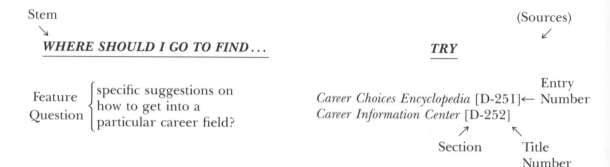

Stem

(Sources)

WHERE SHOULD I GO TO FIND . . .

TRY

Entry
Feature
Question
specific suggestions on
how to get into a
particular career field?
Career Choices Encyclopedia [D-251]← Number
Career Information Center [D-252]

Section   Title
Number

When using Section C, the reader should first select the proper general category and then proceed to the subcategory. Due to the varied approaches that different authors have taken to common topics, it was necessary to craft carefully the feature-questions. Often several feature-questions may appear to be repetitive; upon closer examination, however, important technical differences will be discovered. For the most efficient approach to using Section C, the authors suggest reading all questions related to the subject being researched as a cluster. This will broaden the scope of the inquiry and introduce more possibilities for finding the answer.

Some of the referenced works contain a diversity of facts and, occasionally, there are multiple publications with the same purpose. Although they have a common objective, they usually have subtle differences. If several titles have been listed in response to a feature-question, it is possible that each title may provide different components of the answer. One or more may offer the complete response, while others contain a partial response. All of the titles, either alone or together, will give the full information. This approach permits the reader to identify more materials, even if some are limited.

The feature-questions usually lead the reader to a source that contains the information being sought; other sources, however, provide a selection of titles in which the information can be found. In the latter case the reader is introduced to a variety of information sources.

Trade publications are an important source of industry data. Examples include *Coal Age, Progressive Grocer, Chilton's Iron Age*, and *Advertising Age*. Although space did not permit profiling these many titles, the reader is urged not to overlook the trade journals and trade newspapers, which contain a wealth of industry-related information.

Printed Sources of Information

<u>*WHERE SHOULD I GO TO FIND...*</u>   *TRY*

Accounting/Financial Analysis

Note: For information on taxation, see
also "Taxation" subsection.

Accounting and Auditing Firms

a directory of accounting and auditing   *Consultants and Consulting Organizations*
firms indicating the types of services   *Directory* [D-150]
offered, industries served, contact   *Corporate Finance Sourcebook* [D-153]
person, telephone number, and other
relevant information?

Accounting and Auditing: International

the accounting and auditing   *World Accounting* [D-437] See also the
regulations, standards, and practices   "*Doing Business in ...*" series cited under
of Australia, Belgium, Brazil,   "Business Laws and Practices of Foreign
Canada, France, India, Italy, Japan,   Nations."
Mexico, Philippines, Saudi Arabia,
South Korea, United Kingdom,
United States, and West Germany?

the accounting standards of the   *AICPA Professional Standards* [D-371]
International Accounting Standards   *World Accounting* [D-437]
Committee and the auditing guidelines
of the International Auditing Practices
Committee?

Accounting and Auditing Standards, Guidelines, and Practices

an overview of accounting principles and   *Accountant's Desk Handbook* [D-237]
practices for persons planning to start a   *A Guide for the Foreign Investor* [D-75]
new business?

a ready-reference summary of accounting   *Accountant's Desk Handbook* [D-237]
principles, standards, tax laws, and   *Accounting Desk Book* [D-239]
regulations for the professional
accountant?

<u>*WHERE SHOULD I GO TO FIND...*</u>   <u>*TRY*</u>

Accounting and Auditing Standards, Guidelines, and Practices

an explanation of depreciation rules that are prescribed by ACRS, MACRS, ADR, and the Class Life ADR System?	*Depreciation Guide* [D-260]
an explanation of accounting principles that apply to the management of contracts with the federal government?	*Accounting Guide for Government Contracts* [D-48]
a restatement and explanation of the Generally Accepted Accounting Principles (GAAP)?	*Applying GAAP and GAAS* [D-374] *Miller Comprehensive GAAP Guide* [D-298]
U.S. Auditing Standards, Attestation Standards, International Accounting Standards, and International Auditing Guidelines?	*AICPA Professional Standards* [D-371]
the original accounting standards as set forth by the Financial Accounting Standards Board (FASB)?	*Accounting Standards: Original Pronouncements* [D-240]
a comprehensive practitioner's handbook that addresses the technical operations of an accountant's office?	*AICPA Audit and Accounting Manual* [D-241]
disclosure checklists used in accounting and auditing procedures?	*AICPA Audit and Accounting Manual* [D-241]
guidelines for designing an audit program?	*AICPA Audit and Accounting Manual* [D-241]
illustrative financial statements and working papers used by accountants?	*AICPA Audit and Accounting Manual* [D-241]
a compilation of advice given by the AICPA on technical accounting and auditing matters as requested from accountants in the field?	*AICPA Technical Practice Aids* [D-372]
position statements of the AICPA on accounting and auditing issues?	*AICPA Technical Practice Aids* [D-372]

<u>*WHERE SHOULD I GO TO FIND...*</u>   <u>*TRY*</u>

Accounting and Auditing Standards, Guidelines, and Practices

a restatement and explanation of the
Generally Accepted Auditing Standards
(GAAS)?

Applying GAAP and GAAS [D-374]
Miller Comprehensive GAAS Guide [D-299]

an outline of the steps and procedures to
be followed when conducting an audit?

Miller Comprehensive GAAS Guide [D-299]

the accounting standards of
the International Accounting
Standards Committee and the
auditing guidelines of the International Auditing Practices
Committee?

AICPA Professional Standards [D-371]
World Accounting [D-437]

an explanation of financial accounting
standards that apply to intellectual
property?

Accounting Desk Book [D-239]

Accounting Profession

AICPA's "Code of Professional Ethics"
and "Bylaws"?

AICPA Professional Standards [D-371]

examples of managerial job descriptions
in accounting?

Encyclopedia of Managerial Job Descriptions
[D-403]

Computers and Software: Accounting

how to evaluate and select
microcomputer accounting software
for use in small and medium-size
businesses?

Selecting Business Software [D-99]

descriptive profiles of microcomputer
software packages that perform
accounting functions?

Datapro Directory of Microcomputer Software
[D-387]
Data Sources: Software [D-158]

descriptive and evaluative reviews
of microcomputer spreadsheets
that can be used for financial
planning?

Datapro Reports on Microcomputers [D-391]

guidelines for selecting microcomputer
software for use in accounting?

*Datapro Management of Microcomputer
Systems* [D-388]

WHERE SHOULD I GO TO FIND . . .	*TRY*

Financial Tables

financial tables that are useful to accountants?	*Accountant's Handbook of Formulas and Tables* [D-238] *Accounting Desk Book* [D-239] *Thorndike Encyclopedia of Banking and Financial Tables* [D-326]

Forecasting

how to make financial projections?	*Business Forecasting: Concepts and Microcomputer Applications* [D-52] *Business Plans That Win $$$* [D-53] *Foundations of Financial Management* [D-273] *Handbook of Forecasting* [D-281] *How to Create a Winning Business Plan* [D-411] *Manager's Guide to Business Forecasting* [D-88] *Techniques of Financial Analysis* [D-324]
how microcomputers can be used for financial forecasting?	*Manager's Guide to Business Forecasting* [D-88]
an explanation of techniques used to perform business forecasting and programs written in BASIC for this purpose?	*Business Forecasting: Concepts and Microcomputer Applications* [D-52]
how to evaluate forecasting models and determine the right one to use?	*Manager's Guide to Business Forecasting* [D-88]

Forms and Records

a sample of accounting forms used to organize financial information?	*AMA Handbook of Key Management Forms* [D-373] *Business Forms on File* [D-376] *Ten-Second Business Forms* [D-325]
what records should be set up when establishing a small business?	*How to Set Up Your Own Small Business* [D-290]
a questionnaire that can be used to collect information about a client's system of internal accounting control?	*Miller Comprehensive GAAS Guide* [D-299]

| *WHERE SHOULD I GO TO FIND...* | *TRY* |

Forms and Records

a list of financial information that a small-business manager should maintain?

The Entrepreneur and Small Business Problem Solver [D-269]

a checklist for performing a profit analysis to determine if a profit is being made, and if it is, how much?

The Entrepreneur and Small Business Problem Solver [D-269]

an explanation of the business reporting forms required by the Securities and Exchange Commission?

Accounting Desk Book [D-239]

Government Accounting

an explanation of the principles of municipal accounting and financial reporting?

Accountant's Desk Handbook [D-237]
Accounting Desk Book [D-239]
Municipal Bond Handbook, Vol. 2 [D-306]

a restatement and explanation of the Generally Accepted Accounting Principles for local and state governments (Gvt-GAAP)?

Miller Comprehensive Governmental GAAP Guide [D-300]

cost accounting standards, regulations, techniques, and practices that are followed by the federal government in its relationship with its contractors?

Accounting for Government Contracts [D-370]

Industry Profiles

values of financial and operating ratios by industry?

Almanac of Business and Industrial Financial Ratios [D-20]
American Statistics Index (A guide to U.S. government publications with ratios.) [D-1]
Analyst's Handbook [D-243]
Census of Construction Industries [D-337]
Census of Manufactures [D-338]
Census of Retail Trade [D-340]
Census of Service Industries [D-341]
Census of Wholesale Trade [D-342]
Dow Jones-Irwin Business and Investment Almanac [D-24]
Industry Norms and Key Business Ratios [D-26]

(answer continues)

Industry Profiles

values of financial and operating ratios by industry?	*RMA Annual Statement Studies* [D-27] *Standard & Poor's Industry Surveys* [D-472]
industry norms for each item in a financial statement expressed as a percentage of the aggregate total?	*Industry Norms and Key Business Ratios* [D-26]
aggregate data, by industry, for income account and balance-sheet items?	*Analyst's Handbook* [D-243]
a current and historical analysis of an industry's assets, liabilities, and income data classified according to the size of assets held by firms in that industry?	*RMA Annual Statement Studies* [D-27]
a bibliography of publications that report composite financial data, including financial and operating ratios, for specific industries?	*RMA Annual Statement Studies* [D-27]
reports of interviews with leading CEOs and money managers on financial matters about their industries?	*Wall Street Transcript* [D-458]
a performance analysis of specific industries and major companies within these industries?	*Standard & Poor's Industry Surveys* [D-472]
for each industry, average values per share for each of 13 performance criteria (e.g., profits, earnings, dividends)?	*Analyst's Handbook* [D-243]

New Businesses

how to determine the capital needed to start a business?	*How to Organize and Operate a Small Business* [D-79] *How to Set Up Your Own Small Business* [D-290]
what records should be set up when establishing a small business?	*How to Set Up Your Own Small Business* [D-290]
a list of financial information that a small business manager should maintain?	*The Entrepreneur and Small Business Problem Solver* [D-269]

WHERE SHOULD I GO TO FIND...   *TRY*

Newsletters

a directory of newsletters on accounting
with a nonevaluative description of each?

Newsletters in Print [D-41]
Oxbridge Directory of Newsletters [D-42]

Not-for-Profit Organizations

guidelines and principles for budgeting
and cost analysis in not-for-profit
organizations?

Budgeting for Not-for-Profit Organizations
[D-249]

financial ratios used for hospitals and
other health-care organizations?

Accountant's Desk Handbook [D-237]

Techniques, Formulas, Ratios

how to analyze business financial
statements?

Accounting Desk Book [D-239]
*Dow Jones-Irwin Business and Investment
Almanac* [D-24]
Financial Analyst's Handbook [D-271]
Financial Statement Analysis [D-272]
How to Create a Winning Business Plan
[D-411]
*How to Organize and Operate a Small
Business* [D-79]
Techniques of Financial Analysis [D-324]
Understanding Wall Street [D-327]

a compendium of practical guidance
for solving managerial and cost
accounting problems of private
enterprise, government, and
not-for-profit organiza-
tions?

Managerial and Cost Accountant's Handbook
[D-295]

a listing and explanation of mathematical
formulas used in accounting?

*Accountant's Handbook of Formulas and
Tables* [D-238]
Handbook of Business Formulas and Controls
[D-278]

formulas for financial and operating
ratios that are used for the analysis of
businesses, with an explanation of each
ratio?

*Accountant's Handbook of Formulas and
Tables* [D-238]
Accounting Desk Book [D-239]
The Complete Investor [D-58]
*The Entrepreneur and Small Business
Problem Solver* [D-269]

(answer continues)

WHERE SHOULD I GO TO FIND...	*TRY*

Techniques, Formulas, Ratios

formulas for financial and operating ratios that are used for the analysis of businesses, with an explanation of each ratio?	*Financial Analyst's Handbook* [D-271] *Foundations of Financial Management* [D-273] *Handbook of Business Formulas and Controls* [D-278] *How to Organize and Operate a Small Business* [D-79] *Industry Norms and Key Business Ratios* [D-26] *Ratio Analysis for Small Business* [D-359] *RMA Annual Statement Studies* [D-27] *Techniques of Financial Analysis* [D-324] *Vital Business Secrets for New and Growing Companies* [D-107]
formulas that are used for profit planning, pricing, break-even analysis, and marketing?	*Handbook of Business Formulas and Controls* [D-278]
an explanation of procedures, techniques, and measures used to conduct a financial analysis?	*Accountant's Desk Handbook* [D-237] *Accounting Desk Book* [D-239] *AICPA Audit and Accounting Manual* [D-241] *Applying GAAP and GAAS* [D-374] *Financial Analyst's Handbook* [D-271] *Financial Statement Analysis* [D-272] *Handbook of Business Formulas and Controls* [D-278] *Miller Comprehensive GAAP Guide* [D-298] *Techniques of Financial Analysis* [D-324]
a checklist for performing a profit analysis?	*The Entrepreneur and Small Business Problem Solver* [D-269]

Valuing a Business

an estimate of a company's financial strength and credit rating?	*Dun & Bradstreet Reference Book* [D-171]
how to evaluate an existing business for reasons of purchasing it, and how to determine the price to pay?	*The Entrepreneur and Small Business Problem Solver* [D-269]
changes in the rating of a corporation's debt?	*Barron's* [D-440] *Investor's Daily* [D-449] *Bond Guide* [D-248]

WHERE SHOULD I GO TO FIND...   *TRY*

Valuing a Business

changes in the rating of a corporation's debt?

Security Owner's Stock Guide [D-314]
Wall Street Journal [D-457]

guidelines and techniques for determining the value of a business or professional practice?

The Complete Guide to a Successful Leveraged Buyout [D-57]
Corporate Acquisitions, Mergers, and Divestitures [D-384]
Handbook of Estate Planning [D-280]
How to Price a Business [D-461]
Techniques of Financial Analysis [D-324]
Valuing a Business [D-329]
Valuing Small Businesses and Professional Practices [D-330]
Vital Business Secrets for New and Growing Companies [D-107]

Banking and Finance

Note: See also "Investments" subsection.

Bank Evaluations

a brief explanation of how to evaluate a bank?

Standard & Poor's Industry Surveys (April 1988 issue, page B27) [D-472]

Bank and Savings and Loan Association Rankings

a ranked listing of the world's largest international banks?

Moody's Bank and Finance Manual [D-189]
Rand McNally Bankers Directory: International [D-211]

a list that ranks the largest U.S. banks?

Moody's Bank and Finance Manual [D-189]
Rand McNally Bankers Directory: U.S. [D-212]

periodic international rankings of banks with descriptive financial statistics?

Business Week [D-441]

a ranked list of savings and loan associations?

Moody's Bank and Finance Manual [D-189]
U.S. Savings and Loan Directory [D-230]

a ranking of financial institutions within their SIC industry classification?

Ward's Business Directory, Vol. 3 [D-233]

<u>*WHERE SHOULD I GO TO FIND...*</u>   *TRY*

Bank Operations and Management

a basic operational handbook for the   *Bankers' Handbook* [D-244]
banking industry?

a basic handbook that explains the   *The Loan Officer's Handbook* [D-294]
operational responsibilities of bank loan
officers with information on how to carry
out these duties?

a comprehensive discussion of issues   *Handbook of Mortgage Banking* [D-282]
related to the management of secondary
mortgage banking?

guidelines on how to manage a bank's   *Managing Bank Assets and Liabilities* [D-89]
assets and liabilities for the purpose of
maximizing profits while controlling risk?

Business Planning

instructions and forms for writing a   *Business Plans That Win $$$* (instructions
business plan and loan application?   only) [D-53]
                                                *The Entrepreneur and Small Business Problem
                                                Solver* [D-269]
                                                From Concept to Market [D-73]
                                                How to Set Up Your Own Small Business
                                                [D-290]
                                                *Start-Up Money: How to Finance Your New
                                                Small Business* [D-321]
                                                *Vital Business Secrets for New and Growing
                                                Companies* (business-plan instructions
                                                only) [D-107]

an explanation of the statistical tools   *Accounting Desk Book* [D-239]
and techniques used in financial and/or   *Financial Analyst's Handbook* [D-271]
investment analysis?   *Techniques of Financial Analysis* [D-324]

Capital Sources

how to determine the amount of capital   *How to Organize and Operate A Small
needed to start a business and sources for   Business* [D-79]
borrowing the money?   *How to Set Up Your Own Small Business*
                                                [D-290]

where to obtain the funds needed for   *The Entrepreneur and Small Business Problem
starting or expanding a business?   Solver* [D-269]

WHERE SHOULD I GO TO FIND...   *TRY*

Capital Sources

where to obtain the funds needed for starting or expanding a business?

From Concept to Market [D-73]
Vital Business Secrets for New and Growing Companies [D-107]

the financing alternatives that are available to small and medium-size businesses?

The Entrepreneur and Small Business Problem Solver [D-269]
Handbook for Raising Capital [D-277]
How to Set Up Your Own Small Business [D-290]
Start-Up Money: How to Finance Your New Small Business [D-321]
Vital Business Secrets for New and Growing Companies [D-107]

how to raise foreign capital?

Handbook for Raising Capital [D-277]

Computers and Software: Banking

an analytical discussion of online databases that are available to the banking industry with a detailed critique of each product?

Dow Jones-Irwin Banker's Guide to Online Databases [D-263]

descriptive profiles of microcomputer software packages that serve applications in banking and finance?

Data Sources: Software [D-158]
Datapro Directory of Microcomputer Software [D-387]

Control Boards and Agencies

information on the Federal Reserve System, including the address, telephone number, and names of officials of the System along with a list of the district offices and their locations?

Moody's Bank and Finance Manual [D-189]
Rand McNally Bankers Directory: U.S. [D-212]
U.S. Savings and Loan Directory [D-230]

the names, addresses, and telephone numbers of government agencies that serve the savings and loan industry?

U.S. Savings and Loan Directory [D-230]

the name, address, and telephone number of the chief banking authority in each state?

Consumer's Resource Handbook [D-344]
National Directory of State Agencies [D-199]
State Administrative Officials Classified by Function [D-224]

WHERE SHOULD I GO TO FIND...	*TRY*

Currencies of the World

foreign currency exchange rates?

Barron's [D-440]
Financial Times [D-444]
New York Times [D-454]
Wall Street Journal [D-457]
Other major metropolitan newspapers

exchange rates between the U.S. dollar and currencies of other nations for selected periods?

Europa World Year Book [D-25]
Moody's International Manual [D-191]
Rand McNally Bankers Directory: International [D-211]
Statistical Abstract of the U.S. [D-361]
World Currency Yearbook [D-30]

descriptive information on the currency of individual nations?

World Currency Yearbook [D-30]

Estate Planning

guidelines for estate planning and its financial considerations?

Handbook of Estate Planning [D-280]

"Federal Reserve Data"

an explanation of how to interpret the *Wall Street Journal's* table entitled "Federal Reserve Data"?

Financial Analyst's Handbook [D-271]

Financial Institutions and Service Companies: Listings and Profiles

financial and operating profiles of U.S. banks, savings and loan associations, and other types of financial institutions, including a summary of their financial statements and key financial and operating ratios?

Moody's Bank and Finance Manual [D-189]

a directory of banks in the U.S., with a profile of each that includes location, branches, telephone number, officers, total assets, state and national ranking, and other information?

Rand McNally Bankers Directory: U.S. [D-212]

a directory of Federal Home Loan Banks with addresses, telephone numbers, and names of directors and officers?

Rand McNally Bankers Directory: U.S. [D-212]
U.S. Savings and Loan Directory [D-230]

WHERE SHOULD I GO TO FIND...　　　　　　　　　*TRY*

Financial Institutions and Service Companies: Listings and Profiles

a directory of savings and loan
institutions, with a description of each
that includes address, telephone number,
names of officers with their functions
and titles, financial data, and other
information?

U.S. Savings and Loan Directory [D-230]

a listing of financial institutions, with
the address, telephone number, name
of CEO, and other information for each?

Ward's Business Directory, Vol. 1 [D-231];
Vol. 3 [D-233]

a directory with descriptive profiles of
investment banks, U.S. banks offering
master trust services to corporations,
foreign investment banks in the U.S.,
private insurance and institutional
lenders to corporations, and firms
providing commercial finance and
factoring?

Corporate Finance Sourcebook [D-153]

a directory of specific corporate and
interbank services offered by U.S. banks
in each state?

Rand McNally Bankers Directory: U.S.
[D-212]

a directory of firms that offer pension
management services indicating the
total pension assets being managed,
minimum size of acceptable pension
account, fee structure for accounts,
contact person, telephone number, and
other information?

Corporate Finance Sourcebook [D-153]

a listing of selected U.S. banks and data
corporations that offer cash management
services to corporations, describing
the types of services offered, contact
person, telephone number, and other
information?

Corporate Finance Sourcebook [D-153]

a directory of firms that underwrite
public offerings of equity capital for
small companies?

Pratt's Guide to Venture Capital Sources
[D-209]

a listing of interstate bank holding
companies?

Rand McNally Bankers Directory: U.S.
[D-212]

WHERE SHOULD I GO TO FIND...	*TRY*

Financial Institutions and Service Companies: Listings and Profiles

for individual bank holding companies, a five-year comparison of their growth records, return on assets, return on equity, investment ratios, and their liquidity and leverage ratios?	*Standard & Poor's Industry Surveys* [D-472]
for individual savings and loan holding companies, a five-year comparison of their net income, total assets, price/book value, yield, dividend payout ratio, and price-earnings ratio?	*Standard & Poor's Industry Surveys* [D-472]
a directory of companies that provide electronic information services to the financial services industry?	*Information Sources* [D-185]
the banks in each of the Federal Reserve Districts and their addresses and telephone numbers?	*Federal Staff Directory* [D-177] *Rand McNally Bankers Directory: U.S.* [D-212] *U.S. Savings and Loan Directory* [D-230] *Washington Information Directory* [D-234]

Financial Instruments

a brief explanation of the major money-market instruments?	*Managing Bank Assets and Liabilities* [D-89]
data on the public's use of checking accounts, credit cards, and cash?	*Statistical Abstract of the U.S.* [D-361]

Financial Tables

Note: For additional tables, also see "Investments" and "Real Estate" subsections.

banking and financial tables that are used in transactions involving investing, borrowing, saving, and withdrawals?	*Accountant's Handbook of Formulas and Tables* [D-238] *Accounting Desk Book* [D-239] *The Complete Investor* [D-58] *Thorndike Encyclopedia of Banking and Financial Tables* [D-326]
tables of compound interest for a variety of purposes and periods that show amounts and rates?	*Thorndike Encyclopedia of Banking and Financial Tables* [D-326]

WHERE SHOULD I GO TO FIND...	*TRY*
Financial Tables	
a table that reports the number of days between dates?	*Thorndike Encyclopedia of Banking and Financial Tables* [D-326]
tables of simple interest?	*Accounting Desk Book* [D-239] *Thorndike Encyclopedia of Banking and Financial Tables* [D-326]
a table that reports the effective rate of a loan that requires a compensating balance?	*Thorndike Encyclopedia of Banking and Financial Tables* [D-326]
a table that reports, for construction loans that involve interest and points, the average interest rate for the original loan period and, for delayed repayments, the average rate per month of delay?	*Thorndike Encyclopedia of Banking and Financial Tables* [D-326]
a table that discloses the number of full years that an amount in a savings account, earning at a specified interest rate, will last when subject to a specified size of monthly withdrawals?	*Thorndike Encyclopedia of Banking and Financial Tables* [D-326]
for installment loans, tables that report the payments, for designated periods, necessary to amortize each $100 over the term of the loan, including principal and interest?	*Thorndike Encyclopedia of Banking and Financial Tables* [D-326]
for installment loans, a table that reports, for designated payment periods throughout the term of the loan, the finance charge for each $100 of the loan at a specified annual percentage rate (APR)?	*Thorndike Encyclopedia of Banking and Financial Tables* [D-326]
for installment loans prepaid in full prior to maturity, tables that show the monthly rebate of the unearned finance charge and the monthly cumulative earnings during the period of the loan? (Note: Figures are based on the Rule of 78 and the actuarial method.)	*Thorndike Encyclopedia of Banking and Financial Tables* [D-326]

WHERE SHOULD I GO TO FIND...	*TRY*

Financial Tables

for lease payments, a table that reports the annual percentage rate and finance charge for each $100 of monthly payments made either in arrears or in advance where the payment is a percentage of the capital cost and where a residual may be involved?	*Thorndike Encyclopedia of Banking and Financial Tables* [D-326]
a table that reports the daily rebate value per $100 for each day of the year?	*Thorndike Encyclopedia of Banking and Financial Tables* [D-326]

Forecasts and Performance: Finance Industry

forecasts for the U.S. finance industry?	*Predicasts Forecasts* [D-468]
forecasts for the financial industry in foreign countries?	*Worldcasts* [D-475]
a performance analysis of the finance industry with focus on trends, problems, prospects, developments, and composite statistical data?	*Standard & Poor's Industry Surveys* [D-472] *U.S. Industrial Outlook* [D-367]

Grants and Foundations

grant funds that are available and the information needed to apply for them?	*Foundation Directory* [D-178] *Foundation Grants Index* [D-9]

Information Sources

a subject index to statistical publications of state government agencies and of private organizations that focus on the banking industry?	*Statistical Reference Index* [D-18]
a subject index to U.S. government publications that address banking and finance matters?	*American Statistics Index* [D-1] *Monthly Catalog of U.S. Government Publications* [D-354]
a bibliography of banking directories on subjects in the banking industry?	*Directories in Print* [D-35]
a listing of published research reports on the U.S. and international banking industries?	*Findex* [D-37]

WHERE SHOULD I GO TO FIND...	*TRY*

Information Sources

a bibliography of sources containing banking and monetary statistics?	*A Guide to Statistical Sources in Money, Banking, and Finance* [D-465] *Statistics Sources* [D-473]
a guide to statistical reports issued by the federal government that focus on the performance of the banking industry?	*American Statistics Index* [D-1]

Interest Rates

See also "Financial Tables," above.

current U.S. and selected foreign prime interest rates?	*Barron's* [D-440] *The Economist* [D-443] *Financial Times* [D-444] *Investor's Daily* [D-449] *New York Times* [D-454] *Wall Street Journal* [D-457] Other metropolitan newspapers
current money interest rates (U.S. and foreign), including discount rate of federal funds, Treasury bills, bankers acceptances, certificates of deposit, Eurodollars, and so on?	*Barron's* [D-440] *Financial Times* [D-444] *Investor's Daily* [D-449] *New York Times* [D-454] *Wall Street Journal* [D-457] Other metropolitan newspapers
a weekly listing of selected bank credit cards that are offered nationally with a report of their interest rates and annual fees (if any)?	*Barron's* [D-440]
historical discount rates of foreign central banks?	*Moody's International Manual* [D-191]
average annual money market interest rates and mortgage rates by type of investment for selected years?	*Statistical Abstract of the U.S.* [D-361]

Leveraged Buyouts

information on financing corporate leveraged buyouts?	*The Complete Guide to a Successful Leveraged Buyout* [D-57]

WHERE SHOULD I GO TO FIND...	*TRY*

Loans, Lenders, and Investors

an overview of loan policies and practices of U.S. banks as they apply to new businesses?	*A Guide for the Foreign Investor* [D-75]
what bankers, other lenders, and investors look for when evaluating a financial statement related to a request for funds?	*Vital Business Secrets for New and Growing Companies* [D-107]
what lenders and investors look for when considering a request for funds, other than the financial statement?	*Vital Business Secrets for New and Growing Companies* [D-107]
how to prepare and conduct oneself for a meeting with potential investors in one's company?	*Vital Business Secrets for New and Growing Companies* [D-107]
guidelines for determining how much of the company should be offered to potential investors?	*Vital Business Secrets for New and Growing Companies* [D-107]
instructions and forms for writing a business plan and loan application?	*Business Plans That Win $$$* (instructions only) [D-53] *The Entrepreneur and Small Business Problem Solver* [D-269] *From Concept to Market* [D-73] *How to Set Up Your Own Small Business* [D-290] *Start-Up Money: How to Finance Your New Small Business* [D-321] *Vital Business Secrets for New and Growing Companies* (business plan instructions only) [D-107]
an explanation of the statistical tools and techniques used in financial and/or investment analysis?	*Accounting Desk Book* [D-239] *Financial Analyst's Handbook* [D-271] *Techniques of Financial Analysis* [D-324]
a listing of venture capitalists indicating their areas of investment interest, who to contact, addresses, telephone numbers, an explanation of the venture capital industry, and other related information?	*Complete Information Bank for Entrepreneurs and Small Business Managers* [D-34] *Corporate Finance Sourcebook* [D-153] *Dow Jones-Irwin Business and Investment Almanac* [D-24]

WHERE SHOULD I GO TO FIND...	*TRY*

Loans, Lenders, and Investors

a listing of venture capitalists indicating their areas of investment interest, who to contact, addresses, telephone numbers, an explanation of the venture capital industry, and other related information?

Pratt's Guide to Venture Capital Sources [D-209]
Small Business Sourcebook [D-216]
Who's Who in Venture Capital [D-235]

Newsletters

a directory of published newsletters on banking with a nonevaluative description of each newsletter?

Newsletters in Print [D-41]
Oxbridge Directory of Newsletters [D-42]

Selling a Business

helpful suggestions on how and when to sell a business?

Handbook for Raising Capital [D-277]

Start-Up Capital

how to determine the amount of capital needed to start a business?

How to Organize and Operate A Small Business [D-79]
How to Set Up Your Own Small Business [D-290]

where to obtain the funds needed for starting a business?

The Entrepreneur and Small Business Problem Solver [D-269]
From Concept to Market [D-73]
How to Organize and Operate A Small Business [D-79]
How to Set Up Your Own Small Business [D-290]
Vital Business Secrets for New and Growing Companies [D-107]

Trade Associations: Finance Industry

Note: See also "Business Organizations, Trade Associations, Unions, and Foundations," subsection.

a listing of world banking and related trade associations with their addresses and telephone numbers?

Rand McNally Bankers Directory: International [D-211]

Trade Associations: Finance Industry

a directory of state bankers associations that reports the names of their officers, addresses, and telephone numbers?

Rand McNally Bankers Directory: U.S. [D-212]

a directory of bankers and credit union associations located in Washington, D.C., reporting their addresses and telephone numbers?

Washington Information Directory [D-234]

a directory of the United State League of Savings Institutions, with names, addresses, and telephone numbers?

U.S. Savings and Loan Directory [D-230]

a directory of the state savings and loan leagues, with names, addresses, and telephone numbers?

U.S. Savings and Loan Directory [D-230]

the names, addresses, and telephone numbers of trade associations that are associated with the savings industry?

U.S. Savings and Loan Directory [D-230]

World Banking

a description of the banking system in a foreign nation?

Moody's International Manual [D-191]

a directory of all foreign banks, by nation, that are involved in international trade or exchange, with information about their location, branches, officers, assets, ownership, and other descriptive data?

Rand McNally Bankers Directory: International [D-211]

a directory of major foreign banks, with a descriptive profile of each that includes its capital structure, history, types of service, subsidiaries, names of officers and directors, address, telephone number, consolidated income account, consolidated balance sheet, and other information?

Moody's International Manual [D-191]

WHERE SHOULD I GO TO FIND...   *TRY*

Business Careers

Career Information Sources

a directory of state and local sources for job market and career information?

Occupational Outlook Handbook [D-355]

Employment and the Law

a summary of legal rights pertaining to job discrimination?

Career Information Center [D-252]

an overview of new developments and trends in federal employment law?

Career Information Center [D-252]

Employment Opportunities

a guide that links fields of study with job opportunities?

Career Choices Encyclopedia [D-251]
The Career Guide [D-143]
CPC Annual, Vols. 2 and 3 [D-155]
Peterson's Business and Management Jobs [D-207]
Peterson's Engineering, Science, and Computer Jobs [D-208]

a listing of newspapers, magazines, and trade journals that carry extensive employment advertisements?

Peterson's Business and Management Jobs [D-207]
Peterson's Engineering, Science, and Computer Jobs [D-208]
Professional Job Changing System (newspapers only)

potential opportunities for jobs with profiles of individual companies, including a listing of the types of jobs for which they hire, qualifications for these jobs, compensation, and other related information?

The Career Guide [D-143]
CPC Annual, Vols. 2 and 3 [D-155]
National Job Bank [D-202]
Peterson's Business and Management Jobs [D-207]
Peterson's Engineering, Science, and Computer Jobs [D-208]

advertisements for current job openings?

National Ad Search [D-451]
National Business Employment Weekly [D-452]

WHERE SHOULD I GO TO FIND...	*TRY*

Employment Opportunities

advertisements for current job openings?

New York Times [D-454]
Wall Street Journal [D-457]
Local and out-of-town newspapers, especially the Sunday edition.
Trade and professional journals

a description of career opportunities in real estate?

Barron's Real Estate Handbook [D-245]
See also other career publications cited herein.

Interviewing

guidelines for writing a job résumé and/or preparing for an interview?

The Career Guide [D-143]
Career Information Center [D-252]
CPC Annual, Vol. 1 [D-155]
Executive Jobs Unlimited [D-71]
National Job Bank [D-202]
Occupational Outlook Handbook [D-355]
Peterson's Business and Management Jobs [D-207]
Peterson's Engineering, Science, and Computer Jobs [D-208]
Professional Job Changing System [D-94]
Resume Writing [D-96]
Resumes That Get Jobs [D-97]
What Color Is Your Parachute? [D-108]

how to negotiate a response to employment and salary offers?

The Career Guide [D-143]
Executive Jobs Unlimited [D-71]
Peterson's Business and Management Jobs [D-207]
Peterson's Engineering, Science, and Computer Jobs [D-208]
Professional Job Changing System [D-94]
What Color Is Your Parachute? [D-108]

Job-Hunting Steps

specific suggestions on how to get into a particular career field?

Career Choices Encyclopedia [D-251]
Career Information Center [D-252]

guidelines that explain the steps for finding a job?

CPC Annual, Vol. 1 [D-155]
Executive Jobs Unlimited [D-71]
National Job Bank [D-202]
Professional Job Changing System [D-94]
What Color Is Your Parachute? [D-108]

WHERE SHOULD I GO TO FIND...	*TRY*

Job Market Trends and Projections

employment trends by region of the U.S.?	*Career Information Center* [D-252] *National Business Employment Weekly* [D-452] Local and national newspapers and magazines
labor force projections by the Bureau of Labor Statistics for 1995?	*Career Information Center* [D-252]

Occupations: Titles, Descriptions, and Preparations

a brief description of occupations in the U.S.?	*Dictionary of Occupational Titles* [D-122]
a listing of occupations in each industry?	*Dictionary of Occupational Titles* [D-122]
descriptions of selected occupations that include nature of the work, employment outlook, qualifications, earnings, and related information?	*Career Choices Encyclopedia* [D-251] *Career Information Center* [D-252] *Occupational Outlook Handbook* [D-355] *VGM's Careers Encyclopedia* [D-331]

Placement Firms

names and addresses of employment placement firms and/or executive search firms?	*The Career Guide* [D-143] *Directory of Executive Recruiters* [D-162] *Professional Job Changing System* [D-94]

Résumés

Note: See "Interviewing" in the subsection "Business Careers."

Salaries and Benefits

salaries paid, by occupation?	*American Almanac of Jobs and Salaries* [D-21] Salaries can also be found in several of the directories and handbooks cited in other subsections of "Business Careers," albeit the coverage is not as complete.
a summary of employee benefit plans that are required by law?	*Career Information Center* [D-252]

Training

a listing of occupational education
training programs and facilities by
occupational area and state?

Career Information Center [D-252]
College Blue Book: Occupational Education
[D-144]

Working Conditions

the names and profiles of what have been
described as being the best companies in
America to work for, including ratings of
their principal job factors?

*The 100 Best Companies to Work For in
America* [D-46]

Business Law

Note: This subsection involves not only
laws but also professional standards and
practices that are recognized as proper
procedures, albeit they have not been
legislated. For information about tax
laws, also see "Taxation" subsection.

Accounting and Auditing

the accounting standards of the
International Accounting Standards
Committee and the auditing guidelines
of the International Auditing Practices
Committee?

AICPA Professional Standards [D-371]
World Accounting [D-437]

the accounting and auditing regulations,
standards, and practices of Australia,
Belgium, Brazil, Canada, France, India,
Italy, Japan, Mexico, Philippines, Saudi
Arabia, South Korea, United Kingdom,
United States, and West Germany?

World Accounting [D-437] See also
the *Doing Business in...* series under
"Business Laws and Practices of Foreign
Nations" in this subsection, below.

Business Law, General

an explanation of American business law
that governs daily business practices?

*A Guide to Modern Business and Commercial
Law* [D-274]

an overview of U.S. and foreign
regulations that govern packaging for use
in international trade?

AMA Management Handbook [D-242]

WHERE SHOULD I GO TO FIND...	*TRY*

Business Laws and Practices of Foreign Nations

Note: For intellectual property law, see also "Intellectual Property Law" in this subsection, below.

the laws, regulations, directives, and decisions that regulate doing business in the European Economic Community (Common Market)?	*Common Market Reports* [D-382]
information on the legal aspects of conducting business in individual European Common Market nations and selected other European nations?	*Doing Business in Europe* [D-395]
guidelines on how to conduct business in Russia, including an overview of that nation's regulations for foreign business people?	*How to Do Business with Russians* [D-384]
information on the laws and regulations that govern business transactions in Brazil?	*Doing Business in Brazil* [D-392]
information on the laws and regulations that govern business transactions in Canada?	*Doing Business in Canada* [D-393]
information on the laws and regulations that govern business transactions in the Federal Republic of Germany?	*Business Transactions in Germany* [D-378] *Doing Business in Europe* [D-395]
information on the laws and regulations that govern business transactions in France?	*Doing Business in Europe* [D-395] *Doing Business in France* [D-396]
information on the laws and regulations that govern business transactions in Japan?	*Doing Business in Japan* [D-398] *Japan Business Law Guide* [D-413]
information on the laws and regulations that govern business transactions in Mexico?	*Doing Business in Mexico* [D-399]

WHERE SHOULD I GO TO FIND...	*TRY*

Business Laws and Practices of Foreign Nations

information on the laws and regulations that govern business transactions in the People's Republic of China?	*China Investment Guide* [D-56] *China Laws for Foreign Business* [D-380] *Doing Business in China* [D-394]
information on the laws and regulations that govern business transactions in the Republic of Ireland?	*Doing Business in Europe* [D-395] *Doing Business in Ireland* [D-397]
information on the laws and regulations that govern business transactions in Spain?	*Doing Business in Europe* [D-395] *Doing Business in Spain* [D-400]
information on the laws and regulations that govern business transactions in the United Kingdom?	*Doing Business in Europe* [D-395] *Doing Business in the United Kingdom* [D-401]
the accounting and auditing regulations, standards, and practices of Australia, Belgium, Brazil, Canada, France, India, Italy, Japan, Mexico, Philippines, Saudi Arabia, South Korea, United Kingdom, and West Germany?	*World Accounting* [D-437] See also the *Doing Business in . . .* series cited above.

Consumer Law

an explanation of federal consumer protection laws?	*Consumer Protection Manual* [D-258]
a summary of the deceptive sales practices laws of the individual states?	*Consumer Protection Manual* [D-258]

Corporation Law

federal and state laws that govern the duties of the corporate secretary?	*Corporate Secretary's Guide* [D-385]
corporate reporting requirements as required by federal law and the statutes of each state?	*Corporate Secretary's Guide* [D-385]
the personal liabilities and duties of corporate officers and directors as defined by the federal securities laws?	*17 Code of Federal Regulations 241.18114* [D-343] *Federal Securities Law Reports* [D-404] *Responsibilities of Corporate Officers and Directors Under Federal Securities Laws* [D-311]

WHERE SHOULD I GO TO FIND...	*TRY*

Export and Import Laws, Regulations, and Procedures

a summary of the U.S. government's export regulations?   *Exporters Directory* [D-175]

a summary of U.S. customs regulations and importing procedures?   *Directory of United States Importers* [D-169]

a statement of all U.S. customs regulations?   *19 Code of Federal Regulations* (Chap. 1) [D-343]
Official U.S. Custom House Guide [D-206]

Federal Government: Regulations, Rules, and Procedures

the rules and procedures that control the purchasing of supplies and services by executive agencies of the federal government?   *48 Code of Federal Regulations* [D-343]
Federal Acquisition Regulation [D-270]

a compilation of the regulations in force by the executive departments and agencies of the federal government?   *Code of Federal Regulations* [D-343]

new and proposed regulations of executive departments and agencies of the federal government?   *Federal Register* [D-350]

Insider Trading

provisions of federal securities laws concerning insider trading activities of corporate officers and directors?   *17 Code of Federal Regulations 241.18114* [D-343]
Federal Securities Law Reports [D-404]
Financial Analyst's Handbook [D-271]
Responsibilities of Corporate Officers and Directors Under Federal Securities Laws [D-311]

Insurance Law

the insurance case law of all federal courts and state appellate courts pertaining to policies covering automobiles; fire and casualty; and life, health, and accident insurance?   *Insurance Law Reports* [D-412]

WHERE SHOULD I GO TO FIND...	*TRY*

Intellectual Property Law

information on the intellectual property laws of nations?	*Business Transactions in Germany* [D-378] *Common Market Reports* [D-382] *Doing Business in Brazil* [D-392] *Doing Business in Canada* [D-393] *Doing Business in China* [D-394] *Doing Business in Europe* [D-395] *Doing Business in France* [D-396] *Doing Business in Ireland* [D-397] *Doing Business in Japan* [D-398] *Doing Business in Mexico* [D-399] *Doing Business in Spain* [D-400] *Doing Business in the United Kingdom* [D-401] *Japan Business Law Guide* [D-413] *Patents Throughout the World* [D-418] *Trademarks Throughout the World* [D-434]
the copyright statutes of the various states?	*Copyright Law Reports* [D-383]
the U.S. copyright laws?	*17 U.S. Code* [D-364] *17 U.S. Code Annotated* [D-365] *Code of Federal Regulations* [D-343] *Copyright Law Reports* [D-383] *Forms of Business Agreements and Resolutions* [D-410]
an explanation of U.S. copyright, patent, and trademark laws?	*The Entrepreneur and Small Business Problem Solver* [D-269] *A Guide to Modern Business and Commercial Law* [D-274] *Inventor's Guide to Successful Patent Applications* [D-84] *Patent It Yourself* [D-92]
how corporate names are protected by statute in nations throughout the world?	*Protection of Corporate Names* [D-421]
a directory of published newsletters on patents, copyrights, and trademarks with a non-evaluative description of each newsletter?	*Newsletters in Print* [D-41] *Oxbridge Directory of Newsletters* [D-42]
the full text of the major international copyright conventions to which the U.S. is a party?	*Copyright Law Reports* [D-383]

International Agreements

| the text of the Convention on the Recognition and Enforcement of Foreign Arbitral Awards? | *A Dictionary of Arbitration and Its Terms* [D-116] |

WHERE SHOULD I GO TO FIND...	*TRY*
International Agreements	
the text of the Convention on the Settlement of Investment Disputes Between States and Nationals of Other States?	*A Dictionary of Arbitration and Its Terms* [D-116]
the accounting standards of the International Accounting Standards Committee and the auditing guidelines of the International Auditing Practices Committee?	*AICPA Professional Standards* [D-371] *World Accounting* [D-437]
Labor Law and Judicial Decisions	
a brief guide to federal labor relations law, including explanations of decisions, rulings, and interpretations involving labor union activities, collective bargaining, mediation, and other labor topics?	*Guidebook to Labor Relations* [D-275]
a survey of labor law, including legislation, court decisions, regulations, and rulings?	*Labor Law Course* [D-292]
the full text of the following federal labor statutes? (Note: Reported here are the original statute numbers and citations. Check the *U.S. Code* and *U.S. Code Annotated* for any amendments or revisions.)	*Labor Law Course* [D-292] *Labor Law Reports* [D-414] *Personnel Management, Labor Relations* [D-420] *U.S. Code* [D-364] *U.S. Code Annotated* (See "Popular Name Table") [D-365] *U.S. Statutes at Large* (Cited below as vol. no., Stat., page no.) [D-368]
a. Anti-Injunction Act (Norris-LaGuardia Act), Public No. 72-65	47 Stat. 70
b. Civil Rights Act of 1968 (Interference with Federally Protected Activities), P. L. 90-284	82 Stat. 73-92
c. Clayton Anti-Trust Act, Public No. 63-212	38 Stat. 730
d. Equal Pay Act of 1963, P. L. 88-38	77 Stat. 56

WHERE SHOULD I GO TO FIND...	*TRY*

Labor Law and Judicial Decisions

e. Fair Employment Practices Law (Civil Rights Act of 1964), P. L. 88-352	78 Stat. 241
f. Fair Labor Standards Act, Public No. 75-718	52 Stat. 1060
g. Hobbs Anti-Racketeering Act, Public No. 73-376	48 Stat. 979
h. Labor Management Relations Act (Taft-Hartley Act), P. L. 80-101	61 Stat. 136
i. Labor-Management Reporting and Disclosure Act of 1959, P. L. 86-257	73 Stat. 519
j. National Labor Relations Act, Public No. 74-198	49 Stat. 449
k. Portal-to-Portal Act of 1947, P. L. 80-49	61 Stat. 84
l. Sherman Anti-Trust Act, July 2, 1890	51 Congress, Ch. 647 26 Stat. 209
a digest of leading court decisions regarding labor relations?	*Labor Law Course* [D-292]
a compilation of federal and state labor laws, regulations, decisions, and rulings pertaining to employee-management relations, wages and hours, employment discrimination, child labor, unions, and other areas treated by labor law?	*Employment Coordinator* [D-402] *Labor Law Reports* [D-414] *Personnel Management, Labor Relations* [D-420]
the text of the Uniform Arbitration Act?	*A Dictionary of Arbitration and Its Terms* [D-116]
an overview of new developments and trends in federal employment law?	*Career Information Center* [D-252]
a brief overview of federal labor laws that are of importance to the business person?	*The Entrepreneur and Small Business Problem Solver* [D-269]

Mergers and Acquisitions

basic legal information about tax and nontax issues pertaining to mergers, acquisitions, and divestitures?	*Corporate Acquisitions, Mergers, and Divestitures* [D-384]

WHERE SHOULD I GO TO FIND...	*TRY*

Mergers and Acquisitions

basic legal information about tax and nontax issues pertaining to mergers, acquisitions, and divestitures?	*Responsibilities of Corporate Officers and Directors Under Federal Securities Laws* [D-311] *Tax Transactions Library: Mergers, Acquisitions, and Leveraged Buyouts* [D-431]

Real Estate Law

a descriptive listing of major federal laws that affect real estate?	*Barron's Real Estate Handbook* [D-245]
a summary of governmental regulations that affect the development and operation of condominiums?	*Condominium Development Guide* [D-257]

Securities Law and Judicial Decisions

the U.S. Uniform Securities Act and the securities laws and regulations of each of the fifty states, District of Columbia, Guam, and Puerto Rico?	*Blue Sky Law Reports* [D-375]
the takeover disclosure statutes of the states regarding the acquisition of equity securities of domestic corporations?	*Blue Sky Law Reports* [D-375]
regulations, rulings, and court decisions that annotate the federal laws that govern the securities industry?	*Federal Securities Law Reports* [D-404]
the full text of the major federal statutes that regulate the securities industry?	*Federal Securities Law Reports* [D-404]
a synopsis of the Securities Act of 1933?	*Accounting Desk Book* [D-239]
a synopsis of the Securities Exchange Act of 1934?	*Accounting Desk Book* [D-239]

Tax Law and Judicial Decisions

decisions handed down by federal (excluding U.S. Tax Court) and some state courts regarding federal tax issues?	*American Federal Tax Reports* [D-460] *U.S. Tax Cases* [D-435]
decisions handed down by the U.S. Tax Court?	*Tax Court Memorandum Decisions* [D-427] *Tax Court Reported Decisions* [D-428] *Tax Court Reporter* [D-429] *T. C. Memorandum Decisions* [D-433]

WHERE SHOULD I GO TO FIND...	*TRY*

Tax Law and Judicial Decisions

basic legal information about tax issues pertaining to mergers, acquisitions, and divestitures?	*Corporate Acquisitions, Mergers, and Divestitures* [D-384] *Tax Transactions Library: Mergers, Acquisitions, and Leveraged Buyouts* [D-431]

Business Organizations, Trade Associations, Unions, and Foundations

Note: For information on union collective bargaining negotiations and contracts, see subsection entitled "Personnel Administration."

Abbreviations

standard abbreviations for labor union names, with an explanation of these abbreviations?	*Acronyms, Initialisms, and Abbreviations Dictionary* [D-109] *Directory of U.S. Labor Organizations* [D-170]

Association and Organization Listings and Profiles

the names, addresses, and areas served (authorities) of the shippers' associations?	*Thomas Register's Inbound Traffic Guide* [D-227]
the names and addresses of the trade associations that serve the transportation industry?	*Thomas Register's Inbound Traffic Guide* [D-227]
a listing of association management companies?	*National Trade and Professional Associations of the United States* [D-204]
directories of trade associations, professional associations, and business organizations that indicate their purpose, address, telephone number, and other descriptive information?	*Complete Information Bank for Entrepreneurs and Small-Business Managers* [D-34] *Encyclopedia of Associations, Vol. 1* [D-173] *Encyclopedia of Business Information Sources* [D-36] *Encyclopedia of Information Systems and Services* [D-174] *Exporters Directory* [D-175] *International Directory of Business Information Agencies and Services* [D-466] *National Trade and Professional Associations of the United States* [D-204] *Small Business Sourcebook* [D-216]
a directory of trade and industry organizations in foreign countries with their addresses and telephone numbers?	*Europa World Year Book* [D-25]

WHERE SHOULD I GO TO FIND...   *TRY*

Association and Organization Listings and Profiles

the addresses and telephone numbers
of American Chambers of Commerce
abroad?

*International Directory of Corporate
Affiliations* [D-186]

the addresses and telephone numbers of
foreign trade commissions/chambers of
commerce located in the U.S.?

American Export Register [D-133]
*International Directory of Business
Information Agencies and Services* [D-466]
*International Directory of Corporate
Affiliations* [D-186]

the national addresses, telephone
numbers, and other information on
individual labor organizations?

Directory of U.S. Labor Organizations
[D-170]
Encyclopedia of Associations, Vol. 1 [D-173]
Washington Information Directory [D-234]

the names, addresses, and telephone
numbers of national, regional, state, and
local offices of the AFL-CIO?

Directory of U.S. Labor Organizations
[D-170]

a listing of world banking and related
trade associations with their addresses
and telephone numbers?

*Rand McNally Bankers Directory:
International* [D-211]

a directory of bankers and credit union
associations located in Washington,
DC, that cites purposes, addresses, and
telephone numbers?

Washington Information Directory [D-234]

a directory of the U.S. League of Savings
Institutions with names, addresses, and
telephone numbers?

U.S. Savings and Loan Directory [D-230]

a directory of state savings and loan
leagues, with names, addresses, and
telephone numbers?

U.S. Savings and Loan Directory [D-230]

the names, addresses, and telephone
numbers of trade associations that are
associated with the savings industry?

U.S. Savings and Loan Directory [D-230]

the names, addresses, and telephone
numbers of nongovernmental
organizations in Washington, DC,
arranged according to the subject of their
service?

Washington Information Directory [D-234]

WHERE SHOULD I GO TO FIND...	TRY

Association and Organization Listings and Profiles

a directory of national associations located in Washington, DC, that provide services in the stocks, bonds, and securities industry?	*Washington Information Directory* [D-234]
a directory of national associations located in Washington, DC, that serve the insurance industry?	*Washington Information Directory* [D-234]
a directory of national associations located in Washington, DC, that serve the field of patents, copyrights, and trademarks?	*Washington Information Directory* [D-234]
a directory of national organizations that serve the real estate industry?	*Barron's Real Estate Handbook* [D-245] *Dictionary of Real Estate Terms* [D-213] *Encyclopedia of Associations, Vol. 1* [D-173]
the names and addresses of realtors and state and local boards of realtors who are members of the National Association of Realtors?	*National Roster of Realtors Directory* [D-203]
directories of national, regional, and state radio and television (including cable) networks and groups?	*Spot Radio Rates and Data* [D-218] *Spot Television Rates and Data* [D-219]
a directory of trade and professional associations in Canada?	*Career Information Center* [D-252]
a directory of World Trade Center Clubs located throughout the world with their addresses and telephone numbers?	*American Export Register* [D-133]
a directory of trade and professional associations and user groups that are involved with or interested in computing?	*Computers and Computing Information Resources Directory* [D-148]
a listing of reprographic trade associations, with addresses, telephone numbers, and other descriptive information?	*Datapro Management of Office Automation* [D-389] *Encyclopedia of Associations, Vol. 1* [D-173] *National Trade and Professional Associations of the United States* [D-204]

WHERE SHOULD I GO TO FIND...   *TRY*

Computers and Software: Association Management

a descriptive profile of computer
software packages that have applications for the management of associations and organizations?

Data Sources: Software [D-158]
Datapro Directory of Microcomputer Software
[D-387]

Foundation Grants

a listing of foundations, with a disclosure of their areas of funding interest, size of grants, application guidelines, and other related information?

The Foundation Directory [D-178]
The Foundation Grants Index [D-9]

Business Resources

Business Loan Applications

applications for a Small Business
Administration (SBA) loan or a disaster
loan?

Business Forms on File [D-376]
*The Entrepreneur and Small Business
Problem Solver* [D-269]
From Concept to Market [D-73]
Note: Applications are also
available from the Small Business
Administration.

Buying a Business

the pros and cons of buying an existing
business, and sources that identify
businesses that are for sale?

*The Entrepreneur and Small Business
Problem Solver* [D-269]

how to evaluate an existing business
for purposes of purchasing it, and
how to determine the price to pay for
it?

*The Entrepreneur and Small Business Problem
Solver* [D-269]

a listing of independent corporate
merger and acquisition intermediaries,
indicating their areas of specialization,
form of compensation, contact person,
telephone number, and other relevant
information?

*Consultants and Consulting Organization
Directory* [D-150]
Corporate Finance Sourcebook [D-153]

WHERE SHOULD I GO TO FIND...	*TRY*

Capital Sources

a listing of venture capitalists, with a description of their areas of investment interest, who to contact, information to submit for consideration, and other relevant information?

Complete Information Bank for Entrepreneurs and Small Business Managers [D-34]
Corporate Finance Sourcebook [D-153]
Dow Jones-Irwin Business and Investment Almanac [D-24]
Pratt's Guide to Venture Capital Sources [D-209]
Small Business Sourcebook [D-216]
Who's Who in Venture Capital [D-235]

how to determine the amount of capital needed to start a business and sources for borrowing it?

How to Organize and Operate A Small Business [D-79]
How to Set Up Your Own Small Business [D-290]

where to obtain the funds needed for starting or expanding a business?

The Entrepreneur and Small Business Problem Solver [D-269]
From Concept to Market [D-73]
Small Business Sourcebook [D-216]
Vital Business Secrets for New and Growing Companies [D-107]

Communications

Note: See also "Marketing Media and Services" under the subsection "Marketing."

toll-free "800" business telephone numbers?

AT&T Toll-Free 800 Business Directory [D-136]

a fax phone number in the U.S. or Canada?

Fax Phone Book [D-176]
National Fax Directory (U.S. only) [D-201]

Computers and Software: Business Applications

a listing of sources that identify business databases?

Computers and Computing Information Resources Directory [D-148]
Directories in Print [D-35]
Small Business Sourcebook [D-216]

descriptive profiles of microcomputer software packages that serve office management applications?

Data Sources: Software [D-158]
Datapro Directory of Microcomputer Software [D-387]

WHERE SHOULD I GO TO FIND... | *TRY*

Consultants, Services, and Suppliers

sales catalogs of suppliers that provide such information as products/services offered, design specifications and performance data of products, photographs of products, model numbers, address and telephone number for ordering, and other relevant information?

Thomas Register of American Manufacturers: Catalog File [D-226]

the names, addresses, and telephone numbers of suppliers, with an indication of their products/services?

Corporate Technology Directory [D-154]
Japan Yellow Pages [D-187]
Moody's Industrial Manual [D-190]
Moody's International Manual [D-191]
Moody's OTC Industrial Manual [D-194]
Standard & Poor's Corporation Records [D-220]
Taiwan Yellow Pages [D-225]
Thomas Register of American Manufacturers: Products & Services [D-226]
Trade directories and journals
Yellow-page section of local telephone directories

publications that either list suppliers of equipment, supplies, or services for businesses or report where to locate such lists?

Directories in Print [D-35]
Small Business Sourcebook [D-216]
Thomas Register of American Manufacturers: Products & Services; Catalog File [D-226]
Trade directories and journals
Yellow-page section of local telephone directories

a directory of businesses listed by city and state that cites the nature of the business (product or service) and address?

Moody's Industrial Manual [D-190]
Moody's OTC Industrial Manual [D-194]

a directory of high technology companies that reports the products they manufacture?

Corporate Technology Directory [D-154]

firms that are owned and controlled by members of minority groups and that supply products or provide services?

National Directory of Minority-Owned Business Firms [D-198]
National Directory of Women-Owned Business Firms [D-200]

a directory of imported products and the names of the companies that import them?

Directory of United States Importers [D-169]

WHERE SHOULD I GO TO FIND...	*TRY*
Consultants, Services, and Suppliers	
a directory of exported products and the names of the companies that export them?	*Exporters Directory* [D-175]
a directory of accounting and auditing firms that indicates the types of service offered, industries served, contact person, telephone number, and other information?	*Corporate Finance Sourcebook* [D-153]
a listing of business insurance brokers, reporting the types of insurance offered and kinds of businesses served, special strengths, contact person, telephone number, and other information?	*Corporate Finance Sourcebook* [D-153]
a listing of pension management firms, indicating total pension assets being managed, minimum size of acceptable pension account, fee structure for accounts, contact person, telephone number, and other information?	*Corporate Finance Sourcebook* [D-153]
a listing of selected U.S. banks and data corporations that offer cash management services to corporations and that describes the types of service offered, contact person, telephone number, and other information?	*Corporate Finance Sourcebook* [D-153]
a directory of specific corporate and interbank services offered by named U.S. banks in each state?	*Rand McNally Bankers Directory: U.S.* [D-212]
a directory that reports the names of the public utility companies that provide gas or electricity to each of the principal cities in the U.S. and Canada?	*Moody's Public Utility Manual* [D-196]
the names, addresses, and telephone numbers of nongovernment organizations in Washington, DC, that specialize in services to small business?	*Washington Information Directory* [D-234]

| *WHERE SHOULD I GO TO FIND...* | *TRY* |

Consultants, Services, and Suppliers

a directory of companies that provide information on industry and federal standards and specifications?

Information Sources [D-185]

a directory of online databases that identify companies in sundry industries and the products/services they provide?

Directory of Online Databases [D-261]

a listing of independent corporate merger and acquisition intermediaries, indicating their areas of specialization, form of compensation, contact person, telephone number, and other information?

Consultants and Consulting Organizations Directory [D-150]
Corporate Finance Sourcebook [D-153]

the names, addresses, and telephone numbers of advertising agencies, arranged by the type of products/services being advertised by their clients?

Standard Directory of Advertisers [D-222]

a directory and/or guide to directories of organizations and individuals who either consult for the business community or who serve professional consultants?

Consultants and Consulting Organizations Directory [D-150]
Directories in Print [D-35]
Encyclopedia of Associations, Vol. 1 [D-173]
Information Sources [D-185]
Small Business Sourcebook [D-216]

the names of sales agencies that represent manufacturers along with each agency's address, telephone number, products it sells, name of a key official, and other information?

Directory of Manufacturers' Sales Agencies [D-164]

a directory of firms that offer real-estate consulting services to corporations, indicating the types of service offered, contact person, telephone number, and other information?

Consultants and Consulting Organizations Directory [D-150]
Corporate Finance Sourcebook [D-153]

a directory of firms and individuals who gather information and prepare business research reports for clients?

Directory of Fee-Based Information Services [D-163]

Educational Programs

a listing of educational programs that are available to serve the needs of the business community?

Small Business Sourcebook [D-216]

WHERE SHOULD I GO TO FIND...	*TRY*

Export-Import Resources and Services

a directory of freight carriers, by transportation mode, for domestic and foreign shipments, indicating geographical areas served?	*American Export Register* [D-133] *Official U.S. Custom House Guide* [D-206] *Thomas Register's Inbound Traffic Guide* [D-227]
the names, addresses, and telephone numbers of firms that serve the freight transportation industry, such as customs house brokers, export management companies, export packing services, transportation brokers, shipper's associations, and public warehouses?	*American Export Register* [D-133] *Official U.S. Custom House Guide* (Listed by port of entry) [D-206] *Thomas Register's Inbound Traffic Guide* [D-227]
a directory of U.S. port authorities, with their address, telephone number, and name of contact person?	*American Export Register* [D-133] *Directory of United States Importers* [D-169] *Exporters Directory* [D-175]
a listing of ports of entry in the U.S., Puerto Rico, and the U.S. Virgin Islands?	*Directory of United States Importers* [D-169] *Official U.S. Custom House Guide* [D-206]
a directory of overseas ports with the names of steamship lines that operate between each port and the U.S.?	*American Export Register* [D-133]
a directory of port authorities in foreign countries, stating their address, telephone number, telex number, and name of contact person?	*Directory of United States Importers* [D-169] *Exporters Directory* [D-175]
a listing of Canadian ports of entry?	*Official U.S. Custom House Guide* [D-206]
how to select foreign markets for exporting American-made products?	*Exporters Directory* [D-175]
a directory of exported products and the names of the companies that export them?	*Exporters Directory* [D-175]
a directory of imported products and the names of the companies that import them?	*Directory of United States Importers* [D-169]
a guide to services to American exporters rendered by the U.S. government and foreign governments?	*American Export Register* [D-133] *Exporters Directory* (U.S. government only) [D-175]

WHERE SHOULD I GO TO FIND...	*TRY*

Export-Import Resources and Services

the Schedule of U.S. Tariffs and associated duty rates?

Official U.S. Custom House Guide [D-206]

Federal Agencies: Purchasing Regulations and Procedures

the rules and procedures that control the purchasing of supplies and services by executive agencies of the federal government?

48 Code of Federal Regulations [D-343]
Federal Acquisition Regulation [D-270]

the names and telephone numbers of procurement officers for individual federal departments and agencies?

Washington Information Directory [D-234]

Federal Government Services to Business

the location of business information in federal departments and agencies?

How to Find Business Intelligence in Washington [D-182]
Washington Information Directory [D-234]
See Section H.

a directory of federal laboratories and engineering centers whose expertise, equipment, and facilities are available to assist the business community?

Directory of Federal Laboratory & Technology Resources [D-346]

Foreign Business Resources

how and where to locate information about foreign companies who are prospective suppliers or customers?

How to Find Information About Companies [D-183]
How to Find Information About Foreign Firms [D-287]

how and where to locate information about individual Japanese companies who are potential suppliers or customers?

How to Find Information About Japanese Companies and Industries [D-184]

guidelines on how to select a Japan-based consultant or business partner?

How to Find Information About Japanese Companies and Industries [D-184]

companies in Japan, classified by their product or service, with their addresses and their telephone, cable, and telex numbers?

Japan Yellow Pages [D-187]

<u>*WHERE SHOULD I GO TO FIND...*</u>   <u>*TRY*</u>

Foreign Business Resources

companies in Taiwan, classified by their product or service, with their addresses and their telephone, cable, and telex numbers?

Taiwan Yellow Pages [D-225]

the economic zones and districts in the People's Republic of China that are open to foreign business ventures?

China Investment Guide [D-56]
China Laws for Foreign Business [D-380]

application forms for the registration of authorized agents, foreign enterprises, and joint ventures in the People's Republic of China?

China Investment Guide [D-56]

directories of consulting companies, investment corporations, banks, and airlines in the People's Republic of China, stating their addresses, telephone numbers, and telex numbers?

China Investment Guide [D-56]

profiles of major corporations in the People's Republic of China, including the nature of their businesses, their CEO's names, their addresses and telephone, cable, and telex numbers?

China Investment Guide [D-56]

a listing of custom houses in the People's Republic of China, with their addresses and telephone numbers?

China Investment Guide [D-56]

Forms and Model Clauses

business forms commonly used by firms in the various phases of their operations?

AMA Handbook of Key Management Forms [D-373]
Business Forms On File [D-376]
Ten-Second Business Forms [D-325]

application forms that are required of business firms by federal agencies? (Forms most often requested.)

Business Forms On File [D-376]

model forms that are used for corporate transactions such as incorporating, issuing and transferring stock, replacing stock certificates, declaring dividends, mergers and consolidations, recapitalizations and resolutions?

Corporation Forms [D-386]
Forms of Business Agreements and Resolutions [D-410]

WHERE SHOULD I GO TO FIND...	*TRY*

Forms and Model Clauses

specimen clauses that can be used in various corporation documents?

Corporation Forms [D-386]
Forms of Business Agreements and Resolutions [D-410]

guidelines and specimen forms used in business transactions of non–publicly held corporations?

Forms of Business Agreements and Resolutions [D-410]

forms used for the management of projects?

Project Management Operating Guidelines [D-310]

Franchising

a listing of companies that offer franchise licenses, indicating their type of business, address, telephone number, and other information?

Franchise Opportunities Handbook [D-179]
Rating Guide to Franchises [D-213]
Small Business Sourcebook [D-216]
The Sourcebook of Franchise Opportunities [D-217]

ratings and other evaluations of major U.S. franchisors?

Rating Guide to Franchises [D-213]

a checklist for evaluating a franchise?

Franchise Opportunities Handbook [D-179]
How to Organize and Operate a Small Business [D-79]

a full-text compilation of state and federal franchise statutes along with the "Guide to FTC Franchising Rules"?

Business Franchise Guide [D-377]

recent administrative opinions and court decisions concerning business franchises?

Business Franchise Guide [D-377]

how-to guidelines that address the business and legal issues involved with franchising?

Complete Handbook of Franchising [D-256]

Incorporating

procedures to follow when incorporating?

Corporation Forms [D-386]
The Entrepreneur and Small Business Problem Solver [D-269]
Forms of Business Agreements and Resolutions [D-410]

WHERE SHOULD I GO TO FIND . . .	*TRY*

Incubator Centers for Businesses

a listing of small business incubator centers?

Small Business Sourcebook [D-216]

Information Sources/Services and Statistical Data

publications that either list suppliers of equipment, supplies, and services for businesses, or report where to find such lists?

Directories in Print [D-35]
Small Business Sourcebook [D-216]
Thomas Register of American Manufacturers: Products & Services; Catalog File [D-226]
Trade directories and journals
Yellow-pages section of telephone directories

bibliographies of sources that offer start-up information for small businesses?

Complete Information Bank for Entrepreneurs and Small-Business Managers [D-34]
Small Business Sourcebook [D-216]

bibliographies of reference publications (directories, handbooks, manuals, and so on) concerning the operations of small businesses in specific industries and specific kinds of business?

Small Business Sourcebook [D-216]

bibliographies or directories of trade journals, newsletters, and other trade periodicals?

Business Publication Rates and Data [D-142]
Gale Directory of Publications and Broadcast Media [D-180]
Predicasts Source Directory [D-43]
Small Business Sourcebook [D-216]
Ulrich's International Periodicals Directory [D-44]

sources of statistical data and other business information?

American Statistics Index [D-1]
Directories in Print [D-35]
How to Find Information About Companies [D-183]
Index to International Statistics [D-10]
International Directory of Business Information Agencies and Services [D-466]
Predicasts Basebook [D-467]
Predicasts Forecasts [D-468]
Predicasts F&S Index Europe [D-14]
Predicasts F&S Index International [D-14]
Predicasts F&S Index United States [D-15]

WHERE SHOULD I GO TO FIND...	*TRY*

Information Sources/Services and Statistical Data

sources of statistical data and other business information?	*Small Business Sourcebook* [D-216] *Sourcebook of Global Statistics* [D-471] *Statistical Abstract of the U.S.* [D-361] *Statistical Reference Index* [D-18] *Statistics Sources* [D-473] *Worldcasts* [D-475]
a directory of libraries and special collections on business?	*Directory of Special Libraries and Information Centers* [D-167] *Small Business Sourcebook* [D-216]
a directory of research institutes and information centers whose activities include the field of business?	*Research Centers Directory* [D-214] *Small Business Sourcebook* [D-216]
a newsprint column that answers business questions that have been submitted by readers?	*Nation's Business* [D-453] Note: Many local newspapers also provide this service.
a directory of sources that provide strategic information about individual companies, including financial and operating data?	*How to Find Information About Companies* [D-183]
how to gather intelligence information about competitors and other corporations?	*How to Find Information About Companies* [D-183]
how and where to locate information about individuals in the business community?	*How to Find Information About Executives* [D-286]
how and where to locate information about foreign companies who are prospective suppliers or customers?	*How to Find Information About Companies* [D-183] *How to Find Information About Foreign Firms* [D-287]
special guidelines and sources for getting information about private firms?	*How to Find Information About Private Companies* [D-288]
special guidelines and sources for getting information about service companies?	*How to Find Information About Service Companies* [D-289]
how and where to locate information about individual Japanese companies who are potential suppliers or customers?	*How to Find Information About Japanese Companies and Industries* [D-184]

WHERE SHOULD I GO TO FIND...	*TRY*

Information Sources/Services and Statistical Data

business information to be found in associations, think tanks, and international organizations based in Washington, DC?	*How to Find Business Intelligence in Washington* [D-182] *Washington Information Directory* [D-234]
a listing of published market research reports that focus on financial services?	*Findex* [D-37]
a directory of published newsletters on commercial products, wholesale trade, packaging, rental, warehousing, hardware, or other business subjects, with a nonevaluative description of each newsletter?	*Newsletters in Print* [D-41] *Oxbridge Directory of Newsletters* [D-42]
a guide (index) to magazine articles that describe or evaluate specific office equipment, including telephone systems?	*Consumers Index* [D-7]
an index of magazine articles that report government recalls, warnings, and advisories related to business office products?	*Consumers Index* [D-7]
statistical data on sales volume, operating ratios, capacity, distribution systems, costs, and other normative information that describes the retail trade operations of specific industries, ranging from the national scene to local business districts?	*Census of Retail Trade* [D-340]
descriptive operating data on major retail centers within Standard Metropolitan Statistical Areas (SMSA's)?	*Census of Retail Trade (Major Retail Centers)* [D-340]
descriptive statistics of operating factors in the wholesale trade industry, with coverage that ranges from national summaries to local areas?	*Census of Wholesale Trade* [D-342]
descriptive statistics of operating factors in the service industry?	*Census of Service Industries* [D-341]

WHERE SHOULD I GO TO FIND...	*TRY*

Investors

how to prepare and conduct oneself for a meeting with potential investors in one's company?

Vital Business Secrets for New and Growing Companies [D-107]

Mail Rates

U.S. international mail rates?

Commercial Atlas and Marketing Guide [D-464]
World Almanac [D-29]

rates for parcel post, certified mail, registered mail, special delivery, and postal insurance?

Commercial Atlas and Marketing Guide [D-464]
World Almanac [D-29]

Marketing Media and Services

the names, addresses, and telephone numbers of advertising agencies, arranged by the type of products or services being advertised by their clients?

Standard Directory of Advertisers [D-222]

a directory of radio syndicators, with a description of the program formats they offer?

Spot Radio Rates and Data [D-218]

directories of radio and television stations that include their addresses, telephone numbers, names of key personnel, descriptions of programming facilities, advertising contract terms and rates, and other information?

Gale Directory of Publications and Broadcast Media (Includes rates, not terms.) [D-180]
Spot Radio Rates and Data [D-218]
Spot Television Rates and Data [D-219]

a directory of domestic and international business publications (e.g., magazines and trade newspapers) in the various industries, with a description of each publication, including advertising contract terms and rates, circulation data, printing requirements, names of key advertising executives, addresses, telephone numbers, and other information?

Business Publication Rates and Data [D-142]

WHERE SHOULD I GO TO FIND . . .	*TRY*

Marketing Media and Services

a directory of health care publications, with a description of each publication, including advertising contract terms and rates, circulation data, printing requirements, names of key advertising executives, addresses, telephone numbers, and other information?	*Business Publication Rates and Data* [D-142] *Gale Directory of Publications and Broadcast Media* (Note: Includes only some of these data elements.) [D-180]
a directory of direct-response advertising media, with company descriptions that include advertising contract terms and rates, circulation data, printing requirements, names of key advertising executives, addresses, telephone numbers, and other information?	*Business Publication Rates and Data* [D-142]
a directory of newspapers, with a description of each newspaper, including contract terms, classified rates, frequency of publication, circulation data, printing requirements, names of key advertising executives, addresses, telephone numbers, and other information?	*Gale Directory of Publications and Broadcast Media* (Note: Includes only some of these data elements.) [D-180] *Newspaper Rates and Data* [D-205]
a directory of college and university newspapers and newspapers geared toward black Americans, with a description of each newspaper, including advertising rates, circulation data, frequency of publication, names of key advertising exccutives, addresses, telephone numbers, and other information?	*Gale Directory of Publications and Broadcast Media* [D-180] *Newspaper Rates and Data* [D-205]
a directory of local urban and suburban weekly newspapers and shopping guides, with a description of each publication, including classified rates, printing requirements, circulation data, frequency of publication, names of key advertising executives, address, telephone number, and other information?	*Community Publication Rates and Data* [D-145] *Gale Directory of Publications and Broadcast Media* [D-180]

WHERE SHOULD I GO TO FIND...	*TRY*

Marketing Media and Services

a directory of consumer magazines and consumer card decks, with descriptions that include an editorial profile statement, advertising contract provisions, advertising rates, frequency of publication, circulation data, printing requirements, names of key advertising executives, addresses, telephone numbers, and other information?	*Consumer Magazine and Agri-Media Rates and Data* [D-151]
a directory of farm publications and farm direct-response advertising media, with descriptions that include advertising contract provisions, advertising rates, frequency of publication, circulation data, printing requirements, names of key advertising executives, addresses, telephone numbers, and other information?	*Consumer Magazine and Agri-Media Rates and Data* [D-151] *Gale Directory of Publications and Broadcast Media* (Selected information only) [D-180]
sources for direct-mail lists that are available to purchase for advertising purposes?	*Direct Mail List Rates and Data* [D-159] *Information Sources* [D-185]
providers of support services for direct-mail operations (consultants, suppliers, mail preparation, and so on)?	*Direct Mail List Rates and Data* [D-159]
a directory of firms that provide business co-op mailings and package insert programs, with descriptions that include rates, names of key executives, printing requirements, circulation data, addresses, telephone numbers, and other information?	*Direct Mail List Rates and Data* [D-159]
a listing of published market research reports that focus on financial services?	*Findex* [D-37]

Planning, Organizing, and Managing a Business

how to write a business plan?	*Business Plans That Win $$$* [D-53] *The Entrepreneur and Small Business Problem Solver* [D-269] *From Concept to Market* [D-73]

(answer continues)

WHERE SHOULD I GO TO FIND...   *TRY*

Planning, Organizing, and Managing a Business

how to write a business plan?

How to Create a Winning Business Plan
[D-411]
How to Develop a Business Plan in 15 Days
[D-77]
*How to Organize and Operate a Small
Business* [D-79]
How to Set Up Your Own Small Business
[D-290]
*Start-Up Money: How to Finance Your New
Small Business* [D-321]
*Vital Business Secrets for New and Growing
Companies* [D-107]

steps to follow when organizing a
business?

Business Forms On File [D-376]
*The Entrepreneur and Small Business
Problem Solver* [D-269]
From Concept to Market [D-73]
*How to Organize and Operate a Small
Business* [D-79]

guidelines on how to organize and
manage a small business?

*The Entrepreneur and Small Business
Problem Solver* [D-269]
*How to Organize and Operate a Small
Business* [D-79]
How to Set Up Your Own Small Business
[D-290]
*Vital Business Secrets for New and Growing
Companies* [D-107]

suggestions on how to select a business
name?

How to Set Up Your Own Small Business
[D-290]

tips on selecting the site for a small
business?

How to Set Up Your Own Small Business
[D-290]

suggestions for the physical layout for a
small business?

*How to Organize and Operate a Small
Business* [D-79]

how to evaluate a business lease from the
tenant's point of view?

How to Set Up Your Own Small Business
[D-290]

how to decide if equipment should be
leased or purchased, how to select a
leasing company, and how to negotiate
a lease?

*The Entrepreneur and Small Business
Problem Solver* [D-269]

WHERE SHOULD I GO TO FIND...   *TRY*

Planning, Organizing, and Managing a Business

a directory of firms that offer equipment leasing to corporations, with information on the services provided, industries served, name of contact person, telephone number, and other related information?

Corporate Finance Sourcebook [D-153]

tips on how to prevent theft and bad checks in a small business?

The Entrepreneur and Small Business Problem Solver [D-269]

a checklist of steps to follow when developing or revising credit and collection policies for a small business?

The Entrepreneur and Small Business Problem Solver [D-269]

how to select the right lawyer for a business firm?

How to Set Up Your Own Small Business [D-290]

Pricing

guidelines for setting prices?

AMA Management Handbook [D-242]
The Entrepreneur and Small Business Problem Solver [D-269]
From Concept to Market [D-73]
How to Organize and Operate a Small Business [D-79]

Product Descriptions, Evaluations, and Recall

a guide (index) to magazine articles that describe or evaluate specific office equipment, including telephone systems?

Consumers Index [D-7]

evaluations and comprarisons of business office products?

Buyers Laboratory Test Reports [D-379]
Datapro Office Products Evaluation Service [D-390]
What to Buy for Business [D-459]

an index of magazine articles that report government recalls, warnings, and advisories related to business office products?

Consumers Index [D-7]

Ranking of Companies, Products, and Services

who or what company, product, or
service has been ranked "number one"
according to a selected criterion?

Business Rankings and Salaries Index [D-5]
(Note: Lists many criteria from which to
choose.)

Start–Up Capital

how to determine the amount of capital
needed to start a business, and sources
for borrowing the money?

*How to Organize and Operate a Small
Business* [D-79]
How to Set Up Your Own Small Business
[D-290]

where to obtain the funds needed for
starting or expanding a business?

*The Entrepreneur and Small Business Problem
Solver* [D-269]
From Concept to Market [D-73]
Small Business Sourcebook [D-216]
*Vital Business Secrets for New and Growing
Companies* [D-107]

Stock: Initial Offering

how to take a company public and
the pros and cons associated with this
decision?

Accounting Desk Book [D-239]
*Vital Business Secrets for New and Growing
Companies* [D-107]

Trade Secrets

steps to be taken and forms to be used
when protecting a corporation's trade
secrets?

Corporation Forms [D-386]

Trade Shows, Exhibitions, and Conventions

a directory of industry conventions,
exhibitions, trade shows, and other
meetings with the names and addresses
of sponsors, meeting dates, and other
related information?

Small Business Sourcebook [D-216]
*Trade Shows and Perfessional Exhibits
Directory* [D-228]

Transportation Services

Note: See also "Export-Import Resources
and Services" in this subsection, above.

WHERE SHOULD I GO TO FIND...   *TRY*

Transportation Services

a directory of freight carriers, by transportation mode, for domestic and foreign
shipments, indicating geographical areas
served?

American Export Register [D-133]
Official U.S. Custom House Guide [D-206]
Thomas Register's Inbound Traffic Guide
[D-227]

the airlines that serve each U.S. city?

Commercial Atlas and Marketing Guide
[D-464]

the main routes for each railroad company in the U.S.?

Commercial Atlas and Marketing Guide
[D-464]

| **Computers, Information Processing, and Records Management** |

Associations, Vendors, and Consultants

a directory of firms that provide information products and services, including
databases, software, hardware, information retrieval, reference works, market
research, information brokerage, and
other information?

Data Sources: Data Comm/Telecomm [D-156]
Data Sources: Hardware [D-157]
Data Sources: Software [D-158]
Directory of Fee-Based Information Services
[D-163]
*Encyclopedia of Information Systems and Ser-
vices* [D-174]
Information Sources [D-185]
*Standard & Poor's Register of Corporations,
Directors, and Executives, Vol. 3* [D-221]

a directory of computer, software, and
other high-technology companies with
the products they manufacture?

Corporate Technology Directory [D-154]

a directory of microcomputer software
vendors?

Datapro Directory of Microcomputer Software
[D-387]
Data Sources: Software [D-158]

a directory of vendors for microcomputing, electronic publishing, and/or office
automation products?

*Datapro Management of Microcomputer Sys-
tems* [D-388]
Datapro Management of Office Automation
[D-389]
Datapro Reports on Microcomputers [D-391]
Data Sources: Hardware [D-157]
Data Sources: Software [D-158]

WHERE SHOULD I GO TO FIND...	TRY
Associations, Vendors, and Consultants	
a directory of computer hardware manufacturers?	*Data Sources: Hardware* [D-157]
a listing of computer maintenance companies, with a description of their services?	*Data Sources: Hardware* [D-157]
a listing of data/telecommunications companies, with a profile of each firm?	*Data Sources: Data Comm/Telecomm* [D-156]
the names of consultants in the computing field?	*Computers and Computing Information Resources Directory* [D-148] *Consultants and Consulting Organizations Directory* [D-150]
a listing of reprographic trade associations, with their addresses, telephone numbers, and other descriptive information?	*Datapro Management of Office Automation* [D-389] *Encyclopedia of Associations, Vol. 1* [D-173] *National Trade and Professional Associations of the United States* [D-204]
a directory of companies that provide financial recordkeeping services for specific retail and service trades?	*The Entrepreneur and Small Business Problem Solver* [D-269] Yellow-pages section of local telephone directories
the names and addresses of firms that provide management software for the transportation industry, with an indication of the operational purpose of the software?	*Thomas Register's Inbound Traffic Guide* [D-227]
a directory of trade and professional associations and user groups that are either professionally involved with computing or interested in computing as an avocation?	*Computers and Computing Information Resources Directory* [D-148]
Forecasting	
how microcomputers can be used for financial forecasting?	*The Manager's Guide to Business Forecasting* [D-88]
microcomputer programs written in BASIC that perform business forecasting techniques?	*Business Forecasting: Concepts and Microcomputer Applications* [D-52]

WHERE SHOULD I GO TO FIND...   *TRY*

Hardware, Software, and Databases: Descriptions and Evaluations

guidelines to follow when buying a computer for a business?

Buying a Computer for Your Growing Business [D-55]
Datapro Directory of Microcomputer Software [D-387]
Datapro Management of Microcomputer Systems [D-388]

how to evaluate and select microcomputer software for a business?

Datapro Directory of Microcomputer Software [D-387]
Datapro Management of Microcomputer Systems [D-388]
Selecting Business Software [D-99]

users' ratings of vendor-specific microcomputers, software, and peripherals based on operational criteria?

Datapro Management of Microcomputer Systems [D-388]
Datapro Reports on Microcomputers [D-391]

user comments about computers and software?

Buyers Laboratory Test Reports [D-379]

descriptive and evaluative reviews of microcomputer hardware, software, peripherals, and other related products, including ratings and prices?

Datapro Reports on Microcomputers [D-391]

descriptions, evaluations, and buyer recommendations for word-processing and database-management software for IBM PCs and compatibles?

Buyers Laboratory Test Reports [D-379]

a directory of microcomputer software packages that are available for business applications, with a description of each package?

Datapro Directory of Microcomputer Software [D-387]
Data Sources: Software [D-158]
Directory of Statistical Microcomputer Software [D-168]

a listing of computer databases designed for business applications?

Directory of Online Databases [D-261]
Dow Jones-Irwin Banker's Guide to Online Databases [D-263]
Financial Analyst's Handbook [D-271]
How to Find Information About Companies [D-183]

Hardware, Software, and Databases: Descriptions and Evaluations

descriptions and evaluations of micro-computer software that is available for business use, along with recommenda-tions to buyers?

Datapro Reports on Microcomputers [D-391]
What to Buy for Business [D-459]

a collection of extracts of microcomputer software evaluations that were published in periodicals?

Software Reviews On File [D-456]

a directory of databases that analyze soft-ware and hardware products?

Directory of Online Databases [D-261]

descriptive profiles of computer hard-ware products?

Data Sources: Hardware [D-157]

descriptive profiles of data-communications and telecommunications hardware?

Data Sources: Data Comm/Telecomm [D-156]

what to do with aging PCs?

Datapro Management of Microcomputer Systems [D-388]

guidelines for selecting data management software for microcomputers?

Datapro Management of Microcomputer Systems [D-388]

an explanation of the technical features of the hardware, software, and commu-nications systems that support micro-computing, including guidelines for planning and operating a microcomputer system?

Datapro Management of Microcomputer Systems [D-388]

guidelines for contracting the develop-ment of microcomputer software?

Datapro Management of Microcomputer Systems [D-388]

a description of online databases that provide information used by the invest-ment industry?

Dow Jones-Irwin Investor's Guide to Online Databases [D-265]

guidelines for selecting accounting soft-ware for use with microcomputers?

Datapro Management of Microcomputer Systems [D-388]

microcomputer programs written in BASIC that perform business fore-casting techniques?

Business Forecasting: Concepts and Microcom-puter Applications [D-52]

WHERE SHOULD I GO TO FIND...   TRY

Hardware, Software, and Databases: Descriptions and Evaluations

descriptive profiles of microcomputer software packages that serve applications for government operations?

Datapro Directory of Microcomputer Software [D-387]
Data Sources: Software [D-158]

a table that displays statistical functions and identifies those microcomputer software packages that perform each of these functions?

Directory of Statistical Microcomputer Software [D-168]

guidelines for evaluating and selecting records-management software?

Datapro Management of Office Automation [D-389]

Information Sources

a listing of sources that identify business databases?

Computers and Computing Information Resources Directory [D-148]
Directories in Print [D-35]
Small Business Sourcebook [D-216]

a listing of published market research reports on computers, software, and information systems?

Findex [D-37]

a guide to print and nonprint sources of information on all areas of computers and computing?

Computers and Computing Information Resources Directory [D-148]

directories of vendors of hardware, software, and online products and services?

Directories in Print [D-35]

Newsletters

a directory of published newsletters on computers and information systems, with a nonevaluative description of each newsletter?

Computers and Computing Information Resources Directory [D-148]
Newsletters in Print [D-41]
Oxbridge Directory of Newsletters [D-42]

Office Automation

guidelines for conducting feasibility studies as a preliminary step toward office automation?

Datapro Management of Office Automation [D-389]

an explanation of how to automate an office, with analyses of equipment, systems, software, personnel management, and facilities management?

Datapro Management of Office Automation [D-389]

WHERE SHOULD I GO TO FIND...	*TRY*

Office Automation

how to evaluate and select specific types of equipment for an automated office?	*Datapro Management of Office Automation* [D-389]
reports on solutions to office automation problems?	*Datapro Management of Office Automation* [D-389]
guidelines for estimating the cost and benefit of a new automation system for the office?	*Datapro Management of Office Automation* [D-389]

Officials: Computing Industry

| the names of leaders in the computer information field, with their addresses and telephone numbers? | *Computers and Computing Information Resources Directory* [D-148] |

Organization, Management, and Staffing

guidelines on how to manage information systems?	*AMA Management Handbook* [D-242]
a discussion of issues and guidelines for the management of corporate information systems, including the impact on corporate competitiveness?	*Corporate Information Systems Management* [D-59]
guidelines on how to organize and staff an information center when utilizing microcomputers?	*Datapro Management of Microcomputer Systems* [D-388]
guidelines for training personnel in the use of microcomputer systems?	*Datapro Management of Microcomputer Systems* [D-388]
examples of managerial job descriptions in computer operations?	*Encyclopedia of Managerial Job Descriptions* [D-403]

Records Management

| how to establish a records retention policy? | *Datapro Management of Office Automation* [D-389]
 File Management and Information Retrieval Systems [D-72]
 Handbook of Record Storage and Space Management [D-283]
 Information and Records Management [D-82] |

WHERE SHOULD I GO TO FIND...   *TRY*

Records Management

WHERE SHOULD I GO TO FIND...	TRY
a model schedule for retaining different types of records?	*Datapro Management of Office Automation* [D-389] *Handbook of Record Storage and Space Management* [D-283]
reports on the federal laws and regulations that regulate the retention requirements of business records?	*Federal Register* [D-350]
guidelines for developing, organizing, and managing a records-management system?	*AMA Management Handbook* [D-242] *Business Records Control* [D-54] *Datapro Management of Office Automation* [D-389] *File Management and Information Retrieval Systems* [D-72] *Information and Records Management* [D-82]
sample questionnaires that can be used to conduct a records-management study?	*Information and Records Management* [D-82]
model forms that are used to control records?	*Information and Records Management* [D-82]
tips on how to plan and/or evaluate a records storage system?	*Datapro Management of Office Automation* [D-389] *Handbook of Record Storage and Space Management* [D-283]
guidelines on how to evaluate equipment used for the storage of records?	*Business Records Control* [D-54] *Handbook of Record Storage and Space Management* [D-283]
rules for alphabetic indexing and filing?	*Business Records Control* [D-54] *File Management and Information Retrieval Systems* [D-72]
special considerations that should be addressed when doing computerized indexing of filing systems?	*Business Records Control* [D-54]
helpful hints on how to conduct business with consultants and vendors in matters of records management?	*Information and Records Management* [D-82]

WHERE SHOULD I GO TO FIND...	*TRY*

Trade Shows, Exhibitions, and Conventions

a listing of computer-related conventions, trade shows, and professional exhibitions?

Computers and Computing Information Resources Directory [D-148]
Trade Shows and Professional Exhibits Directory [D-228]

Consumers and Consumerism

Consumer Assistance Organizations and Government Agencies

a directory of government agencies at various levels of government and/or private organizations that provide assistance with consumer complaints, listing their addresses and telephone numbers?

Consumer Protection Manual [D-258]
Consumer Sourcebook [D-152]
Consumer's Resource Handbook [D-344]
Encyclopedia of Associations, Vol. 1 [D-173]
National Directory of State Agencies [D-199]
State Administrative Officials Classified by Function [D-224]
Washington Information Directory [D-234]

consumer programs and services offered by federal agencies, including telephone numbers for acquiring further information about these programs?

United States Government Manual [D-366]

a directory of state agencies for each state with the names, addresses, and telephone numbers of the chief officials?

National Directory of State Agencies [D-199]
State Administrative Officials by Function [D-224]

a directory of Better Business Bureaus?

Consumer's Resource Handbook [D-344]

Consumer Complaints and Their Redress

how to write a consumer's complaint letter?

Consumer Protection Manual [D-258]
Consumer Sourcebook [D-152]
Consumer's Resource Handbook [D-344]

sample letters for expressing one's legal rights in a consumer complaint?

Consumer Protection Manual [D-258]

what to do when wronged in a consumer transaction, and how to pursue a complaint with the provider of consumer goods or services?

Consumer Protection Manual [D-258]

WHERE SHOULD I GO TO FIND...	*TRY*

Consumer Complaints and Their Redress

negotiating strategies for resolving disputes regarding consumer purchases?	*Consumer Protection Manual* [D-258]
the names, addresses, and telephone numbers of consumer-affairs representatives at selected major corporations?	*Consumer's Resource Handbook* [D-344]
the purpose of the small claims court, and how to file a suit in this type of court?	*Consumer Protection Manual* [D-258]

Consumer Credit

a summary of the protection granted under federal laws governing consumer credit, and the rights provided under the Uniform Commercial Code concerning disputes over the balance owed a creditor?	*Consumer Protection Manual* [D-258]
the liability of a credit-card owner when there has been an unauthorized use of his/her card?	*Consumer Protection Manual* [D-258]
a weekly listing of selected low-interest-rate bank credit cards that are offered nationally, with a report of their interest rates and annual fees (if any)?	*Barron's* [D-440]
how to assure the accuracy of a file at a consumer-credit reporting agency, what such an agency must disclose about the file, and remedies available for securing correction of errors found in the file?	*Consumer Protection Manual* [D-258]
the legal rights, obligations, and remedies of collection agencies and debtors regarding collection practices?	*Consumer Protection Manual* [D-258]

Consumer Demographic Data

personal consumption expenditures in the U.S. for selected goods and services during specified years?	*Business Statistics* [D-336] *Historical Statistics of the United States* [D-351]

(answer continues)

WHERE SHOULD I GO TO FIND...	*TRY*

Consumer Demographic Data

personal consumption expenditures in the U.S. for selected goods and services during specified years?	*Statistical Abstract of the United States* [D-361] *Survey of Current Business* [D-363] *World Almanac* [D-29]
data on per capita and family income?	*Census of Population: General Social and Economic Characteristics* [D-339] *Commercial Atlas & Marketing Guide* [D-464] *Historical Statistics of the United States* [D-351] *Sourcebook of Demographics & Buying Power for Every ZIP Code in the USA* [D-470] *Statistical Abstract of the United States* [D-361]
data on urban consumer expenditures?	*Historical Statistics of the United States* [D-351] *Statistical Abstract of the United States* [D-361]
a measure of the potential buying power of consumers in a geographic market compared to other markets?	*Survey of Buying Power Data Service* [D-474]
a measure of household and per capita disposable personal income, reported by market area?	*Survey of Buying Power Data Service* [D-474]

Consumer Prices

Consumer Price Index data?	*BLS News* [D-334] *Business Statistics* [D-336] *CPI Detailed Report* [D-345] *Dow Jones-Irwin Business and Investment Almanac* [D-24] *Historical Statistics of the United States* [D-351] *Statistical Abstract of the United States* [D-361] *Survey of Current Business* [D-363] *Wall Street Journal* [D-457] *World Almanac* [D-29]

WHERE SHOULD I GO TO FIND...	*TRY*

Consumer Prices

retail food prices for selected foods during specified years?	*Historical Statistics of the United States* [D-351] *Statistical Abstract of the United States* [D-361]
retail food price index data for selected years?	*Historical Statistics of the United States* [D-351] *Statistical Abstract of the United States* [D-361]

Consumer Rights, Laws, and Regulations

a summary of consumer rights and obligations under the law?	*Consumer Protection Manual* [D-258]
a summary of the deceptive sales practices laws of the individual states?	*Consumer Protection Manual* [D-258]
an explanation of the rules of the Federal Trade Commission concerning door-to-door sales, advertisements of food stores, and the conduct of book and record clubs?	*Consumer Protection Manual* [D-258]
an explanation of federal and state regulations regarding unordered merchandise?	*Consumer Protection Manual* [D-258]
an explanation of consumer rights under warranties and strategies for recovering damages?	*Consumer Protection Manual* [D-258]
a listing of tenant's rights?	*Consumer Sourcebook* [D-152]

Evaluation: Companies, Products, and Services

who or what is ranked "number one," whether it be a person, company, product, service, region, or some other classification?	*Business Rankings and Salaries Index* [D-5]
ratings of individual insurance companies, based on their profitability and spread of risk?	*Best's Insurance Reports* [D-140]

WHERE SHOULD I GO TO FIND...	*TRY*

Evaluation: Companies, Products, and Services

a guide (index) to magazine articles that provide descriptive information or evaluations on specific products and services?	*Consumers Index* [D-7]
reports of product comparisons and ratings based on test results?	*Consumer Reports* [D-442]
a consumer's guide to software for personal computers that provides descriptive and evaluative information?	*Software Reviews On File* [D-456]
users' ratings of vendor-specific microcomputers, software, and peripherals, based on operational criteria?	*Datapro Management of Microcomputer Systems* [D-388] *Datapro Reports on Microcomputers* [D-391]
user comments about computers and software?	*Buyers Laboratory Test Reports* [D-379]

Financial Planning

guidelines for estate planning?	*Handbook of Estate Planning* [D-280]
financial guidelines for retirement planning?	*Dow Jones-Irwin Guide to Retirement Planning* [D-68]

Information Sources

a subject index to articles in periodicals on consumer topics?	*Business Periodicals Index* [D-4] *Consumers Index* [D-7] *Readers' Guide to Periodical Literature* [D-17]
a subject index to U.S. government publications on consumer related subjects?	*American Statistics Index* [D-1] *Monthly Catalog of United States Government Publications* [D-354]
a bibliography of published market research reports on consumer goods and services?	*Findex* [D-37]
a bibliography of published market research reports on health care providers, regulations, equipment, and drugs?	*Findex* [D-37]
a guide (index) to magazine articles that provide descriptive information or evaluations on specific products and services?	*Consumers Index* [D-7]

WHERE SHOULD I GO TO FIND...	*TRY*

Information Sources

| an index to magazine articles that report government recalls, warnings, and advisories related to consumer products? | *Consumers Index* [D-7] |

Newsletters

| a directory of published newsletters on consumerism with a nonevaluative description of each newsletter? | *Newsletters in Print* [D-41]
Oxbridge Directory of Newsletters [D-42] |

Product Recall

| an index to magazine articles that report government recalls, warnings, and advisories related to consumer products? | *Consumers Index* [D-7] |
| a listing of federal agencies with authority to order recalls of products and the products over which they have oversight? | *AMA Management Handbook* [D-242] |

Purchasing Guidelines

Note: See also "Consumer Rights, Laws, and Regulations" in this subsection.

how to determine the accuracy of claims made by a seller?	*Consumer Protection Manual* [D-258]
how to reject goods either at the time of delivery or after delivery?	*Consumer Protection Manual* [D-258]
guidelines that will help to minimize fraud and errors when purchasing fine gems and jewelry?	*Dow Jones-Irwin Guide to Fine Gems and Jewelry* [D-264]
guidelines to protect against health and medical fraud?	*Consumer Sourcebook* [D-152]
guidelines that will help with the selection of a health club?	*Consumer Sourcebook* [D-152]
ways to minimize closing (settlement) costs when selling a house?	*Consumer Sourcebook* [D-152]
guidelines for purchasing preneed funeral arrangements?	*Consumer Sourcebook* [D-152]

WHERE SHOULD I GO TO FIND...	*TRY*
Purchasing Guidelines	
how to select a travel agent and questions to ask concerning travel arrangements?	*Consumer Sourcebook* [D-152]
Real Estate Matters	
an explanation of the steps involved in purchasing a house?	*Barron's Real Estate Handbook* [D-245]
how to determine the maximum afford-able price that can be paid for a house?	*Barron's Real Estate Handbook* [D-245]
guidelines for selecting a real estate broker?	*Barron's Real Estate Handbook* [D-245]
an explanation of the elements of a residential real estate sales contract?	*Barron's Real Estate Handbook* [D-245]
an explanation of the steps involved with selling a house, including helpful tips on setting the price?	*Barron's Real Estate Handbook* [D-245]
a summary of governmental regulations that govern the development and operation of a condominium?	*Condominium Development Guide* [D-257]
Telephone Service	
a national directory of toll-free "800" business telephone numbers that are available for use by consumers?	*AT&T Toll-Free 800 Consumer Directory* [D-137]
Utility Rates and State Commissions	
the average amount of residential electric bills and charges per kilowatt-hour across the nation during selected years?	*Moody's Public Utility Manual* [D-196] *Statistical Abstract of the United States* [D-361]
the names, addresses, and telephone numbers of state utility commissions?	*Consumer's Resource Handbook* [D-344] *National Directory of State Agencies* [D-199] *State Administrative Officials Classified by Function* [D-224]
Vendor Products and Services	
the name, address, and telephone number of a trade name's manufacturer, marketer, distributor, or importer?	*Brands and Their Companies* [D-113] *Thomas Register of American Manufacturers: Company Profiles, Vol. N–Z* [D-226]

WHERE SHOULD I GO TO FIND...   *TRY*

Vendor Products and Services

the names, addresses, and telephone numbers of companies that provide a particular product or service?

Moody's Industrial Manual [D-190]
Moody's International Manual [D-191]
Moody's OTC Industrial Manual [D-194]
Standard & Poor's Corporation Records [D-220]
Thomas Register of American Manufacturers: Products and Services [D-226]

sales catalogs of companies that contain such information as the products or services offered, design specifications, performance data, product photographs, model numbers, addresses and telephone numbers for ordering and other information?

Thomas Register of American Manufacturers: Catalog File [D-226]

foreign trade names, with the products or services they represent and the company that uses the trade name?

International Directory of Corporate Affiliations [D-186]

a directory of businesses, listed by city and state, that cites each company's address and the products or services provided?

Moody's Industrial Manual [D-190]
Moody's OTC Industrial Manual [D-194]

Corporate Operations, Officials, and Profiles

Acquisitions, Mergers, and Name Changes

information on corporate acquisitions, mergers, and name changes?

Corporate Technology Directory
(Note: Covers high-tech companies only.) [D-154]
Directory of Corporate Affiliations [D-161]
Mergers & Acquisitions [D-450]
Moody's Handbook of Common Stocks [D-303]
Moody's News Reports series [D-192]
Predicasts F&S Index of Corporate Change [D-13]
Standard & Poor's Daily News [D-220]

WHERE SHOULD I GO TO FIND...	*TRY*

Acquisitions, Mergers, and Name Changes

a listing of independent corporate merger and acquisition intermediaries that reports their areas of specialization, method of compensation, contact person, telephone number, and other relevant information?	*Corporate Finance Sourcebook* [D-153]
a directory of merger and acquisition specialists at commercial banks and investment banking firms?	*Institutional Investor* (November issue) [D-447]
guidelines for planning and implementing corporate leveraged buyouts?	*The Art of M&A* [D-50] *The Complete Guide to a Successful Leveraged Buyout* [D-57] *Corporate Acquisitions, Mergers, and Divestitures* [D-384]
how to conduct a search for potential merger or acquisition companies, and where to obtain the necessary information for analyzing these targets?	*The Art of M&A* [D-50] *Corporate Acquisitions, Mergers, and Divestitures* [D-384] *How to Find Information About Acquisition Candidates* [D-285]
how to identify hidden liabilities or undervalued assets of an acquisition or merger company target?	*Corporate Acquisitions, Mergers, and Divestitures* [D-384]
what should be considered before negotiations start for a corporate acquisition or merger?	*Corporate Acquisitions, Mergers, and Divestitures* [D-384]
a comprehensive listing of questions and answers that explain the corporate merger and acquisition processes?	*The Art of M&A* [D-50]
a checklist of things to do when executing a corporate acquisition?	*The Art of M&A* [D-50]
a checklist of basic legal considerations associated with a corporate acquisition?	*Tax Transactions Library: Mergers, Acquisitions and Leveraged Buyouts* [D-431]
basic legal information pertaining to tax and nontax issues regarding corporate mergers, acquisitions, and divestitures?	*Corporate Acquisitions, Mergers, and Divestitures* [D-384]

WHERE SHOULD I GO TO FIND...	*TRY*

Acquisitions, Mergers, and Name Changes

basic legal information pertaining to tax and nontax issues regarding corporate mergers, acquisitions, and divestitures?	*Responsibilities of Corporate Officers and Directors Under Federal Securities Laws* [D-311] *Tax Transactions Library: Mergers, Acquisitions and Leveraged Buyouts* [D-431]
an outline for a corporate merger agreement?	*The Art of M&A* [D-50]
defenses against a corporate tender offer?	*Corporate Acquisitions, Mergers, and Divestitures* [D-384]
an index to articles in journals and newspapers concerning corporate mergers, acquisitions, name changes, and other related activities?	*Predicasts F&S Index of Corporate Change* [D-13]
abstracts of articles in journals and newspapers about corporate acquisitions?	*PROMT* [D-16]
a directory of online databases that contain data records on corporate acquisitions, mergers, and tender offers?	*Directory of Online Databases* [D-261]

Biographical Profiles

biographies of corporate executives, directors, and other notables in the business world?	*Biographical Dictionary of American Business Leaders* [D-111] *Biography and Genealogy Master Index* [D-2] *International Who's Who* [D-126] *Standard & Poor's Register of Corporations, Directors, and Executives, Vol. 2* [D-221] *Who's Who in America* [D-129] *Who's Who in Finance and Industry* [D-130] *Who's Who in the World* [D-131] Consult also one of the U.S regional Who's Who biographical dictionaries, foreign biographical dictionaries, or a Who's Who–type publication in one of the business specialties. (See the next question.)
a bibliography of biographical (Who's Who) dictionaries?	*Directories in Print* [D-35]
how and where to locate information about business executives and others in the business world?	*How to Find Information About Executives* [D-286]

WHERE SHOULD I GO TO FIND...	*TRY*

Compensation

a listing of the highest paid corporate executives in America?

Business Week (See "Executive Compensation Scoreboard" in the May issue.) [D-441]
Forbes [D-445]

an index to information about prevailing salaries in industry, the professions, and occupations?

Business Rankings and Salaries Index [D-5]

guidelines, procedures, and forms followed in the compensation of corporate officers and directors?

Corporation Forms [D-386]
Forms of Business Agreements and Resolutions [D-410]

Corporate Listings, Profiles, and Financial Data

a descriptive profile of U. S. *parent* companies, reporting for each the stock exchange with which it is listed; ticker symbol; types of products or services; approximate sales revenue; SIC codes; board of directors; profile of each division, affiliate, or subsidiary; and other descriptive information?

America's Corporate Families [D-134]
Corporate Technology Directory [D-154]
Directory of Corporate Affiliations [D-161]
Standard & Poor's Register of Corporations, Directors, and Executives, Vol. 1 [D-221]
(See also next question.)

a directory of U.S. businesses with a description of each company that includes address, SIC code, type of business, designation if public or private ownership, names of officers, sales volume, divisions and their lines of business, name of accounting firm and of legal counsel for each, and other descriptive information?

Corporate Technology Directory [D-154]
Million Dollar Directory [D-188]
Moody's Manuals [D-192]
Standard & Poor's Corporation Records [D-220]
Standard & Poor's Register of Corporations, Directors, and Executives, Vol. 1 [D-221]
Ward's Business Directory, Vol. 1 (partial data) [D-231]
Ward's Business Directory, Vol. 2 (partial data) [D-232]
Ward's Business Directory, Vol. 3 (partial data) [D-233]
(See also preceding question.)

Corporate Listings, Profiles, and Financial Data

a directory of businesses in countries throughout the world, with a description of each company that includes the line of business, SIC code, address, telex number or cable address, name and title of senior operating officer, sales volume, name of parent company, and an indication of whether or not the company imports and/or exports?

Principal International Businesses [D-210]
Standard & Poor's Register of Corporations, Directors, and Executives, Vol. 1 [D-221]

a descriptive profile of a foreign parent company or a U.S. parent company with foreign holdings, indicating SIC codes; type of business; names of key personnel; approximate sales; location, telephone number, and line of business of each foreign holding; and other related information?

America's Corporate Families and International Affiliates [D-135]
International Directory of Corporate Affiliations [D-186]
Standard & Poor's Register of Corporations, Directors, and Executives, Vol. 1 [D-221]

the identity of the foreign parent company of a subsidiary, affiliate, or division?

America's Corporate Families and International Affiliates [D-135]
Corporate Technology Directory [D-154]
International Directory of Corporate Affiliations [D-186]
Standard & Poor's Register of Corporations, Directors, and Executives, Vols. 1 and 3 [D-221]

the identification and location of affiliates, subsidiaries, and divisions of foreign parent companies and foreign holdings of American companies?

America's Corporate Families and International Affiliates [D-135]
International Directory of Corporate Affiliations [D-186]
Standard & Poor's Register of Corporations, Directors, and Executives, Vol. 3 [D-221]

the identity of the U.S. parent company of a foreign subsidiary, affiliate, or division?

America's Corporate Families and International Affiliates [D-135]
International Directory of Corporate Affiliations [D-186]

the identity of the U.S. parent company of a subsidiary, affiliate, or division?

America's Corporate Families [D-134]
Corporate Technology Directory [D-154]
Directory of Corporate Affiliations [D-161]

Corporate Listings, Profiles, and Financial Data

the addresses, telephone numbers, and telex numbers of foreign companies or U.S. parent companies with foreign holdings?	*America's Corporate Families and International Affiliates* [D-135] *International Directory of Corporate Affiliations* [D-186] *Standard & Poor's Register of Corporations, Directors, and Executives, Vol. 1* [D-221]
the identification and location of a U.S. parent company's affiliates, divisions, and subsidiaries?	*America's Corporate Families* [D-134] *Corporate Technology Directory* (high-tech operating units only) [D-154] *Directory of Corporate Affiliations* [D-161] *Standard & Poor's Corporation Records* [D-220] *Standard & Poor's Register of Corporations, Directors, and Executives, Vols. 1 and 3* [D-221] *Thomas Register of American Manufacturers: Company Profiles* [D-226]
the address, telephone number, and other communication numbers of a U.S. company?	*America's Corporate Families* [D-134] *Corporate Technology Directory* [D-154] *Directory of Corporate Affiliations* [D-161] *Million Dollar Directory* [D-188] *Moody's Manuals* [D-192] *Standard & Poor's Corporation Records* [D-220] *Standard & Poor's Register of Corporations, Directors, and Executives, Vol. 1* [D-221] *Thomas Register of American Manufacturers: Company Profiles* [D-226] *Ward's Business Directory, Vol. 1* [D-231] *Ward's Business Directory, Vol. 2* [D-232] *Ward's Business Directory, Vol. 3* [D-233] *World Almanac* [D-29]
the location of a company's distributors, engineering or service offices, plants, and sales offices?	*Thomas Register of American Manufacturers: Company Profiles* [D-226]
the names of sales agencies that represent manufacturers along with each agency's address, telephone number, products it sells, name of a key official, and other information?	*Directory of Manufacturers' Sales Agencies* [D-164]

WHERE SHOULD I GO TO FIND...	*TRY*

Corporate Listings, Profiles, and Financial Data

the names of corporate officials?	*America's Corporate Families and International Affiliates* [D-135] *America's Corporate Families* [D-134] *Corporate Technology Directory* [D-154] *Directory of Corporate Affiliations* [D-161] *Dun's Business Rankings* [D-172] *International Directory of Corporate Affiliations* [D-186] *Million Dollar Directory* [D-188] *Moody's Manuals* [D-192] *Standard & Poor's Corporation Records* [D-220] *Standard & Poor's Register of Corporations, Directors, and Executives, Vol. 1* [D-221] *Thomas Register of American Manufacturers: Company Profiles* [D-226] *Ward's Business Directory, Vol. 1* [D-231] *Ward's Business Directory, Vol. 2* [D-232] *Ward's Business Directory, Vol. 3* [D-233]
a listing of companies by industry, using the Standard Industrial Classification (SIC) code system?	*America's Corporate Families and International Affiliates* [D-135] *America's Corporate Families* [D-134] *Corporate Technology Directory* (high-tech companies only) [D-154] *Directory of Corporate Affiliations* [D-161] *International Directory of Corporate Affiliations* [D-186] *Million Dollar Directory* [D-188] *Standard & Poor's Register of Corporations, Directors, and Executives, Vol. 3* [D-221] *Ward's Business Directory, Vol. 3.* [D-233]
a listing of companies classified by industry and product, not using the SIC code system?	*Moody's Industrial Manual* [D-190] *Moody's OTC Industrial Manual* [D-194]
a listing of U.S. companies according to their geographical location?	*Corporate Technology Directory* [D-154] *Directory of Corporate Affiliations* [D-161] *Million Dollar Directory* [D-188] *Standard & Poor's Register of Corporations, Directors, and Executives, Vol. 3* [D-221] *Ward's Business Directory, Vol. 1* [D-231] *Ward's Business Directory, Vol. 2* [D-232]

WHERE SHOULD I GO TO FIND...   *TRY*

Corporate Listings, Profiles, and Financial Data

a listing of high-tech companies with their addresses, telephone numbers, and other information?

Corporate Technology Directory [D-154]
Dow Jones-Irwin Guide to High Tech Investing [D-62]

an unranked listing of U.S. corporations, by industry, that reports financial data for each company regarding sales, profits, earnings per share, and other data?

Business Week (See "Corporate Scoreboard" in the March issue.) [D-441]

major foreign companies, with a comprehensive business and financial profile of each company, including consolidated income account, consolidated balance sheet, excerpts from annual report by the CEO, financial and operating ratios, and other company information?

Moody's International Manual [D-191]
Standard & Poor's Corporation Records (no ratios) [D-220]

a listing of private companies with annual sales of at least $10 million?

Ward's Business Directory, Vol. 2 [D-232]

a listing of private companies with 200–500 employees?

Ward's Business Directory, Vol. 2 [D-232]

data on the financial operations and stock performance of a company, including revenue, financial ratios, capitalization, common-share earnings, sundry per-share data, dividend payout, stock ratings, statement on important developments in the company, and/or other analytical information?

Dow Jones-Irwin Business and Investment Almanac [D-24]
Investor's Daily [D-449]
Moody's Handbook of Common Stocks [D-303]
Moody's Handbook of OTC Stocks [D-304]
Moody's Manuals [D-192]
Standard & Poor's Corporation Records (partial data) [D-220]
Standard & Poor's Stock Reports [D-462]
Stock Market Encyclopedia [D-322]
Value Line Investment Survey [D-436]
Wall Street Transcript [D-458]

the approximate minimum total tangible asset rating of a company?

Thomas Register of American Manufacturers: Company Profiles [D-226]

changes in the rating of a corporation's debt?

Barron's [D-440]
Bond Guide [D-248]
Investor's Daily [D-449]
Moody's News Reports series [D-192]

| *WHERE SHOULD I GO TO FIND...* | *TRY* |

Corporate Listings, Profiles, and Financial Data

changes in the rating of a corporation's debt?

Security Owner's Stock Guide [D-314]
Standard & Poor's Daily News [D-220]
Wall Street Journal [D-457]

an estimate of a public or private company's financial strength and credit rating?

Dun & Bradstreet Reference Book [D-171]

a directory of companies that provide credit-information services?

Information Sources [D-185]

a detailed description of the long-term debt of a company, including the ratings of its corporate stocks and bonds?

Moody's Manuals [D-192]
Standard & Poor's Corporation Records (excludes ratings) [D-220]

a summary of financial statements and key financial and operating ratios for individual companies?

Moody's Manuals [D-192]
Standard & Poor's Corporation Records (excludes ratios) [D-220]
Standard & Poor's Industry Surveys [D-472]

a summary of quarterly earnings of individual corporations?

Barron's [D-440]
Investor's Daily [D-449]
New York Times [D-454]
Standard & Poor's Industry Surveys [D-472]
Wall Street Journal [D-457]
Wall Street Transcript [D-458]

comparative sales and earnings figures for major companies, arranged by industry?

Standard & Poor's Industry Surveys [D-472]

a quarterly comparison of the profits of major corporations?

Standard & Poor's Industry Surveys [D-472]
Wall Street Journal [D-457]

the sales and profits of individual companies in 60 countries?

Business Week (See "International Corporate Scoreboard" in the July issue.) [D-441]

companies that have been the focus of study by investment brokerage houses, and a summary of the reports that have been issued?

Barron's [D-440]
Wall Street Transcript [D-458]

WHERE SHOULD I GO TO FIND...   *TRY*

Corporate Listings, Profiles, and Financial Data

a profile and analysis of small and little-   *Penny Stock Journal* [D-455]
known companies with stocks valued un-
der $10 per share?

profiles of less actively traded over-the-   *Moody's OTC Unlisted Manual*
counter companies that are not listed on   [D-195]
the NASDAQ National Market System?   *Standard & Poor's Corporation Records*
                                                     [D-220]

operating and financial profiles of com-   *Moody's Transportation Manual* [D-197]
panies in the transportation industry?   *Standard & Poor's Corporation Records*
                                                     [D-220]

operating and financial profiles of public   *Moody's Public Utility Manual* [D-196]
utility companies?   *Standard & Poor's Corporation Records*
                                                     [D-220]

information on individual companies   *Predicasts F&S Index Europe* [D-14]
and industries as reported in trade   *Predicasts F&S Index International* [D-14]
journals, newspapers, and other print   *Predicasts F&S Index United States* [D-15]
sources?

the names and profiles of companies   *The 101 Best-Performing Companies in*
that have been described as being the   *America* [D-47]
best performing companies in America
in terms of employee productivity,
capital productivity, creating jobs,
and increasing stockholder wealth?

directories of minority-owned and   *National Directory of Minority-Owned*
women-owned businesses?   *Business Firms* [D-198]
                                                     National Directory of Women-Owned
                                                     Business Firms [D-200]

a directory of American exporting firms   *American Export Register* [D-133]
with a listing of products or services ex-   *Exporters Directory* [D-175]
ported?

a directory of law firms that specialize in   *Official U.S. Custom House Guide* [D-206]
admiralty, customs, and/or international
law?

a directory of companies in the micro-   *Data Sources: Hardware* [D-157]
computer, electronic-publishing, and/or   *Data Sources: Software* [D-158]
office-automation industries?   *Datapro Reports on Microcomputers* [D-391]

WHERE SHOULD I GO TO FIND...	*TRY*

Corporate Listings, Profiles, and Financial Data

a directory of mainframe and microcomputer hardware manufacturers?

Data Sources: Hardware [D-157]

a directory of data/telecommunications companies?

Data Sources: Data Comm/Telecomm [D-156]

a directory of corporate-sponsored research and development centers?

Directory of American Research and Technology [D-160]

a directory of companies that provide financial recordkeeping services for particular retail and service trades?

The Entrepreneur and Small Business Problem Solver [D-269]

a directory of online databases that profile individual corporations by reporting the product or service provided, finances, names of officers, and other information?

Directory of Online Databases [D-261]

guidelines for fulfilling the duties of the corporation secretary, including the federal and state laws and regulations that govern these duties?

Corporate Secretary's Guide [D-385]

the personal liabilities and duties of corporate officers and directors as determined by the federal securities laws?

Federal Securities Law Reports [D-404]
Responsibilities of Corporate Officers and Directors Under Federal Securities Laws [D-311]

guidelines, procedures, and forms concerning the rights and liabilities of corporate officers and directors?

Corporation Forms [D-386]
Forms of Business Agreements and Resolutions [D-410]

Corporations: Group Descriptive Data

the number of public and private companies, respectively, in each state, and the total sales volume and number of employees for each type of firm?

Ward's Business Directory, Vol. 1 [D-231]
Ward's Business Directory, Vol. 2 [D-232]

the number of public and private companies, respectively, in each Standard Industrial Classification (SIC) industry, and the total sales volume and number of employees for each type of firm?

Ward's Business Directory, Vol. 3 [D-233]

WHERE SHOULD I GO TO FIND...	TRY

Defunct Corporate Identities

what has happened to banks and publicly held corporations whose original identities have been lost?

Directory of Obsolete Securities [D-165]

Forms and Model Clauses

specimen forms and clauses for use in corporate transactions such as incorporating, issuing and transferring stock, declaring dividends, merging, consolidations, and leveraged buyouts?

Corporation Forms [D-386]
Forms of Business Agreements and Resolutions [D-410]
Tax Transactions Library: Mergers, Acquisitions and Leveraged Buyouts [D-431]

Incorporating

procedures to follow when incorporating?

Corporation Forms [D-386]
Forms of Business Agreements and Resolutions [D-410]

Information Sources

a bibliography of biographical (Who's Who) dictionaries?

Directories in Print [D-35]

a master index of published sources that report information on individual business firms?

Business Firms Master Index [D-3]

a directory of sources that provide strategic information about individual companies, including financial and operating data?

How to Find Information About Companies [D-183]

an index to information about prevailing salaries in industry, the professions, and occupations?

Business Rankings and Salaries Index [D-5]

an index to articles concerning corporate mergers, acquisitions, name changes, and other related articles in journals and newspapers?

Predicasts F&S Index of Corporate Change [D-13]

a listing of published research reports on the operations of individual companies and their industries?

Findex [D-37]

WHERE SHOULD I GO TO FIND...	*TRY*

Inside Corporate Developments

news about developments taking place in individual corporations?

Barron's [D-440]
Financial Times [D-444]
Forbes [D-445]
Fortune [D-446]
Investor's Daily [D-449]
New York Times [D-454]
Wall Street Journal [D-457]
Wall Street Transcript [D-458]

Intelligence Gathering

a directory of sources that provide strategic information about individual companies, including financial and operating data?

How to Find Information About Companies [D-183]

how to gather intelligence information about competitors and other corporations?

How to Find Information About Companies [D-183]

a directory of state agencies and departments that provide information about companies?

How to Find Information About Companies [D-183]

how and where to locate information about business executives and others in the business community?

How to Find Information About Executives [D-286]

how and where to locate information about individual foreign companies?

How to Find Information About Companies [D-183]
How to Find Information About Foreign Firms [D-287]

guidelines and sources for finding information about private firms?

How to Find Information About Private Companies [D-288]

special guidelines and sources for finding information about service companies?

How to Find Information About Service Companies [D-289]

how and where to locate information about individual Japanese companies and their industries?

How to Find Information About Japanese Companies and Industries [D-184]

a listing of published research reports on the operations of individual companies and their industries?

Findex [D-37]

WHERE SHOULD I GO TO FIND...	*TRY*

Media Enterprises

directories of radio and television stations that include their addresses, telephone numbers, names of key advertising executives, description of programming and facilities, advertising contract terms and rates, and other information?	*Spot Radio Rates and Data* [D-218] *Spot Television Rates and Data* [D-219]
a listing of radio stations that regularly schedule farm programs, programs of interest to black Americans, and/or foreign-language programs?	*Spot Radio Rates and Data* [D-218]
a directory of domestic and international business publications (e.g., magazines and trade newspapers) in the various industries, with a description of each publication, including advertising contract terms and rates, circulation data, printing requirements, names of key advertising executives, address, telephone number, and other information?	*Business Publication Rates and Data* [D-142]
a directory of health care publications, with a description of each publication, including advertising contract terms and rates, circulation data, printing requirements, names of key advertising executives, address, telephone number, and other information?	*Business Publication Rates and Data* [D-142]
a directory of newspapers, with a description of each newspaper, including advertising contract terms, classified rates, frequency of publication, circulation data, printing requirements, names of key advertising executives, address, telephone number, and other information?	*Newspaper Rates and Data* [D-205]
a directory of local urban and suburban weekly newspapers and shopping guides, with a description of each publication, including classified rates, printing requirements, circulation data, frequency of publication, names of key advertising executives, address, telephone number, and other information?	*Community Publication Rates and Data* [D-145]

WHERE SHOULD I GO TO FIND...

TRY

Media Enterprises

a directory of consumer magazines and consumer card decks, with descriptions that include an editorial profile statement, advertising contract provisions, advertising rates, frequency of publication, circulation data, printing requirements, names of key advertising executives, address, telephone number, and other information?

Consumer Magazine and Agri-Media Rates and Data [D-151]

Ranking of Corporations

national, state, and industry rankings of public and private U.S. businesses according to their sales volume and/or number of employees?

Dun's Business Rankings [D-172]

a ranking within Standard Industrial Classification (SIC) industries of U.S. privately-held and publicly-held companies according to their annual sales volume?

Ward's Business Directory, Vol. 3 [D-233]

a ranking of companies based on profitability, growth, and stock-market performance?

Forbes ("Annual Report on American Industry") [D-445]

a ranking of the 500 largest U.S. industrial corporations according to their sales, profits, assets, earnings per share, total return to investors, number of employees, and other criteria?

Fortune (*Fortune* 500 issue) [D-446]

a quarterly ranking of U.S. companies based on the annual amount of change in revenue and income?

Standard & Poor's Industry Surveys [D-472]

a ranking of the 1,000 largest U.S. corporations according to their stock market value?

Business Week (April issue) [D-441]

a ranking of the 1,000 largest public and 1,000 largest private U.S. companies according to annual sales volume?

Ward's Business Directory, Vol. 1 [D-231]

WHERE SHOULD I GO TO FIND...	*TRY*

Ranking of Corporations

| what company is ranked number one according to a selected criterion? | *Business Rankings and Salaries Index* [D-5] (Note: Lists many criteria from which to choose.) |

Real Estate Operations of Corporations

| a directory of officials who are responsible for real-estate acquisitions, leasing, and renting at major U.S. corporations? | *Institutional Investor* (December issue) [D-447] |

Stock: Initial Offering

| how to take a company public and the pros and cons associated with this decision? | *Accounting Desk Book* [D-239] *Vital Business Secrets for New and Growing Companies* [D-107] |

Stockholders

| tips on how corporate officers should prepare for an annual stockholders' meeting, including sample questions often asked by stockholders? | *Corporation Forms* [D-386] |

| guidelines, procedures, and forms associated with calling and conducting stockholders' meetings? | *Corporation Forms* [D-386] *Forms of Business Agreements and Resolutions* [D-410] |

| the names of mutual funds that hold shares of a specified common stock? | *Spectrum 1* [D-315] |

| the identification of beneficial owners of 5 percent or more of outstanding shares of stock of a corporation, along with their addresses, telephone numbers, and number of shares owned? | *Barron's* (Does not report addresses and telephone numbers.) [D-440] *Spectrum 5* [D-319] |

| the names of banks, insurance companies, pension funds, endowments, and foundations that own shares of a specified common stock? | *Spectrum 3* [D-317] |

WHERE SHOULD I GO TO FIND...	*TRY*

Transportation and Utility Companies: Service Areas

system-wide route maps of transportation companies?

Moody's Transportation Manual [D-197]

maps of service regions, pipelines, and transmission lines of public utility companies?

Moody's Public Utility Manual [D-196]

Valuing a Business

guidelines and techniques used to determine the value of a business or professional practice?

The Complete Guide to a Successful Leveraged Buyout [D-57]
Corporate Acquisitions, Mergers, and Divestitures [D-384]
Handbook of Estate Planning [D-280]
How to Price a Business [D-461]
Techniques of Financial Analysis [D-324]
Valuing a Business [D-329]
Valuing Small Businesses and Professional Practices [D-330]
Vital Business Secrets for New and Growing Companies [D-107]

Vendor Products and Services

products or services sold by a company?

Corporate Technology Directory [D-154]
Japan Yellow Pages [D-187]
Million Dollar Directory [D-188]
Moody's Manuals [D-192]
Standard & Poor's Register of Corporations, Directors, and Executives, Vol. 1 [D-221]
Standard Directory of Advertisers [D-222]
Taiwan Yellow Pages [D-225]
Thomas Register of American Manufacturers: Company Profiles. Also in *Catalog File* [D-226]
Ward's Business Directory, Vol. 1 [D-231]
Ward's Business Directory, Vol. 2 [D-232]
Ward's Business Directory, Vol. 3 [D-233]

the types of products or services offered by a company and their associated brand names?

Companies and Their Brands [D-146]
Value Line Investment Survey [D-436]

WHERE SHOULD I GO TO FIND...	TRY

Vendor Products and Services

what kind of product or service is being sold under a given trade name?	*Brands and Their Companies* [D-113] *International Directory of Corporate Affiliations* [D-186] *Standard Directory of Advertisers* [D-222] *Thomas Register of American Manufacturers: Company Profiles, Vol. N–Z* [D-226]
if a trade name is currently being used?	*Brands and Their Companies* [D-113] *International Directory of Corporate Affiliations* [D-186] *Thomas Register of American Manufacturers: Company Profiles, Vol. N–Z* [D-226]
foreign trade names with their associated product or service and company?	*International Directory of Corporate Affiliations* [D-186]
if a company provides export services?	*Million Dollar Directory* [D-188] *Thomas Register of American Manufacturers: Company Profiles* [D-226] *Ward's Business Directory, Vol. 1* [D-231] *Ward's Business Directory, Vol. 2* [D-232] *Ward's Business Directory, Vol. 3* [D-233]
sales catalogs of companies that contain such information as products or services offered, design specifications, performance data, product photographs, model numbers, address and telephone number for placing orders, and other catalog information?	*Thomas Register of American Manufacturers: Catalog File* [D-226]
for each freight-carrier, port, and cargo-transportation service company, the address, names of officials, areas served, intermodal services, special services, special equipment used, and other related information?	*Thomas Register's Inbound Traffic Guide* [D-227]
a listing of companies by industry, using the Standard Industrial Classification (SIC) code system?	*America's Corporate Families and International Affiliates* [D-135] *America's Corporate Families* [D-134]

WHERE SHOULD I GO TO FIND... | TRY

Vendor Products and Services

a listing of companies by industry, using the Standard Industrial Classification (SIC) code system?

Corporate Technology Directory [D-154]
Directory of Corporate Affiliations [D-161]
International Directory of Corporate Affiliations [D-186]
Million Dollar Directory [D-188]
Standard & Poor's Register of Corporations, Directors, and Executives, Vol. 3 [D-221]
Ward's Business Directory, Vol. 3 [D-233]

a listing of companies classified by industry and product, not using the SIC code system?

Moody's Industrial Manual [D-190]
Moody's OTC Industrial Manual [D-194]

Definitions

Acronyms, Abbreviations, and Symbols

the meaning of acronyms and abbreviations used in the business world?

Acronyms, Initialisms, and Abbreviations Dictionary [D-109]
Business Acronyms [D-114]

the meaning of individual stock exchange symbols?

Acronyms, Initialisms, and Abbreviations Dictionary [D-109]
Business Acronyms [D-114]
Symbol Guide [D-323]

abbreviations and acronyms used in finance and investments?

Acronyms, Initialisms, and Abbreviations Dictionary [D-109]
Business Acronyms [D-114]
Dictionary of Finance and Investment Terms [D-120]

how to decipher symbols used by the commodities and options exchanges?

Symbol Guide [D-323]

the meaning of acronyms and abbreviations used with international shipping, foreign customs, duties, and tariffs?

Acronyms, Initialisms, and Abbreviations Dictionary [D-109]
Business Acronyms [D-114]

the meaning of abbreviations of labor union names?

Acronyms, Initialisms, and Abbreviations Dictionary [D-109]

WHERE SHOULD I GO TO FIND...	*TRY*

Acronyms, Abbreviations, and Symbols

the meaning of abbreviations of labor union names?

Directory of U.S. Labor Organizations [D-170]

the meaning of abbreviations and acronyms used to designate federal departments and agencies?

Acronyms, Initialisms, and Abbreviations Dictionary [D-109]
Business Acronyms [D-114]
United States Government Manual [D-366]

Terms, Phrases, and Principles

the definition of terms and phrases used in business and economics?

Dictionary of Business and Economics [D-117]
Dictionary of Finance [D-119]
Dictionary of Finance and Investment Terms [D-120]
Dow Jones-Irwin Dictionary of Financial Planning [D-124]
Encyclopedia of Economics [D-266]
The New Palgrave: A Dictionary of Economics [D-127]
Words of Wall Street: 2,000 Investment Terms Defined [D-132]

a specialized glossary of terms associated with tax havens?

Tax Havens of the World [D-430]

an explanation of the business and economic concepts and related statistical terms that are used in the *Wall Street Journal*?

Dow Jones-Irwin Guide to Using the Wall Street Journal [D-69]

explanations of economic concepts, principles, and philosophies?

The New Palgrave: A Dictionary of Economics [D-127]

definitions of terms and phrases used with computing?

Computer Dictionary [D-115]
Datapro Management of Microcomputer Systems [D-388]
Datapro Reports on Microcomputers [D-391]
Dictionary of Computers, Data Processing, and Telecommunications [D-118]
A Dictionary of Minicomputing and Microcomputing [D-121]

WHERE SHOULD I GO TO FIND...	*TRY*

Terms, Phrases, and Principles

the French and Spanish equivalents of English computing terms?	*Dictionary of Computers, Data Processing, and Telecommunications* [D-118]
definitions of terms and phrases used in the field of information-processing systems?	*American National Dictionary for Information Processing Systems* [D-110]
definitions of terms used to describe hardware and procedures associated with office automation?	*Datapro Management of Office Automation* [D-389]
definitions of terms used in the records-management field?	*Information and Records Management* [D-82]
the meaning of accounting terms used in selected foreign countries?	*World Accounting* [D-437]
the definition of terms and phrases used by the legal profession?	*Black's Law Dictionary* [D-112]
the definition of labor and/or arbitration terms?	*A Dictionary of Arbitration and Its Terms* [D-116] *Labor Law Course* [D-292] *Primer of Labor Relations* [D-308]
the definition of Japanese business and legal terms and phrases?	*Doing Business in Japan* [D-398]
the meaning of foreign investment terms common to individual foreign stock exchanges?	*How to Buy Foreign Stocks and Bonds* [D-76]
a glossary of international-trade terms?	*Exporters Directory* [D-175]
the definition of terms and phrases used in real estate?	*Barron's Real Estate Handbook* [D-245] *Black's Law Dictionary* (legal terms only) [D-112] *Dictionary of Real Estate Terms* [D-123] *Illustrated Encyclopedic Dictionary of Real Estate* [D-125] *Street Talk in Real Estate* [D-128]

WHERE SHOULD I GO TO FIND...   *TRY*

Demographics

Consumer Demographic and Market Data

data on per capita and family income?

Census of Population: General Social and Economic Characteristics [D-339]
Commercial Atlas and Marketing Guide [D-464]
Historical Statistics of the United States [D-351]
Sourcebook of Demographics and Buying Power for Every ZIP Code in the USA [D-470]
Statistical Abstract of the United States [D-361]

demographic data on consumer consumption patterns for state, metropolitan, and television market areas?

Consumer Magazine and Agri-Media Rates and Data [D-151]
Newspaper Rates and Data [D-205]
Spot Radio Rates and Data [D-218]
Spot Television Rates and Data [D-219]
Survey of Buying Power Data Service [D-474]

projections of population, disposable income, retail sales, and Buying Power Index?

Survey of Buying Power Data Service [D-474]

demographic and socioeconomic data for each ZIP code area, including residential and business statistics?

Commercial Atlas and Marketing Guide [D-464]
Sourcebook of Demographics and Buying Power for Every ZIP Code in the USA [D-470]

an index of consumer purchasing patterns for selected consumer items by ZIP code area?

Sourcebook of Demographics and Buying Power for Every ZIP Code in the USA [D-470]

Employment and Labor Force Data

employment trends by region of the U.S.?

Career Information Center [D-252]

labor force projections for 1995 by the Bureau of Labor Statistics?

Career Information Center [D-252]

WHERE SHOULD I GO TO FIND...   *TRY*

Employment and Labor Force Data

statistical data that describe the labor force at the national, state, and selected metropolitan area levels?

Census of Population: General Social and Economic Characteristics [D-339]
Employment and Earnings [D-347]
Historical Statistics of the United States (no metropolitan statistics) [D-351]
Statistical Abstract of the United States [D-361]

average hours worked per week, hourly earnings, and weekly earnings per U.S. industry?

Employment and Earnings [D-347]
Employment, Hours, and Earnings, United States [D-349]
Historical Statistics of the United States [D-351]
Statistical Abstract of the United States [D-361]
Supplement to Employment and Earnings [D-362]
For additional sources, see *Predicasts F&S Index United States* [D-15]

the average hours worked per week, hourly earnings, and weekly earnings for each state and for selected population centers?

Employment and Earnings [D-347]
Employment, Hours, and Earnings, States and Areas [D-348]

for all manufacturing plants, the average hourly earnings of production workers in the U.S. and in individual states?

Census of Manufactures [D-338]

Historical Demographic Data

a compendium of historical annual statistical data on the U.S. population, business, industry, and the economy since colonial times?

Historical Statistics of the United States [D-351]

Information Sources

sources of statistical information pertaining to populations in the U.S. and/or other nations?

American Statistics Index [D-1]
Directories in Print [D-35]
International Directory of Business Information Agencies and Services [D-466]

(answer continues)

WHERE SHOULD I GO TO FIND...	*TRY*

Information Sources

sources of statistical information pertaining to populations in the U.S. and/or other nations?	*Monthly Catalog of United States Government Publications* [D-354] *Sourcebook of Global Statistics* [D-471] *Statistical Abstract of the United States* [D-361] *Statistical Reference Index* [D-18] *Statistics Sources* [D-473]
sources of statistical information about populations at the local and/or regional levels?	*American Statistics Index* [D-1] *Regional Statistics* [D-469] *Statistical Abstract of the United States* [D-361] *Statistical Reference Index* [D-18]
sources of demographic data on individual nations?	*Index to International Statistics* [D-10] *Statistics Sources* [D-473]
an index to information about the populations of foreign nations as reported in trade journals, newspapers, government documents, and other print sources?	*Predicasts F&S Index Europe* [D-14] *Predicasts F&S Index International* [D-14]
an index to information about the U.S. population and its characteristics, as reported in trade journals, newspapers, government documents, and other print sources?	*Predicasts F&S Index United States* [D-15]
a listing of published market research reports on demographic characteristics?	*Findex* [D-37]
a catalog of census documents prepared on demographics and published by the Bureau of the Census?	*Census Catalog and Guide* [D-6]
a directory of online databases that provide demographic information?	*Directory of Online Databases* [D-261]

Population Statistics: Foreign

forecasts of populations and their characteristics in foreign nations?	*Worldcasts* [D-475]
demographic data for foreign nations?	*Countries of the World* [D-22] *Demographic Yearbook* [D-23]

WHERE SHOULD I GO TO FIND...   *TRY*

Population Statistics: Foreign

demographic data for foreign nations?

Europa World Year Book [D-25]
Moody's International Manual [D-191]
Rand McNally Bankers Directory: International [D-211]
Statesman's Yearbook [D-28]
Statistical Abstract of the United States [D-361]
World Almanac [D-29]

Population Statistics: U.S.

population statistics for the U.S.?

Census of Population [D-339]
Commercial Atlas and Marketing Guide [D-464]
Countries of the World [D-22]
Demographic Yearbook [D-23]
Employment and Earnings [D-347]
Historical Statistics of the United States [D-351]
Moody's Municipal and Government Manual [D-193]
Sourcebook of Demographics and Buying Power for Every ZIP Code in the USA [D-470]
Statesman's Yearbook [D-28]
Statistical Abstract of the United States [D-361]
World Almanac [D-29]

historical population data for the U.S.?

Historical Statistics of the United States [D-351]
Predicasts Basebook [D-467]

forecasts of the U.S. population and its characteristics?

Predicasts Forecasts [D-468]

Research Organizations

a directory of governmental agencies and/or private organizations that collect statistical data and make projections on demographic topics?

The GreenBook [D-181]
Information Sources [D-185]
Washington Information Directory [D-234]

WHERE SHOULD I GO TO FIND...	TRY

Economic Analyses and Economists

Analytical Methods and Formulas

the measures that are used to evaluate the accuracy of quantitative economic forecasts, including the formulas for these measures?	*Handbook of Economic and Financial Measures* [D-279]
a listing of technical stock market indicators, with an explanation of how each works?	*Encyclopedia of Technical Market Indicators* [D-268] *Handbook of Economic and Financial Measures* [D-279]
an explanation of the methods and techniques used to determine the forecasting value of various stock market indicators?	*Encyclopedia of Technical Market Indicators* [D-268]
an explanation of the technical methods used in the analysis of the investment market?	*Financial Analyst's Handbook* [D-271]
how to conduct an analysis of an industry?	*Financial Analyst's Handbook* [D-271]

Business and Economic Data for Foreign Nations

export and import data for individual nations during selected years?	*International Financial Statistics* [D-448] *Moody's International Manual* [D-191]
forecasts of the leading foreign economic indicators?	*Worldcasts* [D-475]
industry and product forecasts for foreign nations?	*Worldcasts* [D-475]
forecasts of manufacturers' and retail sales in foreign nations?	*Worldcasts* [D-475]
economic analyses and news reports of political events and conditions in the U.S. and foreign nations?	*Business Week* [D-441] *The Economist* [D-443] *Financial Times* [D-444] *Forbes* [D-445] *Fortune* [D-446]

WHERE SHOULD I GO TO FIND...   *TRY*

Business and Economic Data for Foreign Nations

data on historical changes in consumer   *International Financial Statistics* [D-448]
prices for the world and individual na-   *Moody's International Manual* [D-191]
tions during selected years?

data on foreign direct investments in the   *Survey of Current Business* (August issue)
U.S.?   [D-363]

financial and economic statistical data for   *International Financial Statistics* [D-448]
individual nations and on a worldwide
level?

current prime interest rates for selected   *Barron's* [D-440]
foreign nations?   *The Economist* [D-443]
                                                Financial Times [D-444]
                                                Investor's Daily [D-449]
                                                New York Times [D-454]
                                                Wall Street Journal [D-457]
                                                Other metropolitan newspapers

historical discount rates of foreign central   *Moody's International Manual* [D-191]
banks?

Business and Economic Indicators

values of general business and economic   *Business Statistics* [D-336]
indicators?   *Dow Jones-Irwin Business and Investment*
                                                Almanac [D-24]
                                                Statistical Abstract of the United States
                                                [D-361]
                                                Survey of Current Business [D-363]
                                                World Almanac [D-29]

forecasts of the leading U.S. economic   *Predicasts Forecasts* [D-468]
indicators?

an explanation of the leading indicators   *Financial Analyst's Handbook* [D-271]
of economic activity?   *Handbook of Economic and Financial Mea-*
                                                sures [D-279]
                                                How to Read the Financial Pages [D-80]
                                                Understanding Wall Street [D-327]

reviews of business and economic indica-   *Barron's* [D-440]
tors?   *Business Week* [D-441]
                                                The Economist [D-443]
                                                Forbes [D-445]

(answer continues)

WHERE SHOULD I GO TO FIND...	*TRY*

Business and Economic Indicators

reviews of business and economic indicators?	*New York Times* [D-454] *Survey of Current Business* [D-363] *Wall Street Journal* [D-457]
Consumer Price Index data?	*BLS News* [D-334] *Business Statistics* [D-336] *CPI Detailed Report* [D-345] *Dow Jones-Irwin Business and Investment Almanac* [D-24] *Historical Statistics of the United States* [D-351] *Statistical Abstract of the United States* [D-361] *Survey of Current Business* [D-363] *Wall Street Journal* [D-457] *World Almanac* [D-29]
Producer Price Index data?	*Business Statistics* [D-336] *Historical Statistics of the United States* [D-351] *Producer Price Indexes* [D-358] *Statistical Abstract of the United States* [D-361] *Survey of Current Business* [D-363]
retail Food Price Index data?	*Historical Statistics of the United States* [D-351] *Statistical Abstract of the United States* [D-361]
retail food prices for selected food items during specified years?	*Historical Statistics of the United States* [D-351] *Statistical Abstract of the United States* [D-361]
current prime interest rates for the U.S. and selected foreign nations?	*Barron's* [D-440] *The Economist* [D-443] *Financial Times* [D-444] *Investor's Daily* [D-449] *New York Times* [D-454] *Wall Street Journal* [D-457] Other metropolitan newspapers

Consumer Income and Spending Patterns

personal-consumption expenditures in the U.S. for selected goods and services during specific years?	*Business Statistics* [D-336] *Historical Statistics of the United States* [D-351]

WHERE SHOULD I GO TO FIND...   *TRY*

Consumer Income and Spending Patterns

personal-consumption expenditures in
the U.S. for selected goods and services
during specific years?

Statistical Abstract of the United States
[D-361]
Survey of Current Business [D-363]
World Almanac [D-29]

by ZIP code area, an index of consumer
purchasing patterns for selected consumer items?

*Sourcebook of Demographics and Buying
Power for Every ZIP Code in the USA*
[D-470]

an analysis of personal income at the
state, county, and metropolitan levels?

Survey of Current Business (April issue)
[D-363]

average hours worked per week, hourly
earnings, and weekly earnings per U.S.
industry?

Employment and Earnings [D-347]
*Employment, Hours, and Earnings, United
States* [D-349]
Historical Statistics of the United States
[D-351]
Statistical Abstract of the United States
[D-361]
Supplement to Employment and Earnings
[D-362]
For additional sources, see *Predicasts
F&S Index United States* [D-15]

average hours worked per week, hourly earnings, and weekly earnings for
each state and selected population centers?

Employment and Earnings [D-347]
*Employment, Hours, and Earnings, States
and Areas* [D-348]

for all manufacturing plants, the average hourly earnings of production
workers for the U.S. and individual
states?

Census of Manufactures [D-338]

data on urban consumer expenditures?

Historical Statistics of the United States
[D-351]
Statistical Abstract of the United States
[D-361]

a measure of disposable income for
households and per capita, reported
by market area?

Survey of Buying Power Data Service
[D-474]

<u>*WHERE SHOULD I GO TO FIND...*</u>	<u>*TRY*</u>

Corporations: Group Descriptive Data

the number of public and private companies, respectively, in each state, and the total sales volume and number of employees for each type of firm?	*Ward's Business Directory, Vol. 1* [D-231] *Ward's Business Directory, Vol. 2* [D-232]
the number of public and private companies, respectively, in each Standard Industrial Classification (SIC) industry, and the total sales volume and number of employees for each type of firm?	*Ward's Business Directory, Vol. 3* [D-233]

Currencies of the World

descriptive information on the currency of individual nations?	*World Currency Yearbook* [D-30]

Economists

biographical sketches of notable economists?	*The New Palgrave: A Dictionary of Economics* [D-127] *Who's Who in America* [D-129] *Who's Who in the World* [D-131]

Employment and Labor Force Data

statistical data that describe the labor force at the national, state, and selected metropolitan area levels?	*Employment and Earnings* [D-347] *Historical Statistics of the United States* (no metropolitan data) [D-351] *Statistical Abstract of the United States* [D-361]
average hours worked per week, hourly earnings, and weekly earnings per U.S. industry?	*Employment and Earnings* [D-347] *Employment, Hours, and Earnings, United States* [D-349] *Historical Statistics of the United States* [D-351] *Statistical Abstract of the United States* [D-361] *Supplement to Employment and Earnings* [D-362] For additional sources, see *Predicasts F&S Index United States* [D-15]
average hours worked per week, hourly earnings, and weekly earnings for each state and selected population centers?	*Employment and Earnings* [D-347] *Employment, Hours, and Earnings, States and Areas* [D-348]

WHERE SHOULD I GO TO FIND...	*TRY*

Employment and Labor Force Data

for all manufacturing plants, the average hourly earnings of production workers for the U.S. and individual states?

Census of Manufactures [D-338]

an overview of current wage patterns and other settlement issues in labor contracts?

Collective Bargaining Negotiations and Contracts [D-381]

Federal Budget

information of various kinds on the federal budget?

Budget of the United States Government [D-335]
Dow Jones-Irwin Business and Investment Almanac [D-24]
Historical Statistics of the United States [D-351]
Moody's Municipal and Government Manual [D-193]
Statistical Abstract of the United States [D-361]
World Almanac [D-29]

"Federal Reserve Data"

how to interpret the *Wall Street Journal's* table entitled "Federal Reserve Data"?

Financial Analyst's Handbook [D-271]

General Economic Conditions and Statistics: U.S.

economic analyses and news reports of political events and conditions in the U.S.?

Business Week [D-441]
The Economist [D-443]
Financial Times [D-444]
Forbes [D-445]
Fortune [D-446]

abstracts of selected articles on economic activity that have been reported in trade journals, newspapers, government reports, and other print sources?

PROMT [D-16]

a survey of economic conditions in the U.S. and data on individual industries, along with tables of values for the National Income and Products Accounts (NIPA)?

Business Statistics [D-336]
Survey of Current Business [D-363]

General Economic Conditions and Statistics: U.S.

statistical data on each of a wide array of   *Business Statistics* [D-336]
factors that describe and measure busi-   *Survey of Current Business* [D-363]
ness and economic activity in the U.S.,
and that are used to calculate the Gross
National Product?

the text of interviews with leading CEOs   *Wall Street Transcript* [D-458]
and money managers concerning eco-
nomic matters related to their industries?

analyses of low-priced stock companies in   *Penny Stock Journal* [D-455]
a broad range of industries?

a compendium of decennial statistical   *Census of Population* [D-339]
data on the U.S. population and selected
economic characteristics?

a directory of online databases that pro-   *Directory of Online Databases* [D-261]
vide economic data and economic fore-
casts?

Historical Statistics: General

historical time series statistics for particu-   *Business Statistics* [D-336]
lar industries and products?   *Historical Statistics of the United States*
                                                     [D-351]
                                                     Predicasts Basebook [D-467]
                                                     Survey of Current Business [D-363]

historical data on the annual number of   *Historical Statistics of the United States*
business failures and the size of their lia-   [D-351]
bilities?

a compendium of historical annual sta-   *Historical Statistics of the United States*
tistical data on the U.S. population, busi-   [D-351]
ness, industry, and the economy since
colonial times?

WHERE SHOULD I GO TO FIND...   *TRY*

Industry Profiles

performance analyses and summary data for particular industries?

Business Statistics [D-336]
Census of Manufactures [D-338]
Dow Jones-Irwin Business and Investment Almanac [D-24]
Fortune (*Fortune* 500 issue) [D-446]
Standard & Poor's Industry Surveys [D-472]
Survey of Current Business [D-363]
U.S. Industrial Outlook [D-367]
Wall Street Journal [D-457]
Wall Street Transcript [D-458]

a current and a historical analysis of an industry's assets, liabilities, and income data, classified according to the size of assets held by firms in that industry?

RMA Annual Statement Studies [D-27]

a daily summary of an industry's stock activity, indicating its five-year earnings per share compared with other industries and its stock-price performance compared with other industries for the past year?

Investor's Daily [D-449]

financial and operating ratios by industry?

Almanac of Business and Industrial Financial Ratios [D-20]
American Statistics Index (A guide to U.S. government publications containing ratios) [D-1]
Analyst's Handbook [D-243]
Census of Construction Industries [D-337]
Census of Manufactures [D-338]
Census of Retail Trade [D-340]
Census of Service Industries [D-341]
Census of Wholesale Trade [D-342]
Dow Jones-Irwin Business and Investment Almanac [D-24]
Industry Norms and Key Business Ratios [D-26]
RMA Annual Statement Studies [D-27]
Standard & Poor's Industry Surveys [D-472]

industry norms for each item in a corporate financial statement expressed as a percentage of the aggregate total?

Industry Norms and Key Business Ratios [D-26]

WHERE SHOULD I GO TO FIND...	*TRY*
Industry Profiles	
aggregate data for income account and balance sheet items, by industry?	*Analyst's Handbook* [D-243]
an analytical overview of current conditions in particular industries and an economic forecast for each industry?	*U.S. Industrial Outlook* [D-367]
an analysis of the historical trends and problems of each industry along with its prospects and developments, coupled with an appraisal of the industry's investment outlook?	*Standard & Poor's Industry Surveys* [D-472]
an annual summary, by industry, of the industry's composite market value, sales, profits, assets, and return on invested capital and common equity?	*Business Week* (April issue) [D-441] Note: Some of these and other industry financial statistics may be found in *Statistical Abstract of the United States* [D-361]
a survey of economic conditions in the U.S. and data on individual industries, along with tables of values for the National Income and Products Accounts (NIPA)?	*Business Statistics* [D-336] *Survey of Current Business* [D-363]
industry and product forecasts?	*Predicasts Forecasts* [D-468]
historical time series statistics for particular industries and products?	*Business Statistics* [D-336] *Historical Statistics of the United States* [D-351] *Predicasts Basebook* [D-467] *Survey of Current Business* [D-363]
the text of interviews with leading CEOs and money managers concerning economic matters related to their industries?	*Wall Street Transcript* [D-458]
a bibliography of publications that report composite financial data, including financial and operating ratios, for specific industries?	*RMA Annual Statement Studies* [D-27]
for each industry, the index (average) value per share for each of 13 performance criteria (e.g., profit, earnings, dividends)?	*Analyst's Handbook* [D-243]

WHERE SHOULD I GO TO FIND...	*TRY*

Industry Profiles

a comparison with the movement of the New York Stock Exchange Composite Index of stock price performances of selected industries?	*Moody's Handbook of Common Stocks* [D-303]
average hours worked per week, hourly earnings, and weekly earnings per U.S. industry?	*Employment and Earnings* [D-347] *Employment, Hours, and Earnings, United States* [D-349] *Historical Statistics of the United States* [D-351] *Statistical Abstract of the United States* [D-361] *Supplement to Employment and Earnings* [D-362] For additional sources, see *Predicasts F&S Index United States* [D-15]
statistical data on the operations of the transportation industry, both for individual companies and the aggregate industry?	*Moody's Transportation Manual* [D-197]
financial, economic, and statistical information on the public utility industry, both by company and for the total industry?	*Moody's Public Utility Manual* [D-196] *Standard & Poor's Corporation Records* (by company only) [D-220]
the number of public and private companies, respectively, in each Standard Industrial Classification (SIC) industry, and the total sales volume and number of employees for each type of firm?	*Ward's Business Directory, Vol. 3* [D-233]
a compendium of economic data, collected by the U.S. Bureau of the Census, that describes the activities of individual manufacturing industries in America?	*Census of Manufactures* [D-338]
descriptive data on retail trade activity in the U.S., with operating statistics that describe each retail industry, the scope of which includes national, regional, and local levels?	*Census of Retail Trade* [D-340] *Survey of Buying Power Data Service* [D-474]

WHERE SHOULD I GO TO FIND...	*TRY*

Industry Profiles

descriptive statistics on operating factors in the wholesale-trade industry, with focus on each subsidiary industry and in various U.S. geographical areas?	*Census of Wholesale Trade* [D-342]
descriptive statistics on operating factors in the service industry, with focus on subsidiary industries and in various U.S. geographical areas?	*Census of Service Industries* [D-341]
descriptive statistics on operating factors in the construction industry, with focus on subsidiary industries and in various U.S. geographical areas?	*Census of Construction Industries* [D-337]

Information Sources

sources of statistical information about economic activity in the U.S. and individual foreign nations?	*American Statistics Index* [D-1] *Index to International Statistics* [D-10] *International Directory of Business Information Agencies and Services* [D-466] *Sourcebook of Global Statistics* [D-471] *Statistical Reference Index* [D-18] *Statistics Sources* [D-473]
sources of statistical information about economic conditions at the local (city and county) level?	*American Statistics Index* [D-1] *Regional Statistics* [D-469] *Statistical Reference Index* [D-18]
a bibliography of publications that report composite financial data, including financial and operating ratios, for individual industries?	*RMA Annual Statement Studies* [D-27]
an index to economic data reported in trade journals, newspapers, government reports, and other print sources?	*Predicasts F&S Index Europe* [D-14] *Predicasts F&S Index International* [D-14] *Predicasts F&S Index United States* [D-15]
abstracts of selected articles on economic activity that have been reported in trade journals, newspapers, government reports, and other print sources?	*PROMT* [D-16]

WHERE SHOULD I GO TO FIND...	*TRY*

Information Sources

a listing of published research reports, available for purchase, that focus on economic analyses, forecasting, and consumer spending?

Findex [D-37]

a catalog of census documents prepared on various subjects and published by the U.S. Bureau of the Census?

Census Catalog and Guide [D-6]

a guide to statistical reports, published by federal and state governments and private organizations, that concentrate on the general economy and on conditions in individual industries?

American Statistics Index [D-1]
Statistical Reference Index [D-18]

publications of international intergovernmental organizations that provide statistical data on consumer prices and price indexes in specific foreign nations and world regions?

Index of International Statistics [D-10]

a directory of online databases that provide economic data and economic forecasts?

Directory of Online Databases [D-261]

Investments Abroad

data on U.S. direct investments abroad?

Survey of Current Business (August issue) [D-363]

Market Research Statistics

a ranking and description of television marketing areas, with summary market data?

Spot Radio Rates and Data [D-219]
Spot Television Rates and Data [D-219]
Survey of Buying Power Data Service [D-474]

consumer market data for states and/or metropolitan areas?

Commercial Atlas and Marketing Guide [D-464]
Consumer Magazine and Agri-Media Rates and Data [D-151]
Spot Radio Rates and Data [D-218]
Spot Television Rates and Data [D-219]
Survey of Buying Power Data Service [D-474]

WHERE SHOULD I GO TO FIND...   *TRY*

Market Research Statistics

the five major types of businesses (designated by SIC code) in any local area (ZIP
code region)?

*Sourcebook of Demographics and Buying
Power for Every Zip Code in the USA*
[D-470]

by ZIP code area, an index of consumer
purchasing patterns for selected consumer items?

*Sourcebook of Demographics and Buying
Power for Every Zip Code in the USA*
[D-470]

a potpourri of retail-sales data by geographic market area?

Survey of Buying Power Data Service
[D-474]

a measure of disposable income for
households and per capita, reported by
market area?

Survey of Buying Power Data Service
[D-474]

projections of population, disposable income, retail sales, and Buying Power Index?

Survey of Buying Power Data Service
[D-474]

for each television market (*Area of
Dominant Influence*), the retail sales and
ranking of that market by store group
and merchandise line?

Survey of Buying Power Data Service
[D-474]

National Reserves

data on gold and other reserves of individual nations for selected years?

International Financial Statistics [D-448]
Moody's International Manual [D-191]

| **General Business Reference Sources and General Facts** |

General Business and Economic Conditions

a potpourri of information on business
conditions, investments, and economic
trends?

*Dow Jones-Irwin Business and Investment
Almanac* [D-24]
Predicasts Basebook [D-467]
Predicasts F&S Index Europe [D-14]
Predicasts F&S Index International [D-14]
Predicasts F&S Index United States [D-15]
Statistical Abstract of the United States
[D-361]
See also Section D, subsection titled
"Newspapers, Magazines, and Journals."

WHERE SHOULD I GO TO FIND...	*TRY*

General Business and Economic Conditions

a review of important business events that occurred each day of the preceding year?

Dow Jones-Irwin Business and Investment Almanac [D-24]

a daily newspaper with major coverage of foreign business and economic activity, including developments within companies?

Financial Times [D-444]

comprehensive news coverage of current events in business, finance, and economics?

Barron's [D-440]
Business Week [D-441]
The Economist [D-443]
Financial Times [D-444]
Forbes [D-445]
Fortune [D-446]
Investor's Daily [D-449]
Nation's Business [D-453]
New York Times [D-454]
Wall Street Journal [D-457]

Industry Profiles

annual growth statistics for industries and products?

Predicasts Basebook [D-467]

statistical information on the operations of the transportation industry?

Moody's Transportation Manual [D-197]

statistical information on the operations of the public utility industry?

Moody's Public Utility Manual [D-196]

Information on Individual Companies

information on individual companies as reported in trade journals, newspapers, and other print sources?

Predicasts F&S Index Europe [D-14]
Predicasts F&S Index International [D-14]
Predicasts F&S Index United States [D-15]
PROMT [D-16]

Information Sources

a subject index to journal articles in business and economics?

Business Periodicals Index [D-4]
Readers' Guide to Periodical Literature [D-17]

WHERE SHOULD I GO TO FIND...	*TRY*

Information Sources

bibliographies of business-information sources?	*Business Information: How to Find It, How to Use It* [D-32] *Business Information Sources* [D-33] *Complete Information Bank for Entrepreneurs and Small-Business Managers* [D-34] *Encyclopedia of Business Information Sources* [D-36] *Management Principles and Practice* [D-40] *Where to Find Business Information* [D-45]
sources of business and economic statistical data and other business information?	*American Statistics Index* [D-1] *Directories in Print* [D-35] *Index to International Statistics* [D-10] *International Directory of Business Information Agencies and Services* [D-466] *Predicasts Basebook* [D-467] *Predicasts F&S Index Europe* [D-14] *Predicasts F&S Index International* [D-14] *Predicasts F&S Index United States* [D-15] *Predicasts Forecasts* [D-468] *Small Business Sourcebook* [D-216] *Sourcebook of Global Statistics* [D-471] *Statistical Abstract of the United States* [D-361] *Statistical Reference Index* [D-18] *Statistics Sources* [D-473] *Worldcasts* [D-475]
a subject index to publications issued by the federal government that focus on business, economics, and other subjects?	*American Statistics Index* [D-1] *Federal Government Publications Catalog* [D-8] *Monthly Catalog of United States Government Publications* [D-354] *Statistical Abstract of the United States* (see its guide to primary sources of statistical information) [D-361]
the location of business information to be found in federal departments and agencies?	*How to Find Business Intelligence in Washington* [D-182] *Washington Information Directory* [D-234]

WHERE SHOULD I GO TO FIND...   *TRY*

Information Sources

a subject index to publications that provide statistical data on business, finance,
and economics and that are published
by state government agencies, business
organizations, independent research
organizations, universities, and trade
associations?

Statistical Reference Index [D-18]

a subject index to publications, published
by international intergovernmental organizations, that provide statistical data
on business and economics in which
the scope is national, international, and
worldwide aggregated?

Index to International Statistics [D-10]

an index to magazine articles on business,
office management, office equipment,
and supplies?

Consumers Index [D-7]

a guide to directories of various kinds of
information about specific industries and
types of business?

Directories in Print [D-35]

a bibliography or directory of trade journals?

Business Publication Rates and Data [D-142]
*Gale Directory of Publications and Broadcast
Media* [D-180]
Predicasts Source Directory [D-43]
Small Business Sourcebook [D-216]
Ulrich's International Periodicals Directory
[D-44]

a bibliography of published research reports on international business and finance?

Findex [D-37]

a directory of business information brokers?

Directory of Fee-Based Information Services
[D-163]
Information Sources [D-185]

a directory of firms that provide a variety
of online databases?

Information Sources [D-185]
See also the subsection "Computers, Information Processing, and Records Management."

WHERE SHOULD I GO TO FIND...	*TRY*
Information Sources	
a directory of online serials (periodicals) in business and economics?	*Ulrich's International Periodicals Directory* [D-44]
business information to be found in associations, think tanks, and international organizations based in Washington, DC?	*How to Find Business Intelligence in Washington* [D-182] *Washington Information Directory* [D-234]
Newspapers	
a subject guide to articles that have been published in the *New York Times* on business, economics, and other subjects?	*New York Times Index* [D-11]
the *Wall Street Journal's* publication schedule for its business and economic statistical series, including stock quotations, bond yields, Consumer Price Index, leading economic indicators, and other statistics?	*Dow Jones-Irwin Guide to Using the Wall Street Journal* [D-69]
an index to articles published in the *Wall Street Journal* and *Barron's*?	*Business Periodicals Index* [D-4] *Predicasts F&S Index United States* [D-15] *Wall Street Journal Index/Barron's Index* [D-19]
Phone Numbers	
toll-free "800" business telephone numbers?	*AT&T Toll-Free 800 Business Directory* [D-136]
a fax phone number in the U.S. or Canada?	*Fax Phone Book* [D-176] *National Fax Directory* (U.S. only) [D-201]
Rankings of Companies, Products, and Services	
what product, service, company, region, person, or other item has been ranked "number one" according to a selected criterion?	*Business Rankings and Salaries Index* [D-5] (Note: Lists many criteria from which to choose.)
Standard Industrial Classification (SIC) Code	
an explanation of the Standard Industrial Classification (SIC) coding system?	*Standard Industrial Classification Manual* [D-360]

WHERE SHOULD I GO TO FIND...	*TRY*

General Reference Sources

Information Sources

a subject index to articles that have been published in popular magazines?	*Readers' Guide to Periodical Literature* [D-17]
a subject index to books, articles in periodicals, and other print sources that focus on public-affairs and public-policy issues related to business, finance, economics, political science, and other public-affairs information topics?	*PAIS Bulletin* [D-12]
a bibliography of U.S. books on business, economics, and other subjects that are either in print or soon to be published?	*Books in Print* [D-31] *Forthcoming Books* [D-38]
an international directory of periodicals, annuals, monograph series, and proceedings in business, economics, and other fields, regardless of the frequency of their issuance?	*Ulrich's International Periodicals Directory* [D-44]
a directory of U.S., Canadian, and Puerto Rican broadcast media, newspapers, magazines, trade and technical publications, with descriptive information including address, telephone number, and names of feature editors of the newspapers?	*Gale Directory of Publications and Broadcast Media* [D-180]
a guide to statistical abstracts for individual U.S. states and foreign nations?	*Statistical Abstract of the United States* [D-361]
a bibliography of business, health care, and education publications, with descriptive information about each publication?	*Business Publication Rates and Data* [D-142]
a directory of published newsletters on business and other subjects, with a non-evaluative description of each newsletter?	*Newsletters in Print* [D-41] *Oxbridge Directory of Newsletters* [D-42]

WHERE SHOULD I GO TO FIND...	*TRY*

Information Sources

a catalog of census documents on a variety of subjects and published by the U.S. Bureau of the Census?	*Census Catalog and Guide* [D-6]
a directory of special information collections on business and other subjects, located in corporate libraries, archives, and information centers in the U.S., Canada, and other nations?	*Directory of Special Libraries and Information Centers* [D-167]
a subject index to statistical publications on business, politics, and social trends that are published by state government agencies and private U.S. organizations?	*Statistical Reference Index* [D-18]
a subject index to statistical publications on business, politics, foreign trade, and social conditions, published by international intergovernmental organizations, at the national, international, and worldwide aggregate levels?	*Index to International Statistics* [D-10]

Guide to Governments and Nations

County and Municipal Governments

Note: For information on municipal bonds, see also the subsection "Investments."

sources of information about local government revenues, expenditures, and other financial statistics?	*Regional Statistics* [D-469]
for local units of government in the U.S., details of indebtedness, taxing authority, and an enumeration of outstanding bonds?	*Moody's Municipal and Government Manual* [D-193]
detailed information on individual bonds issued by municipalities to finance industrial-development or pollution-control projects?	*Moody's Municipal and Government Manual* [D-193]

WHERE SHOULD I GO TO FIND...   *TRY*

County and Municipal Governments

an explanation of the principles of municipal accounting and financial reporting?

Accountant's Desk Handbook [D-237]
Accounting Desk Book [D-239]
Municipal Bond Handbook, Vol. 2 [D-306]

a statement and explanation of the generally accepted accounting principles for local and state governments (Gvt-GAAP)?

Miller Comprehensive Governmental GAAP Guide [D-300]

county and municipal government agencies that protect consumers' rights?

Consumer Sourcebook [D-152]

the name, address, and telephone number of local governments that provide services to local businesses that are interested in international trade?

American Export Register [D-133]

Currency-Exchange Rates

current foreign-currency exchange rates?

Barron's [D-440]
Investor's Daily [D-449]
Wall Street Journal [D-457]
See also major metropolitan newspapers.

exchange rates between the U.S. dollar and currencies of individual nations for selected periods of time?

Europa World Year Book [D-25]
International Financial Statistics [D-448]
Moody's International Manual [D-191]
Rand McNally Bankers Directory: International [D-211]
Statistical Abstract of the United States [D-361]
World Currency Yearbook [D-30]

Federal Government: Budget

data on the Federal budget?

Budget of the United States Government [D-335]
Dow Jones-Irwin Business and Investment Almanac [D-24]
Historical Statistics of the United States [D-351]
Moody's Municipal and Government Manual [D-193]
Statistical Abstract of the United States [D-361]
World Almanac [D-29]

WHERE SHOULD I GO TO FIND . . .   *TRY*

Federal Government: Congressional Offices and Officials

names of state delegates to Congress with biographical profiles?	*Congressional Staff Directory* [D-149] *Official Congressional Directory* [D-356]
the names, addresses, and telephone numbers of members of Congress?	*Congressional Staff Directory* [D-149] *Official Congressional Directory* [D-356] *United States Government Manual* [D-366] *Washington Information Directory* [D-234]
names of the members of congressional committees and subcommittees?	*Congressional Staff Directory* [D-149] *Official Congressional Directory* [D-356] *Washington Information Directory* [D-234]
the addresses and telephone numbers of U.S. House and Senate committee offices?	*Congressional Staff Directory* [D-149] *How to Find Business Intelligence in Washington* [D-182] *Official Congressional Directory* [D-356] *Washington Information Directory* [D-234]
the addresses and telephone numbers of federal offices?	*Congressional Staff Directory* [D-149] *Federal Staff Directory* [D-177] *How to Find Business Intelligence in Washington* [D-182] *Official Congressional Directory* [D-356] *United States Government Manual* [D-366] *Washington Information Directory* [D-234]
the names, addresses, telephone numbers, and biographies of the staff members of senators, representatives, and congressional committees and subcommittees?	*Congressional Staff Directory* [D-149]

Federal Government: Executive Branch Programs and Officials, and Independent Agencies

federal government agencies that provide information, procurement assistance, and other services to small businesses?	*International Directory of Business Information Agencies and Services* [D-466] *Small Business Sourcebook* [D-216] *Washington Information Directory* [D-234]
the location of business information in federal departments and agencies?	*How to Find Business Intelligence in Washington* [D-182] *Washington Information Directory* [D-234]

<u>*WHERE SHOULD I GO TO FIND...*</u>   <u>*TRY*</u>

Federal Government: Executive Branch Programs and Officials, and Independent Agencies

the addresses and telephone numbers
of federal offices?

Congressional Staff Directory [D-149]
Federal Staff Directory [D-177]
How to Find Business Intelligence in Washington [D-182]
Official Congressional Directory [D-356]
United States Government Manual [D-366]
Washington Information Directory [D-234]

the names, addresses, and telephone numbers of key executives
and their staffs in the executive
branch, with selected biographical profiles?

Federal Staff Directory [D-177]

the names, addresses, and telephone
numbers of key executives and their
staffs in independent agencies of the
federal government?

Federal Staff Directory [D-177]

a directory of federal laboratories
and engineering centers whose expertise, equipment, and facilities
are available to assist the business
community?

Directory of Federal Laboratory and Technology Resources [D-346]

an explanation of the organization of
the Securities and Exchange Commission, the laws it administers, and
the way it conducts its business?

Financial Analyst's Handbook [D-271]
United States Government Manual [D-366]

the addresses and telephone numbers
of federal offices devoted to consumer
affairs?

Consumer Sourcebook [D-152]
Washington Information Directory [D-234]

the addresses and telephone numbers of regional information centers
and/or other offices of federal departments and agencies?

Consumer's Resource Handbook [D-344]
Federal Staff Directory [D-177]
United States Government Manual [D-366]
Washington Information Directory [D-234]

the names and telephone numbers of
procurement officers for individual federal departments and agencies?

Official Congressional Directory [D-356]
United States Government Manual [D-366]
Washington Information Directory [D-234]

WHERE SHOULD I GO TO FIND...   *TRY*

**Federal Government: Executive Branch Programs and Officials, and
Independent Agencies**

the names and telephone numbers of   *Official Congressional Directory* [D-356]
Equal Employment Opportunity officials   *United States Government Manual* [D-366]
for individual federal departments and   *Washington Information Directory* [D-234]
agencies?

the names and telephone numbers of   *Washington Information Directory* [D-234]
Freedom of Information contacts for the
various federal departments and agencies?

an explanation of the purpose and ser-   *United States Government Manual* [D-366]
vices of individual federal departments   *Washington Information Directory* [D-234]
and agencies?

a map that depicts the area encompassed   *United States Government Manual* [D-366]
within each standard federal region?

the meaning of abbreviations and   *Acronyms, Initialisms, and Abbreviations*
acronyms used to designate federal de-   *Dictionary* [D-109]
partments and agencies?   *Business Acronyms* (business-related only)
                                             [D-114]
                                             United States Government Manual [D-366]

names of key officers, addresses, and   *American Export Register* (no names)
telephone numbers of U.S. foreign em-   [D-133]
bassies and consulates?   *Countries of the World* [D-22]
                                             Exporters Directory [D-175]
                                             Federal Staff Directory [D-177]
                                             *International Directory of Corporate
                                             Affiliations* [D-186]
                                             World Almanac [D-29]
                                             *Worldwide Government Directory with
                                             International Organizations* [D-236]

forecasts of U.S. government programs   *Predicasts Forecasts* [D-468]
and activities?

historical times series statistics on federal   *Historical Statistics of the United States*
programs?   [D-351]
                                             Predicasts Basebook [D-467]

an index to information about programs   *Predicasts F&S Index United States* [D-15]
and activities of federal departments and
agencies as reported in newspapers, trade
journals, government reports, and other
print sources?

| *WHERE SHOULD I GO TO FIND...* | *TRY* |

Federal Government: Executive Branch Programs and Officials, and Independent Agencies

| services provided by the U.S. government to importers and exporters of American products, and the addresses and telephone numbers of U.S. and Foreign Commercial Service district offices? | *American Export Register* [D-133]
Exporters Directory [D-175] |

| the responsibilities of the U.S. Customs Service and the locations of its district offices? | *Directory of United States Importers* [D-169]
Official U.S. Custom House Guide [D-206]
United States Government Manual [D-366] |

Note: For information about port authorities and ports of entry, see the subsection "International Business Transactions."

| a listing of federal agencies with authority to order the recall of products and the products over which they have oversight? | *AMA Management Handbook* [D-242] |

Federal Government: Regulations, Rules, and Procedures

| regulations pertaining to U.S. customs and duty? | *Countries of the World* [D-22] |

| information on obtaining a U.S. passport? | *Countries of the World* [D-22]
United States Government Manual [D-366] |

| the rules and procedures that control the purchasing of supplies and services by departments and agencies of the federal executive branch? | *Federal Acquisition Regulation* [D-270] |

| an explanation of accounting principles that apply to the management of contracts with the federal government? | *Accounting Guide for Government Contracts* [D-48] |

| cost accounting standards, regulations, and practices that are followed by the federal government in its dealings with contractors for goods and services? | *Accounting for Government Contracts* [D-370] |

Federal Government: Regulations, Rules, and Procedures

new and proposed regulations of the fed-   *Federal Register* [D-350]
eral executive branch?

a compilation of the general regulations   *Code of Federal Regulations* [D-343]
in force by the departments and agencies
of the federal executive branch?

abstracts of articles on government reg-   *PROMT* [D-16]
ulations that have been reported in
journals, newspapers, and other print
sources?

application forms required by federal de-   *Business Forms On File* [D-376]
partments and agencies and which are
most frequently requested by businesses?

an explanation of the Basic Information   *Accounting Desk Book* [D-239]
Package (Integrated Disclosure System) of
the Securities and Exchange Commission,
including the various reporting forms
that are required of businesses in their
reporting to the SEC?

Foreign Governments

Note: For information on business laws
in foreign nations, see "Business Laws
and Practices of Foreign Nations" in the
subsection "Business Law."

the addresses and telephone numbers of   *American Export Register* [D-133]
foreign embassies and/or consulates in   *Directory of United States Importers* [D-169]
the U.S.?   *Exporters Directory* [D-175]
                                                   *International Directory of Corporate
                                                   Affiliations* [D-186]
                                                   Official Congressional Directory [D-356]
                                                   Washington Information Directory [D-234]
                                                   World Almanac [D-29]
                                                   *Worldwide Government Directory with
                                                   International Organizations* [D-236]

the names and responsibilities of govern-   *Worldwide Government Directory with Interna-*
ment officials around the world, along   *tional Organizations* [D-236]
with their addresses and telephone, telex,
and cable numbers?

WHERE SHOULD I GO TO FIND...   *TRY*

Foreign Governments

the names of chiefs of state and their cabinet members in governments around the world?

Countries of the World [D-22]
Europa World Year Book [D-25]
The Statesman's Yearbook [D-28]

an "organization manual" for the government of the People's Republic of China, with an explanation of the purpose and responsibilities of each governmental unit?

China Investment Guide [D-56]

the constitution of the People's Republic of China?

China Laws for Foreign Business [D-380]

forecasts of programs and activities of foreign governments?

Worldcasts [D-475]

an index to information about programs and activities of foreign governments as reported in newspapers, trade journals, government reports, and other print sources?

Predicasts F&S Index Europe [D-14]
Predicasts F&S Index International [D-14]

a guide to services rendered by foreign governments to exporters of American products, including information about foreign consumer needs and preferences, laws and customs, entrance requirements, and other related matters of foreign nations?

American Export Register [D-133]

Note: For information about port authorities and ports of entry, see the subsection "International Business Transactions."

a directory of departments of education in Canada?

Career Information Center [D-252]

an overview of the government of Brazil?

Countries of the World [D-22]
Doing Business in Brazil [D-392]

an overview of the legal system in the Republic of Ireland?

Doing Business in Ireland [D-397]

an overview of the legal system in Japan?

Doing Business in Japan [D-398]

WHERE SHOULD I GO TO FIND...	*TRY*

Foreign Governments

an overview of the governmental structure in Spain and the legal system of that country, including an explanation of the roles of lawyers and others in their legal system?	*Countries of the World* (governmental structure only) [D-22] *Doing Business in Spain* [D-400]
an overview of the legal system in the United Kingdom?	*Doing Business in the United Kingdom* [D-401]

General Information About Foreign Nations

descriptive information about individual nations, including the economy, people, political conditions, and other characteristics?	*Countries of the World* [D-22] *Europa World Year Book* [D-25] *Moody's International Manual* [D-191] *The Statesman's Yearbook* [D-28] *World Almanac* [D-29]
the address of a nation's national statistical office?	*International Directory of Business Information Agencies and Services* [D-466] *Statistics Sources* [D-473]
the appropriate kinds of clothes to wear in a foreign country?	*Countries of the World* [D-22]
visa requirements of foreign governments?	*Countries of the World* [D-22]
health information germane to international travel, including immunizations, vaccination certificate requirements, and other health tips for travelers?	*Countries of the World* [D-22]
the dates of public holidays in foreign nations?	*Europa World Year Book* [D-25]
the names and addresses of newspapers and periodicals in foreign nations?	*Europa World Year Book* [D-25]
for banks in foreign nations, the name of a principal executive officer, with address, and telephone number?	*Europa World Year Book* [D-25] *Rand McNally Bankers Directory: International* (includes only banks involved in foreign trade) [D-211]
the names and addresses of stock exchanges in foreign nations?	*Europa World Year Book* [D-25] *How to Buy Foreign Stocks and Bonds* [D-76]

WHERE SHOULD I GO TO FIND...   *TRY*

General Information About Foreign Nations

the names, addresses, and telephone   *Europa World Year Book* [D-25]
numbers of insurance companies in for-
eign nations?

the names, addresses, and telephone   *Europa World Year Book* [D-25]
numbers of trade and industry organi-   *International Directory of Business Informa-*
zations in foreign nations?   *tion Agencies and Services* [D-466]

the economic zones and districts in the   *China Investment Guide* [D-56]
People's Republic of China that are open   *China Laws for Foreign Business* [D-380]
to foreign business ventures?   *Doing Business in China* [D-394]

information on the debt of a foreign na-   *Moody's International Manual* [D-191]
tion, including loan data and bond de-
scriptions with ratings, maturity dates,
interest, security, callable provisions, and
other related information?

information on changes in consumer   *Moody's International Manual* [D-191]
prices for individual nations during se-   *International Financial Statistics* [D-448]
lected years?

information on gold and other reserves   *Moody's International Manual* [D-191]
of nations for selected years?   *International Financial Statistics* [D-448]

descriptive information on the currency   *World Currency Yearbook* [D-30]
of individual nations?

import-export statistics for individual na-   *Moody's International Manual* [D-191]
tions during selected years?   *International Financial Statistics* [D-448]

a directory of telephone codes for for-   *Official U.S. Custom House Guide* [D-206]
eign nations?

financial and economic statistical data for   *International Financial Statistics* [D-448]
individual nations and worldwide aggre-
gate?

an overview of the business and economic   *Countries of the World* [D-22]
environment and the political system in   *Doing Business in Canada* [D-393]
Canada?

an overview of the political and eco-   *Countries of the World* [D-22]
nomic climate for foreign investments   *Doing Business in France* [D-396]
in France?

WHERE SHOULD I GO TO FIND...	*TRY*

General Information About Foreign Nations

an overview of cultural considerations for conducting business in Mexico?	*Doing Business in Mexico* [D-399]
an overview of the business, economic, and political environments in the People's Republic of China?	*China Investment Guide* [D-56] *Doing Business in China* [D-394]
Note: For additional general information about China, see "Foreign Business Resources" in the subsection "Business Resources."	
an overview of the business climate in the Federal Republic of Germany?	*Business Transactions in Germany* [D-378] *Countries of the World* [D-22]

International Organizations

the names and responsibilities of officials of intergovernmental agencies around the world, with their addresses and telephone, telex, and cable numbers?	*Worldwide Government Directory with International Organizations* [D-236]
an index to information about programs and activities of international organizations as reported in newspapers, government reports, and other print sources?	*Predicasts F&S Index Europe* [D-14] *Predicasts F&S Index International* [D-14]
the names of personnel with the European Economic Community's (Common Market) Executive Commission, Council of Ministers, and Court of Justice, along with addresses and telephone numbers?	*Common Market Reports* [D-382]
a subject index to statistical publications of multinational organizations that focus on the business, economic, social, political, education, and health conditions of a national, international, or worldwide significance?	*Index to International Statistics* [D-10]

<u>*WHERE SHOULD I GO TO FIND...*</u>   <u>*TRY*</u>

International Organizations

publications of international intergovernmental organizations that provide statistical data on consumer prices and price
indexes in individual foreign nations and
regions of the world?

Index to International Statistics [D-10]

State Governments

a directory of state government agencies
that provide information, procurement
assistance, and other services to small
businesses?

Small Business Sourcebook [D-216]

the names, addresses, and telephone
numbers of state governmental units that
provide services to businesses interested
in international trade activity?

American Export Register [D-133]

a directory of state agencies and departments that provide information about
individual companies?

How to Find Information About Companies
[D-183]

information on the indebtedness of individual states, including an enumeration
of outstanding bonds?

Moody's Municipal and Government Manual
[D-193]

detailed information on individual bonds
issued by a state to finance industrial-
development or pollution-control
projects?

Moody's Municipal and Government Manual
[D-193]

the names, addresses, and telephone
numbers of elected officials and administrative officers of the individual states,
District of Columbia, and U.S. territories
and possessions?

National Directory of State Agencies [D-199]
*State Administrative Officials Classified by
Function* [D-224]
Washington Information Directory (only the
governors, lieutenant governors, secre-
taries of state, and attorneys general of
each state) [D-234]

an index to information about programs
and activities of state governments, as
reported in newspapers, trade journals,
government reports, and other print
sources?

Predicasts F&S Index United States [D-15]

WHERE SHOULD I GO TO FIND...	*TRY*

State Governments

a directory of state government agencies that protect consumers' rights, listing their addresses and telephone numbers?

Consumer Sourcebook [D-152]
National Directory of State Agencies [D-199]
State Administrative Officials Classified by Function [D-224]

the official holidays of each state?

Employment Coordinator [D-402]

a statement and explanation of the generally accepted accounting principles for state governments (Gvt-GAAP)?

Miller Comprehensive Governmental GAAP Guide [D-300]

Insurance

Business Start-Ups: Insurance

a checklist of insurance considerations when starting a new business?

Business Forms On File [D-376]
The Entrepreneur and Small Business Problem Solver [D-269]

how to select an insurance company and a discussion of the types of insurance available to businesses?

The Entrepreneur and Small Business Problem Solver [D-269]
How to Set Up Your Own Small Business [D-290]

Computers and Software: Insurance

descriptive profiles of microcomputer software packages that serve applications in the insurance industry?

Data Sources: Software [D-158]
Datapro Directory of Microcomputer Software [D-387]

Condominiums: Insurance

information on insurance coverage for condominiums?

Condominium Development Guide [D-257]

Estate Planning

an explanation of life insurance and its role in estate planning?

Handbook of Estate Planning [D-280]

<u>*WHERE SHOULD I GO TO FIND...*</u>   <u>*TRY*</u>

Government Insurance Officials

the name and telephone number of the government regulatory official in charge of the insurance industry in each state and Canadian province?

Best's Agents Guide to Life Insurance Companies [D-138]
Best's Insurance Reports [D-140]
Best's Key Rating Guide: Property–Casualty [D-141]
Consumer's Resource Handbook (U.S. states only) [D-344]
National Directory of State Agencies [D-199]
State Administrative Officials Classified by Function [D-224]

Information Sources

a listing of published research reports on the operations of the insurance industry and individual insurance companies?

Findex [D-37]

a subject index to statistical publications that focus on the insurance industry and which are issued by state government agencies or private organizations?

Statistical Reference Index [D-18]

a subject index to statistical publications of the federal government that focus on the insurance industry?

American Statistics Index [D-1]

Insurance Associations

a directory of national associations located in Washington, DC, that serve the insurance industry?

Washington Information Directory [D-234]

Insurance Company Listings and Profiles

a directory of companies that provide various kinds of insurance, reporting the address, telephone number, name of CEO, and selected descriptive data for each?

Best's Insurance Reports [D-140]
Ward's Business Directory, Vol. 1 [D-231]
Ward's Business Directory, Vol. 3 [D-233]

WHERE SHOULD I GO TO FIND...	*TRY*

Insurance Company Listings and Profiles

descriptive, financial, and operating profiles of insurance companies?	*Best's Agents Guide to Life Insurance Companies* [D-138] *Best's Insurance Reports* [D-140] *Best's Key Rating Guide: Property–Casualty* [D-141] *Moody's Bank and Finance Manual* [D-189] *Standard & Poor's Corporation Records* [D-220]
the distribution of assets of life insurance companies among government securities, corporate securities, mortgages, real estate, policy loans, and other assets, for selected years?	*Best's Insurance Reports* [D-140] *Moody's Bank and Finance Manual* [D-189]
an indication of the relative financial size of an insurance company, based on its policyholders' surplus and conditional reserve funds?	*Best's Agents Guide to Life Insurance Companies* [D-138] *Best's Insurance Reports* [D-140] *Best's Key Rating Guide: Property–Casualty* [D-141]
a listing of business-insurance brokers, indicating the types of insurance and kinds of businesses served, special strengths, contact person, telephone number, and other information?	*Corporate Finance Sourcebook* [D-153]
a directory of insurance companies in foreign nations that reports their addresses and telephone numbers?	*Europa World Year Book* [D-25]
a directory of securities underwriters, with the telephone number of their headquarters?	*Bond Guide* [D-248]

Insurance Industry Statistics

summary operating statistics on the property–casualty insurance industry?	*Best's Aggregates & Averages: Property–Casualty* [D-463]

Insurance and Related Laws

the insurance securities laws and regulations of the 50 states, District of Columbia, Guam, and Puerto Rico?	*Blue Sky Law Reports* [D-375]

WHERE SHOULD I GO TO FIND...   _TRY_

Insurance and Related Laws

an introductory explanation of the law of insurance?

A Guide to Modern Business and Commercial Law [D-274]

the insurance case law of all federal courts and state appellate courts pertaining to policies covering automobiles; fire and casualty; and life, health, and accident insurance?

Insurance Law Reports [D-412]

a separate compilation of the special federal tax laws that apply to the insurance industry?

Federal Taxation of Insurance Companies [D-407]

Insurance Management and State Licensing

guidelines on risk insurance management?

AMA Management Handbook [D-242]

the states in which individual insurance companies are licensed to conduct business?

Best's Agents Guide to Life Insurance Companies [D-138]
Best's Insurance Reports [D-140]
Best's Key Rating Guide: Property–Casualty [D-141]

Insurance Products

the life insurance products offered by individual insurance carriers, with a descriptive analysis of each kind of policy?

Best's Flitcraft Compend [D-139]

the premium rates charged by life insurance companies when issuing substandard or special-class policies?

Best's Flitcraft Compend [D-139]

the guaranteed cash values of life insurance policies of individual carriers?

Best's Flitcraft Compend [D-139]

the dividend history of ordinary life insurance plans of individual insurance companies?

Best's Flitcraft Compend [D-139]

comparative provisions of ordinary life policies issued by insurance companies?

Best's Flitcraft Compend [D-139]

<u>*WHERE SHOULD I GO TO FIND...*</u>   <u>*TRY*</u>

Insurance Products

the current rate being paid on universal   *Best's Flitcraft Compend* [D-139]
life policies by individual insurance carri-
ers?

Newsletters

a directory of published newsletters on   *Newsletters in Print* [D-41]
insurance, with a nonevaluative descrip-   *Oxbridge Directory of Newsletters* [D-42]
tion of each newsletter?

Rankings and Ratings: Insurance Companies

a ranked listing of the largest life insur-   *Best's Agents Guide to Life Insurance*
ance companies?   *Companies* [D-138]
                                                  Moody's Bank and Finance Manual [D-189]

a ranked listing of the leading property–   *Best's Aggregates and Averages: Property–*
casualty insurance companies?   *Casualty* [D-463]
                                                  Best's Key Rating Guide: Property–
                                                  Casualty [D-141]
                                                  Moody's Bank and Finance Manual [D-189]

a ranking of insurance companies within   *Ward's Business Directory, Vol. 3* [D-233]
their Standard Industrial Classification
(SIC) industry?

ratings of individual insurance companies   *Best's Agents Guide to Life Insurance*
regarding their profitability and spread   *Companies* [D-138]
of risk?   *Best's Insurance Reports* [D-140]
                                                  Best's Key Rating Guide: Property–
                                                  Casualty [D-141]

| **International Business Transactions** |

Note: For information on the business
laws and regulations of the U.S. and foreign nations, see the subsection "Business
Law."

WHERE SHOULD I GO TO FIND...	*TRY*

Advertising Agencies

an international directory of advertising agencies, with a descriptive profile of each agency, including location, specialization, and names of account executives?

Standard Directory of Advertising Agencies [D-223]

Computers and Software: Export/Import Industry

descriptive profiles of computer software packages that serve functions associated with the export/import industry?

Data Sources: Software [D-158]

Export/Import Firms and Products

a directory of American exporting firms, with a listing of the products or services they export?

American Export Register [D-133]
Exporters Directory [D-175]

a directory of importers, with descriptive information about each importer?

Directory of United States Importers [D-169]

a directory of imported products and the names of the companies that import them?

Directory of United States Importers [D-169]

a directory of exported products and the names of the companies that export them?

Exporters Directory [D-175]

Export-Import Support Industry

the names, addresses, and telephone numbers of state and local governments and of local associations and organizations that provide services to businesses that are interested in international trade?

American Export Register [D-133]

a listing of custom-house brokers in the U.S.?

American Export Register [D-133]
Official U.S. Custom House Guide (listed by port of entry) [D-206]
Thomas Register's Inbound Traffic Guide [D-227]

<u>*WHERE SHOULD I GO TO FIND...*</u>   *TRY*

Export-Import Support Industry

a listing of custom houses in the People's   *China Investment Guide* [D-56]
Republic of China with their addresses
and telephone numbers?

a directory of freight carriers, by trans-   *American Export Register* [D-133]
portation mode, for domestic and foreign   *Official U.S. Custom House Guide* [D-206]
shipments, indicating geographical areas   *Thomas Register's Inbound Traffic Guide*
served?   [D-227]

a directory of overseas ports, with the   *American Export Register* [D-133]
names of steamship lines that operate
between each port and the U.S.?

the names of airlines, air cargo carriers,   *Official U.S. Custom House Guide* [D-206]
and ocean carriers that serve each of the
U.S. and Canadian ports of entry?

Foreign Business Environments

Note: See also "Export and Import Laws,
Regulations, and Procedures" in the subsection "Business Law."

guidelines on how to conduct business in   *How to Do Business with Russians* [D-284]
Russia?

application forms for the registration of   *China Investment Guide* [D-56]
authorized agents, foreign enterprises,
and joint ventures in the People's Republic of China?

guidelines for conducting business in the   *China Investment Guide* [D-56]
People's Republic of China?   *China Laws for Foreign Business* [D-380]

guidelines for conducting business in   *Japan Business Law Guide* [D-413]
Japan?

Foreign Company Listings

Japanese companies classified by their   *Japan Yellow Pages* [D-187]
product or service and listing their ad-
dresses and telephone, cable, and telex
numbers?

WHERE SHOULD I GO TO FIND...	*TRY*

Foreign Company Listings

companies in Taiwan classified by their product or service and listing their addresses and telephone, cable, and telex numbers?

Taiwan Yellow Pages [D-225]

profiles of major corporations in the People's Republic of China, including the nature of their business, CEO's name, addresses, and their telephone, cable, and telex numbers?

China Investment Guide [D-56]

Foreign Consultants and Partners

guidelines for selecting a Japan-based consultant or business partner?

How to Find Information About Japanese Companies and Industries [D-184]

directories of consulting companies, investment corporations, banks, and airlines in the People's Republic of China, stating their address, telephone number, and telex number?

China Investment Guide [D-56]

Government Regulations and Services: International Trade

services provided to importers and exporters of American products or services by the U.S. government, including the addresses and telephone numbers of U.S. and Foreign Commercial Services district offices?

American Export Register [D-133]
Exporters Directory [D-175]

a guide to services rendered by foreign governments to exporters of American products, including information about foreign consumer needs and preferences, laws and customs, entrance requirements, and other related matters of foreign nations?

American Export Register [D-133]

the names, addresses, and telephone numbers of state and local governments and of local associations and organizations that provide services to businesses that are interested in international trade?

American Export Register [D-133]

WHERE SHOULD I GO TO FIND...	*TRY*

Government Regulations and Services: International Trade

a review of export regulations of the U.S. government?	*Exporters Directory* [D-175]
a summary of U.S. customs regulations and importing procedures?	*Directory of United States Importers* [D-169]
the text of U.S. customs regulations?	*19 Code of Federal Regulations, Ch. 1* [D-343] *Official U.S. Custom House Guide* [D-206]
a listing of foreign ("free") trade zones in the U.S.?	*Directory of United States Importers* [D-169] *Official U.S. Custom House Guide* [D-206]
the Schedule of U.S. Tariffs and associated duty rates?	*Official U.S. Custom House Guide* [D-206]
U.S. international mail rates?	*Commercial Atlas and Marketing Guide* [D-464]

Information About Foreign Companies: Intelligence Gathering

how and where to locate information about foreign companies?	*How to Find Information About Companies* [D-183] *How to Find Information About Foreign Firms* [D-287]
how and where to locate information about Japanese companies?	*How to Find Information About Japanese Companies and Industries* [D-184]

Legal Assistance Regarding Foreign Trade Business

a directory of law firms that specialize in admiralty, customs, and/or international law?	*Official U.S. Custom House Guide* [D-206]

Marketing Abroad

how to select foreign markets for exporting American-made products?	*Exporters Directory* [D-175]
organizations that serve as a source of information for marketing products abroad?	*Exporters Directory* [D-175] *Directory of United States Importers* [D-169]

<u>*WHERE SHOULD I GO TO FIND...*</u>   <u>*TRY*</u>

Newsletters

a directory of published newsletters on
international trade, with a nonevaluative
description of each newsletter?

Newsletters in Print [D-41]
Oxbridge Directory of Newsletters [D-42]

Packaging

an overview of U.S. and foreign regulations that govern packaging used in international trade?

AMA Management Handbook [D-242]

Ports and Port Authorities

a directory of U.S. port authorities, with
the address, telephone number, and
name of contact person for each?

American Export Register [D-133]
Directory of United States Importers [D-169]
Exporters Directory [D-175]

a directory of port authorities in foreign nations, with the address, telephone
number, telex number, and name of contact person for each?

Directory of United States Importers [D-169]
Exporters Directory [D-175]

a directory of overseas ports, with the
names of steamship lines that operate
between each port and the U.S.?

American Export Register [D-133]

a listing of ports of entry in the U.S.,
Puerto Rico, and the U.S. Virgin Islands?

Directory of United States Importers [D-169]
Official U.S. Custom House Guide [D-206]

a listing of Canadian ports of entry?

Official U.S. Custom House Guide [D-206]

a description of U.S. and Canadian ports
of entry, with their physical characteristics and service firms (e.g., custom-house
brokers and warehouses), organizations,
and government agencies that serve each
port?

Official U.S. Custom House Guide [D-206]

Trade Shows, Exhibitions, and Conventions

information about trade shows and exhibitions in Japan?

*How to Find Information About
Japanese Companies and Industries*
[D-184]

| Investments |

Analytical Methods, Techniques, and Formulas

how to analyze corporate financial statements?

Accounting Desk Book [D-239]
The Complete Investor [D-58]
Dow Jones-Irwin Business and Investment Almanac [D-24]
Financial Analyst's Handbook [D-271]
Financial Statement Analysis [D-272]
Understanding Wall Street [D-327]

how to perform an analysis of an industry?

Financial Analyst's Handbook [D-271]

an explanation of the technical methods used for analyzing an investment market?

Financial Analyst's Handbook [D-271]

an explanation of the statistical tools and techniques used in financial and investment analysis?

Financial Analyst's Handbook [D-271]
Techniques of Financial Analysis [D-324]

an explanation of the analytical tools that are used to evaluate the credit worthiness of municipal bonds?

Dow Jones-Irwin Guide to Municipal Bonds [D-64]
Municipal Bond Handbook, Vol. 1 [D-305], *Vol. 2* [D-306]

formulas used for determining bond yields?

The Complete Investor [D-58]
Investment Manager's Handbook [D-291]
Money Market Calculations [D-301]
Municipal Bond Handbook, Vol. 1 [D-305]

an explanation of the methods and techniques used to determine the forecasting value of stock market indicators?

Encyclopedia of Technical Market Indicators [D-268]

formulas used for the different types of money-market calculations, such as interest rates and swap costs?

Investment Manager's Handbook [D-291]
Money Market Calculations [D-301]

WHERE SHOULD I GO TO FIND...   *TRY*

Analytical Methods, Techniques, and Formulas

formulas used when investing in inter-   *Money Market Calculations* [D-301]
national money markets and concerning
differences in strengths of currencies,
estimating swap costs, covered interest
arbitrage, and other factors?

how to assess the volatility of tax-exempt   *Municipal Bond Handbook, Vol. 1* [D-305]
bonds?

Company Financial Profiles and Stock Data

a listing of companies that have increased   *Moody's Handbook of Common Stocks*
their dividend cash payments annually   [D-303]
for at least the past ten consecutive years?

data on the financial operations and stock   *Investor's Daily* [D-449]
performance of a company, including   *Moody's Handbook of Common Stocks*
revenue, financial ratios, capitalization,   [D-303]
common-share earnings, assorted per-   *Moody's Handbook of OTC Stocks*
share data, dividend payout, the stock's   [D-304]
ratings, important developments, and/or   *Moody's Manuals* [D-192]
other information needed by investors?   *Standard & Poor's Corporation Records*
                                                [D-220]
                                               Standard & Poor's Stock Reports [D-462]
                                               Stock Market Encyclopedia [D-322]
                                               Value Line Investment Survey [D-436]
                                               Wall Street Transcript [D-458]

a listing of over-the-counter stocks that   *Moody's Handbook of OTC Stocks* [D-304]
are selling below book value?

changes in the ratings of a corporation's   *Barron's* [D-440]
debt?   *Bond Guide* [D-248]
                                               Investor's Daily [D-449]
                                               Moody's News Reports series [D-192]
                                               Security Owner's Stock Guide [D-314]
                                               Standard & Poor's Daily News [D-220]
                                               Wall Street Journal [D-457]

a quarterly review of the daily and weekly   *Daily Stock Price Record* [D-259]
stock performance of individual stocks?

WHERE SHOULD I GO TO FIND...   *TRY*

Company Financial Profiles and Stock Data

a summary of quarterly earnings of individual corporations?

Barron's [D-440]
Investor's Daily [D-449]
New York Times [D-454]
Standard & Poor's Industry Surveys [D-472]
Wall Street Journal [D-457]
Wall Street Transcript [D-458]

a quarterly comparison of profits of major corporations?

Standard & Poor's Industry Surveys [D-472]
Wall Street Journal [D-457]

companies that have been studied by investment brokerage houses and a summary of the reports?

Barron's [D-440]
Wall Street Transcript [D-458]

a profile and analysis of small and little-
known companies with stocks valued under $10 a share?

Penny Stock Journal [D-455]

a historical daily performance record of
individual stocks since the 1960s?

Daily Price Stock Record [D-259]

a year-end summary of stock performance and earnings per share for each
of more than 900 companies classified by
industry?

Business Week ("The Investment Outlook
Scoreboard" in December issue) [D-441]

a listing of U.S. corporations in foods,
services, transportation, retailing, banking, communications, utilities, and industry, with financial data on each concerning sales, profits, and stock earnings?

Business Week ("Corporate Scoreboard" in
March issue) [D-441]

an estimate of a public or private company's financial strength (credit rating)?

Dun & Bradstreet Reference Book [D-171]

a summary of financial statements, with
key financial and operating ratios for individual companies?

Moody's Manuals [D-192]
Standard & Poor's Corporation Records
(excludes ratios) [D-220]

the full text or summary of CEO and
other management reports to stockholders that review the financial and operating conditions of their companies?

Moody's Manuals [D-192]
Standard & Poor's Corporation Records
[D-220]

WHERE SHOULD I GO TO FIND...   *TRY*

Company Financial Profiles and Stock Data

reports from independent public accoun-   *Moody's Manuals* [D-192]
tants concerning the financial status of
individual companies?

a detailed description of the long-term   *Moody's Manuals* [D-192]
debt of a company, including the ratings   *Standard & Poor's Corporation Records* (ex-
of its corporate stocks and bonds?   cludes ratings) [D-220]

a listing of industrial stock splits and   *Moody's Industrial Manual* [D-190]
their ratios for individual companies dur-   *Moody's OTC Industrial Manual* [D-194]
ing recent years?

a profile of less actively traded over-the-   *Moody's OTC Unlisted Manual* [D-195]
counter companies that are not listed on   *Standard & Poor's Corporation Records*
the NASDAQ National Market System?   [D-220]

a directory of major foreign companies,   *Moody's International Manual* [D-191]
with a comprehensive business and fi-   *Standard & Poor's Corporation Records* (ex-
nancial profile of each, including consol-   cludes ratios) [D-220]
idated income account, consolidated bal-
ance sheet, financial and operating ratios,
long-term debt data, excerpts from report to stockholders, and other company
information?

financial and operating profiles of invest-   *Moody's Bank and Finance Manual*
ment companies, unit investment trusts,   [D-189]
and real estate investment trusts?

the stock exchange symbols of compa-   *Million Dollar Directory* [D-188]
nies?   *Moody's Manuals* [D-192]
                                                 Security Owner's Stock Guide [D-314]
                                                 Standard & Poor's Corporation Records
                                                 [D-220]
                                                 Value Line Investment Survey [D-436]

for corporate common and preferred   *Security Owner's Stock Guide* [D-314]
stocks, their rankings/ratings, call price of
preferred stocks, split ratios, number of
consecutive years for paying dividends,
dividend payment data, earnings per
share for selected years, high/low price
range, and other data?

comparative financial analyses of com-   *Standard & Poor's Industry Surveys* [D-472]
panies and their ranking within their re-
spective industries?

WHERE SHOULD I GO TO FIND...	*TRY*

Computers and Software: Investments

a listing and explanation of computer software that is available for the analysis of investment opportunities?	*Financial Analyst's Handbook* [D-271] *Investment Manager's Handbook* [D-291]
a description of online databases that provide information used by the investment industry?	*Dow Jones-Irwin Investor's Guide to Online Databases* [D-265] *Investment Manager's Handbook* [D-291]
a directory of online databases concerning investments and securities and that are available to the public?	*Directory of Online Databases* [D-261]
descriptions of microcomputer software packages that serve a variety of investment management functions?	*Datapro Directory of Microcomputer Software* [D-387] *Data Sources: Software* [D-158]

Currency Exchange Rates

exchange rates between the U.S. dollar and currencies of other nations for selected periods?	*Europa World Year Book* [D-25] *Moody's International Manual* [D-191] *Rand McNally Bankers Directory: International* [D-211] *World Currency Year Book* [D-30]
how to forecast foreign exchange rates?	*Dow Jones-Irwin Guide to International Securities, Futures, and Options Markets* [D-63]

Defunct Corporate Identities

what has happened to banks and publicly-held corporations whose original identities have been lost?	*Directory of Obsolete Securities* [D-165]

Employee Pension Funds

an annual directory of the 500 largest employee-benefit pension funds, with descriptive information for each fund?	*Institutional Investor* (January issue) [D-447]

Exchanges: Investment Markets

the addresses of major U.S. and selected foreign stock exchanges?	*Dow Jones-Irwin Business and Investment Almanac* [D-24] *Europa World Year Book* [D-25]

WHERE SHOULD I GO TO FIND...	*TRY*

Exchanges: Investment Markets

| an explanation of the NASDAQ system and how it works? | *NASDAQ Handbook* [D-307] |
| a listing of securities and commodity exchanges and securities brokers and dealers with their addresses, phone numbers, and other information? | *Ward's Business Directory, Vol. 3* [D-233] |

Foreign Investments

profiles of foreign stock exchanges that include their addresses; types of securities traded on each exchange; major stock indexes used; domestic securities also traded on the NYSE or AMEX; settlement practices, commissions, and fees; major stock listings; definition of foreign investment terms; and other operating practices and procedures?	*How to Buy Foreign Stocks and Bonds* [D-76]
daily stock quotations on foreign markets?	*Financial Times* [D-444] *Investor's Daily* [D-449] *New York Times* [D-454] *Wall Street Journal* [D-457] Metropolitan newspapers
weekly performance summaries of overseas markets?	*Barron's* [D-440]
historical performance data on foreign stock markets, bonds, and investment indices?	*Dow Jones Investor's Handbook* [D-262]
historical monthly indexes for stock exchanges throughout the world?	*Moody's International Manual* [D-191]
historical yields of long-term bonds issued by foreign governments?	*Moody's International Manual* [D-191]
a descriptive analysis of Asian stock markets?	*Asian Stockmarkets* [D-51]
the names and addresses of the stock exchanges in foreign countries?	*Europa World Year Book* [D-25] *How to Buy Foreign Stocks and Bonds* [D-76]

<u>*WHERE SHOULD I GO TO FIND...*</u>   <u>*TRY*</u>

Foreign Investments

guidelines for investing in foreign capital   *Dow Jones-Irwin Guide to International Secu-*
markets?   *rities, Futures, and Options Markets* [D-63]

background information on specific for-   *Dow Jones-Irwin Guide to International Secu-*
eign investment markets?   *rities, Futures, and Options Markets* [D-63]

how to forecast foreign exchange rates?   *Dow Jones-Irwin Guide to International Secu-*
                                                     rities, Futures, and Options Markets [D-63]

daily announcements of new U.S. and   *Wall Street Journal* [D-457]
non-U.S. security offerings, including
corporates, municipals, mortgages, Eu-
robonds, and others?

guidelines for undertaking business in-   *China Investment Guide* [D-56]
vestments (joint ventures) in the People's   *China Laws for Foreign Business* [D-380]
Republic of China?

a directory of major trust and investment   *China Investment Guide* [D-56]
corporations in the People's Republic of
China?

a directory of major foreign companies,   *Moody's International Manual* [D-191]
with a comprehensive business and fi-   *Standard & Poor's Corporation Records*
nancial profile of each, including consol-   [D-220]
idated income account, consolidated bal-
ance sheet, financial and operating ratios,
long-term debt analysis, and other data?

information on the bonds of foreign na-   *Moody's International Manual* [D-191]
tions, including a description of these
bonds?

an explanation of the Foreign Bond-   *Moody's International Manual* [D-191]
holder's Protective Council, Inc., that
provides information and guidance (not
as a legal agent) to American bondhold-
ers in matters related to the security of
their bonds that have been issued publicly or guaranteed by foreign governments?

for foreign bonds, their S&P ratings,   *Bond Guide* [D-248]
interest rates, due dates, interest dates,
yields to maturity, and other data?

WHERE SHOULD I GO TO FIND...   *TRY*

Foreign Investments

the text of the Convention on the Settlement of Investment Disputes Between States and Nationals of Other States?	*A Dictionary of Arbitration and Its Terms* [D-116]

Industry Profiles

a daily summary of an industry's stock activity and indicating its five-year earnings per share compared with other industries and its stock-price performance compared with that of other industries for the past year?	*Investor's Daily* [D-449]
the text of interviews with leading CEOs and money managers concerning investment matters related to their industries?	*Wall Street Transcript* [D-458]
a year-end summary of stock performance and earnings per share for each of over 900 companies, classified by industry?	*Business Week* ("The Investment Outlook Scoreboard" in December issue) [D-441]
an industry's year-end average stock performance?	*Business Week* ("The Investment Outlook Scoreboard" in December issue) [D-441]
comparative financial analyses of companies and their ranking within their industries?	*Standard & Poor's Industry Surveys* [D-472]
an analysis of the historical trends and problems of each industy, along with its prospects and developments, coupled with an appraisal of the industry's investment outlook?	*Standard & Poor's Industry Surveys* [D-472]
economic forecasts for individual industries?	*U.S. Industrial Outlook* [D-367]

Information Sources

a directory of sources of strategic information about companies that are the target for investment?	*How to Find Information About Companies* [D-183]

WHERE SHOULD I GO TO FIND . . .	*TRY*

Information Sources

special guidelines and sources for getting information about service companies that are the target for investment?	*How to Find Information About Service Companies* [D-289]
a listing of published research reports by investment research firms on individual companies and industries?	*Findex* [D-37]
information on individual companies and industries as reported in trade journals, newspapers, and other publications along with citations to sources with expanded information?	*Predicasts F&S Index Europe* [D-14] *Predicasts F&S Index International* [D-14] *Predicasts F&S Index United States* [D-15]
a directory of companies that provide credit-information services?	*Information Sources* [D-185]
a directory of companies that provide sundry information about financial markets?	*Information Sources* [D-185]

Insider Trading

an explanation of the Insider Trading Doctrine and related issues?	*Financial Analyst's Handbook* [D-271] Note: See also the subsection "Business Law."
information on the inside stock-trading activities of corporate officers, directors, and major stockholders?	*Barron's* [D-440] *Insider's Chronicle* [D-438] *Spectrum 6* [D-320] *Value Line Investment Survey* [D-436] *Vickers Weekly Insider Report* [D-439] *Wall Street Journal* [D-457]

Intelligence Gathering: U.S. Companies

information about developments taking place in individual corporations?	*Barron's* [D-440] *Financial Times* [D-444] *Investor's Daily* [D-449] *New York Times* [D-454] *Wall Street Journal* [D-457] *Wall Street Transcript* [D-458]

WHERE SHOULD I GO TO FIND...   *TRY*

Intelligence Gathering: U.S. Companies

how and where to locate information
about the CEO of a potential investment
target?

How to Find Information About Executives
[D-286]

a directory of sources of strategic information about companies that are the target for investment?

How to Find Information About Companies
[D-183]

special guidelines and sources for getting
information about service companies that
are the target for investment?

*How to Find Information About Service
Companies* [D-289]

information on individual companies
and industries as reported in trade journals, newspapers, and other publications,
along with citations to sources with expanded information?

Predicasts F&S Index Europe [D-14]
Predicasts F&S Index International [D-14]
Predicasts F&S Index United States [D-15]

Intelligence Gathering: Foreign Companies

how and where to locate information
about a foreign company that is an investment target?

How to Find Information About Companies
[D-183]
How to Find Information About Foreign Firms
[D-287]

how and where to locate information
about a Japanese company that is an
investment target?

*How to Find Information About Japanese
Companies and Industries* [D-184]

Investment Advice, Guidelines, and Opportunities

guidelines for investing in foreign capital
markets?

*Dow Jones-Irwin Guide to International Secu-
rities, Futures, and Options Markets* [D-63]

stock-investment advice and a summary
of a stock's performance history?

Moody's Handbook of Common Stocks
[D-303]
Moody's Handbook of OTC Stocks [D-304]
Standard & Poor's Stock Reports [D-462]
Value Line Investment Survey [D-436]
Wall Street Transcript [D-458]

the Hulbert Performance Rating of investment advisory letters?

*Dow Jones-Irwin Business and Investment
Almanac* [D-24]

<u>*WHERE SHOULD I GO TO FIND...*</u>   <u>*TRY*</u>

Investment Advice, Guidelines, and Opportunities

guidelines for investing in fine gems, gold, and collectibles?	*Complete Book of Gold Investing* [D-255] *Dow Jones-Irwin Business and Investment Almanac* [D-24] *Dow Jones-Irwin Guide to Fine Gems and Jewelry* [D-264]
investment guidelines for retirement planning?	*Dow Jones-Irwin Guide to Retirement Planning* [D-68]
questions that an investor in municipal bonds should ask before making a purchase?	*Dow Jones-Irwin Guide to Municipal Bonds* [D-64]
rules for making buy-and-sell decisions on the stock market?	*Encyclopedia of Technical Market Indicators* [D-268]
an explanation of how the gold market works and guidance for investing and trading various gold instruments?	*Complete Book of Gold Investing* [D-255]
an explanation of and guidelines for investing in fixed-income instruments, such as certificates of deposit, Treasury bills, corporate bonds, and other such instruments?	*The Complete Investor* [D-58] *Dow Jones-Irwin Guide to Bond and Money Market Investments* [D-60] *Dow Jones-Irwin Guide to Buying and Selling Treasury Securities* [D-61]
how to evaluate real estate investment opportunities and the value of different types of real estate?	*Dow Jones-Irwin Guide to Real Estate Investing* [D-67]
reference tables for determining the profitability of various kinds of real property?	*Dow Jones-Irwin Guide to Real Estate Investing* [D-67]
key high-tech industries that are potential investment areas and guidelines for investing in them?	*Dow Jones-Irwin Guide to High Tech Investing* [D-62]
guidelines for investing in no-load mutual funds?	*Dow Jones-Irwin Guide to Mutual Funds* [D-65]

WHERE SHOULD I GO TO FIND...	*TRY*

Investment Advice, Guidelines, and Opportunities

daily announcements of new U.S. and non-U.S. security offerings, including corporates, municipals, mortgages, Eurobonds, and others?	*Wall Street Journal* [D-457]
current announcements of new corporate security offerings?	*Moody's News Reports* series [D-192] *Standard & Poor's Daily News* [D-220]
a preview of forthcoming new corporate-debt financing offerings?	*Barron's* [D-440]
a weekly listing of savings institutions around the nation that offer the highest yields on CDs and money-market accounts, reporting their interest rates and minimum required deposits?	*Barron's* [D-440]
announcements of companies going public (initial stock offerings) and where their stock can be purchased and the share price?	*Penny Stock Journal* [D-455]
a weekly review and preview of investment-industry events?	*Barron's* [D-440]
a listing of U.S. savings bonds and Treasury notes that are outstanding?	*Moody's Municipal and Government Manual* [D-193] *Standard & Poor's Corporation Records* [D-220]
information on tax shelters available in nations around the world?	*Tax Havens of the World* [D-430]

Investment Concepts, Instruments, and Practices Explained

how to read the stock exchange quotations?	*Dow Jones-Irwin Business and Investment Almanac* [D-24] *How to Read the Financial Pages* [D-80] *Understanding Wall Street* [D-327]
how to read mutual fund quotations?	*Dow Jones-Irwin Business and Investment Almanac* [D-24] *How to Read the Financial Pages* [D-80]

<u>*WHERE SHOULD I GO TO FIND...*</u>   <u>*TRY*</u>

Investment Concepts, Instruments, and Practices Explained

how to read corporate bond quotations?

Dow Jones-Irwin Business and Investment Almanac [D-24]
How to Read the Financial Pages [D-80]
Understanding Wall Street [D-327]

how to read quotations of U.S. bonds, notes, and bills?

Dow Jones-Irwin Business and Investment Almanac [D-24]
Dow Jones-Irwin Guide to Buying and Selling Treasury Securities [D-61]
How to Read the Financial Pages [D-80]
Understanding Wall Street [D-327]

how to read a bond-yield book?

Municipal Bond Handbook, Vol. 1 [D-305]

an explanation of margin accounts and short selling?

Dow Jones-Irwin Business and Investment Almanac [D-24]
Understanding Wall Street [D-327]

an explanation of the major money-market and fixed-income securities, indicating when interest is paid, rating of marketability, maturity, and the minimum investment allowed?

Dow Jones-Irwin Business and Investment Almanac [D-24]

an explanation of stock options and how to read option quotations?

Dow Jones-Irwin Business and Investment Almanac [D-24]
How to Read the Financial Pages [D-80]
Understanding Wall Street [D-327]

an explanation of how to buy (call) and sell (put) stock options?

Dow Jones-Irwin Guide to Put and Call Options [D-66]
Understanding Wall Street [D-327]

guidelines for trading stock index futures?

Stock Index Futures [D-101]

a comprehensive explanation and analysis of the different types of investments?

The Complete Investor [D-58]
Financial Analyst's Handbook [D-271]

how to obtain current information on the primary international financial markets?

Dow Jones-Irwin Guide to International Securities, Futures, and Options Markets [D-63]

WHERE SHOULD I GO TO FIND...   *TRY*

Investment Concepts, Instruments, and Practices Explained

business and legal guidelines for foreign investors preparing to do business in the U.S.?

A Guide for the Foreign Investor [D-75]

how municipal bonds are insured?

Dow Jones-Irwin Guide to Bond and Money Market Investments [D-60]
Dow Jones-Irwin Guide to Municipal Bonds [D-64]

how to judge the merits of municipal bonds?

Dow Jones-Irwin Guide to Municipal Bonds [D-64]
Municipal Bond Handbook, Vol. 1 [D-305], *Vol. 2* [D-306]

how to evaluate Certificates of Participation?

Dow Jones-Irwin Guide to Municipal Bonds [D-64]

an explanation of the relationship between bond prices and interest rates?

The Complete Investor [D-58]
Municipal Bond Handbook, Vol. 1 [D-305]

a comprehensive guide to the principles and practices of the municipal securities market?

Municipal Bond Handbook, Vol. 1 [D-305], *Vol. 2* [D-306]

a detailed explanation of U.S. bonds, bills, and notes?

The Complete Investor [D-58]
Dow Jones-Irwin Guide to Buying and Selling Treasury Securities [D-61]

a listing of technical stock market indicators, with an explanation of how each works?

Encyclopedia of Technical Market Indicators [D-268]
Handbook of Economic and Financial Measures [D-279]

an explanation of beta forecasts for investment-portfolio management?

The Complete Investor [D-58]
Investment Manager's Handbook [D-291]

a comprehensive guide to investment-portfolio management, including strategies, techniques for measuring and monitoring performances, regulatory agencies, and computer services?

Investment Manager's Handbook [D-291]

strategies for managing bond, real estate, and stock portfolios?

Investment Manager's Handbook [D-291]

| *WHERE SHOULD I GO TO FIND...* | *TRY* |

Investment Concepts, Instruments, and Practices Explained

| a brief explanation of the major money market instruments? | *Managing Bank Assets and Liabilities* [D-89] |

| ratings, prices, yields to maturity, interest payment dates, and other information related to corporate bonds? | *Bond Guide* [D-248]
Moody's Bond Record [D-302] |

| descriptive data on convertible bonds, medium-term notes, obligations of U.S. government and federal agencies, industrial-development revenue bonds, and pollution- and environmental-control revenue bonds? | *Bond Guide* (convertible bonds only) [D-248]
Moody's Bond Record [D-302] |

| an explanation of the NASDAQ system and how it works? | *NASDAQ Handbook* [D-307] |

| descriptive information on individual bond series issued by various states, agencies, or municipalities? | *Moody's Municipal and Government Manual* [D-193] |

| for corporate common and preferred stocks, their rankings/ratings, call price of preferred stocks, split ratios, number of consecutive years for paying dividends, dividend payment data, earnings per share, high/low price range, and other related information? | *Security Owner's Stock Guide* [D-314] |

| for mutual bond funds, their principal objective, type, minimum required shares for initial purchase, maximum sales charge, total net assets, and other related information? | *Security Owner's Stock Guide* [D-314] |

| the steps to follow and forms to be used when establishing and implementing an automatic dividend reinvestment plan? | *Corporation Forms* [D-386] |

Investment Performance

Note: See also "Company Financial Profiles and Stock Data" in this subsection.

WHERE SHOULD I GO TO FIND...	*TRY*

Investment Performance

a quarterly Standard & Poor's (S&P) analysis of representative stocks of the three major exchanges?	*Stock Market Encyclopedia* [D-322]
a listing of companies whose common stocks comprise the Standard & Poor's (S&P) 500 Index?	*Investment Manager's Handbook* [D-291] *Security Owner's Stock Guide* [D-314] *Standard & Poor's Register of Corporations, Directors, and Executives, Vol. 3* [D-221]
charts that summarize the long-term activities of the AMEX Index, Dow Jones Industrial Average, Moody's Daily Commodity Price Index, Moody's Utilities Index, and the NYSE Index?	*Moody's Handbook of Common Stocks* [D-303]
a listing of the companies that comprise the Dow Jones Industrial Average, Dow Jones Transportation Average, and the Dow Jones Utility Average?	*Dow Jones Investor's Handbook* [D-262] *World Almanac* [D-29]
a compilation of the Dow Jones stock averages, covering a range of years, and other stock exchange data?	*Dow Jones Investor's Handbook* [D-262]
historical data for the major stock indexes?	*Dow Jones Investor's Handbook* [D-262] *Statistical Abstract of the U.S.* [D-361]
reference tables for determining the profitability of different types of real property?	*Dow Jones-Irwin Guide to Real Estate Investing* [D-67]
daily quotations for stocks, commodities, options, mutual funds, money rates, U.S. Treasury securities, and other investments?	*Investor's Daily* [D-449] *New York Times* [D-454] *Wall Street Journal* [D-457] Metropolitan newspapers
daily stock quotations on foreign markets?	*Financial Times* [D-444] *Investor's Daily* [D-449] *New York Times* [D-454] *Wall Street Journal* [D-457] Metropolitan newspapers
daily average performances of the AMEX, NYSE, NASDAQ OTC, Dow Jones, and other stock market indexes?	*Investor's Daily* [D-449] *New York Times* [D-454] *Wall Street Journal* [D-457] Metropolitan newspapers

<u>*WHERE SHOULD I GO TO FIND...*</u>   <u>*TRY*</u>

Investment Performance

a quarterly review of the daily and weekly
stock performances of individual stocks?

Daily Stock Price Record [D-259]

weekly performance summaries of U.S.
and foreign stock market indexes?

Barron's [D-440]
The Economist [D-443]

current U.S. and selected foreign prime
interest rates?

Barron's [D-440]
The Economist [D-443]
Financial Times [D-444]
Investor's Daily [D-449]
New York Times [D-454]
Wall Street Journal [D-457]
Metropolitan newspapers

current money interest rates (U.S. and
foreign), including discount rate, federal funds, Treasury bills, bankers acceptances, certificates of deposit, Eurodol-
lars, and others?

Barron's [D-440]
Financial Times [D-444]
Investor's Daily [D-449]
New York Times [D-454]
Wall Street Journal [D-457]
Metropolitan newspapers

weekly performance summaries of stocks,
commodities, futures, options, mutual
funds, U.S. Treasury securities, bonds,
and other investment areas?

Barron's [D-440]

a quarterly review of the daily performances of the major technical stock market indicators for the AMEX, NYSE, and
the OTC?

Daily Stock Price Record [D-259]

a weekly report on the Lipper Mutual
Fund Performance Averages?

Barron's [D-440]

for selected common stocks on the
AMEX, NYSE, and NASDAQ OTC:
(1) their five-year ranking of earnings
growth per share, and (2) their daily relative price change for the past 12 months
compared with stocks of other selected
companies?

Investor's Daily [D-449]

graphic displays of daily stock market
leaders, with summaries of analytical performance statistics?

Investor's Daily [D-449]

WHERE SHOULD I GO TO FIND...	*TRY*

Investment Performance

a daily summary of an industry's stock activity, also indicating its five-year earnings per share compared with other industries, and its stock-price performance compared with that of other industries for the past year?

Investor's Daily [D-449]

a historical daily performance record of individual company stocks since the 1960s?

Daily Stock Price Record [D-259]

quotes on penny stocks and stocks valued from $1 to $10 a share?

Daily Stock Price Record (Over-the-Counter edition) [D-259]
Penny Stock Journal [D-455]

4-week and 52-week performance summaries of the NYSE Composite, Dow Jones Industrials, AMEX Market Value Index, NASDAQ Composite, Wilshire 5000, and the Forbes 500 Index?

Forbes [D-445]

a year-end summary of stock performance and earnings per share for each of over 900 companies, classified by industry?

Business Week ("The Investment Outlook Scoreboard" in December issue) [D-441]

an industry's year-end average stock performance?

Business Week ("The Investment Outlook Scoreboard" in December issue) [D-441]

Moody's average of yields on newly issued corporate and industrial bonds, organized by rating grade for selected years?

Moody's Industrial Manual [D-190]

Moody's average of yields on corporate and industrial bonds, organized by rating grade for selected years?

Moody's Industrial Manual [D-190]

Moody's averages of yield for preferred stocks during selected years?

Moody's Industrial Manual [D-190]

a summary of Moody's Daily Commodity Price Index for selected years?

Moody's Industrial Manual [D-190]

<u>*WHERE SHOULD I GO TO FIND...*</u>	<u>*TRY*</u>

Investment Performance

a listing of industrial stock splits, with ratios for cited companies during recent years?	*Moody's Industrial Manual* [D-190] *Moody's OTC Industrial Manual* [D-194]
a chronological listing of industrial bonds and notes that have or will mature during recent years?	*Moody's Industrial Manual* [D-190]
historical monthly indices for stock exchanges around the world?	*Moody's International Manual* [D-191]
historical yields of long-term bonds issued by foreign governments?	*Moody's International Manual* [D-191]
Moody's bond yield averages for finance company and bank holding company issues during selected years?	*Moody's Bank and Finance Manual* [D-189]
Moody's government and municipal bond yield averages for selected years?	*Moody's Municipal and Government Manual* [D-193]
average annual money-market interest rates and mortgage rates by type of investment for selected years?	*Statistical Abstract of the U.S.* [D-361]
summary statistics on bond and stock yields, security prices, and mutual funds for selected years?	*Statistical Abstract of the U.S.* [D-361]
the end-of-quarter net asset value of mutual funds?	*Spectrum 2* [D-316]

Investment Tables

a table of values for discount securities, showing the price to be paid for a security at a given discount rate and the Coupon Issue Yield Equivalent?	*Thorndike Encyclopedia of Banking and Financial Tables* [D-326]
a table that discloses: (1) the amount to pay for a mortgage at a yield rate (with the yield being to maturity), and (2) the yield to maturity of a mortgage?	*Thorndike Encyclopedia of Banking and Financial Tables* [D-326]

WHERE SHOULD I GO TO FIND...	*TRY*

Investment Tables

a table that discloses: (1) the amount to pay for a mortgage at a yield rate, and (2) the yield of a mortgage, both with the yield being to prepayment?	*Thorndike Encyclopedia of Banking and Financial Tables* [D-326]
a table that shows: (1) the amount to pay for a bond at a yield rate, and (2) the yield of a bond at a given price, both when the yield is to maturity?	*Thorndike Encyclopedia of Banking and Financial Tables* [D-326]
maturity schedules for U.S. Treasury notes and bonds for the years 1988–2016?	*Dow Jones-Irwin Guide to Buying and Selling Treasury Securities* [D-61]

Laws and Regulations: Investments

the "General Regulations Governing U.S. Securities"?	*Dow Jones-Irwin Guide to Buying and Selling Treasury Securities* [D-61]
the "Regulations Governing Book-Entry Treasury Bonds, Notes, and Bills"?	*Dow Jones-Irwin Guide to Buying and Selling Treasury Securities* [D-61]
an explanation of the obligations imposed on the portfolio manager by the Employee Retirement Income Security Act of 1974?	*Investment Manager's Handbook* [D-291]
a discussion of the federal regulations that govern the conduct of investment managers?	*Investment Manager's Handbook* [D-291]
the U.S. Uniform Securities Act and the securities laws and regulations of each of the 50 states, the District of Columbia, Guam, and Puerto Rico?	*Blue Sky Law Reports* [D-375]
the takeover disclosure laws of the various states regarding the acquisition of equity securities of domestic corporations?	*Blue Sky Law Reports* [D-375]
an explanation of Rule 144 under the Securities Act concerning the resale of restricted stock?	*Responsibilities of Corporate Officers and Directors Under Federal Securities Laws* [D-311]

WHERE SHOULD I GO TO FIND...	*TRY*

Laws and Regulations: Investments

an explanation of the Law of Securities?	*A Guide to Modern Business and Commercial Law* [D-274]
a compilation of the federal laws, regulations, rulings, and court decisions that govern the securities industry?	*Federal Securities Law Reports* [D-404]
a synopsis of the Securities Act of 1933?	*Accounting Desk Book* [D-239]
a synopsis of the Securities Exchange Act of 1934?	*Accounting Desk Book* [D-239]

National Associations and Government Offices

addresses and telephone numbers for making inquiries about U.S. Treasury securities?	*Dow Jones-Irwin Guide to Buying and Selling Treasury Securities* [D-61]
a directory of national associations and organizations located in Washington, D.C., that provide services for the investment industry?	*Washington Information Directory* [D-234]

Newsletters and Other Publications

a directory of investment newsletters?	*Newsletters in Print* [D-41] *Oxbridge Directory of Newsletters* [D-42] *The Second Hulbert Financial Digest Almanac* [D-215]
an evaluation of individual investment newsletters?	*The Second Hulbert Financial Digest Almanac* [D-215]
general guidelines on how to assess an investment newsletter?	*The Second Hulbert Financial Digest Almanac* [D-215]
a monthly journal containing articles of interest to the professional investment manager?	*Institutional Investor* [D-447]

WHERE SHOULD I GO TO FIND...	*TRY*

Ranking of Stock Companies

rankings of over-the-counter stock companies according to 12-month and 7-year price-score leaders, high revenues, high net income, high yields, high return on equity, high and low P/E ratios, and low price stocks?	*Moody's Handbook of OTC Stocks* [D-304]
a ranking of companies based on profitability, growth, and stock market performance?	*Forbes* ("Annual Report on American Industry") [D-445]
a ranking of the largest 500 U.S. industrial corporations according to their sales, profits, assets, earnings per share, total return to investors, number of employees, and other criteria?	*Fortune* (*Fortune* 500 issue) [D-446]
a ranking of the largest 1,000 U.S. corporations according to their stock-market value?	*Business Week* (April issue) [D-441]

Ratings of Investment Instruments

Note: See also "Company Financial Profiles and Stock Data" and "Investment Performance" in this subsection.

ratings of a stock's timeliness, safety, and sensitivity to fluctuations of the market (Beta)?	*Value Line Investment Survey* [D-436]
an explanation of the rating systems for corporate, government, and municipal bonds; corporate stock; and commercial paper as developed and used by Standard & Poor's and by Moody?	*Bond Guide* [D-248] *Dow Jones-Irwin Business and Investment Almanac* [D-24] *Dow Jones-Irwin Guide to Bond and Money Market Investments* [D-60] *Dow Jones-Irwin Guide to Municipal Bonds* [D-64] *Moody's Bond Record* [D-302] *Moody's Manuals* [D-192] *Security Owner's Stock Guide* [D-314] *Standard & Poor's Ratings Guide* [D-100] *Standard & Poor's Stock Reports* [D-462]

WHERE SHOULD I GO TO FIND . . .	*TRY*

Ratings of Investment Instruments

an explanation of the analytical tools that are available for evaluating the creditworthiness of municipal bonds?	*Dow Jones-Irwin Guide to Municipal Bonds* [D-64] *The Municipal Bond Handbook, Vol. 1* [D-305], *Vol. 2* [D-306]
how to judge the merits of municipal bonds?	*Dow Jones-Irwin Guide to Municipal Bonds* [D-64] *The Municipal Bond Handbook, Vol. 1* [D-305], *Vol. 2* [D-306]
how to evaluate Certificates of Participation?	*Dow Jones-Irwin Guide to Municipal Bonds* [D-64]
ratings of municipal bonds?	*Bond Guide* [D-248] *Moody's Bond Record* [D-302] *Moody's Municipal and Government Manual* [D-193]
ratings of U.S. government bonds, commercial paper, medium-term notes, convertible bonds, industrial-development revenue bonds, pollution- and environmental-control revenue bonds, and railroad-equipment trust certificates?	*Bond Guide* (only convertible bonds.) [D-248] *Moody's Bond Record* [D-302]
a weekly report on the statistical values of confidence indicators for corporate and government bonds?	*Barron's* [D-440]
S&P ratings of corporate medium-term notes?	*Bond Guide* [D-248]
S&P ratings of equipment certificates of railroads, airlines, and rail-car lessors?	*Bond Guide* [D-248]
S&P ratings of preferred stocks of utility companies?	*Bond Guide* [D-248] *Security Owner's Stock Guide* [D-314]
S&P ratings of pass-through mortgage certificates?	*Bond Guide* [D-248]
for foreign bonds, their S&P ratings, interest rates, interest dates, due dates, yields to maturity, and other related information?	*Bond Guide* [D-248]

WHERE SHOULD I GO TO FIND...   *TRY*

Ratings of Investment Instruments

the names of companies and government   *Bond Guide* [D-248]
units that, due to events or trends, are
subject to potential changes in the ratings of their bonds or other fixed-income
securities?

changes in the ratings of a corporation's   *Barron's* [D-440]
debt?   *Bond Guide* [D-248]
                                            Investor's Daily [D-449]
                                            Moody's News Reports series [D-192]
                                            Security Owner's Stock Guide [D-314]
                                            Standard & Poor's Daily News [D-220]
                                            Wall Street Journal [D-457]

a detailed description of the long-term   *Moody's Manuals* [D-192]
debt of a company, including the ratings
of its corporate stocks and bonds?

for corporate common and preferred   *Security Owner's Stock Guide* [D-314]
stocks, their rankings/ratings, call price of
preferred stocks, split ratios, number of
consecutive years for paying dividends,
dividend-payment data, earnings per
share, high/low price range, and other
related information?

Securities Analysts and Underwriters

a listing of securities analysts by indus- *Corporate Finance Sourcebook* [D-153]
try of specialization, indicating their tele-
phone numbers?

a directory of securities underwriters,   *Bond Guide* [D-248]
with the telephone numbers of their cor-
porate headquarters?

Securities and Exchange Commission

an explanation of the organization of the   *Financial Analyst's Handbook* [D-271]
Security and Exchange Commission, the   *United States Government Manual* [D-366]
laws it administers, and the way it con-
ducts its business?

Stockholders

when the annual meeting of a corpora-   *Moody's Handbook of Common Stocks*
tion's stockholders takes place?   [D-303]

(answer continues)

WHERE SHOULD I GO TO FIND...   *TRY*

Stockholders

when the annual meeting of a corpora-   *Moody's Manuals* [D-192]
tion's stockholders takes place?   *Standard & Poor's Corporation Records*
                                               [D-220]

the number of financial institutions that   *Security Owner's Stock Guide* [D-314]
hold a specified stock and the number of
shares owned?

the identification of beneficial owners of   *Barron's* (Does not include address or
5 percent or more of outstanding shares   phone number.) [D-440]
of stock of a corporation, along with their   *Spectrum 5* [D-319]
addresses, telephone numbers, and num-
ber of shares?

the names of mutual funds that hold   *Spectrum 1* [D-315]
shares of a specified common stock?

the names and amounts of common   *Spectrum 2* [D-316]
stocks that comprise the portfolio of a
specified mutual fund?

a summary of mutual-fund holdings, by   *Spectrum 1* [D-315]
industry group?   *Spectrum 2* [D-316]

the names of banks, insurance compa-   *Spectrum 3* [D-317]
nies, pension funds, endowments, and
foundations that hold shares of a specified common stock?

the names and amount of common stocks   *Spectrum 4* [D-318]
that comprise the portfolio of a specified
bank, insurance company, pension fund,
endowment, or foundation?

Symbols

the meaning of individual stock exchange   *Acronyms, Initialisms, and Abbreviations*
symbols?   *Dictionary* [D-109]
                                               Business Acronyms [D-114]
                                               Symbol Guide [D-323]

the stock exchange symbols of compa-   *Million Dollar Directory* [D-188]
nies?   *Moody's Manuals* [D-192]
                                               Security Owner's Stock Guide [D-314]

WHERE SHOULD I GO TO FIND...	*TRY*

Symbols

the stock exchange symbols of companies?	*Standard & Poor's Corporation Records* [D-220] *Value Line Investment Survey* [D-436] *Wall Street Journal* [D-457]
translations of symbols used by commodities and options exchanges?	*Symbol Guide* [D-323]

U.S. Treasury Bonds, Called

a listing of U.S. Treasury bonds called prior to maturity?	*Moody's Municipal and Government Manual* [D-193]

Management

Note: For information about records management, see the subsection "Computers, Information Processing, and Records Management."

Basic Management Principles and Practices

a comprehensive discussion of the tasks, skills, responsibilities, organization, and strategies of management?	*AMA Management Handbook* [D-242] *The Encyclopedia of Management* [D-267] *Management* [D-86] *Management: Tasks, Responsibilities, Practices* [D-87]
guidelines for managing a corporation after a merger or acquisition?	*Making Mergers Work* [D-85]
an explanation of strategic management principles and practices for the business enterprise?	*AMA Management Handbook* [D-242] *Management* [D-86] *Management: Tasks, Responsibilities, Practices* [D-87] *Strategic Management* [D-102]
guidelines on how to organize and manage a small business?	*The Entrepreneur and Small Business Problem Solver* [D-269] *From Concept to Market* [D-73] *How to Organize and Operate A Small Business* [D-79]

(answer continues)

<u>*WHERE SHOULD I GO TO FIND...*</u>   <u>*TRY*</u>

Basic Management Principles and Practices

guidelines on how to organize and manage a small business?

How to Set Up Your Own Small Business [D-290]
Profit Planning for Small Business [D-95]
Vital Business Secrets for New and Growing Companies [D-107]

how to formulate goals and objectives for a company?

AMA Management Handbook [D-242]
Management [D-86]
Strategic Management [D-102]

checklists of steps, procedures, and considerations involved with planning and managing a business?

Business Forms On File [D-376]

how to set profit goals?

Profit Planning for Small Business [D-95]

principles for the strategic planning and management of capital budgeting?

The Capital Budgeting Handbook [D-250]

an explanation of "operating leverage" and "financial leverage"?

Foundations of Financial Management [D-273]

Computers and Software: Management

descriptive profiles of microcomputer software packages that serve management applications?

Data Sources: Software [D-158]
Datapro Directory of Microcomputer Software [D-387]

Controls, Techniques, and Formulas

a listing and explanation of specific control ratios that can be used in manufacturing, and ways to tailor these to satisfy local conditions?

Handbook of Business Formulas and Controls [D-278]

how to evaluate and control manufacturing activities, and how to decide where there is need for managerial action?

Handbook of Business Formulas and Controls [D-278]

how to test a managerial decision in advance of implementing it?

Handbook of Business Formulas and Controls [D-278]

formulas that are useful when evaluating a prospective manufacturing project and which help decide whether to proceed with the project?

Handbook of Business Formulas and Controls [D-278]

WHERE SHOULD I GO TO FIND...	*TRY*

Controls, Techniques, and Formulas

how to evaluate forecasting models and determine the right one to use?

The Manager's Guide to Business Forecasting [D-88]

a compendium of practical guidance for cost accounting?

Accounting Desk Book [D-239]
Managerial and Cost Accountant's Handbook [D-295]

Information Sources

a list of published research reports that focus on the management of specific companies?

Findex [D-37]

a bibliography/index of literature on management?

Books in Print [D-31]
Business Information Sources [D-33]
Business Periodicals Index (journal articles) [D-4]
Encyclopedia of Business Information Sources [D-36]
Management Information: Where to Find It [D-39]
Management Principles and Practice [D-40]

Job Classification and Descriptions

a model job-classification system?

Dictionary of Occupational Titles [D-122]

model descriptions for occupations in the U.S.?

Dictionary of Occupational Titles [D-122]

examples of managerial job descriptions that are in use in business and industry, classified by functional areas?

Encyclopedia of Managerial Job Descriptions [D-403]

Management and Government Regulations

guidelines on how to manage payroll operations, including the latest government regulations pertaining to payroll issues?

Successful Payroll Management [D-426]

how to comply with OSHA's health and safety regulations?

Employment Coordinator [D-402]
Personnel Management Guide [D-419]
Successful Payroll Management [D-426]

how to protect trade secrets during an OSHA inspection?

Successful Payroll Management [D-426]

WHERE SHOULD I GO TO FIND...	*TRY*

Management of Specific Fields and Functions

a discussion of the issues, policies, and strategies that are of concern to chief financial officers (CFOs)?	*The CFO's Handbook* [D-253]
guidelines for managing a marketing program?	*AMA Management Handbook* [D-242] *Marketing Handbook, Vol. 2* [D-296]
information on management practices in banks?	*Banker's Handbook* [D-244]
guidelines for managing the various phases and components of the manufacturing process?	*AMA Management Handbook* [D-242]
how to evaluate and control manufacturing activities and how to decide where there is need for managerial action?	*Handbook of Business Formulas and Controls* [D-278]
guidelines for managing the purchasing and distribution functions?	*AMA Management Handbook* [D-242]
guidelines on how to manage payroll operations, including the latest government regulations pertaining to payroll issues?	*Successful Payroll Management* [D-426]
comprehensive guidelines that address issues in personnel management?	*AMA Management Handbook* [D-242] *Employment Coordinator* [D-402] *The Entrepreneur and Small Business Problem Solver* [D-269] *Personnel Management Guide* [D-419] See also the subsection "Personnel Administration."
guidelines on risk and insurance management?	*AMA Management Handbook* [D-242]
guidelines on the management of packaging operations?	*AMA Management Handbook* [D-242]
how to manage research and technology?	*AMA Management Handbook* [D-242]
guidelines for managing information systems?	*AMA Management Handbook* [D-242]
comments from professionals on how to manage research and technology?	*AMA Management Handbook* [D-242]

WHERE SHOULD I GO TO FIND...   *TRY*

Management of Specific Fields and Functions

helpful suggestions on how to organize
and manage a sales program?

*The Entrepreneur and Small Business
Problem Solver* [D-269]
Sales Manager's Handbook [D-313]

guidelines for project management, with
answers to problems that arise in the different phases of managing a project?

Project Management Handbook [D-309]
Project Management Operating Guidelines
[D-310]
Successful Project Management [D-103]

checklists, forms, and procedures used in
the management of projects?

Project Management Operating Guidelines
[D-310]

Managing New Ideas

a checklist of criteria for evaluating new
ideas?

From Concept to Market [D-73]
How to Sell New Ideas [D-81]

techniques on how to sell new ideas for
products, services, and operational methods?

How to Sell New Ideas [D-81]

guidelines on how to manage creative
employees?

How to Sell New Ideas [D-81]

Newsletters and Other Publications

a directory of published newsletters that
focus on administration and management, with a nonevaluative description
of each newsletter?

Newsletters in Print [D-41]
Oxbridge Directory of Newsletters [D-42]

a monthly journal that publishes articles
of value to the professional money manager?

Institutional Investor [D-447]

Planning

how to write a business plan?

*The Entrepreneur and Small Business
Problem Solver* [D-269]
From Concept to Market [D-73]
How to Create a Winning Business Plan
[D-411]
How to Develop a Business Plan in 15 Days
[D-77]
*How to Organize and Operate A Small Busi-
ness* [D-79]

(answer continues)

WHERE SHOULD I GO TO FIND...	*TRY*

Planning

how to write a business plan?	*How to Set Up Your Own Small Business* [D-290] *Start-Up Money: How to Finance Your New Small Business* [D-321] *Vital Business Secrets for New and Growing Companies* [D-107]
a guide for managers with responsibility for planning and forecasting business activity?	*The Handbook of Forecasting* [D-281] *How to Create a Winning Business Plan* [D-411] *The Manager's Guide to Business Forecasting* [D-88]
how to set profit goals?	*Profit Planning for Small Business* [D-95]
checklists of steps, procedures, and considerations involved with planning and managing a business?	*Business Forms On File* [D-376]
principles for the strategic planning and management of capital budgeting?	*The Capital Budgeting Handbook* [D-250]

Pricing

guidelines for setting prices?	*AMA Management Handbook* [D-242] *The Entrepreneur and Small Business Problem Solver* [D-269] *From Concept to Market* [D-73] *How to Organize and Operate A Small Business* [D-79]

Well-Run Companies

the basic management practices that have been found by research to distinguish successfully managed companies?	*In Search of Excellence* [D-83]
a listing and description of the best-run companies to work for in America, according to their employees?	*The 100 Best Companies to Work For in America* [D-46]
the names and profiles of companies that have been described as being the best-performing companies in America, according to employee productivity, capital productivity, creating jobs, and increasing stockholder wealth?	*The 101 Best-Performing Companies on America* [D-47]

WHERE SHOULD I GO TO FIND...	*TRY*

Marketing

Note: For information concerning international business transactions, including importing and exporting, see subsection "International Business Transactions."

Advertiser Profiles

a directory of companies, arranged by product or service category, that reports for each company the advertising media it uses, size of advertising budget, month when the advertising budget is decided, names of key management personnel, and the advertising agency that services the account?	*Standard Directory of Advertisers* [D-222]

Advertising Agencies

the names, addresses, and telephone numbers of advertising agencies, arranged by the types of products or services being advertised by their clients?	*Standard Directory of Advertisers* [D-222]
an international directory of advertising agencies, with a descriptive profile of each agency, including the location, specialization, and names of account executives?	*Standard Directory of Advertising Agencies* [D-223]
a listing of advertising agencies that specialize in one or more of the following: markets that serve black Americans and Hispanics, health and medicine, the financial market, direct response, media services, resort and travel, recruitment, or sales promotion?	*Standard Directory of Advertising Agencies* [D-223]
guidelines on how a client firm should work with an advertising agency for the purpose of achieving effective advertising?	*How to Get the Best Advertising from Your Agency* [D-78]

Computers and Software: Marketing

a directory of providers of online marketing databases?	*Information Sources* [D-185]

WHERE SHOULD I GO TO FIND . . .	*TRY*

Computers and Software: Marketing

a directory of online databases that focus on advertising and marketing?	*Directory of Online Databases* [D-261]
descriptive profiles of microcomputer software packages that serve marketing applications?	*Data Sources: Software* [D-158] *Datapro Directory of Microcomputer Software* [D-387]

Federal Agencies: Purchasing Regulations and Procedures

the rules and procedures that control the purchasing of supplies and services by executive branch agencies of the federal government?	*Federal Acquisition Regulation* [D-270]

Franchising

a listing of companies that offer franchise licenses, indicating the type of business, address, telephone number, and other information for each?	*Franchise Opportunities Handbook* [D-179] *Rating Guide to Franchises* [D-213] *Small Business Sourcebook* [D-216] *Source Book of Franchise Opportunities* [D-217]
a checklist for evaluating a franchise?	*Franchise Opportunities Handbook* [D-179] *How to Organize and Operate a Small Business* [D-79]
ratings and other evaluations of major U.S. franchisors?	*Rating Guide to Franchises* [D-213]
a full-text compilation of state and federal franchise statutes along with the "Guide to FTC Franchising Rules"?	*Business Franchise Guide* [D-377]
recent administrative opinions and court decisions regarding business franchises?	*Business Franchise Guide* [D-377]
"how-to" guidelines that address the business and legal issues of franchising?	*Complete Handbook of Franchising* [D-256]

Information Sources and Services

information concerning marketing that is to be found in federal departments and agencies and other Washington-based organizations?	*How to Find Business Intelligence in Washington* [D-182]

WHERE SHOULD I GO TO FIND...   _TRY_

Information Sources and Services

a listing of published market research
reports on industries, companies, and
products?

Findex [D-37]

a subject index to statistical publications
of state government agencies and private organizations that address marketing
matters?

Statistical Reference Index [D-18]

a subject index to statistical publications
of the federal government that address
matters pertaining to marketing?

American Statistics Index [D-1]

Intelligence Gathering: U.S. Companies

how and where to locate information
about prospective customers or clients?

How to Find Information About Companies
[D-183]
How to Find Information About Executives
[D-286]
_How to Find Information About Private
Companies_ [D-288]
_How to Find Information About Service
Companies_ [D-289]

Jobs in Marketing

examples of managerial job descriptions
in marketing and sales?

Encyclopedia of Managerial Job Descriptions
[D-403]

Laws and Regulations: Sales

an overview of federal and state laws on
sales practices?

_A Guide to Modern Business and Commercial
Law_ [D-274]
Consumer Protection Manual [D-258]

Marketing Data

a ranking and description of television marketing areas, with summary
consumer-market data?

Newspaper Rates and Data [D-205]
Spot Radio Rates and Data [D-218]
Spot Television Rates and Data [D-219]

projections of U.S. retail and manufacturers sales?

Predicasts Forecasts [D-468]

WHERE SHOULD I GO TO FIND...	*TRY*

Marketing Data

demographic and socioeconomic data on residential and business communities in each ZIP code area, including age characteristics, household income, employment profile, education, listing of major types of businesses, and a consumer purchasing-potential index for selected consumer items?	*Sourcebook of Demographics and Buying Power for Every ZIP Code in the USA* [D-470]
marketing data on major retail centers within Standard Metropolitan Statistical Areas (SMSAs)?	*Census of Retail Trade* (Major Retail Centers) [D-340] *Survey of Buying Power Data Service* [D-474]
descriptive sales data for each ZIP code area?	*Commercial Atlas & Marketing Guide* [D-464] *Sourcebook of Demographics and Buying Power for Every ZIP Code in the USA* [D-470]
marketing and demographic data for geographic regions?	*Commercial Atlas & Marketing Guide* [D-464] *Survey of Buying Power Data Service* [D-474]
retail-trade patterns in metropolitan and other trading areas?	*Commercial Atlas & Marketing Guide* [D-464] *Survey of Buying Power Data Service* [D-474]
a measure of the potential buying power of consumers in a geographic market compared to other markets?	*Survey of Buying Power Data Service* [D-474]
a measure of disposable personal income for households and per capita, reported by market area?	*Survey of Buying Power Data Service* [D-474]
for each television market (*Area of Dominant Influence*), the retail sales and rankings of that market by store group and merchandise line?	*Survey of Buying Power Data Service* [D-474]
demographic, economic, and sales data that facilitate the setting of sales goals and quotas by market and sales territory?	*Survey of Buying Power Data Service* [D-474]

WHERE SHOULD I GO TO FIND...	*TRY*

Marketing Data

demographic, economic, and sales data that facilitate identifying the sales potential of new markets and new products?	*Survey of Buying Power Data Service* [D-474]
demographic, economic, and sales information that facilitate the identification of test markets, according to criteria selected by the marketer?	*Survey of Buying Power Data Service* [D-474]

Marketing Management

marketing management guidelines?	*AMA Management Handbook* [D-242] *Marketing Handbook* [D-296]
new ideas and practical guidelines for developing and operating a marketing program?	*How to Organize and Operate A Small Business* [D-79] *Marketing Handbook* [D-296]
guidelines for managing sales?	*The Entrepreneur and Small Business Problem Solver* [D-269] *Sales Manager's Handbook* [D-313]
techniques on how to sell new ideas for products and services?	*How to Sell New Ideas* [D-81]
a checklist of considerations when developing a marketing program for small retailers?	*Business Forms On File* [D-376]
techniques and other ideas that have been found to be successful with advertising programs?	*Vital Business Secrets for New and Growing Companies* [D-107]
a listing of warning signals to watch that indicate something is wrong with the new product or new service that has been introduced to the market?	*The Entrepreneur and Small Business Problem Solver* [D-269]
what alternatives are available if a product or service will not sell at the advertised price?	*The Entrepreneur and Small Business Problem Solver* [D-269]
guidelines for marketing new products?	*Marketing Handbook* [D-296] *New Products Handbook* [D-91] *Pioneering New Products* [D-93]

WHERE SHOULD I GO TO FIND...	*TRY*
Marketing Management	
information on marketing banking services?	*Banker's Handbook* [D-244]
Marketing Media and Services	
the names, addresses, and telephone numbers of companies that represent radio and/or television stations for advertising purposes?	*Spot Radio Rates and Data* [D-218] *Spot Television Rates and Data* [D-219]
directories of radio and television stations that include the address, telephone number, names of key personnel, description of programming and facilities, advertising contract terms and rates, and other information about each station?	*Gale Directory of Publications and Broadcast Media* (includes rates, not terms) [D-180] *Spot Radio Rates and Data* [D-218] *Spot Television Rates and Data* [D-219]
a listing of radio stations that regularly schedule farm programs, programs of interest to black Americans, and/or foreign-language programs?	*Consumer Magazine and Agri-Media Rates and Data* [D-151] *Gale Directory of Publications and Broadcast Media* [D-180] *Spot Radio Rates and Data* [D-218]
directories of national, regional, and state radio and television (including cable) networks and groups?	*Spot Radio Rates and Data* [D-218] *Spot Television Rates and Data* [D-219]
a map that depicts cities in the U.S. and its possessions that have television broadcasting stations?	*Spot Television Rates and Data* [D-219]
a directory of domestic and international business publications (e.g., magazines and trade newspapers) in the various industries, with a description of each publication, including advertising contract terms and rates, circulation data, printing requirements, names of key advertising executives, address, telephone number, and other information?	*Business Publication Rates and Data* [D-142]
the names, addresses, and telephone numbers of firms that represent business publications for advertising purposes?	*Business Publication Rates and Data* [D-142]

WHERE SHOULD I GO TO FIND...	*TRY*

Marketing Media and Services

a directory of health care publications, with a description of each publication, including advertising contract terms and rates, circulation data, printing requirements, names of key advertising executives, address, telephone number, and other information?	*Business Publication Rates and Data* [D-142] *Gale Directory of Publications and Broadcast Media* (note: Some of these data elements only) [D-180]
a directory of direct-response advertising media, with company descriptions that include advertising contract terms and rates, circulation data, printing requirements, names of key advertising executives, address, telephone number, and other information?	*Business Publication Rates and Data* [D-142]
a directory of newspapers, with a description of each newspaper, including contract terms, classified rates, frequency of publication, circulation data, printing requirements, names of key advertising executives, address, telephone number, and other information?	*Gale Directory of Publications and Broadcast Media* (some of these data elements only) [D-180] *Newspaper Rates and Data* [D-205]
an explanation of the maximil and minimil rates for newspaper ads?	*Newspaper Rates and Data* [D-205]
a listing of newspaper representatives, with addresses and telephone numbers?	*Newspaper Rates and Data* [D-205]
an explanation of the Standard Advertising Unit System?	*Newspaper Rates and Data* [D-205]
a directory of college and university newspapers and newspapers geared toward black Americans with a description of each newspaper, including advertising rates, circulation data, frequency of publication, names of key advertising executives, address, telephone number, and other information?	*Gale Directory of Publications and Broadcast Media* [D-180] *Newspaper Rates and Data* [D-205]

WHERE SHOULD I GO TO FIND...	*TRY*

Marketing Media and Services

a directory of local urban and suburban weekly newspapers and shopping guides, with a description of each publication, including classified rates, printing requirements, circulation data, frequency of publication, names of key advertising executives, address, phone number, and other information?	*Community Publication Rates and Data* [D-145] *Gale Directory of Publications and Broadcast Media* [D-180]
a directory of consumer magazines and consumer card decks, with descriptions that include an editorial profile statement, advertising contract provisions, advertising rates, frequency of publication, circulation data, printing requirements, names of key advertising executives, address, telephone number, and other information?	*Consumer Magazine and Agri-Media Rates and Data* [D-151]
a directory of farm publications and farm direct-response advertising media, with descriptions that include advertising contract provisions, advertising rates, frequency of publication, circulation data, printing requirements, names of key advertising executives, address, telephone number, and other information?	*Consumer Magazine and Agri-Media Rates and Data* [D-151] *Gale Directory of Publications and Broadcast Media* (selected information only) [D-180]
a directory of firms that represent consumer magazines and farm publications?	*Consumer Magazines and Agri-Media Rates and Data* [D-151]
sources of direct-mail lists that are available to purchase for advertising purposes?	*Direct Mail List Rates and Data* [D-159] *Information Sources* [D-185]
providers of support services for direct-mailing operations (consultants, suppliers, mail preparation, and so on)?	*Consultants and Consulting Organizations Directory* [D-150] *Direct Mail List Rates and Data* [D-159]
a directory of firms that provide business co-op mailings and package-insert programs, with descriptions that include rates, names of key executives, printing requirements, circulation data, address, telephone number, and other information?	*Direct Mail List Rates and Data* [D-159]

WHERE SHOULD I GO TO FIND...	*TRY*

Marketing Media and Services

a directory of market-research firms?
Consultants and Consulting Organizations Directory [D-150]
GreenBook [D-181]
Information Sources [D-185]
Standard & Poor's Register of Corporations, Directors and Executives, Vol. 3 (see SIC category #8732.) [D-221]

names and descriptions of companies that conduct market surveys, consumer research, and product testing?
GreenBook [D-181]

Newsletters

a directory of published newsletters on advertising, marketing, and public relations, with a nonevaluative description of each newsletter?
Newsletters in Print [D-41]
Oxbridge Directory of Newsletters [D-42]

Product Recall

guidelines for managing a product recall?
AMA Management Handbook [D-242]

a listing of federal agencies that can require the recall of a product and the products over which they have oversight?
AMA Management Handbook [D-242]

Trade Shows, Exhibitions, and Conventions

how to make use of trade shows, how to prepare for them, and what to do during the show?
The Entrepreneur and Small Business Problem Solver [D-269]

a directory of industry conventions, exhibitions, trade shows, and other meetings, with the names and addresses of sponsors, meeting dates, and other related information?
Small Business Sourcebook [D-216]
Trade Shows and Professional Exhibits Directory [D-228]

New Products and Services: Invention, Development, and Protection

---

Computers and Software: Intellectual Property

a directory of online databases that are available to the public for conducting patent searches?
Directory of Online Databases [D-261]

WHERE SHOULD I GO TO FIND...	TRY

Consultants and Services

a bibliography of directories that list patent and trademark lawyers?	*Directories in Print* [D-35]
a directory of national associations located in Washington, D.C., that provide services pertaining to patents, copyrights, and trademarks?	*Washington Information Directory* [D-234]
a directory of firms that offer online patent and trademark searches and/or patent information?	*Information Sources* [D-185]
a listing of Patent Depository libraries, with their telephone numbers?	*From Concept to Market* [D-73] *Official Gazette of the United States Patent and Trademark Office* [D-357]
a directory of services provided by the U.S. Patent and Trademark Office, with telephone numbers for the various services?	*Official Gazette of the United States Patent and Trademark Office* [D-357]
the names, addresses, and telephone numbers of attorneys and agents who have been authorized to represent inventors before the U.S. Patent and Trademark Office?	*Attorneys and Agents Registered to Practice Before the U.S. Patent and Trademark Office* [D-332]
a directory of consultants for new product development?	*Consultants and Consulting Organizations Directory* [D-150]
a directory of market research firms that provide concept development and testing, product testing, consumer research, and other related services?	*GreenBook* [D-181]
a listing of companies that build prototypes/models?	*From Concept to Market* [D-73]

Intellectual Property Filings, Guidelines, Laws, and Processes

instructions needed to apply for a patent and the necessary forms?	*Business Forms On File* (applications only) [D-376] *The Entrepreneur and Small Business Problem Solver* [D-269]

WHERE SHOULD I GO TO FIND...	*TRY*

Intellectual Property Filings, Guidelines, Laws, and Processes

instructions needed to apply for a patent and the necessary forms?	*Forms of Business Agreements and Resolutions* [D-410] *From Concept to Market* (no forms) [D-73] *Inventor's Guide to Successful Patent Applications* [D-84] *Patent It Yourself* [D-92]
how to conduct a patent search?	*From Concept to Market* [D-73] *Inventor's Guide to Successful Patent Applications* [D-84] *Patent It Yourself* [D-92]
descriptions of recent U.S. patents, including the claims that have been granted?	*Official Gazette of the United States Patent and Trademark Office* [D-357]
a listing of patents that have expired due to the failure to pay maintenance fees?	*Official Gazette of the United States Patent and Trademark Office* [D-357]
the U.S. copyright laws?	*17 U.S. Code* [D-364] *17 U.S. Code Annotated* [D-365] *Code of Federal Regulations* [D-343] *Copyright Law Reports* [D-383] *Forms of Business Agreements and Resolutions* [D-410]
an explanation of U.S. copyright, patent, and trademark laws?	*The Entrepreneur and Small Business Problem Solver* [D-269] *A Guide to Modern Business and Commercial Law* [D-274] *Inventor's Guide to Successful Patent Applications* [D-84] *Patent It Yourself* [D-92]
the copyright statutes of the states?	*Copyright Law Reports* [D-383]
detailed historical statistics on the number of U.S. copyrights, patents, and trademarks filed and issued or rejected and a distribution of the purposes for the filings?	*Historical Statistics of the United States* [D-351]
guidelines and sources for selecting a trademark?	*Trademark Management* [D-106]

WHERE SHOULD I GO TO FIND...	*TRY*

Intellectual Property Filings, Guidelines, Laws, and Processes

what is registrable as a trademark and how to register it?	*The Entrepreneur and Small Business Problem Solver* [D-269] *Patent It Yourself* [D-92] *Trademark Management* [D-106]
how to use, administer, and police a trademark?	*Trademark Management* [D-106]
information on trademark licensing and franchising?	*Trademark Management* [D-106]
guidelines for selecting, using, and administering trademarks in foreign nations?	*Trademark Management* [D-106]
how corporate names are protected by statute in individual nations throughout the world?	*Protection of Corporate Names* [D-421]
the trademarks that have been either applied for, registered, or abandoned with the U.S. Patent and Trademark Office?	*Compu-Mark Directory of U.S. Trademarks* [D-147] *Official Gazette of the United States Patent and Trademark Office: Trademarks* [D-357] *Trademark Register of the United States* (current registrations only) [D-229]
an application form for a trademark, along with an explanation of the filing requirements?	*Basic Facts About Trademarks* [D-333] *The Entrepreneur and Small Business Problem Solver* [D-269]
an explanation of financial accounting standards that apply to intellectual property?	*Accounting Desk Book* [D-239]
the full text of the major international copyright conventions to which the U.S. is a party?	*Copyright Law Reports* [D-383]
information about the intellectual property laws of individual nations?	*Business Transactions in Germany* [D-378] *China Laws for Foreign Business* [D-380] *Common Market Reports* [D-382] *Doing Business in Brazil* [D-392] *Doing Business in Canada* [D-393] *Doing Business in China* [D-394]

WHERE SHOULD I GO TO FIND...	*TRY*

Intellectual Property Filings, Guidelines, Laws, and Processes

information about the intellectual property laws of individual nations?

Doing Business in Europe [D-395]
Doing Business in France [D-396]
Doing Business in Ireland [D-397]
Doing Business in Japan [D-398]
Doing Business in Mexico [D-399]
Doing Business in Spain [D-400]
Doing Business in the United Kingdom [D-401]
Japan Business Law Guide [D-413]
Patents Throughout the World [D-418]
Trademarks Throughout the World [D-434]

New Product Development, Management, and Marketing

guidelines for developing and marketing new products?

AMA Management Handbook [D-242]
The Entrepreneur and Small Business Problem Solver [D-269]
From Concept to Market [D-73]
Marketing Handbook, Vol. 2 [D-296]
New Products Handbook [D-91]
Patent It Yourself [D-92]
Pioneering New Products [D-93]
That's A Great Idea [D-105]

a checklist of criteria for evaluating new ideas?

From Concept to Market [D-73]
How to Sell New Ideas [D-81]

techniques on how to sell new ideas for products, services, and operational methods?

How to Sell New Ideas [D-81]

how to decide which new product to develop and market?

The Entrepreneur and Small Business Problem Solver [D-269]

sources that are available to assist with the development and marketing of new products?

Consultants and Consulting Organizations Directory [D-150]
The Entrepreneur and Small Business Problem Solver [D-269]
From Concept to Market [D-73]

how to write a business plan for a new product?

How to Create a Winning Business Plan [D-411]

WHERE SHOULD I GO TO FIND...	TRY

New Product Development, Management, and Marketing

how to write project proposals, estimate project costs, and negotiate the contract?	*Project Management Handbook* [D-309] *Project Management Operating Guidelines* [D-310] *Successful Project Management* [D-103]
guidelines on how to manage projects?	*Project Management Handbook* [D-309] *Project Management Operating Guidelines* [D-310] *Successful Project Management* [D-103]
checklists, forms, and procedures used when managing projects?	*Project Management Operating Guidelines* [D-310]
how to manage research and technology?	*AMA Management Handbook* [D-242]
a listing of warning signals to watch that indicate something is wrong with the new product or service that has been introduced to the market?	*The Entrepreneur and Small Business Problem Solver* [D-269]
announcements of new scientific and technological developments?	*Business Week* [D-441]
a directory of federal laboratories and engineering centers that are available to assist the business community?	*Directory of Federal Laboratory & Technology Resources* [D-346]
a directory of nongovernment research and development centers that concentrate on commercially applicable basic and applied research, with a description of each facility?	*Directory of American Research and Technology* [D-160]
the application form of the U.S. Office of Energy-Related Inventions that is used for giving consideration to provide assistance for energy-related inventions?	*Business Forms On File* [D-376]

WHERE SHOULD I GO TO FIND...	*TRY*

Newsletters

| a directory of published newsletters on new products, with a nonevaluative description of each newsletter? | *Newsletters in Print* [D-41] |
| a directory of published newsletters on patents, copyrights, and trademarks, with a nonevaluative description of each newsletter? | *Newsletters in Print* [D-41]
Oxbridge Directory of Newsletters [D-42] |

U.S. Patent and Trademark Office

the address and telephone number of the U.S. Patent and Trademark Office?	*Federal Staff Directory* [D-177] *Official Congressional Directory* [D-356] *United States Government Manual* [D-366] *Washington Information Directory* [D-234]
fees charged by the U.S. Patent and Trademark Office?	*Code of Federal Regulations* [D-343] *Federal Register* [D-350] *From Concept to Market* [D-73] *Inventor's Guide to Successful Patent Applications* [D-84] *Official Gazette of the United States Patent and Trademark Office* [D-357] *Patent It Yourself* [D-92]
how to obtain copies of patents from the U.S. Patent and Trademark Office?	*Official Gazette of the United States Patent and Trademark Office* [D-357]
a directory of services provided by the U.S. Patent and Trademark Office, with telephone numbers for the various services?	*Official Gazette of the United States Patent and Trademark Office* [D-357]
the classes (categories) that constitute the patent classification system of the U.S. Patent and Trademark Office?	*Index to the U.S. Patent Classification* [D-352] *Manual of Classification* [D-353]
the classes (categories) that constitute the trademark classification system of the U.S. Patent and Trademark Office?	*Basic Facts About Trademarks* [D-333] *Official Gazette of the United States Patent and Trademark Office* [D-357] *Trademark Register of the United States* [D-229]

WHERE SHOULD I GO TO FIND...   *TRY*

Personnel Administration

Arbitration

the rules of arbitration as set forth by the American Arbitration Association and the Federal Mediation and Conciliation Service?

A Dictionary of Arbitration and Its Terms [D-116]
See also *29 U.S. Code Annotated,* Sections 171–173.

the text of the Uniform Arbitration Act?

A Dictionary of Arbitration and Its Terms [D-116]

Collective Bargaining and Agreements

abstracts of collective-bargaining agreements?

Collective Bargaining Negotiations and Contracts [D-381]

a summary of the major types of provisions contained in collective-bargaining agreements and the frequency of their use (a norm base)?

Basic Patterns in Union Contracts [D-246]

for issues that have been addressed in labor agreements, a collection of actual clauses found in labor contracts that deal with these issues?

Collective Bargaining Negotiations and Contracts [D-381]

the status of current collective bargaining issues?

Collective Bargaining Negotiations and Contracts [D-381]

the average wage and compensation adjustments that were made under collective bargaining during specified years?

Statistical Abstract of the United States [D-361]

strategies and techniques being used by management and labor unions during the collective bargaining process?

Collective Bargaining Negotiations and Contracts [D-381]

demands and counterproposals that have recently been made during labor negotiations?

Collective Bargaining Negotiations and Contracts [D-381]

how to administer the collective-bargaining agreement, including policing the contract, initiating grievances, and using the arbitration process?

Collective Bargaining Negotiations and Contracts [D-381]

| *WHERE SHOULD I GO TO FIND...* | *TRY* |

Compensation Practices and Pension Funds

an overview of compensation practices and pension plans in the U.S.?

A Guide for the Foreign Investor [D-75]

the kinds of fringe benefits that are being made available to employees around the nation?

Collective Bargaining Negotiations and Contracts [D-381]
Statistical Abstract of the United States [D-361]

a summary of employee benefit plans that are required by law?

Career Information Center [D-252]

the average wage and compensation adjustments that were made under collective bargaining during specified years?

Statistical Abstract of the United States [D-361]

an overview of executive compensation practices in business and industry?

AMA Management Handbook [D-242]

an annual directory of the 500 largest employee benefit pension funds, with descriptive information?

Institutional Investor (January issue) [D-447]

Computers and Software: Personnel Management

descriptive profiles of microcomputer software packages that serve applications in personnel administration?

Datapro Directory of Microcomputer Software [D-387]
Data Sources: Software [D-158]

guidelines for training personnel in the use of microcomputer systems?

Datapro Management of Microcomputer Systems [D-388]

Federal Agencies: Labor Matters

the names, addresses, and telephone numbers of federal agencies that specialize in matters pertaining to labor relations and labor conditions?

Labor Law Reports [D-414]
Personnel Management, Labor Relations [D-420]

the names and telephone numbers of Equal Employment Opportunity officials for individual federal departments and agencies?

Official Congressional Directory [D-356]
United States Government Manual [D-366]
Washington Information Directory [D-234]

WHERE SHOULD I GO TO FIND...	*TRY*

Federal Regulations: Compliance

guidelines on how to comply with the latest income tax withholding regulations?	*Successful Payroll Management* [D-426]
how to comply with OSHA's health and safety regulations?	*Employment Coordinator* [D-402] *Personnel Management Guide* [D-419] *Successful Payroll Management* [D-426]
guidelines for verifying the employment eligibility of employees and instructions for completing Form I-9 (Employment Eligibility Verification Form)?	*Handbook for Employers* [D-276]
a method to prevent over-withholding on sales commissions?	*Successful Payroll Management* [D-426]
guidelines for reporting employees' tips?	*Successful Payroll Management* [D-426]
how to manage federal tax deposits?	*Successful Payroll Management* [D-426]

Holidays

the official holidays in each state?	*Employment Coordinator* [D-402]

Information Sources

sources of information on the labor force in the U.S. and foreign nations?	*American Statistics Index* [D-1] *Sourcebook of Global Statistics* [D-471] *Statistical Reference Index* [D-18] *Statistics Sources* [D-473]
sources of information about the labor force, wages, and other employee-related information at the local level?	*Regional Statistics* [D-469] *Statistical Reference Index* [D-18]
an index to information about prevailing salaries in the different industries, professions, and occupations?	*Business Rankings and Salaries Index* [D-5]

Intelligence Gathering

how and where to locate information about employee candidates?	*How to Find Information About Executives* [D-286]

WHERE SHOULD I GO TO FIND...	*TRY*

Interviewing

| what can and cannot be legally asked during a job interview? | *Employment Coordinator* [D-402]
The Entrepreneur and Small Business Problem Solver [D-269]
How to Organize and Operate A Small Business [D-79]
Personnel Management Guide [D-419]
Successful Payroll Management [D-426] |
| how to ask sensitive questions during a job interview and not violate the law in the process? | *Personnel Management Guide* [D-419]
Successful Payroll Management [D-426] |

Job Classification and Descriptions

a model job-classification system?	*Dictionary of Occupational Titles* [D-122]
model descriptions for occupations in the U.S.?	*Dictionary of Occupational Titles* [D-122]
examples of managerial job descriptions in personnel services?	*Encyclopedia of Managerial Job Descriptions* [D-403]

Labor Economics Statistics

| current economic data that are used in the conduct of collective bargaining, such as the CPI, unemployment rates, productivity indexes, and other data? | *Collective Bargaining Negotiations and Contracts* [D-381]
See also the subsection "Economic Analyses and Economists." |
| by industry, an overview of wage patterns and other trends that are the results of collective bargaining agreements? | *Collective Bargaining Negotiations and Contracts* [D-381] |

Labor Laws and Cases

Note: See also "Labor Law and Judicial Decisions" in the subsection "Business Law."

| an overview of employment laws, compensation practices, pension plans, and executive recruitment in the U.S.? | *A Guide for the Foreign Investor* [D-75] |

WHERE SHOULD I GO TO FIND...	*TRY*

Labor Laws and Cases

a brief summary of federal labor-relations law, including explanations of decisions, rulings, and interpretations involving labor-union activities, collective bargaining, mediation, and other labor topics?	*Guidebook to Labor Relations* [D-275]
a layman's introductory explanation of labor-relations law?	*The Entrepreneur and Small Business Problem Solver* [D-269] *A Guide to Modern Business and Commercial Law* [D-274] *Primer of Labor Relations* [D-308]
a survey of labor law, including regulations, rulings, the full text of some federal legislation, and digests of court decisions?	*Labor Law Course* [D-292]
a compilation and/or explanation of federal and state labor laws, regulations, decisions, and rulings related to employee-management relations, wages and hours, discrimination in unemployment, child labor, unions, and other related matters?	*Employment Coordinator* [D-402] *Labor Law Reports* [D-414] *Personnel Management, Labor Relations* [D-420]
the text of the Uniform Arbitration Act?	*A Dictionary of Arbitration and Its Terms* [D-116]
interpretation of laws and regulations that pertain to personnel management?	*Employment Coordinator* [D-402] *Personnel Management Guide* [D-419]
a condensed explanation of the changes in pension and employee-benefit plans that were made by the Tax Reform Act of 1986?	*Choice of Compensation After Tax Reform* [D-254]
the full text of the following federal labor statutes? (Note: Reported here are the original statute numbers and citations. Check the *U.S. Code* and *U.S. Code Annotated* for any amendments or revisions.)	*Labor Law Course* [D-292] *Labor Law Reports* [D-414] *Personnel Management, Labor Relations* [D-420] *U.S. Code* [D-364] *U.S. Code Annotated* (See "Popular Name Table") [D-365] *U.S. Statutes at Large* (Cited below as vol. no., Stat., page no.) [D-368]

WHERE SHOULD I GO TO FIND...	*TRY*

Labor Laws and Cases

a. Anti-Injunction Act (Norris-LaGuardia Act), Public No. 72-65	47 Stat. 70
b. Civil Rights Act of 1968 (Interference with Federally Protected Activities), P.L. 90-284	82 Stat. 73-92
c. Clayton Anti-Trust Act, Public No. 63-212	38 Stat. 730
d. Equal Pay Act of 1963, P.L. 88-38	77 Stat. 56
e. Fair Employment Practices Law (Civil Rights Act of 1964), P.L. 88-352	78 Stat. 241
f. Fair Labor Standards Act, Public No. 75-718	52 Stat. 1060
g. Hobbs Anti-Racketeering Act, Public No. 73-376	48 Stat. 979
h. Labor Management Relations Act (Taft-Hartley Act), P.L. 80-101	61 Stat. 136
i. Labor-Management Reporting and Disclosure Act of 1959 P.L. 86-257	73 Stat. 519
j. National Labor Relations Act, Public No. 74-198	49 Stat. 449
k. Portal-to-Portal Act of 1947, P.L. 80-49	61 Stat. 84
l. Sherman Anti-Trust Act, July 2, 1890	51 Congress, Ch. 647 26 Stat. 209

Labor Unions and Associations

a directory of labor unions and associations that reports their addresses, telephone numbers, and descriptive information?	*Directory of U.S. Labor Organizations* [D-170] *Encyclopedia of Associations, Vol. 1* [D-173] *Washington Information Directory* [D-234]

<u>*WHERE SHOULD I GO TO FIND...*</u>   <u>*TRY*</u>

Newsletters

a directory of published newsletters on   *Newsletters in Print* [D-41]
collective bargaining, industrial relations,   *Oxbridge Directory of Newsletters* [D-42]
employee benefits, occupational safety
and health, and/or other related topics,
with a nonevaluative description of each
newsletter?

Personnel Policies and Practices

an overview of employment laws, com-   *A Guide for the Foreign Investor* [D-75]
pensation practices, pension plans, and
executive recruitment in the U.S.?

general guidelines pertaining to the dif-   *AMA Management Handbook* [D-242]
ferent areas of human resource manage-
ment?

a description of alternate types of work   *Alternate Work Schedules* [D-49]
schedules for the business environment?

suggestions on how to manage daily   *Managing Human Forces in Organizations*
problems associated with the manage-   [D-90]
ment of people in business organizations?

how to figure wage garnishments?   *Successful Payroll Management* [D-426]

ways to manage overtime?   *Successful Payroll Management* [D-426]

ways to use the Wage-Hour Law to mini-   *Successful Payroll Management* [D-426]
mize absenteeism?

how to manage employees without violat-   *Employment Coordinator* [D-402]
ing the federal equal-employment law?   *Personnel Management Guide* [D-419]
                                                Successful Payroll Management [D-426]

guidelines on how to establish and en-   *Employment Coordinator* [D-402]
force rules in the workplace without vio-   *Personnel Management Guide* [D-419]
lating the law?

tips on how to manage personnel related   *AMA Management Handbook* [D-242]
to the issues of hiring, training, wages,   *Employment Coordinator* [D-402]
benefits, productivity, and safety/security?   *The Entrepreneur and Small Business Problem*
                                                Solver [D-269]
                                                How to Set Up Your Own Small Business
                                                [D-290]
                                                Personnel Management Guide [D-419]

WHERE SHOULD I GO TO FIND...	*TRY*

Personnel Policies and Practices

model forms used in personnel management?

Business Forms On File [D-376]
Employment Coordinator [D-402]
Ten-Second Business Forms [D-325]

how to manage creative employees?

How to Sell New Ideas [D-81]

advice on the use of temporary help?

The Entrepreneur and Small Business Problem Solver [D-269]

Recruiting

an overview of executive recruitment in the U.S.?

A Guide for the Foreign Investor [D-75]

names and addresses of executive search firms?

Consultants and Consulting Organizations Directory [D-150]
Directories in Print (See also "Executive Recruiting Firms") [D-35]
Professional Job Changing System [D-94]
Also, check the yellow-pages section of the telephone directory.

Real Estate

Buying and Selling Guidelines

a buyer's guide to purchasing a house, with an explanation of each step in the process?

Barron's Real Estate Handbook [D-245]

how to determine the maximum affordable price to pay for a house?

Barron's Real Estate Handbook [D-245]

a seller's guide to selling a house, with an explanation of each step, including how to select a broker, setting the price, and understanding the parts of a sales contract?

Barron's Real Estate Handbook [D-245]

Computers and Software: Real Estate

descriptive profiles of microcomputer software packages that serve real estate (including property management) applications?

Data Sources: Software [D-158]
Datapro Directory of Microcomputer Software [D-387]

WHERE SHOULD I GO TO FIND...	*TRY*

Construction-Industry Statistics

descriptive statistics on operating factors in the construction industry, including its component industries and different geographical areas?
Census of Construction Industries [D-337]

Corporate Real Estate Managers

an annual directory of individuals who are responsible for real estate acquisitions, leasing, and renting at major U.S. corporations?
Institutional Investor (December issue) [D-447]

Forms Used in Real Estate Transactions

sample forms that are used in transactions involving real estate?
Barron's Real Estate Handbook (residential properties only) [D-245]
Business Forms On File [D-376]
Illustrated Encyclopedic Dictionary of Real Estate [D-125]
Modern Real Estate Leasing Forms [D-417]
Modern Real Estate and Mortgage Forms: Basic Forms and Agreements [D-416]

model forms of legal documents used with condominium development and operations?
Condominium Development Guide [D-257]

forms and agreements used by the construction and building industry?
Modern Construction and Development Forms [D-415]

Government Regulations: Real Estate

a descriptive listing that summarizes the major federal regulations that pertain to real estate?
Barron's Real Estate Handbook [D-245]

a summary of governmental regulations that affect the development and operation of condominiums?
Condominium Development Guide [D-257]

House Designs and Components

descriptions and illustrations of the different architectural styles of houses?
Barron's Real Estate Handbook [D-245]
Dictionary of Real Estate Terms [D-123]

WHERE SHOULD I GO TO FIND...	*TRY*

House Designs and Components

a cross-sectional drawing of a house, with all of its parts designated and named?	*Barron's Real Estate Handbook* [D-245] *Dictionary of Real Estate Terms* [D-123] *Illustrated Encyclopedic Dictionary of Real Estate* [D-125]

Information Sources

a listing of published research reports on the operations of the real estate industry?	*Findex* [D-37]
an index to real estate statistics published by the federal government?	*American Statistics Index* [D-1]

Investment Analysis Techniques

how to evaluate real estate investment opportunities and the value of different types of real estate?	*Dow Jones-Irwin Guide to Real Estate Investing* [D-67]
how to conduct a real estate investment analysis?	*Barron's Real Estate Handbook* [D-245]
tables for determining the potential profitability of different types of real estate?	*Dow Jones-Irwin Guide to Real Estate Investing* [D-67]
formulas that pertain to financing and measurement in real estate matters?	*Barron's Real Estate Handbook* [D-245] *Dictionary of Real Estate Terms* [D-123]

Jobs in Real Estate

a description of career opportunities in real estate?	*Barron's Real Estate Handbook* [D-245] See also other publications in the subsection "Business Careers."

Newsletters

a directory of published newsletters on real estate, with a nonevaluative description of each newsletter?	*Newsletters in Print* [D-41] *Oxbridge Directory of Newsletters* [D-42]

Real Estate Companies, Consultants, and Organizations

a directory of firms that provide real estate consulting services to corporations,
indicating the types of services, contact
person, telephone number, and other relevant information for each company?

*Consultants and Consulting Organizations
Directory* [D-150]
Corporate Finance Sourcebook [D-153]

a directory of major investors, brokers,
and developers of income-producing
properties, indicating the type of commercial property in which they invest and
the investment range of their purchases?

Directory of Real Estate Investors [D-166]

a directory of companies that provide information to the real estate industry on
such matters as property ownership, most
recent selling price, property descriptions, and other information?

Information Sources [D-185]

a directory of national organizations that
serve the real-estate industry?

Dictionary of Real Estate Terms [D-123]
Encyclopedia of Associations, Vol. 1 [D-173]

financial and operating profiles of real
estate companies and real estate investment trusts?

Moody's Bank and Finance Manual [D-189]

the names and addresses of realtors and
state and local boards of realtors who are
members of the National Association of
Realtors?

National Roster of Realtors Directory [D-203]

Real Estate Development and Management

an overview of the principles associated
with the purchase, management, and development of real estate in the U.S.?

A Guide for the Foreign Investor [D-75]

information on the development (including planning, financing, and marketing),
management, and operation of condominiums?

Condominium Development Guide [D-257]

information on insurance coverage for
condominiums?

Condominium Development Guide [D-257]

WHERE SHOULD I GO TO FIND... | TRY

Real Estate Development and Management

information on tax matters pertaining to condominiums?

Condominium Development Guide [D-257]

guidelines for the conversion of property to a condominium operation?

Condominium Development Guide [D-257]

Real Estate Valuations

residential, commercial, and agricultural real estate values in selected U.S. cities?

Dow Jones-Irwin Business and Investment Almanac [D-24]

how to determine the value of different types of real estate?

Dow Jones-Irwin Guide to Real Estate Investing [D-67]

an evaluation sheet that is used when evaluating a commercial site?

Business Forms On File [D-376]

an evaluation sheet that is used when evaluating a commercial building?

Business Forms On File [D-376]

Tables of Values for Real Estate Transactions

tables of values that are used in transactions involving real estate?

Barron's Real Estate Handbook [D-245]
Thorndike Encyclopedia of Banking and Financial Tables [D-326]

a table that discloses the percent of the principal amount of a loan that is needed each year to retire the loan when there are monthly or quarterly payments that are made either in arrears or in advance?

Thorndike Encyclopedia of Banking and Financial Tables [D-326]

a table that discloses the monthly or quarterly debt service (principal and interest) that is required for each $100 of a mortgage loan at an annual percentage rate (APR)?

Thorndike Encyclopedia of Banking and Financial Tables [D-326]

a table that discloses the total interest charged during the term of the loan for each $100 financed at a designated APR, using monthly level payments made in arrears?

Thorndike Encyclopedia of Banking and Financial Tables [D-326]

WHERE SHOULD I GO TO FIND...	*TRY*

Tables of Values for Real Estate Transactions

a table that discloses for a given loan-to-value ratio and specified APR, when (in terms of years and months) a percent of value has been paid, assuming level monthly payments? → *Thorndike Encyclopedia of Banking and Financial Tables* [D-326]

a table of monthly and quarterly loan amortization schedules? → *Thorndike Encyclopedia of Banking and Financial Tables* [D-326]

a table that discloses the annual percentage rate (APR) of a loan requiring monthly payments when points are deducted from the loan amount at closing? → *Thorndike Encyclopedia of Banking and Financial Tables* [D-326]

tables for determining the potential profitability of different types of real estate? → *Dow Jones-Irwin Guide to Real Estate investing* [D-67]

Taxation

Note: See also the subsection "Accounting/Financial Analysis."

Computers and Software: Tax Accounting

descriptive profiles of microcomputer software packages that serve tax-accounting applications? → *Data Sources: Software* [D-158] *Datapro Directory of Microcomputer Software* [D-387]

Federal Tax Laws and Regulations: Guidelines and Explanations

a general explanation of U.S. tax laws as they apply to corporations? → *A Guide for the Foreign Investor* [D-75]

basic legal information about tax issues pertaining to mergers, acquisitions, and divestitures? → *Corporate Acquisitions, Mergers, and Divestitures* [D-384] *Tax Transactions Library: Mergers, Acquisitions, and Leveraged Buyouts* [D-431]

possible alternative solutions to federal income-tax issues concerning corporate acquisitions, mergers, and leveraged buyouts? → *Tax Transactions Library: Mergers, Acquisitions, and Leveraged Buyouts* [D-431]

a checklist of taxes for which small businesses may be liable? → *How to Organize and Operate A Small Business* [D-79]

WHERE SHOULD I GO TO FIND...   *TRY*

Federal Tax Laws and Regulations: Guidelines and Explanations

the potential effect on certain munici-   *Dow Jones-Irwin Guide to Municipal Bonds*
pal bonds if their tax-exempt status is   [D-64]
removed by the federal government?

the effect of the 1986 Tax Reform Act on   *Dow Jones-Irwin Guide to Municipal Bonds*
municipal-bond investments?   [D-64]

an explanation of tax regulations con-   *Bender's Tax Return Manual* [D-247]
cerning interest earned from U.S.   *Dow Jones-Irwin Guide to Buying and Selling*
securities?   *Treasury Securities* [D-61]
                                                 Federal Tax Coordinator [D-405]
                                                 U.S. Master Tax Guide [D-328]

the annual federal income tax rates since   *Standard Federal Tax Reports* [D-422]
1913?

a condensed explanation of the Tax   *Choice of Compensation After Tax Reform*
Reform Act of 1986 as it affects pension   [D-254]
and employee-benefit plans?

information about tax issues involved in   *Handbook of Estate Planning* [D-280]
estate planning?

an explanation of the Tax Reform Act of   *Accounting Desk Book* [D-239]
1986 (redesignated the Internal Revenue   *General Explanation of the Tax Reform Act of*
Code of 1986) and the Revenue Act of   *1986* [D-74]
1987 (Omnibus Budget Reconciliation   *Revenue Act of 1987: Law and Explanation*
Act of 1987)?   [D-98]
                                                 The RIA Complete Analysis of the '86 Tax
                                                 Reform Act [D-312]

an explanation of depreciation rules that   *Accounting Desk Book* [D-239]
were created by the Tax Reform Act of   *Depreciation Guide* [D-260]
1986 and other legislation?   *Federal Tax Coordinator* [D-405]
                                                 Master Federal Tax Manual [D-297]
                                                 U.S. Master Tax Guide [D-328]

guidelines on how to comply with the   *Successful Payroll Management* [D-426]
latest income tax withholding regula-
tions?

record retention requirements for income   *26 Code of Federal Regulations* [D-343]
tax purposes as prescribed by federal   *Accounting Desk Book* [D-239]
law?

<u>*WHERE SHOULD I GO TO FIND...*</u>	<u>*TRY*</u>

Federal Tax Laws and Regulations: Guidelines and Explanations

information on tax matters concerning condominiums?

Condominium Development Guide [D-257]
See also the general tax guides cited in this category of the subsection "Taxation."

for preparing individual or business federal income tax returns, a condensed guide to the federal income tax law with explanations, tax rate schedules and tax tables, annuity tables, corporation tax rates, tax calendar, checklists, and/or other information?

Bender's Tax Return Manual [D-247]
Lasser's Your Income Tax [D-293]
Master Federal Tax Manual [D-297]
U.S. Master Tax Guide [D-328]
Also contact the Internal Revenue Service for publications.

Federal Tax Laws: Texts

the texts of the Federal Tax Reform Act of 1986 (P.L. 99-514) and the Revenue Act of 1987 (Omnibus Budget Reconciliation Act of 1987) (P.L. 100-203)?

100 U.S. Statutes at Large 2085 (P.L. 99-514) [D-368]
101 U.S. Statutes at Large 1330 (P.L. 100-203) [D-368]
Revenue Act of 1987: Law and Explanation [D-98]
Tax Reform Act of 1986: Law and Controlling Committee Reports [D-104]

the U.S. Internal Revenue Code, with regulations, administrative rulings, and decisions regarding tax issues?

26 U.S. Code Annotated [D-365]
Federal Taxes [D-408]
Federal Tax Coordinator [D-405]
Standard Federal Tax Reports [D-422]
(Note: For an abridged version, see Commerce Clearing House's *Federal Tax Guide* and a similar title by Prentice-Hall.)

Insurance Industry Taxation

a separate compilation of the special federal tax laws that apply to the insurance industry?

Federal Taxation of Insurance Companies [D-407]

Judicial Matters

whether a provision of the Internal Revenue Code has been adjudicated and, if it has, what was the decision of the court?

Federal Taxes [D-408]
Federal Tax Coordinator [D-405]
Standard Federal Tax Reports [D-422]

WHERE SHOULD I GO TO FIND...   *TRY*

Judicial Matters

the litigation history of a tax case and its point of tax law?

Federal Taxes Citator [D-409]
Standard Federal Tax Reports [D-422]

decisions handed down by federal (excluding the U.S. Tax Court) and some state courts concerning federal tax issues?

American Federal Tax Reports [D-460]
U.S. Tax Cases [D-435]

decisions handed down by the U.S. Tax Court?

T. C. Memorandum Decisions [D-433]
Tax Court Memorandum Decisions [D-427]
Tax Court Reported Decisions [D-428]
Tax Court Reporter [D-429]

Newsletters

a directory of published newsletters on taxation, with a nonevaluative description of each newsletter?

Newsletters in Print [D-41]
Oxbridge Directory of Newsletters [D-42]

State and Municipal Taxes

a summary of the kinds of taxes and their rates adopted by the individual states?

Dow Jones-Irwin Business and Investment Almanac [D-24]
Moody's Municipal and Government Manual [D-193]
State Tax Guide [D-424]
Statistical Abstract of the United States [D-361]

the text and explanation of each state's business-related taxes, and the taxes of its municipalities, including their rates?

State and Local Taxes [D-423]
State Tax Reports [D-425] (Note: For an abridged version, see *State Tax Guide* [D-424])

how municipal bonds are treated by various state and local taxing authorities?

Municipal Bond Handbook, Vol. 1 [D-305]

Tax Sanctuaries

an explanation of the major criteria to be considered when selecting the location for a tax sanctuary abroad?

Tax Havens of the World [D-430]

WHERE SHOULD I GO TO FIND...	*TRY*

Tax Sanctuaries

a description of tax and investment incentives offered by individual foreign governments, and a discussion of other related matters pertaining to tax sanctuaries abroad? — *Tax Havens of the World* [D-430]

Tax Services

a directory of companies that provide information on taxation? — *Information Sources* [D-185]

Tax Treaties

income tax, gift tax, and estate tax obligations as required by treaties between the United States and particular foreign governments?

Federal Tax Coordinator [D-405]
Federal Tax Treaties [D-406]
Tax Treaties [D-432]
United States Treaties and Other International Agreements [D-369]

D

Descriptive Profiles of Printed Sources

Having selected in Section C the title of the publication that contains the answer to the question being researched, the reader should now turn to Section D for the complete bibliographic citation and a succinct description of the publication. The profiles in this section expand on the contents of the printed sources, thereby enabling the reader better to judge the suitability of the material that has been targeted. These printed sources have been categorized as follows:

Abstracts and Indexes
Almanacs and Yearbooks
Bibliographies
Books
Dictionaries
Directories
Encyclopedias and Handbooks
Government Documents
Loose-leaf Materials
Newsletters
Newspapers, Magazines, and Journals
Reports
Statistical Digests and Statistics Sources

The categorization of any given title has been based more on what the publication actually is than on the title that it bears. The use of terms in titles occasionally is inconsistent with the standard meaning of the term. Examples include "directory," "encyclopedia," and "handbook." These terms are often used in titles without regard to technical or traditional definitions. Again, the authors have endeavored to classify publications according to their contents; consequently, you might find an "encyclopedia" actually listed under "Directories." And of course there will be some publications that do not fit neatly into any given category.

After deciding on a title, the reader may then proceed to a library, bookstore, or the publisher for a copy. To assist with the latter source, Appendix II provides the addresses and telephone numbers of the publishing houses represented in Sections C and D.

The authors reviewed the latest edition of the publications; nevertheless, in the time required to research, write, and publish this book more recent editions have probably been announced for some of the titles listed here. This should not create a problem because, in most cases, the *kinds* of information probably have not changed. For many of the titles subsequent editions are simply updates of information, such as statistical values.

The date that appears in each bibliographical entry indicates the copyright year of the edition of the publication that was reviewed by the authors. This applies to both serials and nonserials. In terms of serials, these dates do not necessarily correspond with the date of the original edition. It is important for the reader to know which edition or issue was reviewed because the content of publications often change as they evolve into new editions. Thus for serials the reviews represent a "snapshot" in time (the present) for works that have been in publication for years and continue to evolve.

The item entry numbers in Section D correspond to those printed in Section C.

ABSTRACTS AND INDEXES

[D-1] *American Statistics Index (ASI).* 2 vols. Washington, DC: Congressional Information Service, Inc., 1988. Published monthly and cumulated quarterly and annually.

A master index and abstract of statistical publications of the federal government. The publisher, CIS, makes available microfiche copies of most publications indexed and abstracted in *ASI*. Among the subjects covered are business and economics at the national, state, and local levels. Also includes foreign countries in its scope.

Some of the more specific topics covered are business acquisitions and mergers, business cycles, business assets and liabilities, operating ratios, economic analysis, labor characteristics, investments, and other related topics. Categories of materials not to be found in *ASI* include highly technical and scientific data, classified information, and other exceptions as noted by its publisher.

ASI is published in two volumes; namely, the *Index* and the *Abstract*. Indexing is by subjects and names, categories, titles, and agency report numbers. The *Abstract* contains a description of the purpose, content, and format of each statistical publication. *ASI* is a companion to *Index to International Statistics* [D-10] and *Statistical Reference Index* [D-18].

[D-2] *Biography and Genealogy Master Index.* Edited by Barbara McNeil. Detroit: Gale Research Company, 1988. Published annually.

A master index to 55 biographical dictionaries. Although it does not contain biographical sketches, it directs the reader to the biographical source where the profile may be found. This combined index of biographical sketches includes personalities from business and other fields.

[D-3] *Business Firms Master Index.* Edited by Jennifer Mossman and Donna Wood. Detroit: Gale Research Company, 1985.

Contains the titles of published sources that report information about individual companies in the United States. Also includes some foreign firms. A guide to business firms described in directories, buying guides, almanacs, encyclopedias, factbooks, handbooks, periodicals, and yearbooks. This first edition focuses on the communications field (publishers, periodicals, computer companies, advertising agencies, public-relations firms, radio and television stations, cable networks and services, film production companies, online services, telephone companies, newspapers, information systems, and databases.) For each company, indexes only those sources that offer information beyond the firm's name, address, telephone number, and name of the chief operating officer (CEO). Thus it is a master index to sources that provide a variety of meaningful and oftentimes hard-to-find information about companies.

Diverse sources have been indexed, which together can provide a broad profile of a firm. Organized by a single alphabetical listing of companies in which their names are followed by their corporate/institutional affiliation, location, and titles of sources of information. Future editions will cover other subject fields.

[D-4] *Business Periodicals Index.* New York: H. W. Wilson Co. Published monthly, except August, with quarterly and annual cumulations.

A cumulative subject index to approximately 300 English-language periodicals in business and economics. Subjects include accounting, marketing, banking, the chemical industry, communications, computer technology and applications, finance and investments, international business, management, public relations, and other business, industries, and trades. Articles are not indexed by author and the entries are not abstracted; nevertheless, adequate information is provided to facilitate locating the article. Following the subject index is a separate index of book reviews that appear in the journals indexed. Contains a list of indexed journals with their addresses, frequency of publication, and subscription prices.

[D-5] *Business Rankings and Salaries Index.* Compiled by Brooklyn Public Library, Business Library. Detroit: Gale Research Company, 1988.

An index to published lists and rankings of business-related topics. It reports lists and rankings of who or what was ranked number one according to a stated criterion and cites the source of the information. The lists or rankings are of persons, companies, products, services, regions and other categories. "Number one" may be interpreted as being the leading, top, most, poorest, fastest, worst, or some other adjective. Information is organized by subject.

Also indexes published salary surveys that have been conducted by government, trade associations, professional organizations, and other bodies. These surveys are arranged by industry, profession, or occupation.

[D-6] *Census Catalog and Guide.* Compiled by U.S. Bureau of the Census. Washington, D.C.: U.S. Government Printing Office. Published annually.

A catalog of the U.S. Bureau of the Census reports, microfiche, machine-readable files, microcomputer diskettes, and maps that have been issued since January 1980. Contains title, document number, time period of the data, geographic areas covered, abstract of content, Government Printing Office stock number, and the price. Arranged by subject, including chapters on business, construction and housing, manufacturing, transportation, population, and other subjects. A source for identifying the many reports that are based on census data.

[D-7] *Consumers Index to Product Evaluations and Information Sources.* Vol. 15. Ann Arbor, MI: Pierian Press, 1988. Published quarterly with annual cumulation.

An index to articles in more than 100 American, British, and Canadian magazines that provide information on product or service evaluations and general consumer topics. The listings of general consumer articles include brief summaries. Entries for specific products are not annotated. Categories for the indexed articles include food, clothing, the home, health care, transportation, computers, office and business management, and other related consumer subjects. The index citations for specific products indicate whether the reporting article simply describes the product or reports on systematic testing of the product. This book does not publish the findings of product evaluation; instead, it directs the reader to articles where this information can be found.

[D-8] *Federal Government Publications Catalog.* Williamsport, PA: Brodart Company, 1976 to date. Update monthly.

A microform catalog of publications of the U.S. Government Printing Office, arranged by subject, author, and title.

[D-9] *The Foundation Grants Index: A Cumulative Listing of Foundation Grants.* 17th ed. Edited by Ruth Kovacs. New York: The Foundation Center, 1988. Published annually and updated bimonthly with *Foundation Grants Index Bimonthly.*

A listing of foundations that award grants of at least $5,000. Discloses a foundation's limitations on giving and lists its grant awards for the preceding year. Indexes grants by subject (including business and economics) and by state in which the recipient is located. Also includes a summary directory of foundations, with their addresses and the geographical areas to which their grant programs are restricted.

[D-10] *Index to International Statistics (IIS).* 2 vols. Washington, DC: Congressional Information Service, Inc., 1988. Published monthly and cumulated quarterly and annually.

Indexes the contents of English-language statistical publications that are published by the major international intergovernmental organizations (IGOs), such as the United Nations, Organization of American States, the European Community, and approximately 95 other organizations. The scope of the statistical data that appears in these publications and that are indexed by subject, geographic areas, categories, issuing sources, and titles includes business, finance, foreign trade, population, education, health, and other demographic, economic, and political information of nations and regions of the world. The data per se are not reported; instead, the *Index* is a guide to finding the statistical information from IGO sources. This book is a companion to the *American Statistics Index* [D- 1] and the *Statistical Reference Index* [D- 18]. It has a microfiche counterpart.

Volume 1 is the index and volume 2 contains the abstracts. In the latter is to be found a full description of the contents of each of the indexed publications. Again, it describes the statistical data to be found but does not provide the data. The focus is on statistics that are of a national, international, or worldwide scope.

Index to the U.S. Patent Classification. Washington, DC: U.S. Patent and Trademark Office, 1987.
See "Government Documents," [D-352].

Monthly Catalog of United States Government Publications. Washington, DC: U.S. Government Printing Office. Published monthly.
See "Government Documents," [D-354].

[D-11] ***New York Times Index: A Book of Record***. New York: New York Times, 1913 to date. Published semiannually.

A subject index to articles that appear in the *New York Times* newspaper. Offers brief summaries of the articles along with bibliographic reference to the full article. Accesses news-media coverage of current events, including issues related to business and economics. The *New York Times Thesaurus of Descriptors* facilitates locating the information, whether it be manually or by online database searching.

[D-12] ***PAIS Bulletin***. Vol. 74. Edited by Gwen Sloan. New York: Public Affairs Information Service, Inc., 1988. Published monthly and cumulated quarterly, including the annual bound volume.

A subject index to English-language periodicals, books, government documents, monographs, reports of public and private organizations, and other sources published on public affairs and public policy. Contains information that is of interest to the business community in addition to policy researchers, legislators, and others. Indexes policy-oriented literature on economics, management policy-making, business-society issues, finance, political science, demography, and other areas that address contemporary public issues. Excludes topics on the details of business operations. Materials indexed emphasize factual and statistical information.

Bibliographic entries include enough information to allow the reader to determine the purpose of the publication. Also includes the standard bibliographic information that facilitates locating the item. The annual bound volume includes a personal/corporate author index. For a subject index to public affairs information printed in French, German, Italian, Portuguese, and Spanish, see the *PAIS Foreign Language Index*.

[D-13] *Predicasts F&S Index of Corporate Change.* Cleveland, OH: Predicasts, Inc., 1988. Published quarterly and cumulated annually.

An index to periodical and newspaper articles that report on corporate mergers, acquisitions, name changes, and other events that affect corporate structure. Summarizes the event and provides the bibliographical citation for more complete information. Contains an alphabetical company listing, indexing by SIC industrial category, and an index summary by type of event (e.g., name changes, bankruptcies, joint ventures, and foreign operations).

[D-14] *Predicasts F&S Index Europe* and *Predicasts F&S Index International.* Cleveland, OH: Predicasts, Inc., 1988. Published monthly and cumulated quarterly and annually.

These two publications are comprehensive indexes to trade journals, newspapers, government documents, and other miscellaneous print sources. These F&S titles report on information concerning foreign products, industries, and companies. They enable the reader to access periodicals concerning data on an industry, product, or company. *Predicasts F &S Index Europe* covers Europe while *Predicasts F&S Index International* encompasses the remainder of the world, exclusive of the United States.

[D-15] *Predicasts F&S Index United States.* Cleveland, OH: Predicasts, Inc., 1988. Published weekly and cumulated monthly, quarterly, and annually.

A comprehensive index to trade journals, U.S. government documents, newspapers, and special reports concerning information about individual companies and the industries with which they are affiliated. The first section is organized by industry and products while the second section is an alphabetical listing of companies. Both sections are arranged by subject. Thus the reader is able to find concise information about a U.S. company or industry according to subject. The source of information is also reported. This is a major guide to the trade journals and, consequently, to company and industry information.

[D-16] *PROMT.* Cleveland, OH: Predicasts, Inc., 1988. Published monthly and cumulated quarterly and annually.

Predicasts Overview of Markets and Technology (*PROMT*) contains abstracts of selected articles that have been indexed in the various *Predicasts F&S* indexes. These summaries are arranged by subject. They are indexed by company name, product, type of information, and country.

[D-17] *Readers' Guide to Periodical Literature.* New York: H. W. Wilson, Co. Published monthly (January, February, May, June, July, August, and November) and semimonthly (September, October, December, March, and April). Cumulated quarterly and annually.

A subject-author index of periodicals that are of a general public interest vis-à-vis professional and technical journals. Useful to the business and economic researcher who is interested in finding articles concerning business and economics that have been published in popular periodicals. Since these periodicals are not indexed in the *Business Periodicals Index* [D-4], the *Reader's Guide to Periodical Literature* serves as a supplementary index for articles on business and economics.

Statistical Abstract of the United States. 108th ed. U.S. Bureau of the Census. Washington, DC: U.S. Government Printing Office, 1987. Published annually. See "Government Documents," [D-361].

[D-18] ***Statistical Reference Index (SRI).*** 2 vols. Washington, DC: Congressional Information Service, Inc., 1988. Published monthly. The *Index* cumulates monthly, quarterly, and annually.

A subject index to statistical publications that are published by private organizations in the United States and by state government agencies. The statistical publications are on economic conditions, business, industry, finance, government programs, and social trends. The issuing bodies are state government agencies; stock and commodity exchanges, banks, corporations, accounting firms, and other business organizations; commercial publishers of trade-association, business, and industry publications; professional, trade, and other not-for-profit associations and institutes; independent research organizations; and universities and affiliated research centers.

The types of statistical data that are accessed include national, statewide, local, and foreign data. *SRI* does not publish the data per se; instead, it is a guide to the publications in which the data are to be found. The first volume is the *Index*, in which the statistical publications are indexed by: (1) subjects and names, (2) categories, (3) issuing sources, and (4) titles. The *Index* contains full bibliographic citations.

The second volume is the *Abstract*, which contains full descriptions of the publications indexed: that is, the types of statistical data that are to be found in each publication. The publications consist of annual and other recurring reports, periodicals, monographs, and articles.

SRI is part of a series consisting of the *American Statistics Index* [D-1], which indexes statistical publications of the federal government, and the *Index to International Statistics* [D-10] which indexes statistical publications of international intergovernmental organizations. *SRI* has a microfiche companion.

[D-19] ***The Wall Street Journal Index/Barron's Index.*** 2 vols. New York: Dow Jones and Co., 1987. This annual cumulation is of the monthly indexes of the *Journal* and an annual index of *Barron's*.

An index to the *Wall Street Journal* [D-457], final eastern edition, and *Barron's National Business and Financial Weekly* [D-440]. Volume 1 contains corporate news in the *Journal*, arranged by name of corporation. Also within volume 1 is the index to *Barron's*. In volume 2 is the index to general news in the *Journal*, arranged by subject. Entries consist of a concise abstract statement followed by the location of the full article.

Corporate earnings and dividend reports that appeared in the *Journal* are included in the index. Also publishes for each month the daily closing value of the Dow Jones averages. Contains special sections on book reviews, theater reviews, and deaths.

ALMANACS AND YEARBOOKS

[D-20] *Almanac of Business and Industrial Financial Ratios.* Leo Troy. Englewood Cliffs, NJ: Prentice-Hall, Inc., 1988. Published annually.

For 180 industries classified in 16 categories, this almanac reports financial ratios and operating factors expressed as percentages of net sales. The ratios include the current ratio, quick ratio, net sales to net working capital, coverage ratio, asset turnover, and total liabilities to net worth. The operating factor percentages include cost of operations, repairs, bad debts, taxes, interest, and other operating factors. Other financial factors reported as percentages are debt ratio, return on assets, return on equity, and retained earnings to net income.

The tables in this almanac facilitate comparing a company's financial operations with those of others in the same industry. Each industry's sample size is reported. The information is based on statistical data from the Internal Revenue Service. There is usually a three- to four-year lapse between the coverage period of the data and their publication.

[D-21] *The American Almanac of Jobs and Salaries.* John W. Wright. New York: Avon Books, 1987. Published annually.

A guide to American salaries paid in sundry industries and occupations. Also gives job descriptions. Includes salaries in government, the professions, entertainment, science and technology, business, the trades, and other career groups.

[D-22] *Countries of the World and Their Leaders, Yearbook.* 2 vols. Edited by Frank E. Bair. Detroit: Gale Research Company, 1988. Published annually.

A comprehensive guide to the nations of the world, with national profiles that provide descriptions of the people, geography, government, economy, political conditions, culture, appropriate clothing, customs, telecommunications, transportation, and health conditions. Also discloses information and regulations about matters of health in the different countries as they relate to the traveler. Provides guidance concerning passports, visas, duty, and travel warnings.

This yearbook lists the chiefs of state and cabinet members of foreign governments. Also contains a directory of U.S. embassies, counsulates, and foreign service posts. As a yearbook, its annual revision keeps abreast of changes in world situations. Also provides a description of international treaty organizations.

[D-23] *Demographic Yearbook.* Statistical Office of the United Nations. New York: United Nations, 1988. Published annually.

A compendium of worldwide demographic data encompassing approximately 220 countries, this yearbook summarizes characteristics of the population of individual nations and reports on population trends. The data include birth rates, mortality rates, number and size of households, migration rates, illiteracy rates, size of the economically active population, and many other demographic characteristics. Issued under the coordination of the United Nation's Statistical Office and in cooperation with national statistical services around the world.

[D-24] *The Dow Jones-Irwin Business and Investment Almanac.* Edited by Sumner N. Levine. Homewood, IL: Dow Jones-Irwin, 1988. Published annually.

A comprehensive compilation of information that includes topics on the business and economic conditions in selected industries. Also includes information on selected corporations, investment instruments, the stock market, taxes, and a potpourri of other topics concerning entrepreneurs, investors, and others. A source for commencing a search for business and investment information.

[D-25] *The Europa World Year Book.* 2 vols. 30th ed. London: Europa Publications, 1989. Distributed in the United States by Gale Research Company. Published annually.

A collection of profiles of international organizations and countries. For each country this book describes: location, climate, history, language, government, dates of public holidays, currency and exchange rates, statistics on major industries, name of the chief of state and the names of the cabinet members (ministers), major periodicals, listing of banks with their addresses and telephone numbers, listing of trade fairs, identification of the stock exchanges and their addresses, and other descriptive information. Provides a directory of chambers of commerce, industrial associations, and trade unions for the individual countries, along with their addresses, telephone numbers, and names of chief executive officers. Also profiles international organizations.

[D-26] *Industry Norms and Key Business Ratios.* Library edition. Murray Hill, NJ: Dun & Bradstreet Credit Services, 1988. Published annually.

Provides operating financial norms and key business ratios for more than 800 lines of business organized in broad categories. The norms are the percentage that each item in the financial statement is of its respective aggregate total: from this, an industry average has been calculated. These data facilitate comparing a specific business firm with its industry counterparts (norm). Also reports 14 key business ratios for each industry, which indicate solvency, efficiency, and profitability. Includes an explanation of how the ratios were calculated. The database consists of the more than one million financial statements that are contained in the Dun &Bradstreet financial profiles of public and private corporations, partnerships, and proprietorships.

International Financial Statistics. Washington, DC: International Monetary Fund, 1988. Published monthly and with a yearbook edition.
See "Newspapers, Magazines and Journals," [D-448].

[D-27] *RMA Annual Statement Studies.* Philadelphia: Robert Morris Associates, 1987. Published annually.

For 65 years this publication has reported financial norms for industries throughout America. It presently reports current and historical composite financial data for nearly 350 industries. Included are 17 financial and operating ratios and a common-size analysis of assets, liabilities, and income data for each of these industries. Within each industry the data are presented for the total industry and for each of four categories of firms, distinguished by their size of assets. Current and historical comparisons can be made.

The data are presented in five parts, with parts 1–3 addressing the manufacturing industries, wholesale industries, and retailing and service industries. Part 4 focuses on the contractor industries, and part 5 on the finance industry. Also contains a bibliography of other sources that report composite financial data for each industry.

[D-28] *The Statesman's Year-Book.* 125th ed. Edited by John Paxton. New York: St. Martin's Press, 1988. Published annually.

A compilation of profiles of nations. Information includes history, geography, climate, population, government, defense, international relations, economy, currency, banking, energy and natural resources, trade and industry, communications, and other descriptive material. Also provides profiles of the major international organizations.

[D-29] *The World Almanac and Book of Facts 1988.* Edited by Mark S. Hoffman. New York: Newspaper Enterprise Association, 1987. Published annually.

A comprehensive compilation of facts on many subjects, including banking, economics, government finance, stock markets, populations, manufacturing, and others. Also has a directory of major corporations with the address, telephone number, and name of the chief executive officer for each.

[D-30] *World Currency Yearbook.* 25th ed. Edited by Philip P. Cowitt. Brooklyn, NY: International Currency Analysis, Inc., 1989. Published irregularly.

Describes the currencies of the world by continuing the work of *Pick's Currency Yearbook*. The numbering of editions is continuous of *Pick's*. Provides a complete description of each of 145 currencies. These profiles include the currency's history, transferability, developments, varieties, administration, amount in circulation, monthly free- or black-market exchange rate per U.S. dollar for selected years, and other descriptive information. Also reports the ten-year activity record regarding domestic purchasing power, number of devaluations, monetary circulation, and change of free-market value.

BIBLIOGRAPHIES

[D-31] *Books in Print.* New York: R.R. Bowker Company, 1988. Published annually and updated six months after publication via *Books in Print Supplement*.

A bibliography of U.S. books in print or soon to be published. Covers most subjects. The books must be available to the trade or general public for purchase. Excludes bibles, textbooks, professional medical and law books, pamphlets, subscription-only titles, and other books not accessible to the public. Indexed in three ways: author, title, and subject. Also includes a listing of book publishers with their addresses and telephone numbers. The bibliographic data contains title, author, editor, number of volumes, edition number, L. C. (Library of Congress) catalog number, ISBN (International Standard Book Number), price, number of pages, publication date, name of publisher, and other bibliographic information.

[D-32] *Business Information: How to Find It, How to Use It.* Michael R. Lavin. Phoenix, AZ: Oryx Press, 1987.

This is an annotated bibliography of the business reference literature, and more. Its pages contain information on how the business community functions, definitions of business terms and concepts, and a description of the literature cited. The reference materials are prefaced by an explanation of their purpose and how they fit into the business world. Publications are organized according to subject. This is an introduction to business and to the integral role of business reference works. The critical comments in this book are valuable.

[D-33] *Business Information Sources.* Revised ed. Lorna M. Daniells. Berkeley, CA: The Regents of the University of California, 1985. Available through the University of California Press.

This is an annotated bibliography of business information sources. It includes directories, loose-leaf services, bibliographies, handbooks, textbooks, indexes, abstracts, periodicals, dictionaries, government documents, and other reference materials. The author has included many helpful suggestions for finding business information. Covers most major topics in business. Offers a suggested listing of basic reference books for the business researcher. Organized by type of printed material and business subject. The coverage of the literature is extensive.

[D-34] *The Complete Information Bank for Entrepreneurs and Small-Business Managers.* 2d ed. Ron Christy and Billy M. Jones. New York: American Management Association, 1988.

A bibliography of books, periodicals, audiovisual materials, and online data sources that provide information for entrepreneurs of small businesses. Also includes directories of business organizations, venture capital companies, and Small Business Administration regional offices, all of which provide services to small business. This is a sourcebook of information for the small-business community.

[D-35] *Directories in Print.* 2 vols. 6th ed. Edited by Julie E. Towell. Detroit: Gale Research Company, 1989. Published annually. Formerly titled *Directory of Directories.*

An annotated guide to national, regional, and some international directories in numerous fields, including business and industry. These directories are of many kinds, including buyers' guides, suppliers, and professional and scientific rosters. It embraces such business areas as accounting, banking, finance, insurance, real estate, information sciences, automotive parts, construction, discount stores, and others. Profiles of directories report the title, publisher, address, telephone number, scope of the directory, frequency of publication, price, associated online database, and other bibliographic information. Contains subject and title/keyword indexes.

[D-36] *Encyclopedia of Business Information Sources.* 7th ed. Edited by James Woy. Detroit: Gale Research Company, 1988.

Organizes 20,000 printed and nonprinted sources of business information under about 1,000 subjects. When necessary, this publication provides single-sentence descriptions of information sources. These include directories, biographical sources, handbooks, indexes, almanacs, online databases, periodicals, trade associations, professional societies, research centers, and other sources of business information. Prints the names, addresses, and telephone numbers of publishers. Contains a detailed classification of information sources in an encyclopedic format.

[D-37] *Findex: The Directory of Market Research Reports, Studies, and Surveys.* 10th ed. Edited by JoAnne DuChez and Sharon J. Marcus. Bethesda, MD: Cambridge Information Group Directories, Inc., 1988. Published annually and updated mid-year.

An annotated bibliography of published business and market research reports, U.S. and foreign. These reports come from many sources and concern both domestic and foreign economies. The focus of these research reports is on the operations of individual companies and on industries and their specific products. Also contains research reports on corporate management. The profile of each market report includes the title, publication date, publisher, summary, number of pages, price, and a report identification number. This is a major source for identifying commercially available market research reports and for learning where to obtain copies.

[D-38] *Forthcoming Books.* New York: R. R. Bowker Company. Published bimonthly.

This bimonthly publication supplements *Books in Print* [D-31] by announcing book titles that are scheduled to be published in the United States during the ensuing five months. Also lists U.S. titles published since the last issue of *Books in Print.*

A Guide to Statistical Sources in Money, Banking, and Finance. M. Balachandran. Phoenix, AZ: Oryx Press, 1988.
See "Statistical Digests and Statistics Sources," [D-465].

[D-39] *Management Information: Where to Find It.* Marilyn Taylor Thompson. Metuchen, NJ: Scarecrow Press, Inc., 1981.

An annotated bibliography of publications on management. Arranged by subject, it cites information sources concerning general management, specific types of management (financial management, public administration, and other types), and various aspects of management (e.g., organization development). The annotations are brief, yet informative. Most of the entries were published in the 1970s.

[D-40] *Management Principles and Practice: A Guide to Information Sources*. K. G. B. Bakewell. Detroit: Gale Research Company, 1977.

A rich bibliographic guide to the literature in management published before 1977. The entries include books, periodicals, organizations, films, and other audiovisual materials, with descriptive annotations that are one paragraph long. A comprehensive scope of topics is offered, including corporate planning and forecasting; management by objective; operations research; systems analysis; marketing management; production management; financial management; personnel management; and the training, evaluation, and compensation of managers.

[D-41] *Newsletters in Print*. 4th ed. Edited by Brigitte T. Darnay. Detroit: Gale Research Company, 1988. Formerly titled *Newsletters Directory*.

A guide to newsletters published in the U.S. and Canada. Includes a broad range of publications: both newsletters per se and also publications that are only lossely considered as being newsletters. These encompass bulletins, digests, some journals, updates, and other serials that are of a national or regional interest (not local) and that are available to the public (not in-house organs). Contains both printed and electronic (online) newsletters.

Profiles of these newsletters report the title; publisher's name, address, and telephone number; editor's name; description of the purpose, scope, and subjects covered; intended audience; frequency of issues; circulation size; price; whether accessible via online computer; and other descriptive information.

[D-42] *Oxbridge Directory of Newsletters*. 6th ed. Edited by Matthew Manning. New York: Oxbridge Communications, Inc., 1988.

Arranged by subject, this is a bibliography of newsletters with a brief description of each newsletter. Business is one of the areas for which newsletters are listed, and the subjects covered include accounting, advertising and marketing, banking and finance, insurance, international trade, investments, labor, management, manufacturing, real estate, and other business topics.

Within each newsletter's profile is the title; publisher's name, address, and telephone number; description of content; frequency of issue; subscription rate; circulation size; primary readership; whether available in microform or online; and other descriptive information.

[D-43] *Predicasts Source Directory*. Cleveland, OH: Predicasts, Inc., 1988. Published quarterly and cumulated annually.

Lists the trade journals, newspapers, government documents, and other print sources that are indexed in the other Predicasts publications. (See "Abstracts and Indexes" and "Statistical Digests and Statistics Sources" for these titles and their profiles.) They are grouped by SIC industry code and by country.

Regional Statistics: A Guide to Information Sources. M. Balachandran. Detroit: Gale Research Company, 1980.
See "Statistical Digests and Statistics Sources," [D-469].

Sourcebook of Global Statistics. George T. Kurian. New York: Facts On File Publications, 1985.
See "Statistical Digests and Statistics Sources," [D-471].

Statistics Sources. 11th ed. Edited by Jacqueline Wasserman O'Brien and Steven R. Wasserman. Detroit: Gale Research Company, 1987. Published annually.
See "Statistical Digests and Statistics Sources," [D-473].

[D-44] *Ulrich's International Periodicals Directory.* 3 vols. 27th ed. New York: R. R. Bowker Company, 1988. Published annually. Updated quarterly by *Ulrich's Update*.

Beginning with this 27th edition, *Ulrich's* includes all serial publications that were formerly reported in *Ulrich's* and in *Irregular Serials and Annuals*. Thus the new scope encompasses periodicals and other serials that are currently being published and that are being issued regularly and more than once a year. It also includes such serials as annual reviews, monograph series, yearbooks, and proceedings that appear regularly as an annual, or less frequently, or which are published irregularly.

The coverage of serials is international, and its range of subjects embraces business, economics, and other fields. Under the business and economics headings are serial titles on accounting, banking, financing, investments, economic conditions, labor, macroeconomics, management, marketing, small business, and more.

Ulrich's provides full bibliographic information, including where the periodical is indexed and abstracted. It also indicates whether a serial is available online: if there is online access to the serial, the name of the publisher, vendor, and file name is given. The addresses and telephone numbers of the publishers and vendors are also reported.

The three volumes are divided into seven sections: "The Classified List of Serials," "Serials Available Online," "Vendor Listing/Serials Online," "Cessations" (of titles), "Index to Publications of International Organizations," "ISBN Index," and "Title Index."

[D-45] *Where to Find Business Information: A Worldwide Guide for Everyone Who Needs the Answers to Business Questions.* David M. Brownstone and Gorton Carruth. New York: John Wiley & Sons, 1979.

Using more than 2,500 subjects in the field of business, this book refers the reader to English-language books, magazines, business newsletters, computer databases, and other sources for the purpose of finding business information from throughout the world. The first section is the index, which cites, under each subject, the source titles and their identification numbers. In another section is a brief description of each publication along with the publisher's name, address, and telephone number. The price is also quoted. The criteria for inclusion was that each source had to be recently written (or revised) and in publication as of 1979. Dictionaries, encyclopedias, and other materials not frequently revised were excluded. A useful bibliography for materials published in 1979 or earlier.

BOOKS

[D-46] *The 100 Best Companies to Work For in America.* Robert Levering, Milton Moskowitz, and Michael Katz. Reading, MA: Addison-Wesley Publishing Company, 1984.

This is a presentation of the best companies to work for in the opinion of employees, according to the results of one research study. Each of the 100 companies has been profiled concerning its employee practices and policies. The major job factors have been rated on a five-point scale, and the principal positive and negative employee opinions have been reported. This book endeavors to disclose the factors that distinguish these companies from others. Job seekers and managers will find this book of special interest.

[D-47] *The 101 Best-Performing Companies in America.* Ronald N. Paul and James W. Taylor. Chicago: Probus Publishing Company, 1986.

Here is what one research team identified as being the 101 best-performing companies in America, according to employee productivity, capital productivity, creating jobs, and increasing the wealth of stockholders. It analyzes and describes each of these companies in terms of these criteria.

[D-48] *Accounting Guide for Government Contracts.* 9th ed. Paul M. Trueger. Chicago: Commerce Clearing House, 1988.

This book serves as an accounting guide for companies that contract with the federal government. It addresses the many technical and, sometimes, controversial accounting problems that are involved with government contracts. Discusses what the government expects of those with whom it contracts. Subjects covered include types of government contracts, significant clauses found in contracts, cost accounting, allowable and unallowable costs, direct and indirect costs, pricing, profit limitations, fraud, waste, abuse, and other subjects related to government accounting policies and regulations.

[D-49] *Alternative Work Schedules: Selecting, Implementing, and Evaluating.* Simcha Ronen. Homewood, IL: Dow Jones-Irwin, 1984.

Discusses changes that have occurred in the work force and the effect on policies regarding the management of human resources. Presents a descriptive discussion of alternative work schedules: the compressed work week, flexible working hours, part-time employment, and job sharing. Also addresses implementation procedures.

[D-50] *The Art of M & A: A Merger/Acquisition Buyout Guide.* Stanley F. Reed and the staff of Lane and Edson, P.C. Homewood, IL: Dow Jones-Irwin, 1989.

A guide for corporate mergers and acquisitions. Using the question-and-answer format, this publication provides answers to many questions that are asked about this subject. This book is detailed, concise, and informative.

The Art of M & A includes the table of contents for a model merger agreement, with an explanation of each section of this type of agreement. It contains definitions of terms used with mergers and acquisitions. This book addresses the acquisition process, the roles of commercial and investment banks, and the documents involved in the execution of merger and acquisition transactions. There is a discussion of valuation and pricing, financing a leveraged buyout, tax planning, and other issues associated with mergers and acquisitions. Includes a checklist to be followed for the due-diligence process involved with acquisitions.

[D-51] *Asian Stockmarkets: The Inside Story.* Anthony Rowley. Homewood, IL: Dow Jones-Irwin, 1987.

A discussion of the stock markets in Japan, South Korea, Taiwan, Hong Kong, Singapore, Malaysia, Thailand, the Philippines, Indonesia, India, Pakistan, Sri Lanka, Bangladesh, and Nepal. Presents important information for the individual and institutional investor.

[D-52] *Business Forecasting: Concepts and Microcomputer Applications.* Neil Seitz. Reston Publishing Company (Refer to Prentice-Hall, Inc.), 1984.

A technician's manual on how to perform business forecasting. Explains various techniques and then provides programs written in BASIC that will perform forecasting methods using personal computers. A how-to book.

[D-53] *Business Plans That Win $$$: Lessons from the MIT Enterprise Forum.* By Stanley R. Rich and David E. Gumpert. New York: Harper & Row, Inc., 1985.

Explains the dos and don'ts of writing a business plan. It tells what should be emphasized, what should be deemphasized, and what investors look for in a business plan. The authors explain how potential investors evaluate young companies and how they determine what percentage of the company they will need to own to justify their investment. A sample outline of a business plan is included along with a discussion of its elements. There is a chapter that explains how to make financial projections that are to be included in a business plan. Tips are offered on how to target investors and how to present your plan to them.

[D-54] *Business Records Control.* 6th ed. David G. Goodman, Joseph S. Fosegan, and Earnest D. Bassett. Cincinnati, OH: South-Western Publishing Company, 1987.

A comprehensive treatment of business-records management, with a procedural approach. Explains indexing rules and procedures, filing systems and their procedures and controls, records storage and retrieval, equipment used for managing records, and other topics.

The authors offer an extensive explanation of how to alphabetize in various situations. Discusses the characteristics and use of the lastest technology (as of 1987) for managing records in business and industry. Serves as a basic guide for records management.

[D-55] *Buying a Computer for Your Growing Business: An Insider's Guide.* Brooks L. Hilliard. Homewood, IL: Dow Jones-Irwin, 1984.

Provides guidelines to follow when considering the purchase of a computer for a business. Addresses applications, software, security, cost, evaluating business systems, implementation of computer systems, and other important issues.

[D-56] *The China Investment Guide.* Essex, England: Longman Group, Ltd., 1985. Distributed in North America by St. James Press, Inc.

This sourcebook for business ventures in the People's Republic of China updates the 1984–1985 version. Within its pages is a compilation of the business laws of China germane to joint ventures, taxation, imports and exports, foreign exchange control, patents, trademarks, and other regulated areas. It lists names, addresses, and telephone numbers of companies that are of interest to foreign businesspersons who are considering joint ventures in China. A section describes the central government of the People's Republic of China, including the purpose of each ministry and other governmental units. This book guides the foreign businessperson as preparations are being made to conduct business in China.

[D-57] *The Complete Guide to a Successful Leveraged Buyout.* Allen Michel and Israel Shaked. Homewood, IL: Dow Jones-Irwin, 1988.

For managers and investors who are contemplating a corporate leveraged buyout (LBO), this book discusses the issues and guidelines involved with this kind of transaction. Covers a broad array of topics, including how to evaluate an LBO candidate, valuing a company, legal matters, taxation, how to structure the LBO, and other related issues.

[D-58] *The Complete Investor: Instruments, Markets and Methods.* Geoffrey A. Hirt and Stanley B. Block. Homewood, IL: Richard D. Irwin, 1987.

An introduction to forms of investments and their markets. Focuses on fixed-income securities, stocks, real estate, mutual funds, portfolio management, analysis of corporate financial statements, and other topics essential to investing.

[D-59] *Corporate Information Systems Management: The Issues Facing Senior Executives.* 2d ed. James I. Cash, Jr., F. Warren McFarlan, and James L. McKenney. Homewood, IL: Dow Jones-Irwin, 1988.

Discusses the impact of information technology on a corporation's way of doing business. Addresses trends, organizational issues, how information technology changes the way a corporation competes in the marketplace, operations management, multinational issues relating to information technology, and other topics. Provides a bibliography of information-technology literature.

[D-60] *The Dow Jones-Irwin Guide to Bond and Money Market Investments.* Marcia Stigum and Frank J. Fabozzi. Homewood, IL: Dow Jones-Irwin, 1987.

A primer on how to invest in fixed-income instruments, including certificates of deposit; Treasury bills, bonds, and notes; banker's acceptances; commercial paper; money-market funds; municipal securities; corporate bonds; Ginnie Maes; Fannie Maes; and Freddie Macs. Discusses the major issues associated with these instruments. Also includes a description of each, and explains figuring yields, risks, and other subjects that are of concern to investors.

[D-61] *The Dow Jones-Irwin Guide to Buying and Selling Treasury Securities.* 2d ed. Howard M. Berlin. Homewood, IL: Dow Jones-Irwin, 1988.

The investor's practical guide to the U.S. securities market. Explains the nature of Treasury bills, bonds, and notes. Describes how the system works and how to buy, sell, or trade Treasury instruments. Provides an explanation of coupon stripping, Treasury Money-Market and Mutual-Bond Funds, Treasury Options, and options on Treasury Futures. Also discusses tax obligations related to these investment instruments.

[D-62] *The Dow Jones-Irwin Guide to High Tech Investing: Picking Tomorrow's Winners Today.* James B. Powell. Homewood, IL: Dow Jones-Irwin, 1986.

Analyzes selected high-tech industries, with a focus on the interests and needs of investors. Provides guidelines for investing in these industries. Covers such industries as robotics, CAD/CAM and CAE, industrial automation, material-handling systems, semiconductors, communications, computers, energy technology, and others. Provides a directory of more than 1,250 U.S. and foreign public high-tech companies, reporting for each their address, telephone number, stock symbol, and the exchange with which they are listed.

[D-63] *The Dow Jones-Irwin Guide to International Securities, Futures, and Options Markets.* William E. Nix and Susan W. Nix. Homewood, IL: Dow Jones-Irwin, 1988.

A comprehensive guide to investing in international foreign capital markets. Explains the selection of investment criteria, how to determine the actual value of securities, evaluation of foreign currency risks, strategies for portfolio and risk management of international equities and debt securities, and techniques for forecasting foreign exchange rates. This book also discusses the economies of 15 countries and reports commission rates and stock exchange indexes for each of them. A helpful feature is the explanation of how to develop strategies for investing in foreign markets. Includes other related topics not cited in this profile.

[D-64] *The Dow Jones-Irwin Guide to Municipal Bonds.* Sylvan G. Feldstein and Frank J. Fabozzi. Homewood, IL: Dow Jones-Irwin, 1987.

Addresses the concepts and principles that underlie the municipal investment market. Focuses on the bondholder and explains what questions to ask when contemplating purchasing municipal bonds, the criteria for assessing municipal bonds, the differences between types of municipal bonds, the ratings of municipal bonds, and investment strategies. Also discusses specific municipal bonds that have either failed or almost failed. In summary, provides guidelines for the investor in the municipal bond market.

[D-65] *The Dow Jones-Irwin Guide to Mutual Funds.* 3d ed. Donald D. Rugg. Homewood, IL: Dow Jones-Irwin, 1986.

Explains how to establish a no-load mutual-fund investment program. The scope of this publication embraces the types of mutual funds, pros and cons of no-load funds, how to select no-load and money-market funds, timing the market, tax issues related to mutual funds, and other subjects.

[D-66] *The Dow Jones-Irwin Guide to Put and Call Options.* Revised ed. Henry K. Clasing, Jr. Homewood, IL: Dow Jones-Irwin, 1978.

Discusses the strategies and skills needed to engage in the buying and selling of stock options. Addresses the pricing of options, setting strategies, relationship between the degree of risk assumed and reward strategies, spreading, straddles, margin, and taxes.

[D-67] *The Dow Jones-Irwin Guide to Real Estate Investing.* Revised ed. Chris Mader and Jon Bortz. Homewood, IL: Dow Jones-Irwin, 1983.

Provides information on how to analyze investment opportunities in various kinds of real estate. Includes advice about how to assess the effect of inflation and recession on real estate and how to profit from inflation, and gives information that will help make the decision whether to hold or sell property. Also gives guidance on when to refinance or assume a second mortgage.

The authors examine different kinds of real estate investment vehicles and provide reference tables that help determine the profitability of different types of real estate investments under varying conditions.

[D-68] *The Dow Jones-Irwin Guide to Retirement Planning.* 2d ed. Ray Vicker. Homewood, IL: Dow Jones-Irwin, 1987.

Presents guidelines for financial planning for retirement. Gives consideration to determining your net worth, projecting financial needs for retirement, investment plans and opportunities, managing money during retirement, and other important issues.

[D-69] *The Dow Jones-Irwin Guide to Using the Wall Street Journal.* 2d ed. Michael B. Lehmann. Homewood, IL: Dow Jones-Irwin, 1987.

A guide to the business and economic concepts and the statistical terms that are found in the *Wall Street Journal.* The guide explains the business cycle, showing the interrelationships between the different concepts and economic phenomena. Illustrations are provided by reprinting material from the *Journal.* There is an explanation of the various business statistics, what they measure, and how they are computed. Gives historical perspective to current business and economic developments. This book helps the reader gain a greater understanding of the information reported in the *Wall Street Journal* (and other news media too). Lists the publication schedule of the *Journal* for the sundry business and economic statistical series that appear in it at different times.

[D-70] *The Dow Jones-Irwin Guide to Zero-Coupon Investments.* Donald R. Nichols. Homewood, IL: Dow Jones-Irwin, 1986.

Explains the different types of zero-coupon investments and discloses their pros and cons. The reader is instructed on how to manage these investments. Covers different zeros, calculating yields, taxation of zeros, original-issue zero coupons, convertible zero-coupon bonds, municipal bonds as zero-coupon investments, and other related topics.

[D-71] *Executive Jobs Unlimited.* Carl R. Boll. New York: Macmillan Publishing Company, 1979.

A guide to how to get a job. Explains how to write a job résumé, get an interview, conduct an interview, and search for a job in secret. Offers valuable tips on the many aspects of the job search.

[D-72] *File Management and Information Retrieval Systems: A Manual for Managers and Technicians.* Suzanne L. Gill. Englewood, CO: Libraries Unlimited, Inc., 1981.

Covers the fundamentals of file management, with a concentration on the materials that are in a paper medium vis-à-vis micrographics and the electronic format. Teaches the skills for developing a procedures manual for file management. Topics addressed include methods of classification, how to process documents for filing, records retention, equipment and supplies used for filing, and other associated subjects. Microform and computer files are addressed in a cursory manner.

[D-73] *From Concept to Market.* Gary S. Lynn. New York: John Wiley & Sons, 1989.

Explains how to evaluate an innovative idea, prepare for and file a patent application, build a prototype, manufacture, and market an invention. This is a practical guide for the inventor who seeks to take an idea to market. Contains information on how to conduct a patent search, how to document an invention, how to evaluate an invention, names and addresses of organizations that assist with assessing ideas for inventions, and explains how to select a licensee and consummate a licensing agreement.

For inventors who want to establish their own business centered around their inventions, the author discusses how to write a business plan, how these plans are read by investors, where to obtain start-up capital, and how to price the new product. These and other topics are addressed in a style that is easy to read and facilitative for inventive entrepreneurs.

[D-74] *General Explanation of the Tax Reform Act of 1986.* Prepared by the Staff of the Joint Committee on Taxation. Chicago: Commerce Clearing House, 1987.

This Commerce Clearing House publication is a reprint of the report by the same title that was written by the Staff of the Joint Committee on Taxation in consultation with the staffs of the House Ways and Means Committee and the Senate Finance Committee. It resolves differences between the bill that was enacted and committee reports that were issued during the legislative process. This publication discloses the legislative background of the Tax Reform Act of 1986, reasons for this Act, and provides explanations of its various titles.

[D-75] *A Guide for the Foreign Investor: Doing Business in the U.S.* Edited by Robert F. Cushman and Herbert A. Morey. Homewood, IL: Dow Jones-Irwin, 1984.

In the 25 chapters written by experts in their fields, this book presents a comprehensive treatment of those business and legal issues that confront a foreign investor wanting to do business in the United States. The technical guidance found in this publication includes planning for a U.S. operation, ascertaining and assessing acquisition candidates, banking and finance regulations and practices as they pertain to foreign investors, antitrust and other federal laws that should be of special interest to foreign investment in the United States, and tax and accounting rules. The authors of this book also discuss issues concerning real estate, insurance, and other business topics.

[D-76] *How to Buy Foreign Stocks and Bonds: A Guide for the Individual Investor.* Gerald Warfield. New York: Harper & Row, Publishers, 1985.

This is the individual investor's introduction to investing in foreign stocks and bonds. It explains the international securities market, how it works, and how it differs from the U.S. The main portion of this book is devoted to descriptions of individual foreign stock exchanges. A common format is used; however, there are occasional differences due to circumstances unique to a specific exchange. Some profiles are more extensive than others. Information may be found concerning operating practices, policies, and procedures of each stock exchange. There also are definitions of foreign investment terms used on a particular foreign stock exchange. Helpful to the investor are addresses pertaining to investments in the foreign countries covered.

[D-77] *How to Develop a Business Plan in 15 Days.* William M. Luther. New York: American Management Associations, 1987.

A brief guide to writing business plans. Discusses the planning process, how to get organized, 33 market characteristics that have the possibility of having a significant impact on a company's profitability, where to find information sources that are needed for a business plan, and other relevant issues. It should be noted that the author, William Luther, does not mean to imply that a business plan can be written in 15 consecutive days.

[D-78] *How to Get the Best Advertising from Your Agency.* 2d ed. Nancy L. Salz. Homewood, IL: Dow Jones-Irwin, 1988.

Explains how to work in a collaborative mode with an advertising agency. Discusses the roles and responsibilities of each party. A primer for the client-agency relationship. Reveals how an advertising agency works and offers guidelines for the client regarding the daily management of this relationship.

[D-79] *How to Organize and Operate a Small Business.* 8th ed. Clifford M. Baumback. Englewood Cliffs, NJ: Prentice-Hall, Inc., 1988.

A manual on how to organize and manage a small business. Discusses how to make the decision to go into business by addressing the pros and cons, financial and personal risks, causes of business failures, tax burdens, capital shortages, and other considerations. Explains how to prepare a business plan, and provides a checklist for organizing and operating a small business. Discusses the characteristics and intricacies of franchising, and provides helpful information on marketing, manufacturing, organization, financial management, physical-plant layout, taxation, and other relevant issues. A basic source for the neophyte who is about to enter business.

[D-80] *How to Read the Financial Pages.* Peter Passell. New York: Warner Books, Inc., 1986.

A brief explanation of how to read the information found on the financial pages of a newspaper. The explanations include the different stock exchanges, stock-market indexes, government issues (bonds, notes, and bills), tax-exempt bonds, commodity futures, stock options, foreign exchange, prime rate, Consumer Price Index, economic indicators, and other financial and economic data reported on the financial pages.

[D-81] *How to Sell New Ideas, Your Company's and Your Own.* Eugene Raudsepp and Joseph C. Yeager. Englewood Cliffs, NJ: Prentice-Hall, Inc., 1981.

Discusses the ways of promoting innovation and inventiveness in the workplace. This book offers suggestions on how to present new ideas in a manner that will motivate the listener to give serious consideration to them. The authors also present a checklist of criteria that can be used to evaluate new ideas. There is a discussion of the reasons for resistance to new ideas and how to address this resistance. Includes a chapter on how to manage creative persons. The guidelines are applicable to products, services, management techniques, and production procedures.

[D-82] *Information and Records Management: A Decision-Maker's Guide to Systems Planning and Implementation.* Milburn D. Smith, III. Westport, CT: Quorum Books, 1986.

Focuses on the planning and implementation of a records-management system. Addresses information technology, organizing for records management, records inventory, designing a system, imaging systems, computerization, records-retention schedule, working with vendors, and other topics important to records management. Includes model forms and survey questionnaires to be used in records management.

[D-83] *In Search of Excellence: Lessons from America's Best-Run Companies.* Thomas J. Peters and Robert H. Waterman, Jr. New York: Harper & Row, Publishers, 1982.

The authors report on research that identified the management practices that differentiate the successful companies from others. The results of the study have been distilled into eight basic management practices. This is a testimonial book of practices vis-à-vis being one of theory. Its chapters give the reader reason to pause and reflect.

[D-84] *Inventor's Guide to Successful Patent Applications.* Thomas E. DeForest. Blue Ridge Summit, PA: TAB Books, 1988.

Sets forth an explanation of copyrights, patents, and trademarks. Discusses how to read a patent, conduct a patent search, write and file a patent application, and how to reply to actions of the U.S. Patent and Trademark Office. Includes copies of application forms and a schedule of the fees charged by the Office.

[D-85] *Making Mergers Work: A Guide to Managing Mergers and Acquisitions.* Price Pritchett. Homewood, IL: Dow Jones-Irwin, 1987.

Presents how to make the merger or acquisition work. Encompasses avoiding managerial mistakes, managing employees, recognizing and overcoming resistance to change, and other issues that are important to implementing the corporate merger.

[D-86] *Management.* 8th ed. Harold Koontz, Cyril O'Donnell, and Heinz Weihrich. New York: McGraw-Hill Book Company, 1984. Published every four years.

A much-heralded textbook on management that has been published in 16 foreign languages. It presents the concepts, principles, techniques, and art of managing. Coverage includes planning, organizing, staffing, and controlling. Other topics addressed are decision-making, principles of departmentalization, line and staff relationships, appraising managers, motivation, leadership techniques used to plan and control operations, and other aspects of management. Reports illustrative cases.

[D-87] *Management: Tasks, Responsibilities, Practices.* Peter F. Drucker. New York: Harper & Row, 1974.

This major treatise on management focuses on the multidimensional aspects of the art of management. The coverage includes management strategies, planning, design of managerial jobs, how to develop managers, organizational styles, tasks and strategies of top management, managing diversity, and other matters concerning the management of business organizations.

[D-88] *The Manager's Guide to Business Forecasting: How to Understand and Use Forecasts for Better Business Results.* Michael Barron and David Targett. New York: Basil Blackwell, Inc., 1985.

A textbook for business managers who need to understand forecasting but who do not need to become technical experts in it. The purpose is to prepare managers to manage forecasting. Within these pages are guidelines for developing a forecasting system; the concepts, principles, and techniques (overview) of forecasting; how to implement and monitor forecasting activities;

how to appraise forecasts; and how to use them. Thus, the purpose is to explain forecasting to the manager and make it of practical value.

[D-89] *Managing Bank Assets and Liabilities: Strategies for Risk Control and Profit.* Marcia L. Stigum and Rene O. Brauch, Jr. Homewood, IL: Dow Jones-Irwin, 1983.

Examines strategies and tactics for managing a bank's assets and liabilities. The purpose is to maximize profits while controlling liquidity and interest-rate exposure. The authors explain the types of money-market instruments, and how to calculate yields on interest-bearing securities and discount paper. They also explain the operations of banking in the United States and Eurobanking. Coverage includes forecasting of interest rates and other topics. This book may also be useful to managers of thrift institutions.

[D-90] *Managing Human Forces in Organizations.* Madeline E. Heilman and Harvey A. Hornstein. Homewood, IL: Richard D. Irwin, Inc., 1982.

Addresses the daily problems of managing people in organizations. Considers such topics as managing change, building teams, managing conflict, communication, perceiving people, motivation, leadership, exerting influence, and related subjects.

[D-91] *The New Products Handbook.* Edited by Larry Wizenberg. Homewood, IL: Dow Jones-Irwin, 1986.

Explains how to develop and manage new products. Offers guidelines for planning, developing, screening, naming, packaging, and marketing. Discusses the dos and don'ts of new-product management. Gives suggestions on how to manage new products in a competitive environment. Legal issues are also addressed.

[D-92] *Patent It Yourself.* David Pressman. Edited by Stephen Elias. Berkeley, CA: Nolo Press, 1985.

Presents step-by-step instructions for obtaining a patent. Includes the forms necessary for the pre- and post-patent process. Explains the purpose of a patent and how it works. Also explains what can and cannot be patented, the patent search, and what records should be kept by an inventor. The author discusses how to draft claims, how to maintain a patent, the licensing of inventions, and related issues. He also covers international patents.

[D-93] *Pioneering New Products: A Market Survival Guide.* Edwin E. Bobrow and Dennis W. Shafer. Homewood, IL: Dow Jones-Irwin, 1987.

Offers how-to guidelines for identifying ideas for new products and then following through the different stages of development and marketing. Discusses setting goals, establishing product objectives, designing, evaluating new products, preparing a marketing plan for a new product, and pricing. Includes a discussion of the creative process.

[D-94] *The Professional Job Changing System: World's Fastest Way to Get a Better Job.* 9th ed. Robert Jameson Gerberg. Parsippany, NJ: Performance Dynamics, Inc., 1980.

A guide to searching for a professional, managerial, or executive position. It offers valuable tips on how to proceed with the job-hunting task, explaining what to do and not to do. Covers obtaining interviews, how to conduct oneself during an interview, and how to prepare materials for presentation to prospective employers. Also provides advice on how to manage those difficult and, sometimes, embarrassing questions. Lists sample questions that are often asked during an interview. A comprehensive guide to job hunting.

[D-95] *Profit Planning for Small Business.* Robert N. Hogsett. New York: Van Nostrand Reinhold Company, 1981.

Meant for the small-business manager, this book explains how to set goals and objectives and how to establish profit targets. Covers techniques for analyzing business operations and how to interpret the results. Also discusses controls that are available to management. The value of this book is that it addresses issues form the perspective of the small business manager's needs, environment, and skills. Contains a synthesis of many techniques used by large corporations to monitor their business activities, and then reduces these to fit the reality of the small-business operation.

[D-96] *Resume Writing: A Comprehensive How-to-Do-It Guide.* 3d ed. Burdette E. Bostwick. New York: John Wiley & Sons, 1985.

Explains how to write a job résumé, especially for management positions; many of the principles are applicable generally. Discusses the types of résumés, characteristics of a good résumé, and the mechanics of preparing the résumé. Includes many examples.

[D-97] *Resumes That Get Jobs.* 4th ed. Edited by Jean Reed. Englewood Cliffs, NJ: An Arco book. Published by Prentice-Hall Press, 1986.

Explains the purpose and elements of a job résumé. Tells what to include and presents many sample résumés, which enables the reader to select the one that is closest to his/her situation. Discusses how employers read résumés. Also gives consideration to the interview process, focusing on strategy and the employer's perspective of the interview.

[D-98] *Revenue Act of 1987: Law and Explanation.* Chicago: Commerce Clearing House, 1987.

Features complete coverage of the Revenue Act of 1987, and includes the text of amended and added Internal Revenue Code sections. Also presents Controlling Committee Reports and Commerce Clearing House explanations. Contains a table of effective dates for the new provisions; summary table of Code sections that were added, amended, or repealed; and a table of Act sections that did not amend Code sections.

[D-99] *Selecting Business Software.* John W. Yu and David Harrison. Homewood, IL: Dow Jones-Irwin, 1989.

Presents a systematic method for selecting microcomputer software for the business environment. Explains how to assess your business needs for microcomputer software, and then identifies and evaluates software that meets these needs. A broad range of business software is included. These programs encompass database and file management, spreadsheets, word processing, accounting, finance, tax planning, graphics, and other elements to consider. For each of these areas, this book explains what to look for when considering a software package. Illustrative programs are described.

[D-100] *Standard & Poor's Ratings Guide: Corporate Bonds, Commercial Paper, Municipal Bonds, International Securities.* New York: McGraw-Hill Book Company, 1979.

This book reveals the processes that Standard & Poor's follows when it rates debt securities. It explains the organizational structure for implementing this task, the criteria and ratios used, and the methods followed during the financial investigations. The reader is apprised of the analytical considerations and the worksheets that are used.

There are separate sections for corporate and municipal ratings. Each section has chapters that address its different types of ratings. For corporate ratings, these include industrial bonds, public utilities, banks, finance companies, and insurance companies, among others. Municipal ratings include general obligation bonds, revenue bonds, and housing revenue bonds. The operating definitions of the ratings that are used by S&P are reported.

The scope of this book also includes international bond ratings.

[D-101] *Stock Index Futures.* Edited by Frank J. Fabozzi and Gregory M. Kipnis. Homewood, IL: Dow Jones-Irwin, 1984.

Discusses the theory and practice of stock index futures. This includes selection of a brokerage firm, types of orders, margin requirements, and explanation of the averages and indexes used by the futures-index markets, and how stock index futures are priced. In addition, there is an explanation of the risk characteristics of the major stock index futures markets, hedging, speculating, portfolio management, taxation as it relates to stock index futures, and other topics.

[D-102] *Strategic Management: Strategy Formulation and Implementation.* 3d ed. John A. Pearce, II, and Richard B. Robinson, Jr. Homewood, IL: Richard D. Irwin, 1988.

A textbook on strategic management in business. Explains the processes in the strategic management model, how to formulate the company's mission, how to analyze the competitive forces in an industry, and how these forces affect a particular company. Furthermore, the authors explain how to evaluate the multinational environment. The internal analysis of a firm, forecasting, and ways of formulating and implementing strategies are addressed. Sample cases are presented to illustrate the principles associated with strategic management of business organizations.

[D-103] *Successful Project Management: A Step-By-Step Approach with Practical Examples.* Milton D. Rosenau, Jr. New York: Lifetime Learning Publications, Inc./Van Nostrand Reinhold, 1981.

A beginner's manual for project management. Takes the reader through the project-management process in 18 steps. Organized as a how-to reference source, this book discusses the Triple Constraint concept, how to write project proposals, negotiating the project contract, project planning, estimating cost, and organizing the project. It also considers managing change during the project. This book addresses other topics, too, and it is full of examples and illustrations.

[D-104] *Tax Reform Act of 1986: Law and Controlling Committee Reports.* Chicago: Commerce Clearing House, 1986.

Contains the text of the Tax Reform Act of 1986 with the Internal Revenue Code provisions that were added, amended, or repealed by the Act. Also features Amendment Notes and the text of the Controlling Committee Reports.

[D-105] *That's A Great Idea: The New Product Handbook.* Tony Husch and Linda Foust. Oakland, CA: Gravity Publishing, 1986.

Explains how to screen and evaluate the market potential of an idea for a new product. Covers technical feasibility, building of a prototype, financing, legal protection, royalty contracts, and other matters. Most important, it discusses how to decide if the new product idea should be developed or if it should be sold.

[D-106] *Trademark Management: A Guide for Executives.* The United States Trademark Association. New York: Clark Boardman Company, 1981.

Explains the nature, purpose, and function of trademarks. Discusses how to obtain a trademark, and how to use, administer, and police it. This is a brief introduction to trademark protection.

[D-107] *Vital Business Secrets for New and Growing Companies.* L. Joseph Schmoke and Richard R. Allen. Homewood, IL: Dow Jones-Irwin, 1989.

A practical guide to starting and operating a business. The authors have addressed fundamental issues and daily problems that frequently confront entrepreneurs. Here is a practitioner's manual to which the businessperson can turn. Discusses the issues and steps involved with starting a business; where and how to get financing; how much of the company to offer investors and how to conduct oneself in a meeting with them; how to value a new business; and tips on management practices. This book also considers the pros and cons of taking a company public and how to accomplish this feat. Other topics that are addressed include how to write a business plan and what lenders look for in a financial statement. The authors explain business strategies, techniques, and insights that are important to making a business succeed.

[D-108] *What Color Is Your Parachute? A Practical Manual for Job-Hunters and Career Changers.* Richard Nelson Bolles. Berkeley, CA: Ten Speed Press, 1987. Published annually.

A guide to job hunting. Discusses how to assess oneself, set career goals, identify jobs, prepare for and gain an interview, and how to conduct oneself in an interview and conduct negotiations. Cites the titles of other books dealing with job hunting.

DICTIONARIES

[D-109] *Acronyms, Initialisms, and Abbreviations Dictionary.* 13th ed. Edited by Julie E. Towell. Detroit: Gale Research Company, 1988. Published annually.

Serves as a guide to the interpretation of acronyms, abbreviations, contractions, initialisms, and alphabetic symbols in a wide array of fields, including business. Among the terms are advertising slogans, brand names, union names, stock exchange ticker symbols, information systems and services, Moody's bond ratings, Standard & Poor's bond ratings, and many others. Includes domestic and foreign terms.

In addition to the abbreviation or acronym, entries may include the meaning, English translation (for non-English entries), designation of the foreign language to which the term belongs, location or country of origin, subject area, sponsor, and source code.

[D-110] *American National Dictionary for Information Processing Systems.* Developed by the American National Standards Committee, X3, Information Processing Systems. Homewood, IL: Dow Jones-Irwin, 1984.

A dictionary of terms and phrases used in relation to computers, data processing, word processing, data communications, and other similar fields.

[D-111] *Biographical Dictionary of American Business Leaders.* 4 vols. John N. Ingham. Westport, CT: Greenwood Press, 1983.

Contains lengthy biographical profiles of 835 American business leaders from colonial times to 1983. According to the author, the biographees were selected as being "the historically most significant business leaders." For each entry, there is given basic biographical information, a recapitulation of the biographee's business activities, and the importance of the individual to the history of American business. At the end of each biography is a bibliography of additional sources of information on the person.

[D-112] *Black's Law Dictionary.* 5th ed. Henry Campbell Black. St. Paul, MN: West Publishing Company, 1979.

This long-recognized dictionary of legal terms and phrases provides definitions of English and non-English terms and phrases that are used in American and English jurisprudence. Many of the definitions are documented by reference to court cases.

[D-113] *Brands and Their Companies.* 2 vols. 8th ed. Edited by Donna Wood. Detroit: Gale Research Company, 1990. Published annually. Formerly titled *Trade Names Dictionary.*

A dictionary containing approximately 210,000 brand names of consumer products and services. It identifies the product or service that is represented by the trade or brand name and its manufacturer. Emphasizes consumer goods, but includes some industrial and commercial items. In a separate yellow-page section are the addresses and telephone numbers of the companies. The term "brand name" is used synonymously with "trade name" and "trademark." For a composite list of trade names used by a company, see *Companies and Their Brands* [D-146].

[D-114] *Business Acronyms.* Edited by Julie E. Towell. Detroit: Gale Research Company, 1988.

A dictionary of acronyms, abbreviations, and initialisms that are used in the business world. Includes business terms extracted from the *Acronyms, Initialisms, and Abbreviations Dictionary* [D-109] as well as entries taken from other sources. Within *Business Acronyms* are terms used in accounting, advertising, banking, finance, investments, management, marketing, economics, real estate, and other business-related areas. Stock exchange symbols, NASDAQ symbols, and stock and bond ratings are listed. An entry may include the meaning, English translation (for non-English terms), language to which the term belongs, location or country of origin, subject, sponsoring organization, and source code.

[D-115] *Computer Dictionary.* 4th ed. Charles J. Sippl. Indianapolis, IN: Howard W. Sams and Company, 1985.

A comprehensive dictionary of computing terms and phrases, some brief and others more extensive. Illustrations and examples are used when necessary. Photographs and diagrams are used to clarify the meanings.

[D-116] *A Dictionary of Arbitration and Its Terms.* Edited by Katharine Seide. Published for the Eastman Library of the American Arbitration Association. Dobbs Ferry, NY: Oceana Publications, Inc., 1970.

This publication serves several purposes. It contains extended definitions of terms and phrases associated with the arbitration process. As such, it resembles an encyclopedia. It also provides practice and procedural rules for arbitration proceedings and the texts of the Uniform Arbitration Act, United States Arbitration Act, and several international arbitration conventions. The reader is cautioned that these texts may have been amended since the publication of this book in 1970.

[D-117] *Dictionary of Business and Economics.* Revised and expanded ed. Christine Ammer and Dean S. Ammer. New York: The Free Press, 1984.

A dictionary of terms and phrases used in business and economics. Includes charts, graphs, and tables to illustrate the definitions. A useful and recognized dictionary in its field.

[D-118] *Dictionary of Computers, Data Processing, and Telecommunications.* Jerry M. Rosenberg. New York: John Wiley & Sons, 1984.

A dictionary of concise definitions of terminology used in the fields of computers, data processing, and telecommunications. Specifies the relationship between computers, data processing, and telecommunications. Contains an appendix that provides the Spanish and French equivalents of the terms defined in this dictionary.

[D-119] *Dictionary of Finance.* Eitan A. Avneyon. Jerusalem, Israel: G. G. The Jerusalem Publishing House, Ltd., 1988. Available through Macmillan Publishing Company.

Includes the definitions of terms and phrases that are used in banking, marketing, insurance, accounting, economics, public and private financing, investments, and other related areas. Graphs are used, where appropriate, to enhance the definitions.

[D-120] *Dictionary of Finance and Investment Terms.* John Downes and Jordan E. Goodman. Woodbury, NY: Barron's Educational Series, Inc., 1985.

Defines the terminology used in finance and investments. Also includes terms from business law, accounting, economics, taxation, and other related fields. Provides abbreviations and acronyms that are associated with the world of finance and investment.

[D-121] *A Dictionary of Minicomputing and Microcomputing.* Philip E. Burton. New York: Garland Publishing Company, 1982.

Defines computer terms and phrases. In addition to the general dictionary section, contains specialized appendices for terms associated with the areas of structured programming, PASCAL, magnetic-bubble memory technology, printers, automatic control, multiprocessing, data communications, and magnetic recording and storage technology. When necessary, illustrations and examples are used.

[D-122] *Dictionary of Occupational Titles.* 4th ed. Washington, DC: U.S. Employment and Training Administration, 1977. There is a 1986 supplement to this edition. Available from the U.S. Government Printing Office.

Provides definitions for about 20,000 occupations, with descriptions of basic job tasks, purpose of the work, equipment and materials used, products made or services rendered, and other related information.

The occupations are organized according to a coded occupational classification system. This is a comprehensive collection of job occupations. It is systematically organized and offers brief, single-paragraph definitions.

[D-123] ***Dictionary of Real Estate Terms.*** 2d ed. Jack P. Friedman, Jack C. Harris, and J. Bruce Lindeman. New York: Barron's Educational Series, Inc., 1987.

A pocket-size dictionary of real-estate terminology, including terms used in real-estate financing, appraisal, investment, brokerage laws, architecture, planning, and structure. Contains formulas that are used in financing and those that are used for measurement purposes. Pictorial examples, illustrating numerous terms and concepts, are abundant. A directory of national real-estate organizations, with their addresses, appears under "N." This is more than a dictionary—it approaches being a handbook on real estate.

[D-124] ***The Dow Jones-Irwin Dictionary of Financial Planning.*** Robert W. Richards. Homewood, IL: Dow Jones-Irwin, 1986.

Contains definitions of terms and phrases associated with personal financial planning. Provides more than 3,000 definitions used with insurance, home mortgages, retirement planning, income taxes, investments, real estate, and other areas.

[D-125] ***Illustrated Encyclopedic Dictionary of Real Estate.*** 2d ed. Jerome S. Gross. Englewood Cliffs, NJ: Prentice-Hall, Inc., 1978.

A dictionary of real estate terms that is distinguished by two principal features: (1) many illustrations that support narrative definitions, and (2) illustrations of both operational forms used in real estate offices and legal forms. Also contains a directory of national organizations in the real estate field.

To help the real estate professional, there is a cross-section drawing that shows the components of a house. Each part is numbered and named. Since this dictionary was published in 1978, caution should be exercised concerning the possible obsolescence in the legal forms and laws contained in its pages. Remember too that real estate legal requirements may vary by state.

[D-126] ***The International Who's Who.*** London: Europa Publications Limited, 1988. Published annually.

A biographical dictionary that presents profiles of notable persons from around the world and in most areas of endeavor. The biographical sketches include the biographee's nationality, birth date, education, names of parents, marriage, career information, awards, publications, office address, home address, telephone number (home and/or office), and other biographical data.

[D-127] ***The New Palgrave: A Dictionary of Economics.*** 4 vols. Edited by John Eatwell, Murray Milgate, and Peter Newman. New York: Stockton Press, 1987.

This publication is a successor to the esteemed *Dictionary of Political Economy* that was edited by R. H. Inglis. Its history began in 1894, and it has undergone successive editions which included the interim title *Palgrave's Dictionary of Political Economy* (1923–1926). This work has grown through the decades until now it contains nearly 2,000 signed entries that have been authored by more than 900 contributors.

The New Palgrave is an encyclopedic dictionary with extensive explanations that often occupy several pages and which include bibliographies. Its scope encompasses the spectrum of economic thought, and its treatment includes theoretical and applied economics. Among the entries are biographies of 700 major economists that are intermingled with the nonbiographical entries. Arranged in alphabetical order, the subjects are first synthesized in a "List of Entries" for easy identification. Many of the treatises contain formulas and graphs. Here is a classical "dictionary" of economic thought that has been modernized in the recent edition. If the reader is interested in topics that appeared in earlier editions but have been dropped, it is possible to refer to them.

[D-128] *Street Talk in Real Estate.* Bill W. West and Richard L. Dickinson. Alameda, CA: Unique Publishing Company, 1987.

Explains the meaning of terminology commonly used in real estate. There is an emphasis on brokerage and finance. Includes slang and acronyms in the real estate world. The definitions are concise and clearly written.

[D-129] *Who's Who in America.* Wilmette, IL: Marquis Who's Who/Macmillan Directory Division, 1988. Published biennially.

A biographical dictionary of notable persons in the United States. Also includes leading government officials in Canada and Mexico. The biographical sketches include occupation, birth date, names of parents, marriage, education, career data, creative works, civic and political activities, military service, awards, home address, office address, and other biographical information. Also includes listings of retirees, a necrology, and regional and topical listings.

[D-130] *Who's Who in Finance and Industry.* Wilmette, IL: Marquis Who's Who/Macmillan Directory Division, 1987. Published biennially.

A biographical dictionary of notable persons in finance and industry. Biographees include corporate executives and persons from fields related to business, such as professional and trade associations, business researchers, stock exchanges, labor unions, government agencies, and other organizations. The biographical profiles include occupation, home and business addresses, date and place of birth, parents' names, marriage data, education, professional certifications, professional memberships, avocations, and other descriptive information.

[D-131] *Who's Who in the World.* Wilmette, IL: Marquis Who's Who/Macmillan Directory Division, 1988. Published biennially.

Publishes biographical sketches of internationally notable persons who have reference value. The biographees are from nations throughout the world and have achieved in one or more of many different areas of endeavor. Sketches report occupation, birth data, parents' names, education, marriage data, career information, civic and political activities, military record, awards, political affiliation, home and office addresses, and other biographical details.

[D-132] *Words of Wall Street: 2,000 Investment Terms Defined.* Allan H. Pessin and Joseph A. Ross. Homewood, IL: Dow Jones-Irwin, 1983.

Provides explanations of terms and expressions used in the securities industry. Includes "Table of Cross References" that contains synonyms, abbreviations, and terms. Following these are the glossary entries that explain their meanings. This is a source of brief definitions of investment terms.

DIRECTORIES

[D-133] *American Export Register.* 2 vols. New York: Thomas International Publishing Company, 1988. Published annually.

A directory of American exporting firms. Lists companies both alphabetically and by product or service category. Information includes name of company, address, telephone number, cable address, telex number, TWX number, name of person in charge of export sales, products or services offered for exporting, world market areas served, and an indication of a company's interest in developing new overseas markets.

The *American Export Register* indexes product and service categories in eight languages (Arabic, Chinese, English, French, German, Japanese, Portuguese, and Spanish). Lists the addresses and telephone numbers of U.S. and Foreign Commercial Service district offices. Also lists the U.S. embassies, missions, consulates general, and consulates abroad in addition to foreign embassies, consulates general, and consulates in the U.S. Cites services available to American exporters from foreign governments.

Identifies addresses and telephone numbers of World Trade Center Clubs, local governments and organizations that assist businesses with their importing/exporting activities, and U.S. banks with international offices. Also listed are custom-house brokers, U.S. port authorities, overseas ports, steamship lines, international freight forwarders, and air cargo carriers.

[D-134] *America's Corporate Families.* Vol. 1. Parsippany, NJ: Dun's Marketing Services, 1989. Published annually.

A directory of U.S. parent companies and their U.S. divisions and subsidiaries, arranged by corporate family. Provides a cross-reference index between parent companies and their subsidiaries. For a parent company to be included, its net worth must be at least $500,000. The descriptive profile of each company reports location; names of officers; nature of business; names of its accounting firm, bank, and legal counsel; sales volume, and other information. Businesses are also listed by SIC group and geographically. Only corporations that operate from at least two locations and have one or more subsidiaries are included.

[D-135] *America's Corporate Families and International Affiliates.* Vol. 2. Parsippany, NJ: Dun's Marketing Services, 1989. Published annually.

A directory of U.S. corporations and their foreign subsidiaries, arranged by corporate family. Also lists foreign parent companies with their U.S. subsidiaries. Excludes companies that are based either exclusively in the U.S. or totally outside of the U.S. Provides a cross-reference index between subsidiaries and their parent companies. Publishes a profile of corporations that reports the location, telephone number, nature of business, officers, sales volume, export/import activity, and other descriptive information for each.

[D-136] *AT&T Toll-Free 800 Business Directory.* Bridgewater, NJ: AT&T, 1988. Published annually.

A national directory of AT&T toll-free "800" business telephone numbers. These are the numbers assigned for business-to-business use, not for individual consumers. (Note: For the latter, see *AT&T Toll-Free 800 Consumer Directory,* [D-137].) The information also includes the regions, states, and area codes from which a number can be dialed.

[D-137] *AT&T Toll-Free 800 Consumer Directory.* Bridgewater, NJ: AT&T, 1988. Published annually.

A national directory of AT&T toll-free "800" telephone numbers for consumer use. It does not include business-to-business "800" numbers. (Note: for the latter, see *AT&T Toll-Free 800 Business Directory,* [D-136].) The information also includes the regions, states, and area codes from which a number can be dialed.

[D-138] *Best's Agents Guide to Life Insurance Companies.* Oldwick, NJ: A. M. Best Company, 1987. Published annually.

A condensation of *Best's Insurance Reports: Life-Health* [D-140]. It is a guide to life-health insurers in the U.S. For each company, it provides the address, telephone number, names of selected principal officers, financial statistics, states in which the company is licensed to do business, Best's rating, and Best's financial-size category.

[D-139] *Best's Flitcraft Compend.* Oldwick, NJ: A. M. Best Company, 1988. Published annually.

A guide to life insurance policies. Profiles the life insurance products of individual life insurance carriers. Includes a broad array of descriptive data that includes policy provisions, premiums, limitations, restrictions, cash values, history of dividend payouts, substandard (special class) rates, loan values, and other information. Reports on Universal Life plans, annuities, and settlement options. Facilitates comparisons between companies.

[D-140] *Best's Insurance Reports.* Oldwick, NJ: A. M. Best Company, 1988. Published annually and updated via newsletters and monthly journals.

A guide to the insurance industry. It comprises three volumes: (1) *Property-Casualty*, (2) *Life-Health*, and (3) *International Edition*. Presents a detailed description of each insurer that includes its address, telephone number, names of officers and directors, history of the company, assets and liabilities, operating ratios, Best's ratings for profitability and stability, financial-size indicator, and other financial statistics.

[D-141] *Best's Key Rating Guide: Property-Casualty.* Oldwick, NJ: A. M. Best Company, 1987. Published annually.

A condensation of *Best's Insurance Reports: Property-Casualty* [D-140], this is a guide to property-casualty insurers in the U.S. For each company it reports the address, telephone number, name of the president, and the principal types of policies sold. Also summarizes financial and operating data relevant to premiums written, operating income, profitability tests, leverage tests, and liquidity tests. Reports Best's rating and the financial-size indicator.

[D-142] *Business Publication Rates and Data.* 2 vols. Wilmette, IL: Standard Rate and Data Service, 1988. Published monthly.

A directory of domestic and international business publications, also including health care, education, art, music, government, and law. Coverage includes magazines, trade newspapers, direct-response advertising, and other forms of business publications that carry advertisements. Profiles the publication in terms of its editorial policy, circulation size, advertising contract terms, advertising rates, mechanical requirements pertaining to the printing process, deadlines for submitting ads, names of principal advertising executives, address, telephone number, and other relevant information.

[D-143] *The Career Guide: Dun's Employment Opportunities Directory.* Parsippany, NJ: Dun's Marketing Services, 1988. Published annually.

An employment guide for entry-level positions and for experienced job seekers who want to change jobs. Designed primarily for persons with a college education. Contains profiles of 5,000 employers in the U.S., including businesses, financial institutions, non-profit organizations, and government agencies.

The profiles report the employer's name, address, telephone number, person to contact about employment, description of the firm and its products or services, job opportunities, hiring practices, benefits, and career-development programs. Employers are listed alphabetically, geographically, by industry, and by discipline within each state. Also provides a directory of private placement firms. Includes articles on how to write a résumé, conduct an interview, and negotiate a salary.

[D-144] *The College Blue Book: Occupational Education.* 21st ed. New York: Macmillan Publishing Company, 1987. Published biennially.

A profile of occupational education programs organized alphabetically by state. Also lists instructional centers by program area. The profiles indicate the address, telephone number, person to contact, specific occupational programs offered, admission requirements, and other related information.

[D-145] *Community Publication Rates and Data.* Wilmette, IL: Standard Rate and Data Service, 1988. Published semiannually.

A directory of community newspapers and shopping guides. Most are published weekly, but some have other schedules. Describes each publication by reporting its advertising rates, frequency of publication, circulation data, required mechanical measurements, deadlines for submitting ads, names of key executives, address, telephone number, and other related information.

[D-146] *Companies and Their Brands.* 2 vols. 8th ed. Edited by Donna Wood. Detroit: Gale Research Company, 1990. Published annually. Formerly titled *Trade Names Dictionary: Company Index.*

Identifies the types of products or services of various companies and the trade name of each type. Along with this composite list is each firm's address and telephone number. The approximately 40,000 companies are arranged alphabetically by company name. A companion publication to *Brands and Their Companies* [D-113].

[D-147] *The Compu-Mark Directory of U.S. Trademarks.* 7 vols. Washington, DC: Compu-Mark U.S., 1988. Published annually with updates in March, June, and September.

A directory of trademarks pending, registered, renewed, or abandoned with the U.S. Patent and Trademark Office. Reports the name of the trademark, its owner, the date and page number of the *Official Gazette* issue in which it was published, the registration number for registered trademarks, and the serial number for pending trademarks. It does not include graphic illustrations.

[D-148] *Computers and Computing Information Resources Directory.* Edited by Martin Connors. Detroit: Gale Research Company, 1987. Revised every one or two years.

A comprehensive directory of print and nonprint sources of information on all aspects of computers, computing, and data processing. It is a guide to finding sources of computer-related information. These sources include user groups, trade and professional associations, consultants, university computer facilities and research organizations, trade shows, professional exhibits, computer-related association conventions, online database vendors and teleprocessing networks worldwide. The sources also include special libraries and information centers with an emphasis on computers or computer science, as well as journals, newsletters, and computer-oriented directories. Each entry contains the name, address, telephone number, purpose or activities, and other descriptive information for each source. Also contains a directory of some persons in the computer-information field, listing their addresses and telephone numbers.

[D-149] *Congressional Staff Directory.* 30th ed. Edited by Charles B. Brownson. Mount Vernon, VA: Congressional Staff Directory, Ltd., 1988. Published annually.

This is primarily a directory of the staff who work in the offices of the U.S. legislative branch. Includes the offices of senators, representatives, and legislative committees and subcommittees. Provides titles, addresses, telephone numbers, and some biographical sketches. Also reports the addresses, telephone numbers, biographical sketches, and committee assignments of members of Congress. Includes the names and telephone numbers of key personnel in the Library of Congress, General Accounting Office, and other offices.

[D-150] *Consultants and Consulting Organizations Directory.* 2 vols. 9th ed. Edited by Janice McLean. Detroit: Gale Research Company, 1989. Published biennially.

A directory of firms and independent persons who consult. These consultants are profiled by broad subject areas and indexed according to geographical location, subject (field of consulting activity), industries served, personal names, and composite alphabetical listing. The descriptions include address, telephone number, name and title of principal executives, type of consulting service, year founded, and other information. Through its arrangement, a consultant can be identified in the field of interest.

[D-151] *Consumer Magazine and Agri-Media Rates and Data.* Wilmette, IL: Standard Rate and Data Service, 1988. Published monthly.

A directory of consumer magazines and consumer card decks serving various fields. Contains a description of each magazine or card deck that includes advertising rates, printing requirements, names of principal advertising officials, circulation statistics, publication schedule, deadlines for submitting ads, and other information. Also publishes similar descriptions for farm publications and farm direct-response advertising media. Reports demographic data on consumer-purchasing patterns.

[D-152] *Consumer Sourcebook.* 5th ed. Edited by Kay Gill and Robert Wilson. Detroit: Gale Research Company, 1988.

A directory of private organizations and governmental agencies at all levels of government that either advocate and protect consumer rights or provide information, usually free of charge, that assists consumers with their rights. Cites addresses and telephone numbers and, in some cases, names of contact persons. Lists more than 6,200 consumer information sources that have been organized in 26 subject categories that include health care, food and drug safety, insurance, aging, child services, energy, product safety, utilities, and other consumer-interest fields. Also offers guidelines for protection in selected areas of consumer activity.

Consumer's Resource Handbook. 4th ed. Washington, DC: U.S. Office of Consumer Affairs, 1988. Published biennially.
See "Government Documents," [D-344].

[D-153] *The Corporate Finance Sourcebook.* Wilmette, IL: National Register Publishing Company, 1988. Published annually.

A directory for sources of capital funding, including firms and individuals who provide financial and management services. Provides descriptive listings of venture-capital firms, major private lenders, firms that offer commercial finance and factoring, the 100 largest commercial banks with the services they offer corporations, foreign investment banks, leasing companies, securities analysts, CPA firms, and other types of organizations that offer these services. The profiles include the names and telephone numbers of individuals, and they specify the preferred investment fields, range of investments, loan criteria, and other relevant information.

[D-154] *Corporate Technology Directory.* 4 vols. 3d ed. Wellesley, MA: Corporate Technology Information Services, Inc., 1988. Published annually.

Lists public and private U.S. firms and U.S. operating units of foreign companies that manufacture or develop high-technology products. Encompassed within the array of high-technology fields are advanced materials, automation, biotech, chemicals, computers, software, energy, manufacturing, medical, pharmaceuticals, telecommunications, and others. Company profiles include company name, other or former company name(s), address, telephone number, telex, FAX, ownership of the company, ticker symbol, year founded, description of the business activity, annual sales revenue, number of employees, names of executives with their titles and areas of responsibility, product descriptions, SIC codes, detailed Corp Tech product codes, number of Small Business Innovation Research Awards received, and other information. Through the elaborate indexing system, companies can be identified by name, location, parent name, and their high-tech products.

[D-155] *CPC Annual.* 3 vols. Bethlehem, PA: College Placement Council, 1987–1988. Published annually.

A directory that explains the job-hunting process and prints descriptions of companies, not-for-profit organizations, and federal agencies that employ college graduates. The three volumes are: (1) *A Guide to Career Planning, The Job Search, Graduate School, and Work-Related Education,* (2) *A Directory of Employment Opportunities for College Graduates in Administration, Business, and Other Nontechnical Options,* and (3) *A Directory of Employment Opportunities for College Graduates in Engineering, Sciences, the Computer Field, and Other Technical Options.*

  The profiles provide information on employers and includes the nature of their business, occupations for which they hire, address, telephone number, contact person, qualifications, training programs, benefits, and other similar information. There is also an index of recruiting employers arranged by occupational category.

Datapro Directory of Microcomputer Software. 3 vols. Edited by J. Richard Peck. Delran, NJ: Datapro Research Corporation, 1988. Updated monthly.
See "Loose-leaf Materials," [D-387].

[D-156] *Data Sources: Data Comm/Telecomm.* Vol. 3. New York: Ziff-Davis Publishing Company, 1989. Published annually.

A guide to data communications and telecommunications hardware. Provides a directory of data/telecommunications company profiles. Gives a description of each product. These products include network-processor/network-management systems, modems, multiplexors, emulation/conversion equipment, security equipment, PBX/CBX equipment, telephone call-accounting systems, facsimile machines, teleconferencing systems and services, and other telecommunication equipment. Some of the data are displayed in charts that facilitate product comparisons.

[D-157] *Data Sources: Hardware.* Vol. 1. New York: Ziff-Davis Publishing Company, 1989. Published annually.

A guide to computer systems (supercomputers and mainframes, mid-range systems, microcomputers, portable computers, and specialized systems); graphics equipment; printers/COM/card/paper tape equipment; disk/tape/memory equipment; terminals, monitors, teleprinters, and scanners; controllers, PC boards, microcomputer accessories; and media, supplies, support, and power equipment. Profiles each product with appropriate descriptive data. Much of the data are presented in a chart format to permit making product comparisons. Also describes the services of computer maintenance companies. Includes a directory of hardware manufacturers with a profile of each company.

[D-158] *Data Sources: Software.* Vol. 2. New York: Ziff-Davis Publishing Company, 1989. Published annually.

A guide to systems and applications software arranged by field and containing a description of each package. Provides hardware and system requirements, description of functions, and the price. Contains a directory of software companies that profiles each company and includes its location and names of principal officers.

[D-159] *Direct Mail List Rates and Data.* Wilmette, IL: Standard Rate and Data Service, 1988. Updated bimonthly in addition to twice-monthly supplements.

A directory of direct-mail-list sources. Includes owners, compilers, and brokers of business, consumer, and farm lists. Profiles each by reporting the types of lists available, price, credit policy, source of a list, delivery schedule, names of key executives, address, telephone number, and other information.

This directory also cites providers of support services for direct-mail operations. These include consultants, mail preparation, supplies, list maintenance, premium fulfillments, and other services. Contains the names and descriptions of firms that provide business co-op mailing and package insert programs.

Directories in Print. 2 vols. 6th ed. Edited by Julie E. Towell. Detroit: Gale Research Company, 1989. Published annually. Formerly entitled *Directory of Directories.* See "Bibliographies," [D-35].

[D-160] *Directory of American Research and Technology: Organizations Active in Product Development for Business.* 22d ed. New York: R. R. Bowker Company, 1987. Updated annually. (Note: Published prior to the 20th ed. under the title *Industrial Research Laboratories of the United States.*)

A comprehensive guide to research and development facilities that have a focus on commercial applications and that are being operated by corporations and other nongovernment entities. Provides a listing of more than 11,000 R&D centers that reports for each the name, address, and telephone number of the parent company, names of chief officers and principal research personnel, R&D activity fields, size of the professional staff and the scientific disciplines represented by doctorates, and other related information. Subsidiaries are also listed. A classification index enables the reader to identify facilities by R & D activity area.

[D-161] *Directory of Corporate Affiliations.* 2 vols. Wilmette, IL: National Register Publishing Company, 1989. Published annually. Updated bimonthly.

A directory of U.S. parent corporations. Includes information on corporate acquisitions, mergers, and name changes. Offers a cross-index between parent companies and their divisions, affiliates, and subsidiaries. Describes each company by including its location; names of officers and boards of directors; financial information; data on its divisions, affiliates, and subsidiaries; and other information.

[D-162] *Directory of Executive Recruiters.* 16th ed. Edited by James H. Kennedy. Fitzwilliam, NH: Consultant News, 1985. Published annually.

A directory of more than 2,500 executive search firms. These are executive recruiters who are paid by management, not job hunters. Provides the name of the executive search firm, address, contact person, field of specialization, and other information.

Directory of Federal Laboratory and Technology Resources: A Guide to Services, Facilities, and Expertise. Center for the Utilization of Federal Technology. Springfield, VA: National Technical Information Service, 1986. Published biennially. See "Government Documents," [D-346].

[D-163] *Directory of Fee-Based Information Services.* Compiled and edited by Helen P. Burwell. Houston, TX: Burwell Enterprises, 1988. Published annually.

A directory of information specialists who provide their services for a fee. Includes information brokers, freelance librarians, fee-based services of public and academic libraries, and information packagers. Listing encompasses specialists in the U.S. and abroad. Profiles of entries include the name of the firm or individual, address, telephone number, telex and FAX numbers, electronic mail service identification number, name of contact person, subject specialization areas, and types of information services provided (e.g., research, online retrieval, and report writing). Each profile concludes with a descriptive summary.

[D-164] *Directory of Manufacturers' Sales Agencies.* Laguna Hills, CA: Manufacturers' Agents National Association, 1989. Published annually.

Here is a directory of sales agencies that represent manufacturers. It is the membership directory of the Manufacturers' Agents National Association. Organized in three sections; namely, alphabetically by agency name, by state, and by product classification, the reader can identify sales agencies. Profiles of these agencies include address, telephone number, kinds of products being sold, sales territory, name of key officials, warehousing facilities, size of sales staff, and location of branch offices. This directory (1989 edition) includes articles that discuss how to find the right sales agency, descriptions of sales agencies, and articles that cover other topics concerning the relationship between the manufacturer and the sales agency.

[D-165] *Directory of Obsolete Securities.* Boca Raton, FL: Financial Information, Inc., 1988. Published annually.

A cumulative directory of banks and publicly-held companies whose original corporate identities have been lost due to mergers, acquisitions, name changes, bankruptcy, reorganization, dissolution, or charter cancellation. The period of coverage for this edition is cumulative for 1927 to 1987.

Each profile explains (whenever possible) how the identity was lost, the new name (if there is one), the year of the identity loss or change, and whether the stock still has value or if there is any remaining stockholder's equity.

[D-166] *The Directory of Real Estate Investors.* Wilmette, IL: National Register Publishing Company, 1988. Published annually.

An international directory of brokers, investors, and developers of commercial property who have at least $1 million of equity funds to invest. Reports the kind of income-producing properties in which they are interested and the geographic region(s) of their preference. Each company is also described by reporting the address, telephone number, names of contact persons, size of portfolio, investment structure, total funds available, and other relevant information.

[D-167] *Directory of Special Libraries and Information Centers.* 3 vols. 11th ed. Edited by Brigitte T. Darnay. Detroit: Gale Research Company, 1988. Published approximately every two years.

A guide to U.S., Canadian, and other large foreign special information collections that are maintained by special and general libraries, research libraries, company libraries, university libraries, archives, information centers, government agencies, nonprofit organizations, and others.

Each of these special collections is profiled alphabetically, reporting the name of the parent or sponsoring organization, name of the library or information center, principal subject or kind of material in the collection, address, telephone number, name of person in charge, special collections in the holdings, special services provided, and other relevant features. The profiles also indicate whether outsiders may use the special collections.

Subject, geographic, and personnel indexes are provided to access these centers. Augmenting this directory is a five-volume *Subject Directory of Special Libraries and Information Centers* in which the profiles are presented in subject order.

[D-168] *Directory of Statistical Microcomputer Software.* Wayne A. Woodward, Alan C. Elliot, Henry L. Gray, and Douglas C. Matlock, New York: Marcel Dekker, Inc., 1988. Published annually.

Profiles more than 200 statistical software programs that run on microcomputers. These profiles give the program's name; vendor's name, address, telephone number, and contact person; configurations supported; program description; type of program; purpose for which the program was designed; program features; whether it is menu driven; kinds of documentation available; graphic features; data management features; types of statistical functions performed; and other information. Summarized in table form are the various statistical functions and the software packages that support each function.

[D-169] *Directory of United States Importers: 1986–1987.* New York: Journal of Commerce, 1986. Published biennially.

A directory of importers with a profile of each firm. Cites name, address, telephone and telex numbers, cable address, year established, names of principal officers, custom-house broker, port of entry, products imported, and the source nations for the imports. Reviews the U.S. Customs Service regulations and importing procedures. Lists products that are imported and their respective importers. Also cites U.S. and foreign embassies and consulates, international banks in the U.S., trade associations, and ports of the world.

[D-170] *Directory of U.S. Labor Organizations.* Edited by Courtney D. Gifford. Washington, DC: Bureau of National Affairs, 1986. Published biennially.

Contains a listing of U.S. labor organizations, with the addresses and telephone numbers of their national headquarters and the names of national officers, average membership size, frequency of national conventions, names of official publications, historical notes, and other information. Also includes information on the organizational structure of the AFL-CIO and the addresses and telephone numbers of its offices and the names of officials.

   This directory reports sundry labor statistics and contains a glossary of labor-union abbreviations with their definitions.

[D-171] *Dun & Bradstreet Reference Book.* 4 vols. Murray Hill, NJ: Dun & Bradstreet Credit Services, 1988. Updated bimonthly.

Available only to D&B subscribers. Lists, by state and city, public and private U.S. and Canadian firms with the SIC number for their line of business, telephone number, branches, and codes that indicate the Estimated Financial Strength and the Composite Credit Appraisal for each company. This is one part of Dun & Bradstreet's "Business Information Reports" service.

[D-172] *Dun's Business Rankings.* Parsippany, NJ: Dun's Marketing Services, 1987. Published annually.

A directory of U.S. public and private businesses that ranks companies by sales volume and/or number of employees. Rankings are at the national and state levels and by industry. There is a composite ranking for public and private firms and then separate rankings for each of these categories. Includes the names of chief executive officers, sales executives, finance executives, and purchasing officers.

[D-173] *Encyclopedia of Associations. Vol. 1. National Organizations of the U.S.* Edited by Karin E. Koek, Susan B. Martin, and Annette Novallo. Detroit: Gale Research Company, 1989. Published annually.

A directory of national and international organizations headquartered in the U.S. that have voluntary memberships. Includes trade, labor, business, and commercial organizations in addition to those in other fields. Encompasses advertising, building industries, chemicals, consulting, engineering, finance, industrial equipment, manufacturers' representatives, real estate, sales, warehousing, and others. The organization profiles disclose the organization's name, acronym, address, telephone number, name and title of chief operating official, founding date, membership size, purpose, size of operating budget, computer-based services that are offered, official publications, date and location of annual convention, and other descriptive information.

[D-174] *Encyclopedia of Information Systems and Services.* 3 vols. 9th ed. Edited by Amy Lucas. Detroit: Gale Research Company, 1988. Published annually. Vol. 1: *United States Listings.*Vol. 2: *International Listings.*Vol. 3: *Indexes.*

These three volumes are a guide to organizations, systems, and services in the electronic-information industry. The entries are of those who produce, distribute, access, or service this industry. Descriptive listings include those organizations, systems, and services that are of a regional, national, or international scope. The type of entries include database producers, online companies, CD-ROM publishers, videotex/teletex information services, information networks, information-retrieval software, service companies, trade associations in the information industry, and other related entries. Profiles report name, address, telephone number, name of administrator, descriptions of systems and services provided, types of information stored, description of computer-based products and services, listing of user groups, and other information for each listing. This is one of the major sources for identifying vendors in the electronic-information industry in the U.S. and abroad.

[D-175] *Exporters Directory/U.S. Buying Guide: 1987–1988.* 2 vols. New York: Journal of Commerce, 1986. Published biennially.

A directory of American exporters. Lists firms alphabetically and by product. Also contains a brand-name index. Profiles of exporting firms include name, address, telephone number, telex number, cable address, names of key officers, number of employees, year established, ports of exit, products exported, countries served, and international freight forwarder. Also describes export-related services provided by the U.S. Department of Commerce. Lists U.S. and foreign embassies and consulates, international banks in the U.S., trade associations, and ports of the world.

[D-176] *Fax Phone Book.* Deerfield Beach, FL: Dial-A-Fax Directories Corp., 1988. Published annually.

A directory of fax phone numbers for companies, arranged alphabetically by state and Canadian province. Entries include the company's name, address, voice phone number, and fax phone number. The listing also includes public fax-service bureaus. Information is provided on dialing international fax phone numbers.

[D-177]   *Federal Staff Directory.* 7th ed. Edited by Charles B. Brownson and Anna L. Brownson. Mt. Vernon, VA: Congressional Staff Directory, Ltd., 1988. Published annually. Updated between editions by the *CSD Federal Executive Update.*

Lists key executives and their staff assistants in the executive branch of the federal government. Includes their names, titles, addresses, and telephone numbers. Prints selected biographical profiles. Entries are from the Office of the President; cabinet departments; independent agencies; and quasi-official, non-government, and international organizations. Serves as a telephone directory for the executive branch.

[D-178]   *The Foundation Directory.* 11th ed. Edited by Loren Renz and Stan Olson. New York: Foundation Center, 1987. Published biennially.

A directory of foundations and their activities. Lists foundations alphabetically by state. Reports for each foundation its address, telephone number, purpose, types of projects funded, financial data, application information, who to write, and the names of officers and trustees. Foundations are indexed by subject area of giving, geographical location, type of support awarded, and alphabetically. Specifies the geographical scope of a foundation's activities.

[D-179]   *Franchise Opportunities Handbook.* 21st ed. Andrew Kostecka. Washington, DC: U.S. Government Printing Office, 1988. Published annually.

A directory of firms that offer business franchises. The description of each company states its address, name of franchising contact person, description of the business, number of franchisees, equity capital required, financial and managerial assistance available, and the training provided to franchisees.

The author discusses the issues associated with franchising, including risks, guidelines when considering a franchise, checklist for evaluating a franchise, and the code of ethics of the International Franchise Association. Lists field offices of the Minority Business Development Agency, U.S. International Trade Administration, and the Small Business Administration. Cites addresses and telephone numbers of these offices.

[D-180]   *Gale Directory of Publications and Broadcast Media.* 3 vols. 122nd edition. Edited by Donald P. Boyden and John Krol. Detroit: Gale Research Company, 1990. Published annually. Former titles have been *Gale Directory of Publications*, *Ayer Directory of Publications*, and *IMS Directory of Publications*.

A guide to newspapers, magazines, journals, and other related publications in addition to television stations, cable systems, and radio stations. Includes those newspapers, magazines, journals, and related publications of the United States, Canada, and Puerto Rico that publish at least four issues per year. Excludes most in-house publications and those of primary and secondary schools and houses of worship. Reports limited descriptive information on communities in which the publications are located/circulated.

Information for each print publication includes address; telephone number; fax number; names of the publisher, editor, and national advertising manager; base advertising rate; circulation; subscription price; frequency of publication; and other descriptive information. Contains a classification index of the publications.

Profiles of radio stations, television stations, and cable systems report address, telephone number, fax number, station format, call letters/frequency/channel/cable company name, network affiliations, owner/operator, ADI, operating hours, advertising rates, and other information.

Volume Three contains maps of the United States, individual states, Canadian provinces, and Puerto Rico. This volume provides sixteen indexes to the print publications according to particular type or subject, and one index to radio stations by format (e.g., adult programs, classical music, etc.). It also cites the names, addresses, and telephone numbers of feature editors of daily newspapers that have a circulation of at least 50,000.

[D-181] *The GreenBook: International Directory of Marketing Research Companies and Services.* New York: American Marketing Association, New York Chapter, 1987. Published annually.

A directory of firms in 53 countries that provide market research services. For each company it reports address, telephone number, names of principal officers, and a description of services offered. The companies are indexed by service, geographically, and alphabetically. Some of the services included are advertising research, concept development and testing, consumer research, idea generation, interviewing services, name development, package development, and product testing.

[D-182] *How to Find Business Intelligence in Washington.* 9th ed. Washington, DC: Washington Researchers Publishing, 1988.

This directory is a guide to the business-related data that are to be found in federal offices and Washington-based organizations. Within its pages are the names, addresses, and telephone numbers of offices and persons with expertise, the latter identified by their topical specialty. Reports the kinds of industry data that are collected by each department or agency. Lists published and unpublished sources. Also identifies the Freedom of Information Act office for each federal department or agency and reports its address and telephone number.

[D-183] *How to Find Information About Companies: The Corporate Intelligence Source Book.* 6th ed. Washington, DC: Washington Researchers Publishing, 1988. Published annually.

A directory of information sources for gathering corporate intelligence, with guidelines for conducting this kind of activity. Features printed, nonprint, and online sources of information on individual companies, public and private. The scope of sources covers libraries; federal, state, and local governments; courts; associations; private investigation services; and others. It addresses the issue of ethics, how to interview for corporate information, and ways to organize for the purpose of collecting strategic information about corporate competitors.

[D-184] *How to Find Information About Japanese Companies and Industries.* Washington, DC: Washington Researchers Publishing, 1984.

Designed to provide sources of information concerning the economic, commercial, and political situations in Japan, with special focus on Japanese companies and industries. This book is useful for learning about either existing or new markets in Japan, becoming informed about Japanese competitors, and identifying prospective trade partners in Japan. The sources of information include government agencies in the U.S. (federal, state, and local), Japanese sources of information in the U.S. and Japan, international organizations, trade associations, private-sector organizations, and published materials.

Explains how to prepare for a trip to Japan to gather business intelligence, where to get information on Japanese business customs, and tips on how to conduct on-site research. This publication contains a directory of organizations with their addresses and telephone numbers.

[D-185] *Information Sources: The Annual Directory of the Information Industry Association.* Edited by Barbara E. Van Gorder. Washington, DC: Information Industry Association, 1988. Published annually.

The membership directory of the trade association of the information industry. Company listings represent a broad spectrum of products and services in this industry, including database vendors, software producers, information brokers, and publishers of reference books and periodicals. Includes full-page company ads that describe each company, encompassing address, telephone number, products or services, and so on. Companies can be identified by the product/service index. The listing is limited to members of the Information Industry Association.

The International Directory of Business Information Agencies and Services. Detroit: Gale Research Company, 1986.
See "Statistical Digests and Statistics Sources," [D-466].

[D-186] *International Directory of Corporate Affiliations.* Wilmette, IL: National Register Publishing Company, 1988. Published annually.

A directory of foreign parent companies with their domestic and international holdings and of U.S. parent companies with their foreign subsidiaries, affiliates, and divisions. Contains a cross-reference index between parent companies and their divisions, affiliates, and subsidiaries. Company descriptions include address, telephone number, names of officers, line of business, and location and business focus of affiliates, divisions, and subsidiaries. Lists companies by country. Also provides addresses and telephone numbers of foreign consulates in the U.S., U.S. embassies, American Chambers of Commerce abroad, and foreign trade commissions and chambers of commerce.

[D-187] *Japan Yellow Pages.* Tokyo, Japan: Japan Yellow Pages Ltd., 1988. Distributed in America by Croner Publications, Inc. and others. Published annually.

This is the yellow pages of the telephone directory for selected cities in Japan. It lists businesses by their product or service. Contains informative advertisements that assist with locating suppliers and buyers. Provides address, telephone number, cable address, telex, and fax number.

[D-188] *Million Dollar Directory: America's Leading Public and Private Companies.* 5 vols. Parsippany, NJ: Dun's Marketing Services, 1988. Published annually.

A directory of U.S. businesses, arranged alphabetically, with a description of each firm. Includes the address, telephone number, names of officers and directors, sales volume, line of business, divisions, indication of public ownership, state of incorporation, and other information. To be included, a company must have a net worth exceeding $500,000, and it must be the headquarters site or operate at a single location. Divisions are not listed separately.

Many types of businesses are included, but some industries are underemphasized, such as credit agencies, consulting and professional organizations, engineering firms, hospitals, some types of financial institutions, and foreign-owned corporations. Includes alphabetical, geographical, and industrial listings of companies.

[D-189] *Moody's Bank and Finance Manual.* Robert P. Hanson, editor-in-chief. 3 vols. (beginning with the 1988 edition there will be 4 volumes). New York: Moody's Investors Service, 1987. Published annually, with semiweekly updating via *Moody's Bank and Finance News Reports.*

One of the eight *Moody's Manuals*, it profiles institutions in the U.S. finance industry: banks, savings and loan associations, investment companies, insurance companies, real estate companies, real estate investment trusts, unit investment trusts, and other financial enterprises. The extent of coverage contained in the profiles depends on the amount of coverage purchased.

Basically, the data include history, location, names of officers and directors, consolidated financial statement, financial and operating ratios, debt structure, letters to shareholders, list of securities held in trust, record of income and principal distribution, and other financial information that is appropriate to the type of financial institution. There is also a "Special Features" section that displays summary statistics for the finance industry.

[D-190] *Moody's Industrial Manual.* 2 vols. Robert P. Hanson, editor-in-chief. New York: Moody's Investors Service, 1987. Published annually, with semiweekly updating via *Moody's Industrial News Reports.*

One of the eight *Moody's Manuals*, it reports on publicly held industrial companies that are listed on the New York, American, and regional stock exchanges. Contains comprehensive information, the extent of which depends on the level of coverage purchased by the company. Profiles often include the capital structure, history of the company, subsidiaries, nature of the business, principal properties, names of officers and directors, excerpts from the annual report to stockholders, consolidated income account, consolidated balance sheet, financial and operating ratios, detailed description of stocks and bonds issued, month of the annual stockholders' meeting, and other information.

A "Special Features" section of blue pages provides summary information, such as Moody's bond yield averages and preferred stock yield averages.

[D-191] *Moody's International Manual.* 2 vols. Robert P. Hanson, editor-in-chief. New York: Moody's Investors Service, 1987. Published annually, with weekly updating via *Moody's International News Reports*.

One of the eight *Moody's Manuals*, it reports on major publicly-held foreign corporations and national and supranational institutions. The latter are listed as world corporations, such as the Asian Development Bank, European Economic Community, International Monetary Fund, and other development organizations.

Corporations and financial institutions are arranged by country, with the level of coverage in a profile depending on the extent of coverage purchased. Profiles often include the capital structure, history of the company, subsidiaries, nature of the business, principal properties, names of officers and directors, excerpts from the annual report to stockholders, consolidated income account, consolidated balance sheet, financial and operating ratios, detailed descriptions of stocks and bonds issued, month of the annual stockholders' meeting, and other information.

Contains a description of the debts of foreign countries and their outstanding bonds. Among other data about a foreign nation are its banking system, political organization, international transactions, economy, people, and geography.

A blue-page "Special Features" section presents statistical tables and lists that summarize a variety of international investment, financing, and trade data.

[D-192] *Moody's Manuals.* 8 titles. Robert P. Hanson, editor-in-chief. New York: Moody's Investors Service, 1987. Published annually, with weekly or semiweekly updates for each title via the *News Reports* series. Also, the *Complete Corporate Index*, published three times yearly, centrally indexes companies in all the *Manuals*.

This set of eight manuals, plus index and updates, reports current financial and other information on publicly-held companies, banks, utilities, and governments (federal, state, and local). The component manuals, arranged by type of organization, are

> *Bank and Finance Manual* [D-189]
> *Industrial Manual* [D-190]
> *International Manual* [D-191]
> *Municipal and Government Manual* [D-193]
> *OTC Industrial Manual* [D-194]
> *OTC Unlisted Manual* [D-195]
> *Public Utilities Manual* [D-196]
> *Transportation Manual* [D-197]

These publications include financial-statement data and narrative reviews. The information was obtained from corporations, Securities and Exchange Commission reports, reports to stockholders, and other sources.

The scope includes thousands of companies and government bond-issuing agencies. There are four levels of coverage in the profiles, depending on the level that was purchased. Descriptions are arranged by coverage level and, in some of these titles, by geographic location or type of company. A blue section in the center provides special features that are usually summary statistics or special lists, depending on the manual's subject. For more on the information contained in individual manuals, see the biobliographic sketch for each title.

[D-193] *Moody's Municipal & Government Manual.* 2 vols. (commencing with the 1988 edition there will be 3 volumes). Robert P. Hanson, editor-in-chief. New York: Moody's Investors Service, 1987. Published annually, with semiweekly updating via *Moody's Municipal & Government News Reports.*

One of the eight *Moody's Manuals*, it reports on federal, state, and municipal government financing. Publishes extensive information about bond issues. This is a source to find out about pollution-control bonds, industrial-development bonds, and other bonded indebtedness of government units at all levels of government and for whatever purpose the bonds were issued. Also presents financial statistics for each state, including descriptions of revenue sources, taxing authority and limitations, and state tax rates.

[D-194] *Moody's OTC Industrial Manual.* 1 vol. Robert P. Hanson, editor-in-chief. New York: Moody's Investors Service, 1987. Published annually, with semiweekly updating via *Moody's OTC Industrial News Reports.*

One of the eight *Moody's Manuals*, it reports on publicly held industrial companies that are actively traded over-the-counter as part of the NASDAQ system. Contains comprehensive information, depending on the level of coverage purchased by the company. Profiles often include the capital structure, history of the company, subsidiaries, nature of the business, principal properties, names of officers and directors, excerpts from the annual report to stockholders, consolidated income account, consolidated balance sheet, financial and operating ratios, detailed description of stocks and bonds issued, month of the annual stockholders' meeting, and other information. A blue-page "Special Features" section contains a geographical index of companies, classification of companies by industry and product, and a listing of OTC industrial stock splits.

[D-195] *Moody's OTC Unlisted Manual.* 1 vol. Robert P. Hanson, editor-in-chief. New York: Moody's Investors Services, 1987. Published annually, with weekly updating via *Moody's OTC Unlisted News Reports.*

One of the eight *Moody's Manuals*, it reports on over-the-counter stocks that are less actively traded and that are not listed on the NASDAQ National Market System. Often contains financial and operating information on each company, the extent of coverage depending on the level of coverage purchased. Profiles may include nature of the business, history of the company, subsidiaries, principal properties, names of officers and directors, names of the auditor and legal counsel, consolidated income account, consolidated balance sheet, description of long-term debt, excerpts from the auditor's report, and other information. Contains a geographical index of companies.

[D-196] *Moody's Public Utility Manual.* 2 vols. Robert P. Hanson, editor-in-chief. New York: Moody's Investors Service, 1987. Published annually, with semiweekly updating via *Moody's Public Utility News Reports.*

One of the eight *Moody's Manuals*, it profiles companies in the public utility industry. These include gas and electric utilities, gas transmission companies, telephone companies, and water companies. The level of coverage depends on the level purchased by the company.

The data often include the corporate history, address and telephone number, names of officers and directors, description of business activities, annual report to stockholders, subsidiaries, physical properties, financial statistics, consolidated income account, consolidated balance sheet, financial and operating ratios, descriptions of long-term debt (including bond ratings), and other information. For many companies, it displays maps of their service regions and their pipe or transmission lines. A "Special Features" section reports summary statistics on the public utility industry.

[D-197] *Moody's Transportation Manual.* 1 vol. Robert P. Hanson, editor-in-chief. New York: Moody's Investors Service, 1987. Published annually, with weekly updating via *Moody's Transportation News Reports.*

One of the eight *Moody's Manuals*, it profiles companies in the transportation industry. These include railroads, airlines, trucking, steamship, automobile/truck leasing and rental companies, oil pipelines, bus lines, and bridge companies. The level of coverage for each company depends on the coverage purchased.

The information usually includes corporate history, company business activities, annual report to stockholders, address and telephone number, names of officers and directors, consolidated income account, consolidated balance sheet, notes to financial statements, structure of long-term debt and bond ratings, and other information. For some of the major companies, a map of their routes is displayed. A "Special Features" section presents summary statistics of the transportation industry.

[D-198] *National Directory of Minority-Owned Business Firms.* Lombard, IL: Business Research Services, Inc., 1988. Published annually.

A directory of business firms owned by minorities. According to the directory's publisher, a minority-owned business is one that "is beneficially owned and actively controlled by one or more members of the (listed) groups" (p. iii). These groups are black American, Hispanic American, Hasidic Jew, American Indian and Native American, Asian Pacific American, and women. It lists firms according to their Standard Industrial Classification (SIC) category and alphabetically. The company profiles include the business's name, address, telephone number, nature of the business, contact person, minority group, number of employees, sales volume, and other descriptive information.

[D-199] *The National Directory of State Agencies.* Edited by Sharon J. Marcus. Bethesda, MD: Cambridge Information Group Directories, Inc., 1989. Published annually.

Lists the elected officials and administrative officers of the individual states. The directory identifies these persons by their functional areas and reports their addresses and telephone numbers. The arrangement by area of responsibility is by state and by composite of all states. Includes standing committees of the legislatures. Also provides a directory of national associations that represent state government officials. Contains a section that serves as a national telephone directory for state government officials and administrative officers.

[D-200] *National Directory of Women-Owned Business Firms.* Lombard, IL: Business Research Services, Inc., 1988. Published annually.

A directory of business firms that are beneficially owned and controlled by women (that is, women own at least 51 percent of the business and exercise control over it). Profiles of firms are arranged by Standard Industrial Classification (SIC) category. Each profile reports the business's name, address, telephone number, nature of the business, contact person, minority type, number of employees, sales volume, and other information. Also provides an alphabetical listing of the firms.

[D-201] *National Fax Directory.* Detroit: Gale Research Company, 1989. Data compiled by General Information, Inc. Published annually.

A directory of fax numbers for U.S. companies, organizations, libraries, and government agencies. Companies are listed by subject, using the SIC code and, in another section, alphabetically along with organizations, libraries, and government agencies. Also includes addresses and voice phone numbers.

[D-202] *National Job Bank.* 4th ed. Edited by Brandon Toropov. Boston: Bob Adams, Inc., 1988. Published annually.

A directory of U.S. companies, with a profile of each that reports the company's name, address, telephone number, contact person or position (title), nature of the business, professional job positions for which each company commonly hires, educational qualifications, and fringe benefits provided. Designed to assist the job hunter. Explains how to conduct a job search, write a résumé, and interview for a job.

[D-203] *National Roster of Realtors Directory.* 2 vols. Cedar Rapids, IA: Stamats Communications, Inc., 1988. Published annually.

Lists the names and addresses, by city and state, of realtors who are members of the National Association of Realtors. Also lists the addresses and telephone numbers of state and local boards of realtors.

[D-204] *National Trade and Professional Associations of the United States.* 22d ed. Edited by John J. Russell and Patricia B. Lee. Washington, DC: Columbia Books, Inc., 1987. Published annually.

A directory of national trade and professional associations, labor unions, scientific or technical societies, and other selected national organizations. Describes each by stating its address, telephone number, name and title of the chief operating officer, membership size, titles of publications, date and place of annual meeting, annual budget, and historical facts about the organization. Associations are indexed alphabetically and by subject, geography, budget size, and acronym. Includes a listing of association-management companies.

Newsletters in Print. 4th ed. Edited by Brigitte T. Darnay. Detroit: Gale Research Company, 1988. Formerly titled *Newsletters Directory*.
See "Bibliographies," [D-41].

[D-205]   *Newspaper Rates and Data.* 2 vols. Wilmette, IL: Standard Rate and Data Service, 1988. Published monthly.

A directory of national, regional, and local newspapers plus college/university newspapers and newspapers geared toward black Americans. Profiles of these publications include advertising rates, mechanical measurements, circulation, and other related information. Explains the Standard Advertising Unit System and maximil/minimil rates. Includes demographic consumer marketing data. Part 2 reports a detailed analysis of a newspaper's circulation and penetration. Gives extensive market data.

Official Congressional Directory. Washington, DC: U.S. Government Printing Office. Published biennially to coincide with each new Congress.
See "Government Documents," [D-356].

[D-206]   *Official U.S. Custom House Guide.* Edited by Joe Douress. Philadelphia: North American Publishing Company, 1987. Published annually.

A guide to the major North American ports of entry. Profiles each of these ports, both seaports and airports. The profiles state the name of the port, address, telephone number, director's name, and the names of the airlines or ocean cargo carriers that serve the port. There is also a physical description of the port, including various water depths for seaports. For each port there is reported the address and telephone number of the local U.S. Customs Service district office, Chamber of Commerce, and International Trade Administration Office. Port descriptions also include the trucking services, air-freight services, warehousing services, courier services, railroads, customs house brokers/freight forwarders, packing and container services, and other services that are available at the port of entry. Identifies nearby foreign trade zones and foreign consulate offices.

The *Official U.S. Custom House Guide* lists law firms that specialize in admiralty, customs, and/or international law. It also has a directory of air and ocean cargo carriers.

Reprints U.S. Customs rules and regulations. An important feature of this directory is its inclusion of the U.S. tariff schedule and the duty rates for articles entering the U.S. Explains the U.S. Customs Service, including its functions and the services it provides. Publishes a directory of the names and titles of key officials of the Service and the addresses and telephone numbers of district offices. The addresses and telephone numbers of the International Trade Administration district offices are also included. The reader will find the telephone code for each country.

Oxbridge Directory of Newsletters. 6th ed. Edited by Matthew Manning. New York: Oxbridge Communications, Inc., 1988.
See "Bibliographies," [D-42].

[D-207] *Peterson's Business and Management Jobs.* Edited by Christopher Billy and Mark Geoffroy. Princeton, NJ: Peterson's Guides, Inc., 1988. Published annually.

An extensive listing of employers in the U.S. and Canada who offer entry-level jobs to college graduates with baccalaureate and/or advanced degrees in business and management and/or in the humanities and social sciences.

Employer (companies and government agencies) profiles explain the nature of the business, the number of new employees planned to be hired, starting salaries, training programs, starting locations, benefits, summer employment, opportunities for experienced personnel, opportunities for business/management graduates, and other information of interest to job hunters. Also includes a linkage between academic disciplines and job opportunities, a listing of news media that print extensive employment ads, and guidelines for writing a résumé and preparing for an interview.

[D-208] *Peterson's Engineering, Science, and Computer Jobs.* Edited by Christopher Billy and Mark Geoffroy. Princeton, NJ: Peterson's Guides, Inc., 1988. Published annually.

An extensive listing of employers in the U.S. and Canada who offer entry-level jobs to college graduates with baccalaureate and/or advanced degrees in engineering, the physical and biological sciences, and in computer science. Profiles each employer (companies and government agencies) by explaining the nature of the business, the number of new employees planned to be hired, starting salaries, training programs, starting locations, benefits, summer employment, opportunities for experienced personnel, majors sought and assignments offered, etc. Also includes a linkage between academic disciplines and job opportunities, a listing of news media that publish extensive employment advertisements, and guidelines for writing a résumé and preparing for an interview.

[D-209] *Pratt's Guide to Venture Capital Sources.* Edited by Stanley E. Pratt and Jane K. Morris. Wellesley Hills, MA: Venture Economics, Inc., 1987. Published annually.

This serves as a guide to venture capital in the U.S. and Canada by offering a directory of venture capital firms and individuals. Provides a brief description of each source that includes address, telephone number, industry and project preferences, and other related information. Also includes a list of firms that underwrite public offerings for equity capital in small businesses.

[D-210] *Principal International Businesses.* Parsippany, NJ: Dun's Marketing Services, 1987. Published annually.

A directory of the most prominent and largest businesses in countries around the world (according to Dun and Bradstreet International). Lists firms alphabetically within country and in a composite list for all countries. Also organizes them by line of business (SIC Code). Entry profiles include address, SIC code, name of parent company, name of senior operating officer, and other information.

[D-211] *The Rand McNally Bankers Directory: International.* Chicago: Rand McNally & Company, 1988. Revised semiannually.

Part of a three-volume set that is in its 224th edition, this third volume of *The Rand McNally Bankers Directory* focuses on foreign international banks. It includes only those banks that are involved with foreign exchange or trade. Lists head offices, branches, agencies, and representative offices located outside the U.S. Profiles of banks vary in the kinds of information, but the data usually include location, telephone number, names of officers and their functional areas, branches, affiliates, financial data, association memberships, worldwide correspondents, and other descriptive information. Banks are listed alphabetically within city by country. Demographic information is provided for each country.

[D-212] *The Rand McNally Bankers Directory: United States.* 2 vols. Chicago: Rand McNally & Company, 1988. Revised semiannually.

Part of a three-volume set, these two volumes of *The Rand McNally Bankers Directory* have individual listings for U.S. chartered national banks, state banks, industrial banks, trust companies, banking Edge Act corporations, and mutual-savings banks. Excludes Federal Reserve banks (except in the "Reference and Banking Information" section) and thrift institutions.

The amount of detailed information in the profiles varies, but the data usually include address, telephone number, branches and their managers, names of officers and their functional titles, directors, holding company, parent company, name of automated clearinghouse, name of paper clearinghouse, routing number, state and national rankings of bank based on total assets, financial data, principal correspondents, and other information.

Also provides directories for the Federal Reserve system, automated clearinghouses, paper clearinghouses, U.S. banking and related trade associations, Federal Home Loan Banks, the Federal Deposit Insurance Corporation (FDIC), other federal government banking-regulatory agencies, and state-bank officials and associations. There is also a directory of specific corporate and interbank services that are offered by named U.S. banks.

[D-213] *The Rating Guide to Franchises.* Dennis L. Foster. New York: Facts on File Publications, 1988.

Profiles the leading franchisors in the U. S. Presents ratings and other evaluations of franchising companies. Each franchisor is rated on industry experience, franchising experience, training and services, financial strength, satisfied franchisees, and fees and royalties.

The profiles also include a discussion of the nature of the business, type of person wanted by the franchisor to be a franchisee, projected earnings for a franchisee, services provided the franchisee, advertising, major provisions of the franchise contract, franchisee's initial investment, fees and royalties charged by the franchisor, and other related topics. Franchisors are arranged by industry. Addresses and telephone numbers are cited.

[D-214] *Research Centers Directory.* 2 vols. 12th ed. Edited by Peter D. Dresser. Detroit: Gale Research Company, 1987. Published annually.

A directory of permanently established research centers, institutes, bureaus, and other similar nonprofit research organizations in business and other fields. Descriptive information in each entry includes the address, telephone number, director's name, sources of support, fields of research, specialized collections and databases, publications, and other related information. Indexes by names of the research centers, acronyms of the centers, names of sponsoring institutions, subject, and special capabilities (equipment, databases, collections, and other service capabilities).

[D-215] *The Second Hulbert Financial Digest Almanac.* Mark Hulbert. Washington, DC: Minerva Books, Inc., 1988.

An evaluative guide to approximately 90 investment newsletters. Explains the services of each newsletter, its strengths and weaknesses, graphs the performance of the investment portfolio recommended by the newsletter and compares it with the performance of the S&P 500 index, and discusses other features.

Ranks each investment newsletter according to: (1) clarity and completeness of its advice, and (2) riskiness (volatility) of its investment recommendations. Reports the newsletter's address, telephone number, editor's name, subscription rate, and whether it offers a telephone hotline update.

[D-216] *Small Business Sourcebook.* 2 vols. 2d ed. Edited by Robert J. Elster. Detroit: Gale Research Company, 1987.

A valuable and comprehensive sourcebook of information for anyone starting or operating a small business. It offers *sources* of information, by industry. These sources include federal and state government services to small business, trade associations, franchising organizations, suppliers, statistical references, trade periodicals, sources of finance, consultants, trade shows, and others.

[D-217] *The Source Book of Franchise Opportunities.* Robert E. Bond. Homewood, IL: Richard D. Irwin, Inc., 1988.

A directory of franchising firms in more than 40 fields. Presents profiles of franchisors that include address, telephone number, contact person, description of the business, year company was established, number of company-owned and franchised units, geographical distribution of operating units, cash investment required of the franchisee, total investment (cash and debt) required, initial franchise fee, contract period for the original franchise agreement and the first renewal period, financial assistance available from the franchisor, services provided by the franchisor to the franchisee, and other information.

[D-218] *Spot Radio Rates and Data.* Wilmette, IL: Standard Rate and Data Service, 1988. Published monthly.

A directory of the radio industry, with an alphabetical listing, by state and U.S. possession, of radio stations. The station profiles include address, telephone number, call letters, names of key personnel, advertising contract terms and spot rates, and other information about the station. Also indicates radio stations that regularly schedule farm programs, foreign-language programs, and programs geared toward black Americans. Reports descriptions and rankings of television market areas. Contains a listing of program syndicators and firms that represent radio stations.

[D-219] *Spot Television Rates and Data.* Wilmette, IL: Standard Rate and Data Service, 1988. Published monthly.

A directory of the television industry, with an alphabetical listing, by state and U.S. possession, of television stations. It provides a description of each station indicating its address, telephone number, call letters, names of key personnel, advertising contract terms and spot rates, and other information. Also reported are descriptions and rankings of television market areas. Among other kinds of information contained in this publication are data on consumer markets, a map that depicts the cities that have television broadcasting stations, and a listing of firms that represent television stations.

[D-220] *Standard & Poor's Corporation Records.* 7 vols. New York: Standard & Poor's Corporation, 1988. First six volumes are titled *Standard Corporation Descriptions* and are updated semimonthly. The seventh volumn, *Daily News*, is published daily.

This directory, in loose-leaf form, compiles financial and operational profiles of publicly-held corporations. It includes industrials, transportation companies, utilities, over-the-counter stock companies, and the larger and more active financial institutions. Also cites foreign firms. The corporate profiles are in the six *Standard Corporation Descriptions* volumes. The extent of coverage depends on the level of coverage purchased.

Profiles report capitalization, nature of the business, corporate history, stock data, bond descriptions, earnings and finances, names of corporate officers and directors, address, telephone number, month of annual stockholders' meeting, and other descriptive information.

The *Daily News* reports daily corporate activities, such as changes in bond ratings, mergers, acquisitions, new securities offerings, and other daily business developments.

The *Standard & Poor's Corporation Records* includes an index of firms classified by SIC code number. There is also a "Cross-Reference" index to subsidiaries.

[D-221] *Standard & Poor's Register of Corporations, Directors and Executives.* 3 vols. 62d ed. New York: Standard & Poor's Corporation, 1989. Published annually.

This directory of the international business community provides a descriptive listing of corporations. In volume 1 is reported for each corporation the address, telephone number, officers, directors, SIC code, line of business, primary bank, primary law firm, stock exchange on which its stock is traded, annual sales, number of employees, and other descriptive information. Volume 2 contains brief biographical sketches of directors and executives, which include business and residential addresses, birth date, college from which they graduated, fraternal membership, principal business affiliations, and other information.

In volume 3 is an assortment of indexes. One of these lists the categories of the Standard Industrial Classification (SIC) system and explains this code system. Another index lists the companies profiled in volume 1 according to their SIC subject code. Companies are arranged in another index germane to their geographical location, and, finally, there is a cross-reference index that links parent companies with their divisions and subsidiaries. This volume concludes with an obituary section of directors and executives who have died in the time since their biographical profiles appeared in the previous edition.

[D-222] *Standard Directory of Advertisers: Classified.* Wilmette, IL: National Register Publishing Company, 1988. Published annually and updated via biweekly ad changes and five cumulative supplements.

A directory of corporations that advertise regionally or nationally. Profiles each company and provides the name, address, and telephone number of its advertising agency. The companies are listed alphabetically by category of product or service. Reports the size of companys' advertising budgets and the months when they are decided. Also indicates the media various companies use for advertising. Gives a list of the largest advertisers and advertising agencies. A geographical edition is published in the spring that lists advertisers by city and state.

[D-223] *Standard Directory of Advertising Agencies: The Agency Red Book.* Wilmette, IL: National Register Publishing Company, 1988. Published in February, June, and October of each year.

An international guide to the advertising industry. Lists advertising agencies alphabetically and profiles each agency by reporting its address, telephone number, specialization, annual gross billings by media, names of accounts, names of management and account executives, and other information. Also provides a geographical index of agencies and a "Special Market Index" that identifies agencies that specialize in selected markets.

[D-224] *State Administrative Officials Classified by Function.* Lexington, KY: Council of State Governments, 1989. Published biennially.

A directory of state government officials, both elected and appointed. Information is arranged by state within function. Cites names of officials, addresses, and telephone numbers. Includes all of the states, the District of Columbia, and U.S. possessions and territories.

[D-225] *Taiwan Yellow Pages.* Edited by Mei Yun Shih. Taipei, Taiwan: Taiwan Yellow Pages Corp., 1988. Distributed in America by Croner Publications, Inc. Published annually.

As indicated by the title, this is the yellow-page telephone directory for Taiwan, Republic of China. It lists businesses by their product or service. Contains informative advertisements that help the reader identify suppliers and buyers. Provides address, telephone number, cable address, telex number, fax number, name of an officer, and the products or services offered.

[D-226] *Thomas Register of American Manufacturers and Thomas Register Catalog File.* 21 vols. 78th ed. New York: Thomas Publishing Company, 1988. Published annually.

A directory of American manufacturers arranged in three major sections; (1) "Products and Services" (vols. 1–12), (2) "Company Profiles" (vols. 13–14), and (3) "Catalog File" (THOMCAT) (vols. 15–21). Volume 21 also contains the *Thomas Register's Inbound Traffic Guide* [D-227].

This 78th edition of *Thomas Register* lists the names, corporate descriptions, and products or services offered by more than 145,000 American companies: it tells who manufactures what. Contains a collection of product catalogs from more than 1,400 firms. Volume 14 includes an index of brand names, and volume 21 has a directory of freight carriers and other companies that serve the inbound freight transportation industry. *Thomas Register* is the directory of the American manufacturing community, where suppliers and products can be found.

[D-227] *Thomas Register's Inbound Traffic Guide.* New York: Thomas Publishing Company, 1988. Published annually. Available either as the final section in the last volume of *Thomas Register of American Manufacturers and Thomas Register Catalog File* [D-226] or as a separate publication.

A directory of the freight transportation industry. For the different modes of transportation (airlines, barges, trucks, railway, and steamships), it identifies the carriers and providers of support services (custom house brokers, export management, export packing services, freight-auditing services, ports, public warehouses, and transportation brokers). It also cites providers of managerial software and the names of shippers' associations and trade associations for the shipping industry. There is a descriptive profile of each company. This is a handy reference tool for a firm seeking to identify the right inbound transportation mode and carrier.

[D-228] *Trade Shows and Professional Exhibits Directory.* 2d ed. Edited by Robert J. Elster. Detroit: Gale Research Company, 1986. Published annually.

A directory of exhibitions, trade shows, conventions, and other types of meetings designed to foster direct sales and trade contacts. Lists these meetings by general subject categories. Each entry includes such information as the name, address, and telephone number of the sponsor; name of the exhibits manager; cosponsors; expected attendance; targeted participants; charges to exhibitors; and dates and location of the meeting. The indexes include geographic locations of meetings, chronology of meeting dates, sponsoring organizations, products or services displayed, and an alphabetical listing of trade shows and exhibitions by name.

[D-229] *Trademark Register of the United States.* Washington, DC: Trademark Register. Published annually.

Although privately published, this publication serves as an index to the *Official Gazette-Trademarks* [D-357] of the U.S. Patent and Trademark Office. It contains a listing of U.S. trademarks currently registered and renewed. The listing is cumulative since 1881. It covers all classes of goods, services, and products. For each entry, arranged by Patent and Trademark Office class, it provides the trademark name, registration number, date of registration, and class designation.

United States Government Manual. Office of the Federal Register. Washington, DC: U.S. Government Printing Office, 1988. Published annually.
See "Government Documents," [D-366].

[D-230] *The U.S. Savings and Loan Directory.* 2 vols., 7th ed. Chicago: Rand McNally and Company, 1988. Published annually.

Contains an alphabetical listing, by state, of savings and loan institutions, with a profile of each institution that includes address, telephone number, names of officers, total assets, total deposits, total loans, net worth, and other financial statistics. This directory publishes information on the savings industry, including the associations and government agencies that serve the industry. Reports state demographic information and data on a state's financial industry.

[D-231] *Ward's Business Directory of U.S. Private and Public Companies: Over $11.5 Million in Sales.* Vol. 1. Detroit: Gale Research Inc., 1989. Published annually. (Note: The next edition will have four volumes, and these will not be divided by levels of sales.)

Volume 1 of a three-volume set, this is a directory of the largest U.S. private companies and selected public firms. Most entries are privately held. To be included, a company must have an annual sales volume over $11.5 million. Reports name of company, address, telephone number, type (public or private), name of CEO, SIC code, number of employees, annual sales volume expressed in millions of dollars, year founded, and whether the company imports and/or exports. Companies are listed alphabetically and by geographic region (states, cities, and ZIP code).

Entries include manufacturers, wholesale and retail firms, service companies, financial institutions, insurance companies, and other businesses. A special section lists the 1,000 largest publicly held U.S. companies, ranked by sales volume (excludes financial institutions), the 1,000 largest privately held U.S. companies, ranked by sales volume, and the 1,000 largest U.S. employers, ranked by number of employees. This section also includes an analysis of public and private companies in each state using sundry statistical data. Also provides the names of companies that appear in volume 2 of this publication [D-232].

[D-232] *Ward's Business Directory of U.S. Private and Public Companies: $.5 to $11.5 Million in Sales.* Vol. 2. Detroit: Gale Research Inc., 1989. Published annually.

Volume 2 of a three-volume set, this is a directory of U.S. private companies and selected public firms whose annual sales are between $500,000 and $11.5 million. Most entries are privately held. The information reported for a company is its address, telephone number, type (public or private), name of CEO,

SIC code, number of employees, annual sales volume expressed in millions of dollars, year founded, and whether the company imports and/or exports. Companies are listed alphabetically and by geographic region (cities, states, ZIP code).

Entries include manufacturers, wholesale and retail firms, service companies, and other businesses. A special section lists private firms with at least $10 million in annual sales, private companies with 200–500 employees, and presents an analysis of public and private firms by state.

[D-233] Ward's Business Directory of U.S. Private and Public Companies: Ranked by Sales Within Industry. Vol. 3. Detroit: Gale Research Inc., 1989. Published annually.

Volume 3 of a three-volume set, this is a directory of U.S. private companies and selected public firms, listed by SIC industry, whose annual sales are at least $500,000. These companies are ranked within their industry by annual sales volume. The information reported for each company includes the sales-volume rank, annual sales volume expressed in millions of dollars, address, telephone number, name of CEO, SIC classification, number of employees, year founded, and whether the company imports and/or exports.

Entries include manufacturers, wholesale and retail firms, service companies, financial institutions, insurance companies, and other businesses. Describes each SIC industry by reporting the number of public and private companies, total sales volume, and number of employees.

[D-234]   Washington Information Directory. Washington, DC: Congressional Quarterly, Inc., 1987. Published annually.

Arranged by subject, this is a directory for governmental and nongovernmental sources of information in Washington, DC. Includes federal departments and agencies along with private organizations. Reports for each entry a statement of purpose, address, and telephone number. Contains directories of foreign embassies, U.S. ambassadors, selected state officials, mayors of major cities, and federal regional information offices. For federal departments and agencies, discloses the names and telephone numbers of procurement officers, Freedom of Information contacts, Equal Employment Opportunity contacts, and other selected officials. Also includes organizations and agencies that serve consumer affairs.

[D-235] Who's Who in Venture Capital. A. David Silver. New York: John Wiley & Sons, 1987. Usually published annually.

A directory of venture capitalists that reports their address, telephone number, investment interests, names of principals with their educational and business experiences, and size of the investment fund along with the average amount per investment. Includes venture capitalists in the U.S., U.K., and Canada. Discusses the criteria often used by venture capitalists when contemplating the investment decision.

[D-236] *Worldwide Government Directory with International Organizations.* Bethesda, MD: National Standards Association, 1988. Published annually.

A telephone directory for the governments of the world. Also includes United Nations agencies and other intergovernmental organizations. Reports the address, telephone number, telex number, and cable address of principal departments and agencies. Provides the names and titles of major elected and appointed government officials in 175 nations, along with the positions and responsibilities of those officials. For each country there is reported the central bank or currency-issuing bank, with a listing of its officers.

ENCYCLOPEDIAS and HANDBOOKS

[D-237] *Accountant's Desk Handbook.* 3d ed. Albert P. Ameiss and Nicholas A. Kargas. Englewood Cliffs, NJ: Prentice-Hall, Inc., 1988.

A comprehensive ready-reference handbook for the accountant. Features sections titled "Financial Accounting," "Managerial Accounting," and "Standards, Procedures, and Reports for Auditing and Accounting." Includes a discussion of new accounting pronouncements from the Financial Accounting Standards Board (FASB), Governmental Accounting Standards Board (GASB), the Securities and Exchange Commission (SEC), American Institute of Certified Public Accountants (AICPA), and other professional bodies.

Topics in this handbook embrace the wide array of accounting areas, including international accounting procedures, unique disclosure formats and contents for small and developing businesses, computerized management-information systems, zero-base budgeting, accounting principles for health care organizations and municipalities, the Tax Reform Act of 1986, and other accounting subjects.

[D-238] *Accountant's Handbook of Formulas and Tables.* 2d ed. Lawrence Lipkin, Irwin K. Feinstein, and Lucile Derrick. Englewood Cliffs, NJ: Prentice-Hall, Inc., 1973.

A compilation of formulas used in business accounting. Includes formulas for simple and compound interest, annuities, inventory, depreciation, bond values, marketing, cost and production, ratio analysis, and other purposes. Explains the purpose of each formula. Also includes an assortment of tables of values used by accountants.

[D-239] *Accounting Desk Book: The Accountant's Everyday Instant Answer Book.* 9th ed. Tom M. Plank and Douglas L. Blensly. Englewood Cliffs, NJ: Prentice-Hall, Inc., 1989.

A comprehensive reference book that provides information on accounting, taxation, finance, and other related topics. Addresses accounting principles and practices, analysis and interpretation of financial statements, internal controls, cost accounting, fund accounting, the organization of the Securities and Exchange Commission (SEC), the filing requirements of the SEC, the Tax Reform Act of 1986, and other related matters. Also contains: (1) a discussion of the advantages and disadvantages of different accounting methods, (2) a guide to the retention requirements for income-tax records, and (3) financial-planning tables.

[D-240] *Accounting Standards: Original Pronouncements.* 2 vols. Norwalk, CT: Financial Accounting Standards Board, 1988. Published annually.

Here are the original pronouncements of standards for the accounting profession as promulgated by the Financial Accounting Standards Board. These standards form the operating guidelines for the practice of accounting.

[D-241] *AICPA Audit and Accounting Manual.* American Institute of Certified Public Accountants. Chicago: Commerce Clearing House, 1987. Also available in loose-leaf form that is updated periodically.

This is a practical reference manual for the small and medium-size accounting practice. It explains techniques and procedures that are used in the practice of accounting and auditing. Although billed as a nonauthoritative source, it is a handy reference tool that addresses how to plan and administer an audit engagement, internal control, sample working papers useful to an accountant, disclosure checklists, financial statements, accounting reports, and related topics. Replete with illustrations.

[D-242] *AMA Management Handbook.* 2d ed. Edited by William K. Fallon. New York: American Management Associations, 1983.

A comprehensive treatment of the field of management. Contains thoughtful contributions from more than 200 experts whose writings encompass the subdisciplines of management. The approach is practical. Among the management areas covered are finance, manufacturing, purchasing, transportation, distribution, marketing, human-resources management, employee benefits, and others. Examples of more specific topics covered are cost accounting, materials management, energy management, database management, and packaging regulations for international trade. The articles have been written to educate and facilitate the manager in whatever area of a corporation he/she is to be found.

[D-243] *Analyst's Handbook.* New York: Standard & Poor's Corporation, 1988. Published annually with monthly supplements.

A handbook devoted to reporting the performance of each of more than 70 industries. This is accomplished by analyzing per-share data, composite income-account and balance-sheet statistics, and financial ratios. The index data per share are reported for each year from 1956 to date, as applied to the S&P stock price indexes per industry group. Performance criteria include sales, operating profit, earnings per share, earnings as percent of sales, dividends, P/E ratio, and book value. Eight financial ratios are reported for each industry.

[D-244] *The Bankers' Handbook.* 3d ed. Edited by William H. Baughn, Thomas I. Storrs, and Charles E. Walker. Homewood, IL: Dow Jones-Irwin, 1988.

A collection of 85 articles dedicated to a broad range of subjects important to the banking industry. The authors are specialists in their fields. Subjects include boards of directors (recruitment and functions), organization, financial management, capital planning, internal auditing, assessing financial performance, management of a bank's investment portfolio, managing credit services, agricultural lending, trust services, and other banking topics.

[D-245] *Barron's Real Estate Handbook.* 2d ed. Jack C. Harris and Jack P. Friedman. New York: Barron's Educational Series, Inc., 1988.

This is a handy reference book on real estate for buyers, sellers, and realtors. It contains definitions of real-estate terminology, formulas used in financial transactions, guidelines for buyers and sellers of residential property, a summary of federal laws that affect real estate, explanations of how to estimate income and returns on a real estate investment, and other basic information on real estate transactions.

Barron's Real Estate Handbook also includes finance tables that are necessary for buyers and sellers. It discusses career opportunities in real estate, including descriptions of various positions and the responsibilities, educational requirements, and opportunities for advancement. Replete with illustrations of terms and concepts.

[D-246] *Basic Patterns in Union Contracts.* 11th ed. Washington, DC: Bureau of National Affairs, 1986. Published irregularly.

Based on a sample of 400 collective-bargaining agreements from industries across the nation, the Bureau of National Affairs has provided a descriptive summary of the major types of provisions contained in these contracts and the frequency of their appearance. This norm allows negotiators to compare their bargaining proposals or agreements with practices in their industry, as of the time of publication. Topics addressed include contract reopeners, contract renewal, negotiations, discharge procedures, appeal procedures, insurance, grievances and arbitration, holidays, overtime, rights of management and unions, seniority, strikes and lockouts, wages, and other collective-bargaining issues.

Oftentimes the frequency of use of certain contract provisions is reported, categorized separately for manufacturing and nonmanufacturing agreements. Also noted are practices common to individual industries.

[D-247] *Bender's Tax Return Manual.* Ernest D. Fiore, Jr., Roger V. Russell, and Matthew Bender's Tax Staff. New York: Matthew Bender & Company, 1988. Published annually.

Provides a detailed analysis and explanation, line-by-line, of all major federal tax forms pertaining to individual and business tax returns. Contains tax legislation and how it affects the different lines of each tax form. Includes more than 100 blank IRS forms and schedules with instructions. Full of illustrative examples.

Addresses returns for individuals, corporations, small businesses, partnerships, and others. A guide for the tax preparer.

[D-248] *Bond Guide.* New York: Standard & Poor's Corporation, 1988. Published monthly.

Reports on the ratings, yields, interest-payment dates, redemption provisions, and other descriptive information on corporate bonds. Provides similar kinds of data for foreign bonds, convertible bonds, and selected municipal bonds. Contains S&P ratings for equipment certificates, corporate medium-term notes, utility preferred stocks, and pass-through mortgage certificates. The *Bond Guide* includes a "CreditWatch" for companies and government units that have the possibility for a change in the ratings of their bonds or other fixed-income securities because of events or trends that have caused them to come under special surveillance by S&P.

[D-249] *Budgeting for Not-for-Profit Organizations.* Robert D. Vinter and Rhea K. Kish. New York: Free Press, 1984.

Explains the principles and methodologies used in budgeting for not-for-profit organizations. Addresses the process, organization, functional budgeting, cost centers, financial records, revenue and expense management, cost-analysis procedures, and other related topics.

[D-250] *The Capital Budgeting Handbook.* Edited by Mike Kaufman. Homewood, IL: Dow Jones-Irwin, 1986.

Designed for the businessperson involved with capital budgeting. Includes a compilation of 29 technical chapters on strategic planning for capital expenditures, preparation of the capital budget, the use of mathematical programming for allocating capital, evaluating a prospective capital project, determining risk, financing capital projects, and other associated topics.

[D-251] *Career Choices Encyclopedia: Guide to Entry-Level Jobs.* Career Associates. New York: Walker and Company, 1986.

Explores occupations in the different industries by explaining the overall nature of the industry, new job opportunities and competition for jobs, principal geographic centers for jobs in a given career field, how to break into a field, qualifications, career paths, job responsibilities, salaries, working conditions, internships, and sources of additional information. Includes a table that links fields of study with job opportunities.

[D-252] *Career Information Center.* 13 vols. 3d ed. Mission Hills, CA: Glencoe Publishing Company, 1987.

This set of occupational profiles is organized by grouping jobs according to occupational interest area. This cluster approach allows the reader to become familiar with a number of related jobs. Each volume focuses on a separate occupational field. The last volume is a master index and appendix.

The occupational profiles report on the nature of the work, training and education requirements, how to get the job, employment and advancement prospective, compensation, working conditions, and sources of additional information. Each career-field volume contains an overview of its field. Summary statistical data are in volume 13.

[D-253] *The CFO's Handbook.* Edited by Richard F. Vancil and Benjamin R. Makela. Homewood, IL: Dow Jones-Irwin, 1986.

A compendium of 31 authoritative articles written on topics of interest to corporate financial officers (CFOs). These treatises take a conceptual approach intended to stimulate the thinking of these officers. Topics include analysis of market competitiveness, setting corporate financial goals, developing financial policies, debt financing, international risk management, relationships with regulatory agencies, managing financial management, budgeting, internal auditing, and other related topics.

[D-254] *Choice of Compensation After Tax Reform.* Isidore Goodman. Chicago: Commerce Clearing House, 1987.

Presents a brief explanation of the impact of the Tax Reform Act of 1986 on pension and employee benefit plans. Discusses the tax treatment of different categories of compensation, including fringe benefits and deferred compensation. Also addresses tax reform concerning uniform distribution rules affecting tax-favored retirement plans, individual retirement accounts (IRAs), and other matters associated with tax reform and compensation.

[D-255] *The Complete Book of Gold Investing.* Jeffrey A. Nichols. Homewood, IL: Dow Jones-Irwin, 1987.

Explains the workings of the gold market and describes the different instrumentalities of gold, such as bullion coins, gold bullion, gold-mining equities, futures, and options. It explores the relationship between gold prices and the economy. Provides guidance for investing and trading in gold.

[D-256] *The Complete Handbook of Franchising.* David D. Seltz. Reading, MA: Addison-Wesley Publishing Company, 1982.

Offers comprehensive guidelines on franchising. Explains franchising and covers planning, franchise feasibility for the franchisee and the franchisor, table of organization, financing, site selection, recruitment, training, legal matters, and other subjects.

[D-257] *Condominium Development Guide: Procedures, Analysis, Forms.* Revised ed. Keith B. Romney and Brad Romney. Boston: Warren, Gorham and Lamont, 1983. Updated annually with cumulative supplements.

This reference book and its annual cumulative supplements contain information and recommendations on the development of condominiums. Although the primary emphasis is on first-home residential condominiums, attention is also given to other types of condominium development; namely, commercial, conversion, resort, manufactured-home, and timesharing. It addresses the pros and cons of condominiums, how to determine market feasibility, and analysis of development cost and the potential for profit. This guide also considers planning, site selection, financing condominium development, marketing, management, legal documents used in the development and operation of condominiums, insurance, taxation, and other related matters.

This is a valuable handbook for developers, lenders, lawyers, salespersons, and others who are involved with condominiums.

[D-258] *The Consumer Protection Manual.* Andrew Eiler. New York: Facts On File Publications, 1984.

A guide for consumers. It explains strategies and remedies for securing redress of consumer complaints. Contains an overview of federal and state laws that affect consumers and sellers. Provides procedural steps for seeking redress for fraud, mistakes, improper sales practices, consumer-credit and collection abuses, and violation of warranties. *The Consumer Protection Manual* offers alternative recourses for solving consumer problems. It explains how to handle a billing error. It also explains how to learn the contents of a consumer's credit file. Lists government agencies that safeguard consumer rights, with an explanation of what these agencies can do to help consumers. This handbook presents fundamental rules and strategies that are involved in the conduct of consumer affairs.

[D-259] *Daily Stock Price Record.* New York: Standard & Poor's Corporation, 1988. Published quarterly.

Consists of three editions; (1) *Daily Stock Price Record: New York Stock Exchange* (NYSE), (2) *Daily Stock Price Record: American Stock Exchange* (ASE), and (3) *Daily Stock Price Record: Over-the-Counter* (OTC). Each of these editions is published quarterly.

The NYSE and ASE editions report for each listed corporation the daily volume of shares traded, high/low, and closing price. Weekly performance statistics are also reported. The stock profiles show the average quarterly dividend yield, earnings per share, and the most recent quarterly dividend paid.

The OTC edition discloses volume, high/low, and close for NASDAQ National Market Issues. Volume, bid, and asked are reported for all other OTC issues. Reports the historical record of stock performances for OTC stocks, including industrial stocks, mutual funds, and banks and insurance stocks.

The *Daily Stock Price Record* contains statistics on the major stock market technical indicators, such as Barron's Confidence Index, the Dow Jones Averages, Standard & Poor's Averages, NYSE and AMEX Advances and Declines, Barron's Low Price Stock Index, and others.

[D-260] *Depreciation Guide.* Chicago: Commerce Clearing House, 1987.

Explains the depreciation rules that have been set down by the Accelerated Cost Recovery System (ACRS), Modified Accelerated Cost Recovery System (MACRS), Asset Depreciation Range (ADR), and the Class Life Asset Depreciation Range System. Provides the texts of the ADR regulations and the Asset Guideline Classes (Revenue Procedure 83-35). Also includes depreciation decimal tables.

[D-261] *Directory of Online Databases.* New York: Cuadra-Elsevier. Published quarterly.

An international guide to databases that are available online to the public. These databases encompass many subjects. Those related to business include accounting; advertising; management; business and industry directories (domestic and foreign); specific industries; copyrights, patents, and trademarks; corporate finance (domestic and foreign); currency-exchange rates; marketing; securities; and others.

Each database profile reports the subject and content; name, address, and telephone number of the producer and of the online vendor; requirements for accessing and using the database; geographic coverage; time span of the data; updating frequency; and other relevant information. Provides information on gateways in the online database industry.

[D-262] *The Dow Jones Investor's Handbook.* Edited by Phyllis S. Pierce. Homewood, IL: Dow Jones-Irwin, 1988. Published annually.

Presents a wide array of data pertaining to U.S. and foreign stock exchanges. These data include the Dow Jones averages for industrial, transportation, and utility stocks for varying periods of time. Also reports Barron's Confidence Index for eight years, trading data for bonds listed on the AMEX and NYSE for the preceding year, OTC stocks, U.S. Treasury bonds and notes, and NASDAQ indices. Contains foreign indices and closing prices for selected issues on foreign markets.

[D-263] *The Dow Jones-Irwin Banker's Guide to Online Databases.* J. Thomas Monk, Kenneth M. Landis, and Susan S. Monk. Homewood, IL: Richard D. Irwin, Inc., 1988.

The banking industry's guide to online information systems that are available for the industry's various operating needs. It discusses the issues associated with the electronic gathering of data and the risks entailed, the vocabulary of the information industry, why and when to go online, and other related topics. Contains profiles of online databases in which are described the contents of each database and how it is accessed. A valuable resource for bankers who require business information.

[D-264] *The Dow Jones-Irwin Guide to Fine Gems and Jewelry.* David Marcum. Homewood, IL: Dow Jones-Irwin, 1986.

A guide for consumers and investors in fine gems and jewelry. Offers buying tips, suggestions on what to look for and questions to ask, describes gemstones, provides tips to consumers for each type of gemstone, discusses diamond grading and how to understand the grading report, addresses appraisals and pricing, and covers other related matters.

[D-265] *The Dow Jones-Irwin Investor's Guide to Online Databases.* J. Thomas Monk, Kenneth M. Landis, and Susan S. Monk. Homewood, IL: Richard D. Irwin, Inc., 1988.

A handbook that addresses the information requirements of professional investors and indentifies the online databases that are available to serve their needs. It reports the names of vendors and their online database products. Provides a profile of each database that describes its content and how it is accessed.

Encyclopedia of Associations. Vol. 1. National Organizations of the U.S. Edited by Karin E. Koek, Susan B. Martin, and Annette Novallo. Detroit: Gale Research Company, 1988. Published annually.
See "Directories," [D-173].

Encyclopedia of Business Information Sources. 7th ed. Edited by James Woy. Detroit: Gale Research Company, 1988.
See "Bibliographies," [D-36].

[D-266] *Encyclopedia of Economics.* Edited by Douglas Greenwald. New York: McGraw-Hill, 1982.

A compilation of articles covering 310 subjects in economics. Contains in-depth definitions of terms and phrases used in this field. The articles have been prepared by authorities on their subjects. References are cited at the end of each article. A valuable reference tool for the economist and the businessperson.

   This publication includes terms and concepts applicable to banking, financial instruments, government fiscal policy, economic history, labor unions, econometrics, taxation, statistical techniques, stocks, and other related subjects.

[D-267] *The Encyclopedia of Management.* 3d ed. Edited by Carl Heyel. New York: Van Nostrand Reinhold Company, 1982.

A single-volume source for the person seeking information on a topic in management. With contributions from hundreds of recognized authors, this encyclopedia serves as a ready-reference tool. Its scope encompasses basic concepts in management, corporate planning, legal issues confronted by managers, financial management of corporations, project management, manufacturing, labor relations, personnel administration, and other areas associated with the management function. The articles are signed and contain valuable reference sources.

[D-268] *The Encyclopedia of Technical Market Indicators.* Robert W. Colby and Thomas A. Meyers. Homewood, IL: Dow Jones-Irwin, 1988.

Provides a technical description of more than 100 stock market indicators. Explains how to calculate and interpret these measures. Through a series of chapters, the authors analyze the forecasting value of these indicators. Presents buy-and-sell decision rules for operating in the stock market.

[D-269] *The Entrepreneur and Small Business Problem Solver: An Encyclopedic Reference and Guide.* William A. Cohen. New York: John Wiley & Sons, Inc., 1983.

A compendium of essential information for entrepreneurs of small business. Designed to be a one-stop source for finding answers to questions that are often asked, it is organized by areas of business activity. Some of these categories are legal matters involved with starting and running a business, sources of capital, planning, recruiting employees, protecting an idea, setting up records, financial management, advertising, pricing, and other concerns. This is a handy reference for the person who is going into business. The practical value of this publication is enhanced by its inclusion of model forms used in business, directories, source bibliographies, and photographs.

[D-270] *Federal Acquisition Regulation (FAR).* Chicago: Commerce Clearing House, 1988. Published annually.

Contains the purchasing regulations followed by the Department of Defense, General Services Administration, and the National Aeronautics and Space Administration. *FAR* serves as a guide for companies wanting to sell to the federal government. It explains terminology used by the government, contracting methods and requirements, types of contracts, contract management, and other topics related to the federal government's purchasing process.

[D-271] *The Financial Analyst's Handbook.* 2d ed. Edited by Sumner N. Levine. Homewood, IL: Dow Jones-Irwin, 1988.

A comprehensive handbook for financial analysts and money managers. Covers economic analysis, the analysis of equity investments, fixed-income investments, portfolio management, statistical techniques used in financial analysis, insider trading, and other topics of vital interest to financial executives. Its 56 articles, written by authorities, are technically oriented for use by practitioners.

[D-272] *Financial Statement Analysis: Theory, Application, and Interpretation.* 4th ed. Leopold A. Bernstein. Homewood, IL: Richard D. Irwin, Inc., 1988.

This publication facilitates investing and lending decisions by explaining how to analyze financial statements. It focuses on understanding business data and the methods that are employed to analyze and interpret these data. The primary targeted audiences include accountants, credit analysts, investors, lending officers, managers, and security analysts.

Part 1 addresses the interplay between financial analysis and accounting with its conventions and techniques. Part 2 concentrates on an in-depth analysis of financial statements and their preparation. Finally, part 3 examines the primary objectives of the users of financial statements and the analytical tools and techniques used to arrive at decisions.

[D-273] *Foundations of Financial Management.* 5th ed. Stanley B. Block and Geoffrey A. Hirt. Homewood, IL: Richard D. Irwin, Inc., 1989.

Explains the concepts, theories, and practices of financial management. Addresses financial analysis and planning, financial forecasting, operating and financial leverage, capital budgeting, insider trading, international financial management, and other similar topics. Provides formulas that are the working tools of the financial manager. Examples are used to enhance explanations. The emphasis is on basics vis-à-vis advanced theories and applications.

Franchise Opportunities Handbook. 21st ed. Andrew Kostecka. Washington, DC: U.S. Government Printing Office, 1988. Published annually.
See "Directories," [D-179].

[D-274] *A Guide to Modern Business and Commercial Law: A Comprehensive and Practical Handbook.* Bernard M. Kaplan. Chicago: Commerce Clearing House, 1985.

A comprehensive introduction to U.S. business and commercial law. Its scope encompasses many business-law subjects. The format highlights legal principles, commentary, and case illustrations. Among topics covered are contracts, agency, corporations, partnerships, negotiable instruments, labor law, insurance law, bankruptcy, and protection of intellectual property.

[D-275] *Guidebook to Labor Relations.* 24th ed. Commerce Clearing House Staff. Chicago: Commerce Clearing House, 1987.

A brief summary of federal labor-relations law. Covers the full spectrum of labor law, including areas of federal regulation, labor rights, bargaining units, unfair labor practices, labor-union activities, collective bargaining, mediation, and conciliation of labor disputes. Cites laws, administrative opinions, court decisions, and interpretations. This is a ready-reference handbook for finding information.

[D-276] *Handbook for Employers: Instructions for Completing Form I-9.* Chicago: Commerce Clearing House, 1987.

A guide for helping the employer comply with the Immigration Reform and Control Act of 1986. It provides directions on how to verify the employment eligibility of employees and instructions on how to complete the Employment Eligibility Verification Form (I-9).

[D-277] *Handbook for Raising Capital.* Edited by Lawrence Chimerine, Robert F. Cushman, and Howard D. Ross. Homewood, IL: Dow Jones-Irwin, 1987.

A comprehensive treatment of ways to secure capital for the small and medium-size business. The alternatives are explained by authors who are recognized authorities. These alternatives include bank loans, venture capital, corporate joint ventures, federal and state government-assisted financing, foreign capital, selling stock, mergers and acquisitions, Employee Stock Ownership Plan, and other options.

[D-278] *Handbook of Business Formulas and Controls.* Spencer A. Tucker. New York: McGraw-Hill, 1979.

Provides formulas that are used to analyze and control business operations. In section 1 there are 127 formulas and equations, along with 592 practical business problems with solutions. Addresses basic, unit, incremental, and advanced profit-planning formulas, along with formulas for operating decisions. Considers such operational areas as pricing, marketing, scarce-factor product evaluations, time value of money, break-even analysis, and investments.

Section 2 presents 251 control ratios for manufacturing and explains how to evaluate and control business activities from the grass roots to top-level management. Discusses how decisions can be tested in advance, how to ascertain where there is need for managerial action, and how to correct adverse situations.

[D-279] *The Handbook of Economic and Financial Measures.* Edited by Frank J. Fabozzi and Harry I. Greenfield. Homewood, IL: Dow Jones-Irwin, 1984.

A comprehensive guide to the standard measures of economic and financial activity. Describes the background of each measure, how it is used, weaknesses, and how it is constructed. Interprets economic indicators that are commonly reported in the news media.

[D-280] *The Handbook of Estate Planning.* Edited by D. Larry Crumbley. Homewood, IL: Dow Jones-Irwin, 1988.

A guide to estate planning. Addresses how to select an executor, trustee, or attorney; avoiding probate; federal estate and gift taxes; valuation problems; annuities; life insurance; trusts; providing for children and the elderly; and other topics involved in estate planning.

[D-281] *The Handbook of Forecasting: A Manager's Guide.* Edited by Spyros Makridakis and Steven C. Wheelwright. New York: John Wiley & Sons, Inc., 1982.

A handbook that presents the concepts, principles, and methodologies used in business forecasting. Designed for managers, it discusses the context in which forecasting takes place. Using separate authors for each chapter, a variety of ideas are presented. Forecasting is examined as it applies to sales, operations planning and control, capacity planning, finance, industrial products, services, and other business areas. Discusses what needs to be forecasted, guidelines for using the results of forecasting, and other topics important to the manager's responsibilities for planning and forecasting.

[D-282] *The Handbook of Mortgage Banking: A Guide to the Secondary Mortgage Market.* Edited by James M. Kinney and Richard T. Garrigan. Homewood, IL: Dow Jones-Irwin, 1985.

Provides an analysis of the secondary-mortgage market and related guidelines for management decisions. Stresses how to manage a mortgage banking business. Includes essays that discuss Fannie Maes, Freddie Macs, Ginnie Maes, rating agencies, legal and regulatory matters, financial management of secondary mortgages, determining yields, and related subjects.

[D-283] *Handbook of Record Storage and Space Management.* C. Peter Waegemann. Westport, CT: Quorum Books, 1983.

A handbook on space planning and management for records storage. Explains how to evaluate equipment used to store records (this includes lateral files, drawer cabinets, mobile shelving, microfilm, and others). Discusses the cost of managing records. Also addresses records retention; that is, how to formulate a policy that determines how long to keep records. A records-retention schedule is included.

[D-284] *How to Do Business With Russians: A Handbook and Guide for Western World Business People.* Misha G. Knight. New York: Quorum Books, 1987.

Explains the strategies, protocols, techniques, and procedures for doing business in the Soviet Union. Discusses how the Russians conduct business at home and abroad. Topics covered include an outlook of Soviet business conditions and export prospects, how to establish a business office in Russia, elements of the negotiation process in Russia, USSR trade fairs, Soviet customs procedures and tariffs, and other related topics.

This handbook lists the Soviet organizations that accredit foreign corporations and provides their addresses. It gives an example of the costs associated with opening an office, contains sample documents and forms that are used in business transactions with the Soviets, and explains special commercial terminology that is used by Russians in foreign trade.

[D-285] *How to Find Information About Acquisition Candidates.* Washington, DC: Washington Researchers Publishing, 1987.

Contains guidelines on how to organize and conduct corporate acquisition research. Discusses ways to identify merger/acquisition candidates and techniques for evaluating them. To guide the researcher, ten key questions are provided along with suggested sources for finding the answers. These sources are both general and industry-specific. Although all industries could not be included, basic methods and types of sources are offered. These can be applied to any industry that is being studied in the search for acquisition candidates. The sources include publications, computer databases, and government agencies. Explains the steps to be taken in the acquisition research process, from how to get started to how to recognize legal problems that could result from a corporate acquisition.

[D-286] *How to Find Information About Executives.* Washington, DC: Washington Researchers Publishing, 1986.

A guide to how and where to find information about executives in the business community. Explains procedures and places. Targets may be the competitor's business manager, plant manager, or others. Useful for locating information about prospective customers or clients, prospective employees, suppliers, the CEO of a company in which an investment is being considered, and other persons.

The sources of information are governmental agencies, the Securities and Exchange Commission, courts, trade and professional associations, labor unions, publications, databases, and other references. Also explains how to conduct telephone interviews when seeking information about persons.

[D-287] *How to Find Information About Foreign Firms.* Washington, DC: Washington Researchers Publishing, 1987.

A guide to how and where to locate information about foreign companies. Explains the special considerations that are necessary when conducting research on a foreign firm. Lists questions that should be asked and suggests guidelines for the investigation. Discusses sources of information such as publications; federal, state, and municipal governments; international intergovernmental organizations; private organizations; databases; and other sources.

[D-288] *How to Find Information About Private Companies.* Washington, DC: Washington Researchers Publishing, 1987.

Researching private companies often requires special techniques and sources. This publication explains how to conduct research on private firms and discusses sources of information. These sources include government (federal, state, and local), labor unions, trade and professional associations, private monitoring organizations, publications, databases, and others. A valuable tool for learning how to gather information on private companies.

[D-289] *How to Find Information About Service Companies.* Washington, DC: Washington Researchers Publishing, 1987.

Conducting intelligence gathering on companies that provide a service requires special procedures and sources. This publication discusses the special research methodology for collecting information on the service industry. Strategies, developing source leads, and other considerations are addressed. Provides special information sources such as government agencies (federal, state, and local), publications, databases, private monitoring organizations, trade associations, unions, and others.

[D-290] *How to Set Up Your Own Small Business.* 2 vols. Max Fallek. Minneapolis: American Institute of Small Business, 1985.

This handbook offers tips on how to establish and operate a small business. It takes a practical approach, discussing matters such as how to prepare a business plan, how to select a business name, how to choose an attorney for your business, how to determine the amount of capital that will be needed to start the business, where to secure the financing, what records are needed when setting up a business, how to select the location for the business, and other vital concerns. There is also a discussion of sales forecasting and personnel management.

[D-291] *The Investment Manager's Handbook.* Edited by Sumner N. Levine. Homewood, IL: Dow Jones-Irwin, 1980.

Designed for professional investment managers of endowments, mutual funds, pension funds, trusts, and the internal portfolios of insurance companies and saving institutions. Provides information on how to manage the different types of investment portfolios. Also discusses the federal regulations that govern investment management.

[D-292] *Labor Law Course.* 26th ed. Chicago: Commerce Clearing House, 1987.

Provides an introduction to labor law, with a focus on federal statutes. Addresses all principal areas of labor law. Includes the full text of major federal labor legislation. Also provides a digest of significant court decisions affecting labor relations.

[D-293] *Lasser's Your Income Tax.* J. K. Lasser Tax Institute. Edited by Bernard Greisman. New York: Simon & Schuster, 1987. Published annually.

This publication has been around for more than 50 years. It is one of the guides for helping complete the individual federal income-tax report. Its pages contain a succinct summary of federal income-tax law coupled with authoritative opinions, rulings, and decisions by the IRS, federal courts, and others.

Lasser's Your Income Tax has helpful explanations and instructions on how to complete Form 1040 and other forms used for individual filings. It addresses such topics as dividend income, interest income, capital gains and losses, retirement and annuity income, deductions, tax savings plans, and other tax matters. It also includes checklists for reducing taxes, tax worksheets and forms, tax tables, and tax-rate schedules. Updated annually to reflect changes in the federal income-tax laws and regulations.

[D-294] *The Loan Officer's Handbook.* Edited by William J. Korsvik and Charles O. Meiburg. Homewood, IL: Dow Jones-Irwin, 1986.

This is a basic guide for bank loan officers. It is a compilation of 42 essays that offer guidance to these officers in the various responsibilities of their job. It includes a discussion of loan-portfolio management, analytical tools (e.g., financial-statement analysis, forecasting funds flow, and product life cycle), making the loan decision, regulatory issues, and other topics concerning the loan officer.

[D-295] *The Managerial and Cost Accountant's Handbook.* Edited by Homer A. Black and James Don Edwards. Homewood, IL: Dow Jones-Irwin, 1979.

A compendium of 42 articles that were written by teams comprised jointly of accounting executives and accounting educators. These articles provide practical guidance for dealing with accounting problems confronted by managers and cost accountants. Articles address the environments of business, government, and not-for-profit organizations. The range of topics is broad, including cost components, costs related to pricing, cost accounting and organizational style, methodology of cost and managerial accounting, cost accounting for manufacturers, cost accounting for state and local governments, and cost accounting for not-for-profit organizations.

[D-296] *Marketing Handbook. Vol. 1, Marketing Practices; Vol. 2, Marketing Management.* Edited by Edwin E. Bobrow and Mark D. Bobrow. Homewood, IL: Dow Jones-Irwin, 1985.

These two volumes form a comprehensive treatment of the field of marketing. Volume 1 focuses on applied marketing by addressing such topics as strategic marketing in different types of markets, responding to change, product life cycle, market research, marketing planning, packaging, advertising, sales forecasting, pricing strategy, and other related subjects. Volume 2 addresses organizing a product-management system, improving the productivity of marketing, developing and managing new products, legal considerations in marketing, and other issues.

[D-297] *Master Federal Tax Manual.* New York: Research Institute of America, 1988. Published annually.

A condensed guide to the federal income, excise, gift, and estate-tax laws. Contains an explanation of the Internal Revenue Code and regulations. Provides special editorial comments classified as "Observations" (commentary), "Cautions" (alert), "Illustrations" (clarification), and "Recommendations" (courses of action). Provides tax rates and tax tables. This is a desktop handbook for quick referencing of the federal tax laws.

[D-298] *Miller Comprehensive GAAP Guide.* Martin A. Miller. San Diego: Harcourt Brace Jovanovich, 1988. Published annually.

Contains a restatement of the promulgated Generally Accepted Accounting Principles. Also includes many of the nonpromulgated accounting principles that are in practice. The material is presented in a concise format, and this guide has examples for illustrative purposes. Includes accounting principles for specialized industries such as banking and thrift institutions, entertainment, franchise-fee revenue, insurance industry, mortgage banking, oil- and gas-producing companies, real estate, and regulated industries. Presents the background for each accounting principle.

[D-299] *Miller Comprehensive GAAS Guide.* Martin A. Miller and Larry P. Bailey. San Diego: Harcourt Brace Jovanovich, 1987. Published annually.

A comprehensive handbook on auditing. Includes the promulgated and many nonpromulgated auditing standards, procedures, and practices. Encompasses GAAS, SAS, SSARS, SEC Auditing Releases, Statements on Quality Control Standards, Specialized Industry Audit Guides, and the Code of Professional Ethics. Also provides an internal accounting control questionnaire and a model audit program. The *Guide* addresses the auditor's plan for an audit, principles and practices for conducting an audit, legal liabilities of auditors, and other matters related to executing an audit.

[D-300] *Miller Comprehensive Governmental GAAP Guide.* Larry P. Bailey. San Diego: Harcourt Brace Jovanovich, 1987. Published annually.

Contains the promulgated accounting principles that guide financial reporting by local and state governments. Analyzes and restates the original promulgations of the Governmental Accounting Standards Board, the National Council on Governmental Accounting, and the American Institute of Certified Public Accountants.

This guide covers the underlying concepts, principles, and standards of accounting and financial reporting by governmental units. The scope embraces all state and local government entities, including hospitals, colleges and universities, and certain nonprofit organizations (e.g., libraries, museums, and research and scientific organizations).

[D-301] *Money Market Calculations: Yields, Break-Evens, and Arbitrage.* Marcia Stigum. Homewood, IL: Dow Jones-Irwin, 1981.

Presents the formulas that are used when making the many different calculations involved with money-market transactions. Formulas are for discount securities, interest-bearing securities, futures contracts, and interest arbitrage. Provides formulas to calculate yield to maturity, security prices, accrued interest, break-even point on a trade, and for other investment purposes.

[D-302] *Moody's Bond Record: Corporates, Convertibles, Governments, Municipals, Commercial Paper Ratings, Preferred Stock Ratings.* New York: Moody's Investors Service, 1988. Published monthly.

As the title indicates, this monthly publication reports descriptions and/or ratings of corporate, municipal, and U.S. government bonds, convertible bonds, commercial paper, and preferred stocks. Profiles of U.S. corporate bonds and Canadian provincial and municipal obligations include name of the issuer and the issue, interest dates, current bond price, current call price, Moody's rating, yield to maturity, price-range history, amount outstanding, amount of the sinking fund, federal tax status, date issued, and other data.

    This publication also reports Moody's ratings of municipal bonds, commercial paper, medium-term notes, convertible bonds, preferred stocks, obligations of U.S. government and federal agencies, industrial-development revenue bonds, pollution- and environmental-control revenue bonds, and railroad-equipment trust certificates. For the industrial-development and the pollution-control revenue bonds, this guide also reports the date of sale, amount issued, issuer, interest rate, maturity date, lessee or guarantor, and underwriter. Features charts that summarize sundry debt securities.

[D-303] *Moody's Handbook of Common Stocks.* New York: Moody's Investors Service, 1988. Published quarterly.

Publishes a brief profile of more than 900 stocks that have popular investor interest. These one-page profiles include ten-year statistics covering gross revenue, operating profit margin, return on equity, net income, shares outstanding, earnings per share, dividends paid per share, P/E (price/earnings) ratio, and percentage average yield. This handbook also reports on recent developments in and prospects for the company. The quality of the common stock is evaluated and assigned a grade. Finally, there are listings of corporations according to various criteria.

[D-304] *Moody's Handbook of OTC Stocks.* New York: Moody's Investors Services, 1988. Published quarterly.

Provides financial and business information on 593 companies whose common stocks are traded over-the-counter. There are one-page descriptive summaries that include the NASDAQ symbol, line of business, the approximate dividend yield, whether the stock can be purchased on margin, a long-term price chart, Moody's 7-year and 12-month stock-price scores, dividends per share, earnings per share, capitalization, annual financial data, and recent developments in the company. Also includes summaries of OTC stocks.

[D-305] *The Municipal Bond Handbook. Vol. 1.* Edited by Frank J. Fabozzi, Sylvan G. Feldstein, Irving M. Pollack, and Frank G. Zarb. Homewood, IL: Dow Jones-Irwin, 1983.

A compendium of articles on topics that encompass the breadth of the municipal-bond market. Addresses the different kinds of municipal bonds, tax issues, guidelines for determining credit risk, yield levels, pricing of bond insurance, municipal bond portfolio management, and the regulatory environment.

[D-306] *The Municipal Bond Handbook. Vol. 2.* Edited by Sylvia G. Feldstein, Frank J. Fabozzi, and Irving M. Pollack. Homewood, IL: Dow Jones-Irwin, 1983.

Contains a collection of essays on the municipal bond industry that focus on the legal framework for general obligation and revenue bonds. Also addresses the methods for analyzing selected types of municipal, hybrid, and special bonds. Discusses credit analysis of municipal notes and the technicalities of municipal accounting and financial reporting.

[D-307] *The NASDAQ Handbook.* National Association of Security Dealers. Chicago: Probus Publishing Company, 1987.

Explains the NASDAQ system, that is, how the over-the-counter system works and how it differs from the stock exchanges. This handbook describes the roles of the different participants who constitute the NASDAQ system and the services and regulations of the system. This is a valuable guide for the investor who trades in over-the-counter stocks.

Occupational Outlook Handbook. U.S. Bureau of Labor Statistics. Washington, DC: U.S. Government Printing Office, 1988. Published biennially. Updated by *Occupational Outlook Quarterly.*
See "Government Documents," [D-355].

[D-308] *Primer of Labor Relations.* 23d ed. John J. Kenny. Washington, DC: Bureau of National Affairs, 1986.

Summarizes the law of labor relations. Explains the law in clear and basic language for the layperson. The *Primer* addresses the rights of employees to organize, as prescribed by law, and outlines the legal procedure to follow when organizing a bargaining unit. It also explains the provision of the law germane to job actions, the processes for settling labor disputes, operations of unions, and other labor matters. Includes a "Table of Cases," which are those cases that have been important to labor relations.

[D-309] *Project Management Handbook.* Edited by David I. Cleland and William R. King. New York: Van Nostrand Reinhold Company, 1983.

A practical guide to project management. Explains the concepts and techniques needed to solve problems associated with managing projects in public and private organizations. Its scope encompasses large and small projects, with emphasis on managing projects in a comprehensive managerial system.

The *Project Management Handbook* contains a collection of articles written by experienced professionals. Among the topics addressed are project evaluation, selection, planning, organization, control, and other aspects of project management.

[D-310] *Project Management Operating Guidelines: Directives, Procedures, and Forms.* Harold Kerzner and Hans J. Thamhain. New York: Van Nostrand Reinhold Company, 1986.

A manual on project management that contains procedures, forms, and checklists. It provides policy directives for each phase of project management. Focuses on project initiation, bid proposals, planning, cost control, management, and other phases of project management.

Ratio Analysis for Small Business. Richard Sanzo. Washington, DC: Small Business Administration, 1977. Available from the U.S. Government Printing Office. See "Government Documents," [D-359].

[D-311] *Responsibilities of Corporate Officers and Directors Under Federal Securities Laws.* 3d ed. Chicago: Commerce Clearing House, 1988.

Discusses the duties and personal liabilities of corporate officers and directors as prescribed by federal securities laws. The coverage includes laws, rules, administrative interpretations, and court decisions. Topics encompass liabilities germane to the registration of securities, fraud violations, insider trading and tipping, filing of corporate reports, regulation of takeovers and tender offers, short-swing profit, resale of restricted stock (Rule 144), and other liabilities of corporate officers and directors.

[D-312] *The RIA Complete Analysis of the '86 Tax Reform Act.* New York: Research Institute of America, 1986.

A comprehensive explanation of the Tax Reform Act of 1986. Contains a discussion of all provisions. A table clearly indicates those sections of the Internal Revenue Code that were affected by the Act.

[D-313] *Sales Manager's Handbook.* Edited by Edwin E. Bobrow and Larry Wizenberg. Homewood, IL: Dow Jones-Irwin, 1983.

A compendium of 31 essays written by authorities on sales management. Offers suggestions, strategies, and practical guidance in this field. The chapters discuss how to structure the sales organization, approaches to selling in the marketplace, communication, sales forecasting, sales campaigns, recruiting and training a sales force, motivation, legal considerations in sales management, accounting, and other related topics.

[D-314] *Security Owner's Stock Guide.* New York: Standard & Poor's Corporation, 1988. Published monthly.

A guide to common and preferred stocks. Reports a broad range of descriptive data on each stock. Profiles of the stocks include the stock exchange on which the stock is listed, ticker symbol, principal business of the company, stock split ratios during the past five years, ranking of a common stock and rating of a preferred stock, years of consecutive dividend payments, dividend payment statistics, earnings per share, high/low price range, call price of preferred stocks, and other descriptive information. The *Guide* discloses changes in the rating/ranking of stocks.

In a separate section, comparable profiles are provided for mutual bond funds.

[D-315] *Spectrum 1: Investment Company Stock Holdings Survey.* Rockville, MD: Computer Directions Advisors Investment Technologies, Inc., 1988. Published quarterly.

Contains an alphabetical listing, by stock name, of all common stocks held by all mutual funds. These holdings include issues on the New York Stock Exchange, American Stock Exchange, and over-the-counter. The data reported include the identity of the management company of each mutual fund, amount of change in shareholdings during the most recent quarter, and the total shares owned at the end of the quarter. Contains a "Summary of Fund Holdings by Industry Group" and a listing of the 100 largest (by dollar value) purchases, sales, and holdings. Includes domestic and European mutual funds.

[D-316] *Spectrum 2: Investment Company Portfolios.* Rockville, MD: Computer Directions Advisors Investment Technologies, Inc., 1988. Published quarterly.

An alphabetical listing of all common stocks held by mutual funds, organized by name of fund. The data include name of the mutual fund, amount of increase or decrease in shareholdings of a stock during the last quarter, number of shares owned of a stock at the end of the most recent quarter, market value of shares owned of each stock, net assets of the fund at the end of the quarter, and the name of the fund's management company. Also reports a "Summary of Fund Holdings by Industry Group" and a listing of the 100 largest purchases, sales, and holdings, all by dollar value. Includes domestic and European funds. *Spectrum 2* differs from *Spectrum 1* in its organization of the data.

[D-317] *Spectrum 3: Institutional Stock Holdings Survey.* Rockville, MD: Computer Directions Advisors Investment Technologies, Inc., 1988. Published quarterly.

A listing of the equity holdings, and changes in these holdings, of institutions that are required to file Form 13F with the Securities and Exchange Commission. These institutions include banks, insurance companies, pension funds, endowments, foundations, and others. The information is arranged by name of stock. For each institution, *Spectrum 3* reports the companies in which stock is held, the number of shares owned at the end of the quarter, and changes that occurred in shareholdings during the past quarter. For these institutional portfolios, includes a summary of holdings by industry group. Also discloses the stocks that comprise the top 100 holdings, sales, and purchases for these Form 13F institutions.

[D-318] *Spectrum 4: Institutional Portfolios.* Rockville, MD: Computer Directions Advisors Investment Technologies, Inc., 1988. Published quarterly.

An alphabetical listing of all common stocks held in portfolios by banks, insurance companies, pension funds, endowments, and foundations, arranged by institutional owner. These institutions must file Form 13F with the Securities and Exchange Commission. The reported data include changes in shareholdings of a stock during the past quarter, number of shares held at the end of the quarter, and the market value of these shares. For these institutional portfolios, there is reported a summary of holdings by industry group. Discloses the stocks that constitute the top 100 holdings, sales, and purchases for these Form 13F institutions.

[D-319] *Spectrum 5: Five Percent Ownership.* Rockville, MD: Computer Directions Advisors Investment Technologies, Inc., 1988. Published monthly.

A listing of beneficial owners of 5 percent or more of the outstanding stock of a corporation that is traded in the United States. Owners include individuals, partnerships, corporations, or others, both foreign and domestic. The sources of data are Schedules 13G, 13D, and 14D-1, which must be filed with the Securities and Exchange Commission.

Spectrum 5 is divided into three sections; (1) new 5 percent beneficial owners (Schedules 13D and 14D-1), (2) a cumulative listing of all 5 percent beneficial owners (Schedules 13G, 13D, and 14D-1), and (3) a directory that lists 5 percent beneficial owners with their addresses and telephone numbers. In sections 1 and 2 can be found the amount of prior and current shareholdings.

[D-320] *Spectrum 6: Insider Holdings.* Rockville, MD: Computer Directions Advisors Investment Technologies, Inc., 1988. Published semiannually.

A listing of all corporate officers and directors who own stocks or bonds in their company. Also identifies the 10 percent principal bond or stockholders of a corporation. The data were derived from Forms 3 and 4 of the Securities and Exchange Commission. Includes the names of inside holders, the number of shares held by each, and the date and amount of the recent trade.

[D-321]   *Start-Up Money: How to Finance Your New Small Business.* Mike P. McKeever. Berkeley, CA: Mike P. McKeever, 1984. Available from Nolo Press.

Designed to assist the entrepreneur who wishes to raise money to either start or expand a small business. Offers detailed instructions on how to write a business plan and prepare a loan application. Discusses how to assess your idea for a new or expanded business, sources of funds for starting a small business, how to prepare a cash flow and capital spending forecast, ways to present your business plan to a financier, and other helpful hints on getting started in business.

[D-322] *Stock Market Encyclopedia.* Vol. 10, no. 3. New York: Standard & Poor's Corporation, August, 1988. Published quarterly.

Contains financial profiles of 750 companies that are representative of those that have been described in *Standard & Poor's Stock Reports* [D-462]. These 750 are large and actively traded stocks either on the American Stock Exchange, New York Stock Exchange, or NASDAQ.

The profiles include major income-account and balance-sheet data, dividends, earnings, and price history. These profiles have focal sections titled "Current Outlook," "Important Developments," "Business Summary," and "Review of Operations." This is a brief yet comprehensive summary of a firm's financial operations and its stock's performance. Descriptions of stock include the P/E (price/earnings) ratio, seven-year market-action chart, per-share data, annual dividend-payment data, and other information.

The *Stock Market Encyclopedia* also offers summary data for the American Stock Exchange, New York Stock Exchange, and NASDAQ by ranking stocks on different criteria, whereas the *Stock Reports* does not provide this summary. The latter has a separate edition for each stock exchange. Thus the *Encyclopedia* reports the same kind of financial statistics for individual companies, but limits its profiles to the 750 most actively traded stocks on the AMEX, NYSE, and NASDAQ.

[D-323] *Symbol Guide.* Mt. Laurel, NJ: ADP Brokerage Information Services Group, 1988. Published semiannually, with supplements between each issue.

Provides an alphabetical listing of symbols used on the securities, futures, and options exchanges in the U.S. and Canada. These include the New York Stock Exchange, American Stock Exchange, NASDAQ, the regional stock exchanges, and other types of exchanges. Coverage includes U.S. stocks, mutual funds, money market funds, commodities, bonds, Treasury notes, and U.S. options on equities and nonequities. The *Symbol Guide* also includes Canadian securities, OTC issues, futures, and options.

This is an operations manual for the publisher's online service; consequently, for technical reasons, the symbols of some NASDAQ–OTC stocks have been modified by the publisher to accommodate its online system.

[D-324] *Techniques of Financial Analysis.* 6th ed. Erich A. Helfert. Homewood, IL: Richard D. Irwin, Inc., 1987.

A handbook containing the technical tools used for financial analysis. It contains ratio formulas, techniques for projecting operating performance and financial requirements, methods for managing operating funds, how to assess the cost of capital, an analysis of financing alternatives for business, and other topics germane to corporate financial analysis.

[D-325] *Ten-Second Business Forms.* Robert L. Adams. Boston: Bob Adams, Inc., 1987.

Designed to facilitate business record keeping. Presents a collection of business forms that address most areas of business management that require the organization of information. Its array includes forms for quotes, bids, estimates, proposals, work orders, and packing slips. Also includes credit/debit notices, salesperson's daily record forms, invoices, balance sheet, daily cash record, accounts-receivable aging chart, account record, office communication forms, personnel records (e.g., time sheets, payroll records, and employment applications), profit-and-loss statement, straight-line depreciation schedule, inventory control forms, and other types of forms that are used in business. The reader is informed as to the kinds of information that should be maintained.

[D-326] *Thorndike Encyclopedia of Banking and Financial Tables.* 3d ed. David Thorndike. Boston: Warren, Gorham & Lamont, 1987. Published annually.

A compilation of banking and financial tables that are used in the U.S. These tables are grouped according to: (1) Loan Payment and Amortization, (2) Compound Interest and Annuity, (3) Interest, (4) Savings and Withdrawal, (5) Installment Loan, Leasing, and Rebate, and (6) Investment. Provides instructions on how to use each table. Also contains definitions of financial terms.

[D-327] *Understanding Wall Street.* 2d ed. Jeffrey B. Little and Lucien Rhodes. Blue Ridge Summit, PA: TAB Books, Liberty House Division, 1987.

A guide to the workings of Wall Street. Explains stocks and their transactions, how to read investment tables on the financial pages, how to interpret corporate financial statements, the principles and practices of investing and trading, bonds and bond tables, stock options, and many other features of Wall Street. This is a basic handbook for the investor.

[D-328] *U.S. Master Tax Guide.* 71st ed. Chicago: Commerce Clearing House, 1987. Published annually.

This is a condensed guide to the federal income-tax laws. It has been written for laypersons and professionals who prepare tax returns. Contains a variety of checklists (e.g., Taxable Income Items; Medical Expenses; Business Deductions, Merchants and Professional Persons; Losses; and Investors' Expenses). There is an extensive explanation of the Internal Revenue Code, including examples. Includes cross references to paragraphs in the *Standard Federal Tax Reports* [D-422]. Provides numerous tables, including tax-rate schedules, tax tables, and corporate income tax rates.

[D-329] *Valuing a Business: The Analysis and Appraisal of Closely-Held Companies.* Shannon P. Pratt. Homewood, IL: Dow Jones-Irwin, 1981.

Discusses the theory and practice of valuing a business, especially medium-size and large closely-held businesses. Explains how to conduct the appropriate financial analysis, including comparative ratio analysis. Addresses the issues involved in the sale of full or partial interest in a business. Focuses on how to gather the necessary data, how to prepare the written appraisal report, and other topics related to buying or selling a business.

[D-330] *Valuing Small Businesses and Professional Practices.* Shannon P. Pratt. Homewood, IL: Dow Jones-Irwin, 1986.

Explains how to appraise the value of small businesses and professional practices in the U.S. and Canada. Discusses common errors that occur in the valuation process. Topics covered include different values for different purposes, the difference in the appraisal of large and small businesses, financial analysis of the company, methods used to determine value, appraising a professional practice, valuing for various types of litigation and estate planning, appraising intangible assets, and other related topics.

[D-331] *VGM's Careers Encyclopedia.* 2d ed. Edited by Craig T. Norback. Lincolnwood, IL: National Textbook Company, 1988.

An encyclopedic guide to career information. Profiles occupations by reporting the nature of the work, qualifications and training required, advancement potential, compensation, working conditions, and sources of additional information for the profiled occupation.

Government Documents

[D-332] *Attorneys and Agents Registered to Practice Before the U.S. Patent and Trademark Office.* U.S. Patent and Trademark Office. Washington, DC: U.S. Government Printing Office, 1988. Published annually.

A directory of names, addresses, and telephone numbers of attorneys and agents who have been registered to practice before the U.S. Patent and Trademark Office. Reports their registration number. Includes persons in the U.S. and in foreign countries.

[D-333] *Basic Facts About Trademarks.* U.S. Patent and Trademark Office. Washington, DC: U.S. Government Printing Office, 1988.

Gives an explanation of a trademark and the benefits of registering one. Describes the filing requirements in detail, and lists the international classes of trademarks used for goods and services. Contains trademark application forms and reports the required registration fees.

[D-334] *BLS News.* U.S. Bureau of Labor Statistics. Washington, DC: U.S. Government Printing Office. Published monthly.

A newsletter series that announces economic statistics, such as the Consumer Price Index for the nation and by region. Published by the U.S. Bureau of Labor Statistics for the purpose of providing a timely release of economic data.

[D-335] *Budget of the United States Government.* U.S. Office of Management and Budget. Washington, DC: U.S. Government Printing Office, 1988. Published annually.

This is the official annual budget message of the U.S. government's executive branch, with an overview of the president's budget proposal. It contains the president's economic outlook, economic assumptions, and priorities for the nation during the forthcoming fiscal period. Within this document is to be found revenue estimates for the new fiscal year and actual budget data for previous years. It covers federal receipts by source, federal programs by function, and displays the proposed budget for each federal agency and function within the agency.

[D-336] *Business Statistics.* 25th ed. U.S. Bureau of Economic Analysis. Washington, DC: U.S. Government Printing Office, 1987. Published biennially.

A supplement to *Survey of Current Business* [D-363], *Business Statistics* reports a wealth of historical economic statistics for the more than 1,900 economic data series that are used by the Bureau of Economic Analysis to calculate the Gross National Product and which are reported in the *Survey*. *Business Statistics* contains monthly data for the past four years and annual statistics for the past 25 years concerning general business indicators, economic indicators, and individual industry characteristics such as production, sales, inventories, and import and export data. Monthly data are reported for 267 selected series covering 22 years. Also provided are quarterly and annual data extending over 31 years for National Income and Product Accounts, New Plant and Equipment Expenditures, and U.S. International Transactions.

With this extensive array of data on the economy at large and on individual industries, *Business Statistics* is a valuable source with which to initiate a search for historical economic data. The information is updated monthly with the *Survey of Current Business*.

[D-337] *Census of Construction Industries.* U.S. Bureau of the Census. Washington, DC: U.S. Government Printing Office, 1982. Revised every five years.

One of the components of the quinquennial economic census, this series reports descriptive data on different areas of the construction industry. These include general contractors (residential and nonresidential), operative builders, special contractors (e.g., electricians, plumbers, heating, carpenters), and subdividers and developers of real estate. The data are reported for the entire U.S., by state, and for selected SMSAs. Illustrative of the data are receipts, employment, payrolls, hours worked, payments for materials and supplies, payments for fuels and rentals, value added, and other data.

[D-338] *Census of Manufactures.* U.S. Bureau of the Census. Washington, DC: U.S. Government Printing Office, 1982. Revised every five years, with annual partial updates published in the *Annual Survey of Manufactures*.

A component of the quinquennial economic census of the Bureau of the Census. The *Census of Manufactures* reports on the manufacturing industry of the U.S. Industry statistics are summarized for the U.S., each state, MSAs, counties, and places with populations of at least 2,500. These industry data are also arranged by Standard Industrial Classification (SIC) industry group.

Included among the comprehensive data are total employment, payroll, production-worker hours and wages, value added by manufacture, value of shipments, beginning-of-year and end-of-year inventories, new-capital expenditures, selected operating ratios, and other data that describe the industrial activity of America. Includes a table that displays an array of historical statistics for the different product classes.

[D-339] *Census of Population.* U.S. Bureau of the Census. Washington, DC: U.S. Government Printing Office, 1980. Revised decennially.

This title actually represents an extensive series of reports that describe the population of the U.S. and its possessions. Included are such subtitles as "Number of Inhabitants," "General Population Characteristics," "General Social and Economic Characteristics," and others. Reports the number of persons living in the U.S. and describes them in terms of age, race, sex, marital status, education, income, labor force, occupation, and other demographic variables. The data are summarized for the U.S. and detailed by state.

[D-340] *Census of Retail Trade.* U.S. Bureau of the Census. Washington, DC: U.S. Government Printing Office, 1982. Revised every five years and partially updated with monthly and annual surveys.

As part of the quinquennial economic census, this series provides a statistical analysis of retail business in the U.S. It focuses on retail trade defined as businesses that primarily sell merchandise for personal or household consumption or that render services related to these sales. The *Census of Retail Trade* consists of the *Geographic Area Series, Major Retail Centers Series,* and the *Industry Series.*

The retail-trade industry is described by reporting the kinds of businesses according to their Standard Industrial Classification (SIC) code group and the number of enterprises in each group, sales volume, first quarter and annual payroll, and the number of employees. Furthermore, a diversity of statistics are provided for selected industries, with the data being unique to the activity of each retail industry. Examples of the kinds of data that are reported include the dollar value of sales per square feet of selling space, the average cost per meal charged by restaurants in selected SMSAs, sales of gallons of gasoline by type of dispensing system per SMSA, and data on lease departments in main stores. Again, due to the large diversity of industries in retail trade, the array of data is extensive.

The arrangement of data is for the total U.S. and by state, SMSA, county, and for places with populations of more than 2,500. Descriptive data are also given for shopping centers, malls, and other neighborhood business districts. The *Census of Retail Trade* is a significant source of information on retail trade germane to sales volume, operating costs, capacity, operating ratios, physical plant variables, and other related factors. These are presented in a scope that ranges from national summaries to local shopping centers.

[D-341] *Census of Service Industries.* U.S. Bureau of the Census. Washington, DC: U.S. Government Printing Office, 1982. Revised every five years and partially updated annually.

A component of the quinquennial economic census series, *Census of Service Industries* provides descriptive statistical data on the service industry of the U.S.; that is, those businesses that offer services to individuals and/or other businesses. The data cover the different service-industry categories in the Standard Industrial Classification (SIC) system. Excludes elementary and secondary schools, institutions of higher education, labor unions, political organizations, religious organizations, governmental organizations, hospitals, and private households. Includes the service classifications of hotel, automotive repair, legal services, social services, health services (excluding hospitals), recreation services, and others.

Data are presented for the total U.S., individual states, SMSAs, counties, places with a population of at least 2,500, and areas within a state that are outside of the SMSAs. Among the data reported are the number of service establishments, receipts, expenses, payroll, and selected operating ratios.

[D-342] *Census of Wholesale Trade.* U.S. Bureau of the Census. Washington, DC: U.S. Government Printing Office, 1982. Revised every five years and partially updated in between by intervening surveys.

As part of the U.S. quinquennial economic census, the *Census of Wholesale Trade* specializes in businesses that sell merchandise to retail stores, other wholesalers, farms, institutions, and other professional users. It describes wholesale-trade activity by providing statistical data reported for the total U.S. and each state, SMSA, county, and place with a population of at least 2,500. Also reports data by type of wholesaler and line of commodity. The kinds of data published for Standard Industrial Classification (SIC) industries are sales volume, payroll, operating expenses, inventories, operating ratios, and other data for wholesale trade.

[D-343] *Code of Federal Regulations.* Office of the Federal Register. Washington, DC: U.S. Government Printing Office, 1988. Revised at least once each calendar year, with the component titles issued on a quarterly schedule. Supplemented five days weekly by the *Federal Register* [D-350].

Often cited as *CFR*, the *Code of Federal Regulations* consists of 50 titles that are a compilation of the general and permanent regulations in force by executive departments and agencies of the federal government. Most of these rules were first published in the *Federal Register*. To determine the latest version of a rule, refer to the *CFR* and then to subsequent issues of the *Federal Register*, because the latter updates the *CFR*. Each of the 50 titles specializes on specific subjects. The titles are divided into chapters, parts, and sections.

[D-344] *Consumer's Resource Handbook.* 4th ed. Washington, DC: U.S. Office of Consumer Affairs, 1988. Published biennially.

A guidebook for consumers. It explains how to make a consumer complaint, including guidance for writing a complaint letter. Discusses major sources of help that are available to consumers. Furnishes a "Consumer Assistance Directory" that lists federal, state, county, and city government consumer protection/assistance offices with their addresses and telephone numbers. The reader can also identify the names of consumer-affairs representatives for major corporations. Includes a directory of local better-business bureaus.

[D-345] *CPI Detailed Report.* U.S. Bureau of Labor Statistics. Washington, DC: U.S. Government Printing Office, 1988. Published monthly.

This monthly report follows the movement of the U.S. consumer prices for the nation at large, by region, and for selected cities. Two price indexes are reported: the Consumer Price Index for All Urban Consumers (CPI-U) and the Consumer Price Index for Wage Earners and Clerical Workers (CPI-W). These indexes are based on data for the U.S. city average and selected metropolitan areas. Provides current and historical CPI statistics. Indexes are reported for expenditure categories and for commodity and service groups. There are special indexes, such as all items exclusive of food, all items exclusive of shelter, commodities excluding food, and services excluding selected categories of service. This is an important source of current information on the Consumer Price Index.

[D-346] *Directory of Federal Laboratory and Technology Resources: A Guide to Services, Facilities, and Expertise.* Center for the Utilization of Federal Technology. Springfield, VA: National Technical Information Service, 1986. Published biennially.

A directory of federal laboratories and engineering centers. Provides a brief description of each, including address, telephone number, name of contact person, and an explanation of at least one of the following: services, expertise, facility, or information services. These resource centers are indexed by subject, state, available resources, and agency.

Dictionary of Occupational Titles. 4th ed. Washington, DC: U.S. Employment and Training Administration, 1977. There is a 1986 supplement to this edition. Available from the U.S. Government Printing Office.
See "Dictionaries," [D-122].

[D-347] *Employment and Earnings.* U.S. Bureau of Labor Statistics. Washington, DC: U.S. Government Printing Office, 1988. Published monthly.

A primary source for obtaining statistical data on the employed and unemployed populations. Reports data at the national, state, and industry levels. Offers information on the general population and specially targeted populations, with statistics for the average number of hours worked per week, hourly and weekly earnings, productivity data, and other statistics. Distinguishes between seasonally adjusted and nonseasonally adjusted data.

There is a listing of special reports that are issued each year and the monthly issue in which each is scheduled to appear.

[D-348] *Employment, Hours, and Earnings: States and Areas, 1939–1982.* 2 vols. U.S. Bureau of Labor Statistics. Washington, DC: U.S. Government Printing Office, 1984. Revised approximately every four or five years.

For specified years, reports for each state and selected metropolitan areas the number of employees, average weekly hours worked, and average hourly and weekly earnings. These historical time series are arranged by Standard Industrial Classification industry group, both statewide and within each metropolitan area. The data are delimited to nonfarm industries.

[D-349] *Employment, Hours, and Earnings: United States, 1909–1984.* 2 vols. U.S. Bureau of Labor Statistics. Washington, DC: U.S. Government Printing Office, 1985. Revised periodically and updated annually with the *Supplement to Employment and Earnings* [D-362].

A historical databook on employment, hours, and earnings for each nonagricultural industry. Reports the total number of employees per industry and the number of women employees. Also reports, for specified years and on monthly and annual bases, the average hours worked per week and the average hourly and weekly earnings paid per industry. Industries are those identified in the Standard Industrial Classification system. This is a major source of historical employment data, especially for wages paid in each industry.

[D-350] *Federal Register.* Office of the Federal Register. Washington DC: U.S. Government Printing Office, 1988. Published five days a week.

Publishes the *proposed* rules and regulations of the departments and agencies of the executive branch of the federal government. It is the first place that new regulations are published. Serves as the daily supplement to the *Code of Federal Regulations* [D-343]. The *Federal Register* is the daily publication that announces operating rules of federal executive offices, and it publishes notices of orders and opinions of these departments and agencies.

Franchise Opportunities Handbook. 21st ed. Andrew Kostecka. Washington, DC: U.S. Government Printing Office, 1988. Published annually.
See "Directories," [D-179].

[D-351] *Historical Statistics of the United States, Colonial Times to 1970, Bicentennial Edition.* 2 vols. U.S. Bureau of the Census. Washington, DC: U.S. Government Printing Office, 1975.

A companion to the *Statistical Abstract of the United States* [D-361], this publication provides the historical "trail of data" for many of the statistical series that are found in the *Statistical Abstract.* The scope of data is extensive; it presents the characteristics of the U.S. population and a vast array of variables related to business, industry, and the economy from colonial days to recent times. Industry-specific statistics are included, as are those for the economy at large. The reporting covers vital statistics, migration figures, and social statistics. Within its pages are interesting data that describe economic events of colonial America. This is a significant source of annual figures that reflect the history of the U.S.

[D-352] *Index to the U.S. Patent Classification.* U.S. Patent and Trademark Office. Washington, DC: U.S. Government Printing Office, 1987. Updated annually.

Also available for use at one of the Patent Depository Libraries. For a directory of these libraries, see *Official Gazette of the United States Patent and Trademark Office* [D-357].

Serves as an index to the classes and subclasses of the patent classification system used by the U.S. Patent and Trademark Office. This index is an alphabetical listing of subject headings that refer to the classes. It functions as an entry into the patent-classification system. After identifying the classes and subclasses of interest in the *Index*, the reader then refers to the *Manual of Classification* [D-353] for further refinement of the patent search: that is, to determine the precise applicable class or subclass.

[D-353] *Manual of Classification.* U.S. Patent and Trademark Office. Washington, DC: U.S. Government Printing Office, 1988. Updated semiannually.

Provides the descriptive titles and numbers of all classes and subclasses that comprise the patent classification system of the U.S. Patent and Trademark Office. Also lists unofficial subclasses. Explains how the patent classification system works.

[D-354] *Monthly Catalog of United States Government Publications.* Washington, DC: U.S. Government Printing Office. Published monthly.

An index of publications issued by the federal government. Provides a bibliographical description of the documents. Indexes them by title, author, subject, and series/report number. The *Cumulative Subject Index to the Monthly Catalog of United States Government Publications* is the composite index to the *Monthly Catalog* for the period 1900–1971.

[D-355] *Occupational Outlook Handbook.* U.S. Bureau of Labor Statistics. Washington, DC: U.S. Government Printing Office, 1988. Published biennially. Updated by *Occupational Outlook Quarterly*.

Presents detailed descriptions for about 225 occupations and summary descriptions for about 125 additional occupations. The detailed profiles include discussion of the nature of the work, working conditions, training, earnings, related occupations, employment outlook, and sources of additional information.

Provides suggestions for writing a job résumé and how to prepare for an interview. Includes a directory of state and local sources for job-market and career information. For each occupation that is listed, cites the occupational code assigned in the *Dictionary of Occupational Titles* [D-122].

[D-356] *Official Congressional Directory.* Washington, DC: U.S. Government Printing Office. Published biennially to coincide with each new Congress.

The official membership directory of the U.S. Congress. It publishes a brief biography of each member, states the district of each representative and the counties and ZIP codes that comprise that congressional district, lists the state delegations, and provides the names of the members and staff of Senate and House committees and subcommittees. Also reports the names of staff members for each member of Congress. The *Official Congressional Directory* contains a directory of names, addresses, and telephone numbers of officers of the Congress and officials in the executive branch and independent agencies.

Prints brief biographies of members of the U.S. Supreme Court and other federal courts. Lists the names, addresses, and telephone numbers of foreign diplomatic representatives to the U.S. and locations of foreign consular offices in the U.S. Also gives the names of U.S. ambassadors to foreign countries and the location of U.S. embassies and consular offices. There is a directory of international organizations, with their addresses, telephone numbers, and names of member nations and, in some cases, the names of officials.

[D-357] *Official Gazette of the United States Patent and Trademark Office.* 2 vols. Washington, DC: U.S. Government Printing Office, 1988. Published weekly.

The official listing of patents and trademarks pending or recently registered, renewed, cancelled, or amended with the U.S. Patent and Trademark Office. Published in two volumes: (1) *Patents* and (2) *Trademarks*. The patent descriptions and trademark designs are included along with the owner's name and the Patent and Trademark Office's identification number. Also included are notices of the office regarding patents and trademarks. Contains a directory of services provided by the office and the telephone number for each service.

[D-358] *Producer Price Indexes.* U.S. Bureau of Labor Statistics. Washington, DC: U.S. Government Printing Office, 1988. Published monthly. Formerly titled *Producer Prices and Price Indexes*.

This monthly report discloses movements in producer prices. Producer Price Indexes are reported for selected industries, commodity groupings and individual items within them, by stage of processing, and for other special categories. Annual averages are reported in an annual supplement.

[D-359] *Ratio Analysis for Small Business.* Richard Sanzo, Small Business Administration. Washington, DC: U.S. Government Printing Office, 1977.

Discusses the ratios that are used to conduct financial analyses of small businesses. Gives formulas and explains how to interpret and evaluate these ratios.

[D-360] *Standard Industrial Classification Manual.* U.S. Office of Management and Budget. Springfield, VA: National Technical Information Service, 1987.

The Standard Industrial Classification (SIC) system is a standardized categorization of types of business and economic activity. This four-digit hierarchical system was developed by the U.S. Office of Management and Budget. It permits the classification of industries and their subunits. The SIC is used for the systematic collection, analysis, and dissemination of statistical business and economic data. This manual contains the official definitions of the SIC groups.

[D-361] *Statistical Abstract of the United States.* U.S. Bureau of the Census. Washington, DC: U.S. Government Printing Office, 1988. Published annually.

Summarizes social, political, and economic statistics of the United States; consequently, it is a major source of statistical information. The *Statistical Abstract* also functions as a guide to other sources of statistical information through its source notes, section introductions, and Appendix 1.

The focus is primarily on national data, but regional, state, and local data can also be found. Reports population statistics, education data, labor force, employment earnings, finances of state and local governments, price indexes, business activity, vital statistics on manufacturing, comparative international statistics, and other statistical data. Contains a bibliography of sources of statistical information available from the federal government, individual states, selected nations, and nongovernment sources.

For historical statistical data that do not appear in an edition of *Statistical Abstracts*, see *Historical Statistics of the United States* [D-351].

[D-362] *Supplement to Employment and Earnings.* U.S. Bureau of Labor Statistics. Washington, DC: U.S. Government Printing Office, 1988. Published annually.

This publication updates *Employment, Hours, and Earnings: United States 1909– 1984* [D-349] by providing monthly and annual averages for the size of employment and weekly hours of productivity, and the average hourly and weekly earnings. It reports data for the current and previous five years for each nonagricultural industry, categorized by Standard Industrial Classification code.

[D-363] *Survey of Current Business.* U.S. Bureau of Economic Analysis. Washington, DC: U.S. Government Printing Office, 1988. Published monthly.

This periodical is a major source of information on U.S. business and economic statistics. It is the principal publication for obtaining values on the National Income and Product Accounts (NIPA). Updates, monthly, the statistical data contained in the biennial *Business Statistics* [D-336].

In fulfilling its purpose, *Survey of Current Business* provides tables that cover the more than 1,900 major economic data series used by the U.S. Bureau of Economic Analysis (BEA) to calculate the Gross National Product (GNP). Business and leading economic indicators are reported along with individual-industry data. Also published in this title are the special reports of studies conducted by the BEA. These reports appear at different times of the year; a schedule of release dates appears on the back cover of the monthly issues.

[D-364] *United States Code.* 1982 ed. Supplement 4. Washington, DC: U.S. Government Printing Office, 1987. Periodic editions are published, plus cumulative annual supplements.

Contains "the general and permanent laws of the U.S." It is an informal presentation of these laws, organized in 50 titles (broad subjects). For example, Title 12 is "Banks and Banking," Title 15 is "Commerce and Trade," and Title 26 is "Internal Revenue Code." The laws are published verbatim, there being minor editorial changes of a nonsubstantive nature. Thus, the *USC* is a restatement of the federal laws.

[D-365] *United States Code Annotated.* St. Paul, MN: West Publishing Company, 1988. Updated annually with cumulative pocket parts that are based on a quarterly pamphlet series. New editions of the *USCA* are published periodically.

Contains U.S. laws of a general and permanent nature arranged under the same 50 titles as in the *United States Code* [D-364]. The additional feature of the *USCA* is that it provides annotations of these laws. The annotations are digests of federal and state court decisions, and those of the U.S. comptroller general and the U.S. Merit Systems Protection Board. Opinions of the U.S. attorney general are also included.

[D-366] *United States Government Manual.* Office of the Federal Register. Washington, DC: U.S. Government Printing Office, 1988. Published annually.

Focusing on programs and activities, this is the official handbook of the federal government. It contains information on the legislative, executive, and judicial branches, including departments, committees, commissions, quasi-official agencies, and boards. Also includes information on international organizations of which the U.S. is a member.

  The profiles report the legislative or executive authority for the governmental unit, its purpose and history, and a description of its programs and activities. Contains the names of principal officials, the addresses and telephone numbers of the main and field offices of the governmental unit, and other related information.

[D-367] *U.S. Industrial Outlook.* U.S. International Trade Administration. Washington, DC: U.S. Government Printing Office, 1988. Published annually.

Consisting of signed narrative analyses and statistical data, this guide to individual American industries provides an overview of current conditions, an outlook for the forthcoming year, and a five-year forecast. Statistical data are reported for (1) "total industry" output per industry and (2) product totals, regardless of the industry that produced the product. The "total industry" production data include all output, even for products that are primarily classified under another SIC industry code.

  Information for an industry includes dollar value of shipments, total employment, number of production workers, average hourly earnings, value of imports and exports, and other relevant data. This is a major U.S. government publication that analyzes U.S. industries and provides both historical performance data and economic forecasts. Individual companies are not discussed.

[D-368] *United States Statutes at Large.* Washington, DC: U.S. Government Printing Office, 1988. Published at the conclusion of each session of the U.S. Congress.

Contains the verbatim text of public and private laws passed by the Congress, along with concurrent resolutions, proclamations, and Constitutional amendments. This is the primary source for finding federal laws because its text of the laws has not been edited.

[D-369] *United States Treaties and Other International Agreements.* Washington, DC: U.S. Government Printing Office, 1988. Published annually.

Contains the full text of treaties and other international agreements (diplomatic notes, declarations, and others) between the U.S. and other nations. Indexes by country and subject. This is the bound form of the *Treaties and Other International Acts Series*, starting with T.I.A.S. No. 2010.

Loose-Leaf Materials

[D-370] *Accounting for Government Contracts: Cost Accounting Standards.* Lane K. Anderson. New York: Matthew Bender & Company, 1988. Updated annually.

A loose-leaf service that keeps abreast of the standards of cost accounting, regulations, techniques, and practices that are used in the determination of allowable costs by the federal government in its dealings with contractors. For each standard of cost accounting there is a discussion of its purpose, fundamental requirement, techniques for application, exemptions, definitions, and an explanation of other matters related to the standard. There is also an explanation of the pronouncements of the Cost Accounting Standards Board.

[D-371] *AICPA Professional Standards.* 2 vols. American Institute of Certified Public Accountants. Chicago: Commerce Clearing House, 1988. Updated irregularly.

This loose-leaf service, prepared by the American Institute of Certified Public Accountants, reports U.S. professional accounting standards, the Statements of International Accounting Standards of the International Accounting Standards Committee, the International Auditing Guidelines, and the International Statements on Auditing of the International Auditing Practices Committee.

Volume 1 contains U.S. auditing standards. These include general standards, field-work standards, and reporting standards. Also includes attestation engagement standards and standards pertaining to services of accountants on prospective financial information. This volume concludes with auditing interpretations.

Volume 2 contains accounting and review services, the AICPA's Code of Professional Ethics, and its bylaws. Also appearing in this volume are the International Accounting Standards and the International Auditing Guidelines.

[D-372] *AICPA Technical Practice Aids.* 2 vols. American Institute of Certified Public Accountants. Chicago: Commerce Clearing House. Updated irregularly.

Volume 1 of this loose-leaf service contains selected responses of the Technical Information Service of the American Institute of Certified Public Accountants to inquiries that have been submitted by professional accountants related to accounting and auditing matters. Topics include specialized industry problems, specialized organizational problems, presentation of financial statements, assets, liabilities, auditor's reports, and other topics that have been confronted.

Volume 2 reports positions that have been taken by the Accounting Standards Division and the Auditing Standards Division of the AICPA on different issues germane to for-profit and not-for-profit organizations and to government accounting.

[D-373] *The AMA Handbook of Key Management Forms.* Edited by David M. Brownstone and Irene M. Franck. New York: American Management Association, 1987.

A sample of model forms used by private businesses for performing internal management activities. Organized by functional area, these forms are used for personnel management (activities such as hiring, training, supervision, compliance, and payroll), benefits and fringes, financial operations, sales and marketing, purchasing, plant operations, communications, and other aspects of management.

[D-374] *Applying GAAP and GAAS.* 2 vols. Paul Munter and Thomas A. Ratcliffe. New York: Matthew Bender & Company, 1988. Updated semiannually.

This loose-leaf service provides a complete guide to the generally accepted accounting principles and the generally accepted auditing standards. It includes pronouncements of the Financial Accounting Standards Board (FASB), American Institute of Certified Public Accountants (AICPA), and other organizations. The scope is comprehensive.

[D-375] *Blue Sky Law Reports.* 4 vols. Chicago: Commerce Clearing House, 1984 to date. Updated bimonthly.

Usually referred to as *Blue Sky Law Reporter*, it publishes the full text of the 1956 and 1985 U.S. Uniform Securities Acts and the securities laws and regulations of the fifty states, District of Columbia, Guam, and Puerto Rico. Also reports the takeover disclosure statutes of the states, which govern the acquisition of equity securities of domestic corporations. The *Blue Sky Law Reports* contains, for the individual states, the insurance securities laws, in full text, that govern the sales and issuance of insurance securities.

This is the publication for finding the regulations, rules, orders, policy statements, and rulings issued by Blue Sky regulatory authorities. Starting with the first Blue Sky Act in 1911, it reports federal and state court decisions, attorneys-general opinions, and administrative decisions that have interpreted state Blue Sky legislation.

[D-376] *Business Forms On File.* Edited by Richard P. Zeldin. New York: Facts On File Publications, 1987. Updated annually.

A loose-leaf compilation of business forms and checklists that are frequently used in business. The forms include some of those used by different federal departments and agencies, such as the Small Business Administration, Department of Labor, Internal Revenue Service, General Services Administration (GSA), and others. These include forms used when applying for an SBA business loan or an SBA disaster loan. Other government forms include SBA business-plan forms, various forms used by the GSA in its procurement programs, a form to request that the Office of Energy-Related Inventions evaluate an energy-related invention, and other forms used by federal departments and agencies.

Among the forms provided are a balance sheet, monthly cash-disbursements journal, real-estate lease, employee-evaluation form, employment application, contract, promissory note, general-partnership agreement, and other forms that are used to operate a business. Also of value to the business person are check-lists for various purposes, such as matters to be considered when purchasing insurance for a small business, steps to be taken when organizing a small business, considerations and actions involved in developing a marketing program, a list of financial ratios when engaged in financial analysis, and other important checklists for managing a business.

[D-377] *Business Franchise Guide.* 2 vols. Chicago: Commerce Clearing House, Inc. Updated monthly.

This loose-leaf service provides the full text of state and federal statutes that are of general application concerning business franchises. It also digests laws that apply to special industries and includes FTC regulations that pertain to franchising. The monthly updates keep the subscriber current on the laws, proposed legislation, administrative opinions, and judicial decisions that affect the franchising industry.

[D-378] *Business Transactions in Germany (FRG).* 4 vols. Edited by Bernd Rüster. New York: Matthew Bender & Company, 1988. Updated annually.

Covers the business laws and regulations in the Federal Republic of Germany. Reports on the political and socioeconomic conditions in that country. The legal topics addressed include the legal system, foreign investments in Germany, contract law, commercial law, partnerships, labor contracts, taxation, accounting principles and practices, banking, and others. Also discusses government incentives for industrial development and contains the text of major German statutes that govern business activity.

[D-379] *Buyers Laboratory Test Reports: Reports on Office Products.* Edited by Burt Meerow. Hackensack, NJ: Buyers Laboratory, Inc., 1988. Updated monthly.

This loose-leaf service reports the results of laboratory tests, user surveys, and in-house use tests on office equipment and supplies. The "Data Analysis Reports" give a description of the office product and its specifications, pricing schedule, and length of warranty. "Test Reports" disclose the Buyers Laboratory's recommendation and description of a product, general appraisal, test observations, and other technical information.

The categories of office equipment and supplies that are reviewed include dictating equipment, facsimile equipment, furniture, computer printers, computers/word processors, software, copiers, typewriters, postage-meter machines, and general office supplies. Also keeps subscribers abreast of the results of retests.

The semimonthly newsletter *Update* publishes comments from users and other current information about office products.

[D-380] ***China Laws for Foreign Business.*** 5 vols. Sidney, Australia: CCH Australia Limited, 1987, and Beijing, China: China Prospect Publishing House, 1987. Distributed in America by Commerce Clearing House. Updated four to eight times a year.

Contains the laws, regulations, rules, notices, and announcements of the People's Republic of China regarding foreign economic and trade activities in mainland China. Addresses business regulations, taxation, customs, and special economic zones and cities. Prints both the official Chinese text and the English translation. Through its updating service, the subscriber to this loose-leaf service is kept current of new legal developments that affect foreign businesses in China.

[D-381] ***Collective Bargaining Negotiations and Contracts.*** 2 vols. Washington, DC: Bureau of National Affairs, 1988. Updated biweekly. Supplemented by *What's New in Collective Bargaining Negotiations and Contracts*, a biweekly newsletter, and *Facts For Bargaining*, a quarterly newsletter.

A rich source of information on the strategies, techniques, and processes associated with collective bargaining. It provides background economic statistics, such as the Consumer Price Index, productivity indexes for selected industries, unemployment rates for different industries, wage patterns by industry, and other data used in collective bargaining.

Two volumes comprise this loose-leaf service: *Techniques and Trends, Current Settlements* (vol. 1), and *Basic Patterns, Clause Finder* (vol. 2). The first volume reports on demands and counterproposals that have been made in collective bargaining sessions in individual industries, along with an abstract of specific contract settlements.

In the second volume can be found the full text of selected labor contracts. Furthermore, it provides thousands of clauses from negotiated labor agreements that cover almost all pertinent subjects. The array of topics includes wages, overtime, pensions, income maintenance, promotion and demotion, working conditions, seniority, union security, and others.

Collective Bargaining Negotiations and Contracts offers current information on techniques and strategies, background data for collective bargaining, industry trends regarding demands and settlements, and excerpts from agreements that serve as models. The supplementary newsletters keep the subscriber abreast of new developments and summaries concerning issue-specific data, such as median-wage increases. This is a one-stop reference source.

[D-382] ***Common Market Reports.*** 4 vols. Chicago: Commerce Clearing House, 1988. Updated bimonthly.

A guide to business laws affecting the conduct of business in the European Economic Community (Common Market). It keeps the subscriber of this loose-leaf service current regarding developments in the laws, regulations, directives, and court decisions that govern business activities in the EEC. There are texts of the Treaty of Rome, regulations, and directives. Also includes annotations of decisions by the Executive Commission and the European Court of Justice. Provides explanations and editorial comments. Lists names, addresses, and telephone numbers for contacting personnel who are with the Executive Commission, Council of Ministers, and the Court of Justice.

[D-383] *Copyright Law Reports.* 2 vols. Chicago: Commerce Clearing House, 1988. Updated monthly.

Commonly referred to as *Copyright Law Reporter*, this loose-leaf service is a guide to the U.S. copyright law. It contains the full text of the Copyright Revision Act of 1976 (Public Law 94-553) and its predecessor, the Copyright Act of 1909 (Public No. 60-349). Also reports the copyright statutes of the individual states. *Copyright Law Reports* includes the regulations of the Copyright Office, the Copyright Royalty Tribunal, and other federal agencies as they relate to copyrights. Provides information on federal and state court decisions concerning copyrights. The subscriber is kept current of developments regarding regulatory trends, notices of hearings, and other matters on copyrights.

[D-384] *Corporate Acquisitions, Mergers and Divestitures.* Paramus, NJ: Prentice Hall Information Services, 1988. Updated monthly.

This is a comprehensive source of information on corporate acquisitions, mergers, and divestitures. Reports basic legal information, and offers suggestions for acquisition strategies. Focuses on problems and solutions for one-step and multistep acquisitions, in addition to divestitures of assets or subsidiaries. Addresses tax and nontax issues. A source for remaining abreast of legal developments concerning corporate acquisitions, mergers, and divestitures.

[D-385] *Corporate Secretary's Guide.* 3 vols. Chicago: Commerce Clearing House, 1988. Updated monthly.

A guide for fulfilling the duties and responsibilities of the corporate secretary. This loose-leaf service provides the federal and state laws and regulations that affect the corporate secretary. Its scope encompasses corporate and securities laws, registration, reporting requirements, proxies, broker-dealer regulations, securities transfers, individual liabilities, takeovers, and other relevant subjects. A semimonthly newsletter, *Corporate Directions*, accompanies this subscription service.

[D-386] *Corporation Forms.* 2 vols. Paramus, NJ: Prentice Hall Information Services, 1988. Updated monthly.

Provides guidelines, forms, and specimen clauses for the full scope of transactions associated with publicly-held corporations. Includes procedures and forms for incorporating, issuing stocks, calling annual stockholders' meetings, preparing resolutions, entering into mergers and consolidations, compensating officers and directors, and many other corporate activities. Explains the use for each form. Includes model corporate documents such as articles of incorporation and bylaws. There are tips on how to protect trade secrets and how to avoid oversights in corporate minutes.

[D-387] *Datapro Directory of Microcomputer Software.* 3 vols. Edited by J. Richard Peck. Delran, NJ: Datapro Research Corporation, 1988. Updated monthly.

This loose-leaf service provides a comprehensive directory of microcomputer software that is available for purchase. Arranged by subject, most of the categories pertain to business. These include accounting, banking and finance, insurance, real estate, manufacturing, sales, and other subjects.

The profiles of microcomputer software programs include the product name; vendor's name, address, and telephone number; major function that is supported by the software; compatible hardware; minimum amount of internal memory that is recommended; operating system; peripherals required; source language used; pricing; training; documentation; and other items of information. Also includes a directory of vendors, with their addresses and telephone numbers.

[D-388] *Datapro Management of Microcomputer Systems.* 2 vols. Edited by J. Richard Peck. Delran, NJ: Datapro Research Corporation, 1988. Updated monthly.

Offers two principal services: (1) an explanation of the concepts, principles, implications, and insights into the world of microcomputers—past, present, and future; and (2) practical advice and guidelines for the planning, installation, and operation of microcomputer systems. The subscriber to this loose-leaf service can find recommendations on the justification, selection, installation, and use of microcomputers, with attention given to financial and operational considerations. The focus is on issues and problems associated with the management of microcomputers in the business environment. Thus, these two volumes explain microcomputer hardware components, explore software options, discuss data communications that involve microcomputers, and address data-processing concepts and applications.

Includes a directory of vendors in the microcomputers industry that gives their addresses, telephone numbers, and a description of the products and services they provide.

[D-389] *Datapro Management of Office Automation.* 2 vols. Edited by J. Richard Peck. Delran, NJ: Datapro Research Corporation, 1988. Updated monthly.

A guide to automating the office; also addresses the problems that arise in the automated-office environment. Discusses the available technology and its impact, synthesizes information to help solve problems in the automated office, and reports on new solutions.

Subscribers learn about the current thinking on designing and managing an automated office, including advice on evaluating and selecting systems, improving productivity, personnel management, systems and operations management, and other issues. Contains articles that discuss word-processing systems, facsimile systems, information-storage systems, estimating the cost of new automation systems, data processing, and other topics related to office automation.

[D-390] *Datapro Office Products Evaluation Service.* 2 vols. Edited by J. Richard Peck. Delran, NJ: Datapro Research Corporation, 1988. Updated monthly.

Examines the functions and performance of copiers, electronic typewriters, and facsimile machines. Reports specifications and prices of these office products, along with user ratings and product test results. This is a reference tool for learning about product evaluations and comparisons between models and brands.

Also includes training guidelines. A monthly newsletter supplements the up-dates.

[D-391] *Datapro Reports on Microcomputers.* 3 vols. Edited by J. Richard Peck. Delran, NJ: Datapro Research Corporation, 1988. Updated monthly.

A consumer's guide to microcomputers that examines hardware, software, pe-ripherals, and services. As a loose-leaf service, it keeps the subscriber abreast of new developments and changes. Explains how to plan and select microcomput-ers. Provides a comparison of user ratings on hardware, software, peripherals, communications, and other related products. This gives the reader evaluative information that is independent of that provided by vendors.

There are also descriptive and evaluative reviews (separate from user rat-ings) of microcomputer systems, monitors, printers, expansion cards, database-management software, spreadsheets, graphics, system software, word process-ing, and other microcomputer products. Narrative and table formats are used. The analysis of software is more extensive here than in *Datapro Directory of Mi-crocomputer Software* [D-387], but there are more descriptive reviews in the latter publication.

[D-392] *Doing Business in Brazil.* Pinheiro Neto. New York: Matthew Bender & Company, 1988. Updated semiannually and with a monthly newsletter entitled *Monthly Legal Letter.*

Reports on the business laws and regulations of Brazil. In addition to describ-ing the Brazilian legislative and judicial systems, this loose-leaf publication pro-vides information on the kinds of business organizations in Brazil, regulations that govern establishing a business, import/export controls, foreign-investment regulations, commercial contracts, taxation, insurance, intellectual property, in-dustrial property, labor laws, trade regulations, financial institutions, and other topics of interest to foreign investors.

[D-393] *Doing Business in Canada.* 3 vols. H. Heward Stikeman and R. Fraser Elliott, editors-in-chief. New York: Matthew Bender & Company, 1988. Updated semiannually.

Reports on business laws and regulations in Canada. Contains an overview of the Canadian government and political system, along with an introduction to that nation's business and economic environment. Addresses such legal topics as the regulation of foreign investments, import/export regulations, contracts, property, laws regulating the establishment of businesses, franchising, intellec-tual property, accounting, banking, taxation, securities laws and regulations, and other legal issues of importance to persons doing business in Canada. Also discusses the incentives for foreign investment in Canada.

[D-394] *Doing Business in China.* William P. Streng and Allan Wilcox. New York: Matthew Bender & Company, 1989. Updated annually.

Presents the laws and regulations that govern business activities in the People's Republic of China and discusses the politico-economic-business environment in which they operate. The laws and regulations address import/export transactions, intellectual property, joint ventures, financing, taxation, energy development, labor, restrictions on foreign business executives, and other matters related to conducting business in mainland China.

[D-395] *Doing Business in Europe.* Chicago: Commerce Clearing House, 1988. Updated monthly.

A guide to the laws, regulations, and selected general information that is needed to conduct business in the individual member countries of the European Common Market and in other selected European nations. Although other European countries may be added in the future, those presently included are Austria, Belgium, Denmark, France, Germany, Britain, Greece, Ireland, Italy, Luxembourg, the Netherlands, Portugal, Spain, Sweden, and Switzerland.

The topics covered for each country include establishing a business, foreign investment, licensing, patent and trademark laws, antitrust, court systems, taxes, company laws, and other related topics. For each country, there is a topical index.

[D-396] *Doing Business in France.* 2 vols. Siméon Moquet Borde & Associés. New York: Matthew Bender & Company, 1988. Updated semiannually.

Reports the business laws and regulations that are followed in France, and addresses the politico-economic climate. Focuses on the laws and regulations that pertain to direct investments in France, exchange controls, immigration laws, franchising, corporate law, contracts, mail-order sales, products liability, labor relations, banking and finance, taxation, accounting, import/export trade, patents and trademarks, and other business activities. Also discusses France's investment incentives.

[D-397] *Doing Business in Ireland.* Edited by Patrick Ussher, Brian J. O'Connor, and Charles McCarthy. New York: Matthew Bender & Company, 1989. Updated annually.

Reports on the laws and regulations that govern business activity in the Republic of Ireland. It explains the government incentives to attract business investments. The laws and regulations that are addressed focus on incorporating a business in Ireland, contracts, franchising, intellectual property, employment, banking, taxation, and other matters affecting business activity.

[D-398] *Doing Business in Japan.* 10 vols. Edited by Zentaro Kitagawa. New York: Matthew Bender & Company, 1987. Updated semiannually.

Covers the laws and regulations that govern business transactions in Japan. Includes the full text of major statutes such as the Foreign Exchange and Foreign Trade Control Act, the Commercial Code, General Designation of Unfair Business Practices, and other statutory documents. These volumes provide guidance to the laws and regulations regarding contracts, intellectual property, taxation, loans, leases, advertising, checks, credit cards, property, joint ventures, securities, antimonopoly restrictions, and numerous other matters concerning business activity.

[D-399] *Doing Business in Mexico.* 3 vols. Edited by Susan K. Lefler. New York: Matthew Bender & Company, 1988. Updated semiannually.

Reports on the business laws and regulations of Mexico. Contains an overview of the sociopolitical environment of Mexico and the cultural considerations when transacting business in that country. Addresses Mexican law regarding contractual formalities, foreign-investment procedures, taxation of foreign residents, immigration policy, labor relations, import/export transactions, foreign-exchange controls, antitrust, real property, loan agreements, trust laws, and other topics. Discusses Mexico's industrial investment tax incentives. *Doing Business in Mexico* also covers the application of U.S. laws when doing business in Mexico.

[D-400] *Doing Business in Spain.* Edited by Fernando Pombo. New York: Matthew Bender & Company, 1988. Updated annually.

Reports the laws and regulations that govern business activity in Spain. Includes topics on contracts, exchange controls, foreign investments, property ownership, shared titles of property, performance guarantees, intellectual property, advertising, unfair competition, products liability, technology transfer, accounting principles and rules, taxation, labor law, import/export transactions, insurance, banking, and other topics. Also provides selected sample forms used in Spain for sundry types of business transactions. A "Table of Statutes" organizes Spanish laws by topic and cites their location in the text.

[D-401] *Doing Business in the United Kingdom.* 3 vols. Clifford Chance. New York: Matthew Bender & Company, 1988. Updated semiannually.

Reports on the laws and regulations that govern business activity in the United Kingdom. Presents a summary of the legal system in the U.K. and then provides coverage of the laws pertaining to setting up a new business, acquiring an existing business, contracts, agency, real property, intellectual property, information technology, taxation, accounting, labor, import/export restrictions, and other business topics.

[D-402] *Employment Coordinator.* 17 vols. New York: Research Institute of America, 1988. Updated with monthly supplements and a biweekly newsletter titled *Employment Alert.*

A loose-leaf service that keeps its subscribers informed about developments in employment law regarding compensation, benefits, safety in the workplace, labor relations, employment practices, and personnel policy and administration. Contains explanations of federal and state laws that govern employment. Among its contents are checklists that help prevent the employer from overlooking important points of law, model forms used in personnel administration, sample language for employee handbooks, and other related valuable tools.

[D-403] *The Encyclopedia of Managerial Job Descriptions.* Vols. 1 and 2. Lawrence Stessin and Carl Heyel. New York: Business Research Publications, Inc., 1981. Vol. 3. Carl Heyel, 1986 (updates the two previous volumes).

A helpful guide to developing managerial-position descriptions for a business organization. It explains how to accomplish this task and then presents more than 400 examples of managerial-job descriptions that were received from a large variety of companies in different industries. The range includes the board chairman and goes through staff and service positions.

These actual functioning job descriptions report the purpose of the position, duties and responsibilities, to whom the position reports, what other positions report to the position being described, work performed, and other information. The functional areas addressed include executive officers, production, marketing and sales, personnel, accounting and control, computer operations, and administrative services. This publication gives the reader an opportunity to see how others in the industry view a given managerial position, thereby providing a basis for structuring an appropriate job description.

[D-404] *Federal Securities Law Reports.* 7 vols. Chicago: Commerce Clearing House, 1988. Updated weekly.

Also cited as *Federal Securities Law Reporter*, this loose-leaf subscription service functions as a guide to federal regulations of the securities industry. It contains the pertinent laws, regulations, court decisions, rulings, and forms. Within its pages are the full texts of the Securities Act of 1933, Securities Exchange Act of 1934, Public Utility Holding Company Act, and the Investment Company Act of 1940. Also provides the full texts of regulations, SEC releases, and official forms. This is a comprehensive source of materials concerning the federal regulation of the securities industry.

[D-405] *Federal Tax Coordinator.* 33 vols. 2d ed. New York: Research Institute of America, 1988. Updated weekly.

Addresses federal income, gift, estate, and excise taxes by providing a subject instead of an Internal Revenue Code approach to explaining taxes. Most of the presentation is narrative with the Code and regulations being cited verbatim in a separate section of each volume. References to rulings and judicial decisions are in footnotes. On points of law, the narrative discussions include, where appropriate, "Observations" (analysis or commentary), "Cautions" (alert to dangers and what should be done), "Illustrations" (clarification), and "Recommendations" (guidelines for legally minimizing taxes). In this loose-leaf service, judicial decisions are not reported in full text.

[D-406] *Federal Tax Treaties.* 3 vols. Paramus, NJ: Prentice Hall Information Services, 1988. Updated monthly.

This loose-leaf subscription service reports on the tax laws as prescribed by treaties between the U.S. and other nations. Includes the full text of every tax treaty, supplementary treaty, and protocol regarding income taxes, estate taxes, and gift taxes. Reports changes in these laws and associated rulings and case decisions.

[D-407] *Federal Taxation of Insurance Companies.* Dennis P. Van Mieghem and Thomas M. Brown. Paramus, NJ: Prentice Hall Information Services, 1988. Updated bimonthly.

Reports on the federal tax laws, regulations, rulings, and major case decisions that pertain to the taxation of insurance companies. This loose-leaf subscription service is divided into three principal sections: (1) Life Insurance Companies, (2) Property and Liability Insurance Companies, and (3) General Tax Concepts for Insurers. Its comprehensive coverage of topics includes insurance reserves, tax-accounting methods, investment income, consolidated returns, overview of state taxes, and other topics concerned with taxation of the insurance industry.

[D-408] *Federal Taxes.* 14 basic vols. Paramus, NJ: Prentice Hall Information Services, 1988. Updated weekly.

This loose-leaf subscription service is a comprehensive reporting of the federal tax laws, regulations, rulings, and court decisions. Included are the Internal Revenue Code (full text), interpretations, and explanations. The judicial history of tax cases can be followed. Information is arranged by Code section. Contains tax-rate tables, an index to selected tax articles appearing in periodicals, a "Transactions Index," and sections on the different provisions of the federal tax Code.

[D-409] *Federal Taxes Citator.* Series 1 (1863–1954). Series 2 (1954 to present). 4 bound volumes and 2 loose-leaf volumes. Paramus, NJ: Prentice Hall Information Services, 1988. Updated monthly.

Through coded listings, this publication facilitates tracing the history of a federal tax case and ascertaining later cases and rulings in which the case was cited. Identifies the nature of subsequent citations in terms of how the later court decision(s) regarded the decision of the original case. Also reports on the point of law that was the subject of later cases in which the original case was cited.

[D-410] *Forms of Business Agreements and Resolutions.* 3 vols. Paramus, NJ: Prentice Hall Information Services, 1988. Updated quarterly.

This loose-leaf service provides guidelines and forms for use in publicly-held corporations, close corporations, partnerships, joint ventures, foundations, and other types of business organizations. These materials address the full spectrum of business transactions, including getting organized, operations, employment agreements, settlements, franchises, intellectual property, and others.

[D-411] *How to Create a Winning Business Plan.* James W. Taylor. Westbury, NY: Asher-Gallant Press, 1986.

A loose-leaf manual that explains how to write a business plan. Includes instructions, examples, and forms. It takes the reader step by step through the process. The explanations cover financial concepts, financial statements, how to identify the entrepreneur's strengths and weaknesses, how to prepare an operating budget, and how to prepare a new-product business plan. A salient feature of this manual is its working forms.

[D-412] *Insurance Law Reports.* 3 vols. Chicago: Commerce Clearing House, 1988. Each volume is updated per the following schedule: *Automobile Law Reports,* biweekly; *Fire and Casualty Law Reports*, biweekly; and *Life, Health, and Accident Law Reports*, monthly.

Also cited as *Insurance Law Reporter*, this three-volume loose-leaf subscription service reports the full text of federal and state court decisions on insurance cases. Topical indexes provide direct access to the cases according to their subject.

[D-413] *Japan Business Law Guide.* 2 vols. Sydney, Australia: CCH Australia Limited, 1988. Distributed in America by Commerce Clearing House. Updated quarterly.

This loose-leaf service keeps the subscriber current on business laws and regulations in Japan. It addresses topics that include contracts, intellectual property, labor, taxation, investments, export/import controls, banking, commercial litigation and arbitration, and many other subjects that concern the person wanting to do business in Japan or with a Japanese company.

[D-414] *Labor Law Reports.* 16 vols. Chicago: Commerce Clearing House, 1988. Updated weekly.

Also known as the *Labor Law Reporter*, this loose-leaf service reports the full text of principal federal labor statutes and the text or digest of state statutes. Also includes regulations, decisions, and rulings. Coverage encompasses all aspects of labor law, such as collective bargaining, unions, wages, hours, and discrimination. These volumes are organized according to (1) *Labor Relations* (6 vols.), *Wages-Hours* (2 vols.), *State Laws* (3 vols.), *Employment Practices* (4 vols.), and the *Quick Finder* (1 vol.). A source for keeping abreast, on a weekly basis, of developments in labor law.

[D-415] *Modern Construction & Development Forms.* 2d ed. Jack Kusnet and Owen T. Smith. Boston: Warren, Gorham & Lamont, Inc., 1988. Updated semiannually.

A loose-leaf service that provides the forms and agreements used during the construction of a project. All kinds of construction projects are covered. The updates introduce new forms and agreements that are being used.

[D-416] *Modern Real Estate and Mortgage Forms: Basic Forms and Agreements.* 3d ed. Edited by Alvin L. Arnold. Boston: Warren, Gorham & Lamont, Inc., 1988. Updated semiannually.

Presents forms that are used in real estate transactions of all types. This collection includes forms for contract of sale, mortgage notes, leasing, equity financing, and many others. As new forms are introduced into practice, the updates bring these to the attention of the subscribers to this loose-leaf service.

[D-417] *Modern Real Estate Leasing Forms.* Jack Kusnet and Robert Lopatin. Boston: Warren, Gorham & Lamont, Inc., 1988. Updated annually.

Provides a complete collection of forms used for leasing real estate. Explains the legal and tax consequences of leasing transactions. A valuable part of this loose-leaf publication is the specimen lease clauses, with explanations of how to customize a lease to the advantage of the lessor or the lessee.

[D-418] *Patents Throughout the World.* Edited by Alan Jacobs. New York: Clark Boardman Company, 1988. Updated three times per year.

Contains digests of the patent laws of more than 200 nations. Follows a standard format for all countries. This loose-leaf service reports the legal citations of patent statutes, duration of patents, protection given by a patent, who may be a patentee, what may be patented, fees, and other related information for each country. Also provides the texts of the different international patent conventions.

[D-419] *Personnel Management Guide.* Paramus, NJ: Prentice Hall Information Services, 1988. Updated quarterly and with a monthly newsletter titled *Personnel Management Guidelines*.

Offers current information on all areas of employee management. Addresses wages, benefits, hiring, training, rules in the workplace, productivity, and safety/security. Its comprehensive coverage also focuses on equal employment, evaluating job applications and résumés, reducing turnover, discipline, motivation, how to keep good workers, health-care cost containment, use of the company car, and many more issues. This is a subscription service.

[D-420] *Personnel Management, Labor Relations.* 3 vols. Paramus, NJ: Prentice Hall Information Services, 1988. Updated weekly.

Volume 1 of this loose-leaf service explains the federal and state labor laws. Addresses such subjects as fair employment practices, wages and hours, equal pay, labor relations, and working conditions. Contains a section on cost-of-living indexes. State labor laws are presented in digest form.

Volume 2 provides the full text of major federal labor laws, orders, wage and hour regulations, and other federal rules and regulations. Volume 3 reports on OSHA standards and procedures. *Personnel Management, Labor Relations* also summarizes important court cases pertaining to labor.

Predicasts Basebook. Cleveland, OH: Predicasts, Inc., 1988. Updated annually. See "Statistical Digests and Statistics Sources," [D-467].

Predicasts Forecasts. Cleveland, OH: Predicasts, Inc., 1988. Updated quarterly and cumulated annually. See "Statistical Digests and Statistics Sources," [D-468].

[D-421] *Protection of Corporate Names: A Country by Country Survey.* United States Trademark Association. New York: Clark Boardman Company, 1987. Updated annually.

Seventy-one nations responded to a survey conducted by the United States Trademark Association regarding the statutory protection given to corporate names by those nations. This publication reports their responses.

The questionnaire addressed five major areas: the relationship between corporate names and trademarks; registration and other ways of protecting corporate names; commonly used designations for different forms of business ventures; limitations on how corporate names may be used; and limited rights of a subsidiary to use a corporate name. This loose-leaf service also keeps the subscriber abreast of statutory changes in the protection of corporate names in these countries.

Standard & Poor's Corporation Records. 7 vols. New York: Standard & Poor's Corporation, 1988.
See "Directories," [D-220].

Standard & Poor's Stock Reports (*American Stock Exchange, New York Stock Exchange, Over the Counter*). New York: Standard & Poor's Corporation, 1988. Published quarterly as a paperback and as a loose-leaf service. The latter is updated weekly. See "Reports," [D-462].

[D-422] ***Standard Federal Tax Reports***. 15 vols., contained in 18 loose-leaf binders. Chicago: Commerce Clearing House, 1988. Published annually with weekly updates.

Also cited as the *Standard Federal Tax Reporter*, this guide to federal income-tax law began with the enactment of the U.S. income tax in 1913. Contains the text of the Internal Revenue Code and legislative changes made to it. Organized by Code section, it also includes tax regulations, decisions of the federal courts and Board of Tax Appeals, revenue rulings and procedures, and other IRS releases.
Volumes 1–9 contain the Code, regulations, court decisions, rulings, and Commerce Clearing House's explanations. These are arranged by Code sections. Volume 10 features current developments regarding regulations, legislation, new rulings, and court decisions. Among the other volumes are the full texts of the Internal Revenue Code (*Internal Revenue Code*) and the decisions of federal courts concerning tax cases (*U.S. Tax Cases Advance Sheets*). Additionally, the *Citator* coordinates the litigation history of points of tax law, commencing in 1913.

[D-423] ***State and Local Taxes***. 48 vols. Paramus, NJ: Prentice Hall Information Services, 1988. Updated weekly.

This loose-leaf tax service reports on the tax laws, regulations, rulings, and court decisions for the individual states, District of Columbia, and local units of government. Includes the full text of state tax statutes and regulations. The comprehensive coverage embraces license and occupation taxes, property taxes, income taxes, sales taxes, franchise taxes, special city and county taxes, and other related matters. There are explanations and interpretations of these taxes.

[D-424] ***State Tax Guide***. 2 vols. Chicago: Commerce Clearing House, 1988. Updated bimonthly.

This loose-leaf state tax guide is an abridged version of CCH's *State Tax Reports* [D-425]. It is a quick access to the taxes of the individual states and the District of Columbia. This overview of state taxes is organized by state and by tax. Designed to be used with *State Tax Reports*.

[D-425] *State Tax Reports.* Chicago: Commerce Clearing House, 1988. A separate volume for each of the fifty states and the District of Columbia. Updated monthly, except bimonthly for New York and California. A weekly *State Tax Review* is published for each state.

Also cited as the *State Tax Reporter*, this is a loose-leaf service guide to the taxes of each state and the District of Columbia. Contains the texts of statutes and regulations, and explanations, opinions, and court decisions pertaining to state and municipal tax laws. Some of the taxes covered are property, income, franchise, sales, use, gasoline, and liquor taxes.

[D-426] *Successful Payroll Management.* Paramus, NJ: Prentice Hall Information Services, 1988. Updated monthly.

A loose-leaf service that provides guidelines and tips on how to save costs when managing a payroll. Includes the latest federal rules and regulations concerning the hiring and management of employees. Topics cover a wide range of payroll-related issues.

[D-427] *Tax Court Memorandum Decisions.* Chicago: Commerce Clearing House, 1988. Updated weekly.

A loose-leaf service that reports the full text of the memorandum decisions of the U.S. Tax Court. The loose-leaf pages are bound semiannually.

[D-428] *Tax Court Reported Decisions.* Paramus, NJ: Prentice Hall Information Services, 1988. Updated weekly.

Provides the full text of reported decisions by the U.S. Tax Court. It is a companion to the *T. C. Memorandum Decisions* [D-433].

[D-429] *Tax Court Reporter.* 3 vols. Chicago: Commerce Clearing House, 1988. Updated weekly.

Contains the full text of the regular (reported) decisions of the U.S. Tax Court.

[D-430] *Tax Havens of the World.* 3 vols. Walter H. Diamond and Dorothy B. Diamond. New York: Matthew Bender & Company, 1988. Updated quarterly.

This loose-leaf service presents information on how to select the site for an overseas tax sanctuary and describes actions taken by 54 national governments to create tax shelters for foreign investment. Provides information on the laws, regulations, and conditions in each of these countries pertaining to their tax sanctuaries. The profiles discuss such topics as "Tax Exemptions and Reductions," "Investment and Capital Incentives," "Political and Economic Stability," "Transfer of Funds and Guarantees," "Banking and Foreign Exchange," and "Free Trade Zones." Other topics are also addressed. A comprehensive source for identifying tax shelters around the world.

[D-431] *Tax Transactions Library: Mergers, Acquisitions and Leveraged Buyouts.*
4 vols. Martin D. Ginsburg, Jack S. Levin, *et al.* Chicago: Commerce Clearing
House, 1989. Updated bimonthly. (Note: These four volumes are only part of
the expanding *Tax Transactions Library.*)

A loose-leaf subscription service that addresses the federal income-tax issues
associated with corporate acquisitions, mergers, and leveraged buyouts. This
publication uses the transactional approach: that is, it presents the different tax
problems associated with an acquisition, merger, or leveraged buyout and then
discusses the alternative solutions. It also cites specific sections of the Internal
Revenue Code that pertain to these solutions.

   Coverage includes securities laws, antitrust reporting, state corporate law, accounting, contract terms, and fraudulent-conveyance law. Publishes a checklist
of basic legal considerations in an acquisition. Sample forms used for mergers, acquisitions, and leveraged buyouts are provided. The problem-solving approach makes this a valuable reference tool.

[D-432] *Tax Treaties.* 3 vols. Chicago: Commerce Clearing House, 1988. Updated
monthly.

Here are the texts of treaties between the U.S. and foreign countries regarding
income and estate taxes. This loose-leaf subscription service also includes rulings, regulations, judicial decisions, and explanations of the provisions of these
treaties.

   The treaties are arranged alphabetically, by country. Includes U.S. regulations
that pertain to the articles of these treaties. The mandated withholdings under
the income-tax provisions of the treaties may be found herein.

[D-433] *T. C. Memorandum Decisions.* Paramus, NJ: Prentice Hall Information
Services, 1988. Updated weekly.

Contains the full text of memorandum decisions of the U.S. Tax Court. This is
part of a loose-leaf service that includes *Tax Court Reported Decisions* [D-428], but
the latter remains in unbound form, whereas the *T. C. Memorandum Decisions* are
bound at the end of each year.

[D-434] *Trademarks Throughout the World.* Edited by Alan Jacobs. New York:
Clark Boardman Company, 1988. Updated three times per year.

Provides digests of the trademark laws of more than 200 countries. It uses a
standard format for all nations as it reports the legal citations of trademark
statutes; definitions of trademarks, service marks, and trade names; who may
apply; what can be registered; what is not registrable; required documents; procedures; duration and renewal; and other related information for each country.
This loose-leaf service also contains the texts of international conventions on
trademarks.

[D-435] *U.S. Tax Cases.* Chicago: Commerce Clearing House, 1988. First published weekly in loose-leaf form in a volume titled *U.S. Tax Cases Advance Sheets*
that is a component of *Standard Federal Tax Reports* [D-422], and then semiannually in bound form under the title *U.S. Tax Cases.*

Reports the full text of decisions by the federal courts concerning federal tax laws. Excludes decisions of the U.S. Tax Court. (For the latter, see CCH's *Tax Court Memorandum Decisions* [D-427] and *Tax Court Reporter* [D-429], and Prentice-Hall's *Tax Court Reported Decisions* [D-428] and *T. C. Memorandum Decisions* [D-433].) Also includes decisions of state courts that involve federal tax laws.

[D-436] *The Value Line Investment Survey.* New York: Value Line, Inc., 1988. Published weekly.

This loose-leaf investment advisory service is published in three parts: part 1, "Summary and Index"; part 2, "Selection and Opinion"; and part 3, "Ratings and Reports." It provides in-depth coverage of 1,700 stocks classified in 91 industries. For each stock, the information includes such items as the recent price; P/E (Price/Earnings) ratio; relative P/E ratio; dividend yield; the different rankings of the stock; rating for timeliness; safety rating; Beta Coefficient (market sensitivity); relative price strength; indexes of price stability, persistence of price growth, financial strength, and earnings predictability; per-share quarterly earnings; statement on recent company developments; and other vital financial information. Company profiles are updated quarterly, by industry, on a rotating basis.

[D-437] *World Accounting.* 2 vols. John P. McAllister, Larry L. Orsini, and Rajeev N. Parikh. New York: Matthew Bender & Company, 1988. Updated annually.

These two loose-leaf volumes contain the accounting and auditing regulations, standards, and practices for Australia, Belgium, Brazil, Canada, France, India, Italy, Japan, Mexico, the Philipines, Saudi Arabia, South Korea, the U.K., the U.S., and West Germany. They explain the customary, recommended, and required financial-statement disclosures of each nation. A standard format is followed in each country's chapter, enabling the reader to compare accounting and auditing treatments between nations. For example, "Intangible Assets" is always section .17, therefore, both CAN.17 (Canada) and IND.17 (India) address this topic.

For each balance-sheet category there is an explanation of the differences between tax and financial statement treatments. A listing is provided of those items that should be placed in each balance-sheet category. For each nation included there is a disclosure of any accounting practices that are unique to that nation. Finally, this publication contains sample financial statements and, irregularly, uniform charts of accounts, accounting terms and acronyms, and other information in the appendixes. A comprehensive source for information on international accounting.

Worldcasts. 8 vols. Cleveland, OH: Predicasts, Inc., 1988. Updated quarterly. See "Statistical Digests and Statistics Sources," [D-475].

Newsletters

Newsletters have become a widely used medium for communicating business information. They are usually only a few pages, specialized, and, although some are published on a regular schedule, others are issued irregularly. There are thousands of them; some are written by individuals in their homes or small offices while others are published by large and sophisticated organizations. Their purposes are many. Some concentrate on investment matters while others target specific industry developments, patent activities, taxation, collective bargaining, and a host of other subjects in the business arena.

Due to the voluminous number of newsletters and their equally diverse purposes, it was not feasible to profile them in this edition. For bibliographies that specialize in profiling newsletters in business and other fields, the reader is referred to *Newsletters in Print* [D-41] and the *Oxbridge Directory of Newsletters* [D-42]. An exception has been made by including in this subsection the profiles of two newsletters on insider trading because of the current interest on this subject in the business community.

[D-438] *The Insider's Chronicle*. Edited by William Mehlman. Boca Raton, FL: Financial Information, Inc., 1988. Published weekly with a quarterly summary.

Reports on the inside trading of a corporation's stock by its officers. Lists the names of the insiders along with the price, volume, and date of their trade. It also discloses the notices of intent to sell restricted securities (SEC "144 letter stock").

[D-439] *Vickers Weekly Insider Report*. Edited by Edwin A. Buck. Brookside, NJ: Vickers Stock Research Corp., 1988. Published weekly.

This investment newsletter reports on the inside stock transactions of corporate officers, directors, and major stockholders, as reported to the Securities and Exchange Commission. Stocks are those of publicly-held corporations on the New York Stock Exchange, American Stock Exchange, and those traded over-the-counter. The data reported includes the trade date, prices, shares bought or sold, and the number of shares owned by the insider. Also publishes a sell-buy ratio that measures the bearish-bullish activities of corporate insiders. This newsletter includes the "Top Ten" and the "Least Liked" stocks of this group of investors.

Newspapers, Magazines, and Journals

Newspapers, magazines, and journals are important sources of information on current developments in the business world. Their scopes vary depending on their purposes. Some are quite general, while others specialize on a particular industry or subject. These publications are too multitudinous for all to be listed here, but a few of the more recognized ones are profiled below.

A very important and valuable source of information about an industry is the trade journal. This type of journal publishes trends, developments, statistical data, information about individual companies, quarterly and/or year-end financial and operating data, and other information about a specific industry. Many trade journals carry extensive advertising that is valuable to suppliers and buyers. There are thousands of these journals and their counterparts, the trade newspapers. The reader's attention is called to the importance of such sources for business information. Trade journals and trade newspapers should be consulted when needing industry-specific information.

Some excellent references list and describe these publications. The reader is directed to *Predicasts Source Directory* [D-43], *Gale Directory of Publications and Broadcast Media* [D-180], *Business Publication Rates and Data* [D-142], and *Ulrich's International Periodicals Directory* [D-44].

PROFILES

[D-440] *Barron's National Business and Financial Weekly.* New York: Dow Jones. Published weekly.

A highly regarded weekly that reports on topics of interest to investors. Prints extensive tables of securities quotations and financial statistics. As a weekly, *Barron's* publishes investment data and activities for the preceding week and previews the forthcoming week. It includes weekly summaries of stocks, securities, commodities, futures, bonds, and other investment vehicles. Also reports economic indicators, bank credit-card rates at selected financial institutions, world stock market indexes, foreign exchange rates, and the many stock-price indexes. The reader can also find information on insider stock transactions as reported to the Securities and Exchange Commission. There are analytical articles on subjects of interest to the investment community.

Printed sources that help identify and locate the articles include *Barron's Index* [D-19], *Business Periodicals Index* [D-4], and *Predicasts F&S Index United States* [D-15].

[D-441] *Business Week.* New York: McGraw-Hill. Published weekly.

A comprehensive magazine reporting on activities in the business community, with focus primarily on the U.S. but also encompassing foreign business and economic developments. Coverage includes economic trends, business outlook, finance, an array of summary statistics on investment activity, new scientific and technological developments, corporate activities, profiles of corporate leaders, information processing, marketing, and other news events of the business world. Some of the indexing services that index articles in this magazine are *Business Periodicals Index* [D-4], *Predicasts F&S Index United States* [D-15], and *PAIS Bulletin* [D-12].

[D-442] *Consumer Reports.* Mt. Vernon, NY: Consumers Union of U.S., Inc. Published monthly.

This magazine reports on the results of product testing by Consumers Union. Major brands of product categories are evaluated and rated, based on characteristics common to that type of product. Ratings are also assigned to different models of a brand. There are articles on consumer services, such as auto insurance services and premiums. A special annual issue, published in December of each year, is the *Buying Guide*, which updates earlier product reviews.

CPI Detailed Report. U.S. Bureau of Labor Statistics. Washington, DC: U.S. Government Printing Office, 1988. Published monthly.
See "Government Documents," [D-345].

[D-443] ***The Economist***. London, England: The Economist Newspaper, Ltd. Published weekly.

A weekly magazine that reports on economic, business, finance, and political affairs in the U.K., Europe, Asia, America, and other regions of the international community. Contains articles that focus mainly on the U.K. but also address other nations. Includes a regular section titled "Economic and Financial Indicators" that concentrates on selected countries. Some of the indexing services that index articles in this magazine are *Business Periodicals Index* [D-4], the *Predicasts F&S Indexes* [D-13–15], and *PAIS Bulletin* [D-12].

Employment and Earnings. U.S. Bureau of Labor Statistics. Washington, DC: U.S. Government Printing Office, 1988. Published monthly.
See "Government Documents," [D-347].

[D-444] ***Financial Times*** *(London)*. New York: FT Publications, Inc. Published daily except Sundays and holidays.

An international business newspaper that reports general and business news regarding major world events, financial and economic activities, news about companies, quotations on world stock markets, commodities, currency-exchange rates, and other business information. Although its major focus is on the U.K.'s financial, economic, and company news, it also reports American and European matters. There are several editions of the *Financial Times*, including the U.S. edition described herein. This newspaper serves as a daily window onto the world's business scene.

[D-445] ***Forbes***. New York: Forbes, Inc. Published biweekly, except in April and October during which months an extra issue is published.

A business magazine that publishes a potpourri of feature articles and special reports of interest to the business community. Highlights domestic and international business issues. Topics include investments, marketing, industry news, company profiles, science and technology, careers of business leaders, and other subjects. Known for its special reports that include the "Annual Report on American Industry," "Annual Directory Issue," and "Special Report on International Business."
Forbes discloses the highest-paid business executives and reports the ranked performances of businesses according to selected criteria. It also reviews the performances of the leading stock indexes. Among the indexing services that

index articles in this magazine are *Business Periodicals Index* [D-4], *Predicasts F&S Index United States* [D-15], and *Readers' Guide to Periodical Literature* [D-17].

[D-446] *Fortune.* New York: Time, Inc. Published biweekly.

A general business magazine that encompasses a wide array of business topics. Its articles report on economic issues, individual corporate performance, executive profiles, management, politics, trade, international business and economic events, new technology, and other business topics. A special April issue, the "Fortune 500" ranks the largest 500 U.S. industrial corporations. The listing offers a consolidated ranking and also a ranking by industry. The criteria for ranking include sales, profits, assets, earnings per share, total return to investors, market value, stockholders' equity, and the number of employees. Among the indexing services that index articles in this magazine are *Business Periodical Index* [D-4], *Predicasts F&S Index United States* [D-15], and *Readers' Guide to Periodical Literature* [D-17].

[D-447] *Institutional Investor.* New York: Institutional Investor, Inc. Published monthly.

Written for the professional investment manager, this journal publishes articles on investor relations, corporate finance, pension management, portfolio strategy, stock markets, real estate, banking, and other subjects of interest to the money manager. Features a variety of annual articles, such as (1) a directory of real-estate operations managers at major U.S. corporations, (2) names of merger and acquisition specialists at commercial and investment banks and foreign institutions, and (3) a directory of the largest employee benefit pension funds. There also is the "International Edition" that addresses the interests of international investment managers.

[D-448] *International Financial Statistics.* Washington, DC: International Monetary Fund. Published monthly and with a yearbook edition.

An important source of current and historical statistical information on business and economic activity in individual nations and worldwide. Country profiles report data on currency exchange rates, international liquidity, money and banking, consumer prices, production, weekly wages, interest rates, imports and exports, and other national financial statistics. Whereas the monthly publication reports recent changes for key data series, the *Yearbook* publishes changes in annual data for thirty years.

[D-449] *Investor's Daily.* Los Angeles: Investor's Daily, Inc. Published every business day.

A business newspaper that publishes news for the investor. Provides extensive financial statistical data. Includes individual stock and other investment performances, as well as summaries of the AMEX, NYSE, and OTC. Reports activities on foreign markets, U.S. securities, money rates, new corporate investment offerings, changes in corporate debt ratings, and foreign exchange rates. The activities of individual companies are reported in *Investor's Daily*, along with a section on industry and corporate analyses. There are extensive graphic displays of stock market leaders.

[D-450] *Mergers & Acquisitions.* Philadelphia: MLR Publishing Company. Published bimonthly.

This journal reports on the mergers and acquisitions of corporations in the U.S. Includes profiles of these transactions, disclosing the names and locations of the corporate parties, revenues of each corporation, terms of the agreement, nature of the business of each corporate party, and the effective date of the merger or acquisition. There are articles that survey corporate mergers and acquisitions, discussing the various aspects of this activity.

[D-451] *The National Ad Search.* Milwaukee, WI: National Ad Search, Inc. Published weekly.

Offers a national review of available job openings. Prints a sample of help-wanted advertisements selected from major newspapers. The focus is primarily on professional, managerial, and technical jobs. Ads are organized by job category. Publishes articles that survey the national job market.

[D-452] *National Business Employment Weekly.* New York: Dow Jones & Co. A special weekly edition of the *Wall Street Journal.*

This weekly newspaper reprints job ads from the four regional editions of the *Wall Street Journal.* In addition to providing a national scope of the employment market, each issue contains articles that address various aspects of the job search and the career market. These articles offer job-seeking tips and overviews of job opportunities.

[D-453] *Nation's Business.* Washington, DC: Chamber of Commerce of the U.S. Published monthly.

A popular magazine that reports on business, economic, and political events. Includes a section on small business. The "Direct Line" feature allows readers to send in their business questions and have the answers published. Some of the indexing services for articles in this magazine are *Business Periodicals Index* [D-4], *Predicasts F&S Index United States* [D-15], and *Readers' Guide to Periodical Literature* [D-17].

[D-454] *The New York Times.* New York: New York Times, Inc. Published daily.

One of the leading newspapers in America with an extensive business section. Provides a broad range of news coverage that includes current business events, company news, changes of corporate executives, stock quotations, market indicators, money rates, and other business and economic features. Also publishes job ads that are from New York and other states around the nation. Articles are indexed in the *New York Times Index* [D-11].

[D-455] *The Penny Stock Journal.* New York: Dalton Communications. Published monthly.

This monthly newspaper focuses on small and, often, little-known companies with low-priced stocks from a wide range of industries. Each issue reports more than 7,000 stock quotations for penny stocks and stocks valued between $1.00 and $10.00. Company profiles and analyses are offered, including in-depth reports. Announces first-time stock offerings, where to buy them, and their per-share price. Lists the 100 stocks most actively traded along with the 100 that increased the most and the 100 that declined the most.

Producer Price Indexes. U.S. Bureau of Labor Statistics. Washington, DC: U.S. Government Printing Office. Published monthly. Formerly titled *Producer Prices and Price Indexes*.
See "Government Documents," [D-358].

[D-456] ***Software Reviews On File***. Edited by Scott F. Wight. New York: Facts On File, Inc. Published monthly.

Reprints extracts of microcomputer software reviews that have appeared in periodicals. Also provides a description of each package as written by the software's publisher, and, in a concise format, reports the author, producer, package components, system requirements, and price. The scope includes various areas of business, communications, computers, desktop publishing, education, entertainment, word processing, and personal use. The monthly issues are cumulated in a loose-leaf binder.

Survey of Current Business. U.S. Bureau of Economic Analysis. Washington, DC: U.S. Government Printing Office. Published monthly.
See "Government Documents," [D-363].

[D-457] ***Wall Street Journal***. New York: Dow Jones & Company. Published daily except Saturdays, Sundays, and general legal holidays.

Widely regarded as the leading daily business and financial newspaper in the U.S. It reports on the activities of the national and international business communities. The coverage includes world market events, the performance of corporate stocks and the major stock market indexes, U.S. government securities, bonds, money rates, commodities, futures, analyses of statements of corporate earnings, synopsis of business/finance news, developments within major companies, activities of foreign stock exchanges, corporate insider stock trading (once a week), credit rating of companies, foreign exchange rates, announcements of new securities issues, and analytical articles on selected topics. Articles are indexed in the *Wall Street Journal Index* [D-19].

[D-458] ***The Wall Street Transcript***. New York: Wall Street Transcript Corporation. Published weekly.

Reports extensively on financial conditions and developments in companies and industries. Reprints the full text of brokerage house reports on individual corporations ("Broker Reports") and highlights other brokerage reports ("Wall Street Roundup"). Also publishes the full text of interviews with CEOs and money managers regarding matters relating to their industries. Technical analyses are provided. Profiles an industry's outstanding CEOs and announces executive promotions. Contains a cumulative composite index for year-to-date.

[D-459] *What to Buy for Business.* Rye, NY: What to Buy, Inc. Published bimonthly.

A magazine that contains buyer's guides for evaluating and comparing computers, printers, software, copiers, fax machines, telephone systems, and typewriters. Includes product profiles and recommendations. Each issue is devoted to one of these classes of products.

Reports

[D-460] *American Federal Tax Reports.* First and Second Series. Paramus, NJ: Prentice Hall Information Services, 1988. Published annually.

Reports unabridged texts of federal tax decisions handed down by federal courts, except the U.S. Tax Court. Also includes the full texts of decisions, rendered under federal tax law, by state courts. Through a paragraph-numbering system, there is a tie-in of cases between this series and Prentice-Hall's *Federal Taxes* [D-408]. The First Series reports federal tax decisions through 1957, and the Second Series reports decisions since 1958.

[D-461] *How to Price a Business.* Raymond C. Miles. Englewood Cliffs, NJ: Institute for Business Planning, 1982.

A special report that explains the fundamental principles of pricing a business, including determining benchmark values, how to set the price, types of payment arrangements, taxes related to the sale of a business, and other matters.

[D-462] *Standard & Poor's Stock Reports.* New York: Standard & Poor's Corporation, 1988. Published quarterly as a paperback and weekly as a loose-leaf service.

This set of reports is published in three editions: *American Stock Exchange (ASE)*, *New York Stock Exchange (NYSE)*, and *Over the Counter (OTC)*. Each edition profiles the companies that are traded on the referenced stock exchange. *OTC* includes nearly 1,600 companies that are traded over the counter or that are listed on regional stock exchanges.

The two-page descriptions include such information as the company's ticker symbol; percentage yield; S&P ranking; beta value; summary of business operations; important developments; current outlook of earnings and dividends; ten-year book value, earnings, dividends, and P/E ratio; dividend data; capitalization; number of shareholders; address and telephone number of the company; and the names of principal officers and directors.

Statistical Digests and Statistics Sources

American Statistics Index (ASI). 2 vols. Washington, DC: Congressional Information Service, Inc., 1988. Published monthly and cumulated quarterly and annually.
See "Abstracts and Indexes," [D-1].

[D-463] *Best's Aggregates & Averages: Property-Casualty.* Oldwick, NJ: A. M. Best Company, 1988. Published annually.

Presents summary annual statistics on the operations of the property-casualty insurance industry. Data are for stock companies, mutual companies, reciprocal exchanges, and Lloyd's organizations. Information includes consolidated balance-sheet and operating statistics, time-series data for the industry, and cumulated financial data by line of business. Lists the leading property-casualty insurance companies and groups.

Business Statistics. 25th ed. U.S. Bureau of Economic Analysis. Washington, DC: U.S. Government Printing Office, 1987. Published biennially.
See "Government Documents," [D-336].

[D-464] *Commercial Atlas & Marketing Guide.* 119th ed. Chicago: Rand McNally & Company, 1988. Published annually.

Contains a collection of U.S. maps augmented by a substantial array of commercial, economic, and population statistics, all organized for marketing purposes. The scope of the economic and commercial data is broad, encompassing per-capita income, sales data by industry, buying-power index, median household income, and other relevant statistics. Ranks the largest American corporations, by industry. Displays specialized commercial maps, such as the "Map of Retail Sales," "Map of Manufacturing" (value added), "Map of Trading Areas." The geographic focus encompasses the nation, individual states, counties, and towns.

The business person can find mileage and driving-time maps, airlines serving each city, main routes for individual railroads, telephone area codes, a ZIP code map of the United States, population and sales data for each ZIP code region, and postal information.

For each state, the *Commercial Atlas & Marketing Guide* provides a statewide map and reports data for each place; that is, incorporated and unincorporated places; "no pop." areas, which are railroad stations, factories, mines, and other places in the open country; and other place classifications. For each named place, the data may include, depending on the characteristics, population, county, airlines and railroads serving it, presence of hospital(s), whether the place has been designated a Principal Business Center, and other information. This atlas contains a cornucopia of marketing data, and it is a valuable information source for the marketer.

CPI Detailed Report. U.S. Bureau of Labor Statistics. Washington, DC: U.S. Government Printing Office, 1988. Published monthly.
See "Government Documents," [D-345].

Demographic Yearbook. Statistical Office of the United Nations. New York: United Nations, 1988. Published annually.
See "Almanacs and Yearbooks," [D-23].

Employment and Earnings. U.S. Bureau of Labor Statistics. Washington, DC: U.S. Government Printing Office, 1988. Published monthly.
See "Government Documents," [D-347].

Employment, Hours, and Earnings: States and Areas, 1939–1982. 2 vols. U.S. Bureau of Labor Statistics. Washington, DC: U.S. Government Printing Office, 1984. Revised approximately every four or five years.
See "Government Documents," [D-348].

Employment, Hours, and Earnings: United States, 1909–1984. 2 vols. U.S. Bureau of Labor Statistics. Washington, DC: U.S. Government Printing Office, 1985. Revised periodically and updated annually with the *Supplement to Employment and Earnings* [D-362].
See "Government Documents," [D-349].

[D-465] *A Guide to Statistical Sources in Money, Banking, and Finance*. M. Balachandran. Phoenix, AZ: Oryx Press, 1988.

An annotated bibliography of reference publications that report banking and monetary statistics for the U.S. and other nations. These references are arranged by state, regional, and national sources; foreign nation; and international sources. They address interest rates, foreign-exchange markets, capital and credit markets, money supply, currency, consumer finance and credit cards, bank deposits and loans, treasury operations, and the profitability of financial institutions. Contains the addresses of U.S. and foreign government agencies and private publishers of banking and monetary statistics.

Historical Statistics of the United States, Colonial Times to 1970, Bicentennial Edition. 2 vols. U.S. Bureau of the Census. Washington, DC: U.S. Government Printing Office, 1975.
See "Government Documents," [D-351].

How to Find Business Intelligence in Washington. 9th ed. Washington, DC: Washington Researchers Publishing, 1988.
See "Directories," [D-182].

Index to International Statistics. 2 vols. Washington, DC: Congressional Information Service, Inc., 1988. Published monthly and cumulated quarterly and annually.
See "Abstracts and Indexes," [D-10].

[D-466] *The International Directory of Business Information Agencies and Services.* Detroit: Gale Research Company, 1986.

An international guide to sources of business information in 23 nations and international organizations. Organized by nation, with a separate chapter on international organizations, this publication lists chambers of commerce, government organizations, independent organizations, research organizations, business libraries, organizations that promote foreign trade, and other sources of statistical information. The profiles of organizations include address, telephone number, fax number, name of principal official, summary of purpose and activities, names of publications issued, and other related information.

International Financial Statistics. Washington, DC: International Monetary Fund, 1988. Published monthly and with a yearbook edition.
See "Newspapers, Magazines, and Journals," [D-448].

[D-467] *Predicasts Basebook.* Cleveland, OH: Predicasts, Inc., 1988. Published annually. Loose-leaf format.

A comprehensive composite of time-series statistics for each of the major industries and the general economy. The years of coverage vary with each annual edition. Includes 14 years of data for almost 30,000 series. These statistical series focus on plant and equipment expenditures, production, consumption, wages, labor force, exports/imports, and other data. Sources of the statistical data are cited. Although this book is published annually, the database is updated quarterly and is available via its online counterpart, *PTS U.S. Time Series* [F-118]. Additional time-series data can be accessed through this online service.

[D-468] *Predicasts Forecasts.* Cleveland, OH: Predicasts, Inc., 1988. Updated quarterly and cumulated annually. Loose-leaf format.

A comprehensive guide to U.S. business and economic forecasts. Arranged by industry, it contains projections of many variables regarding products and other industry activities. For each prediction it provides the source publication; consequently, it serves as an abstract of trade journals, government reports, and other printing sources that provide forecast statistics.

 Predicasts Forecasts cites short- and long-range data, annual growth for the criterion, and the base year. Voluminous sources have been analyzed and the forecasting information abstracted. Using the bibliographical citations, the reader can locate the report or article and search for additional information. Also includes forecasts for the major economic indicators.

Producer Price Indexes. U.S. Bureau of Labor Statistics. Washington, DC: U.S. Government Printing Office, 1988. Published monthly. Formerly titled *Producer Prices and Price Indexes.*
See "Government Documents," [D-358].

[D-469] *Regional Statistics: A Guide to Information Sources.* M. Balachandran. Detroit: Gale Research Company, 1980.

A bibliographic guide to sources of socioeconomic data at the local (state, county, and municipal) level. The sources are arranged according to general data sources, housing and construction, population, labor, industrial statistics, business directories, financial data, energy, and transportation. The unique feature is its focus on sources of small-area (local) statistics.

[D-470] *Sourcebook of Demographics and Buying Power for Every ZIP Code in the USA.* Fairfax, VA: CACI, Inc., 1988. Published annually.

Describes the demographic and socioeconomic characteristics of each ZIP Code region in the United States. Includes residential and business statistics. Residential descriptors include post-office name; county FIPS (Federal Information Processing Standard) Code; age distribution of the population; median age; race; total population for 1970, 1980, 1986, and projected for 1993; number of households; housing profile; household income; per-capita income; average family size; education; employment profile; purchasing potential index for selected types of consumer items; and other residential characteristics of the ZIP code area.

The business descriptors for each ZIP code region include the number of firms; estimated employment; and the top five types of businesses, by SIC group, ranked according to the number of employees in each group. Also includes state-summary data.

[D-471] *Sourcebook of Global Statistics.* George T. Kurian. New York: Facts On File, Inc., 1985.

A bibliography of 209 publications that provides statistical information on topics concerning regions throughout the world. Does not contain the statistics per se; instead, it serves as a guide to sources of statistical information: publications issued by public and private organizations, including those at the national and international levels. The types of publications include annuals, books, irregular serials, and monthly issues. Profiles of these publications contain the standard bibliographical information, in addition to the table of contents, sources of the data, language of the text, and other relevant features.

[D-472] *Standard & Poor's Industry Surveys.* 2 vols. New York: Standard & Poor's Corporation, 1988. Published annually with quarterly updates.

Offered both as a loose-leaf service and in a bound softcover edition (the form can be selected by the subscriber), this is a comprehensive guide to the major domestic industries of America. It surveys the performance history and current status of each industry and its principal components. Along with composite financial and operating data for individual industries, there is statistical information on each of 1,200 individual companies. These data include financial and operating ratios for the industry and individual companies within it.

Reports trends, prospects, and new developments for the industries. Provides financial comparisons between companies and five-year performance data for each. Industry analyses appear in a "Basic Analysis" section that is prepared annually and in the "Current Analysis" section that is updated quarterly. An "Earnings Supplement" section summarizes the latest quarterly and annual earnings of individual companies, listed by industry.

Statistical Abstract of the United States. 108th ed. U.S. Bureau of the Census. Washington, DC: U.S. Government Printing Office, 1987. Published annually. See "Government Documents," [D-361].

Statistical Reference Index (*SRI*). 2 vols. Washington, DC: Congressional Information Service, Inc., 1988. Published monthly. The *Index* cumulates monthly, quarterly, and annually.
See "Abstracts and Indexes," [D-18].

[D-473] ***Statistics Sources.*** 12th ed. Edited by Jacqueline Wasserman O'Brien and Steven R. Wasserman. Detroit: Gale Research Company, 1989. Has been published annually, but recently, biennially.

A guide to national and international sources of statistical information. Does not contain the statistical data; instead, it is a guide to publications, government agencies, organizations, trade and professional associations, and international bodies that furnish information. Includes sources of statistics for the U.S. and other nations covering business, financing, industry, education, and other subjects. Topics are arranged alphabetically. For each nation there is cited the name and address of the national statistical office and the titles of the major printed sources of statistical information. The scope also includes publications of the United Nations and the International Monetary Fund.

Supplement to Employment and Earnings. U.S. Bureau of Labor Statistics. Washington, DC: U.S. Government Printing Office, 1988. Published annually.
See "Government Documents," [D-362].

[D-474] ***The Survey of Buying Power Data Service.*** New York: Sales & Marketing Management Magazine, 1987. Published annually.

A comprehensive statistical source of marketing and sales data, this is an expansion of the "Survey of Buying Power" that appears in the *Sales & Marketing Management Magazine* in July and October of each year. Contains population figures; demographic and economic characteristics; retail sales for major cities, counties, states, and MSAs.

An important and useful feature is the Effective Buying Income (EBI), which is an index of disposable personal income that is reported for households and per capita by major city, MSA, county, and state. Another measure of significance is the Buying Power Index (BPI), which is expressed in four forms. It is a measure of a market's (state, region, county, metropolitan market, or TV-coverage area) potential consumer buying power, figured as a percentage of a composite U.S. potential.

This publication reports geographic-market retail sales by retail store group. Also, it reports the Merchandise Line Sales for specified merchandise categories. These are arranged by major city, state, and television markets (ADIs).

Contains maps of states, counties, and metro markets. This book is a principal source of marketing and sales information for current activities and projections. It makes possible the setting of sales goals and quotas, the identification of test markets according to criteria selected by the marketer, and the determination of the sales potential of a new market and a new product.

Survey of Current Business. U.S. Bureau of Economic Analysis. Washington, DC: U.S. Government Printing Office, 1988. Published monthly.
See "Government Documents, [D-363].

U.S. Industrial Outlook. U.S. International Trade Administration. Washington, DC: U.S. Government Printing Office, 1988. Published annually.
See "Government Documents," [D-367].

[D-475] *Worldcasts*. 8 vols. Cleveland, OH: Predicasts, Inc., 1988. Updated quarterly. Loose-leaf format.

A comprehensive guide to foreign (international) business and economic forecasts. Four of the volumes are organized by world region: (1) West Europe; (2) East Europe, Africa, and Middle East; (3) Americas (excluding the U.S.); and (4) Asia and Oceania. Another four volumes are arranged by product or industry: general economics, utilities, and services; agriculture, mining, forestry, food, textiles, wood, and paper; chemicals, polymers, drugs, oil, rubber, stone, clay, and glass; and primary metals, machinery, electronics, and transportation equipment.

Provides short-range and long-range forecasts for major foreign economic indicators and products and industries outside of the U.S. The source journal from which each forecast figure was obtained is reported; therefore, this is a comprehensive review of printed sources, with the forecasted data having been abstracted from them. Following the composite regional data are forecasts for each country within the region.

E

Where Should I Go to Find Information in Online Databases?

Information Contained in Section E

In this Section are business questions the answers to which can be found by using online databases.

What Is a Database?

A database, simply stated, is a collection of information organized in a selected arrangement. Usually all the pieces of information are arranged in the same way in a given database, whether the information is about a company, person, product, or other data element. A mail-order catalog is an example of a database, because it consists of information arranged so that each item in the catalog has a description, an order number, a price, and, perhaps a picture and other data.

A typical online database is stored in a database vendor's computer. Telephone lines connect the vendor's computer with the computers of people who are looking for information in the database. People might use terms like "computer database" or just "database" to mean "online database."

What Is the Relationship Between Books and Databases?

Many databases are available on paper, often as books. An example is the D & B – MILLION DOLLAR DIRECTORY database. In book form it is called the *Million Dollar Directory*. Information in some online databases and their book counterparts is very much the same. But the information in other online databases differs somewhat, or even a great deal, from the books of the same name. A reason for the differences is that publishers can update a database much more rapidly and frequently than they can publish new editions of books. There are other reasons, too. The intended users of the database might not be the same group of people as the intended users of the book. The database could actually correspond to two or more books, or one book could be marketed in computerized form as several databases. There are online databases like ABI/INFORM that are published only as databases and have no paper counterpart. The important point is that information available in an online database often is in some way different—in content or in presentation—from the information found in books.

Sometimes the confusing result of these differences is that an online database can have a name very much like or very different from its book counterpart. It is customary to use all upper-case letters when writing the name of an online database. When an upper-case title is used in this book, it means that an online database is being described.

Added confusion regarding a database name comes from the fact that a database often is available from more than one vendor. Such a vendor, often called an online vendor, sells access to the database. Each vendor might have its own name for the database. These vendor names could even differ from the publisher's name for the database. (The publisher is the firm that creates or produces the database, much as a book publisher produces books.) Whenever possible, the publisher's name is used here for each database, but Section F also provides information about vendor designations for databases.

Which Databases Are Listed in This Book?

The online databases in this Section and in Section F are available for use through companies that are vendors of online databases. There are many such companies; for the purposes of this book, five online database services have been chosen from three of the most important vendors of business databases. Taken as a group, these five services have provided the business community with a large variety of well-known business databases. The five services and their vendors are:

Service	Vendor
After Dark	BRS Information Technologies
BRS Search Service	BRS Information Technologies
CompuServe	CompuServe Information Service
Dialog	Dialog Information Services
Knowledge Index	Dialog Information Services

By subscribing to the appropriate service, the reader may obtain the information stored in the databases described in the next few pages. See the following paragraphs, "For Further Information," to find out more about how to subscribe.

This book profiles databases that primarily address business activities in the U.S. All the databases listed here are important to the American business community, but many more online databases are available. Each of the database services listed above offers other business databases, as well as many databases in other fields of interest. There are also other vendors of databases that are important to those interested in business. Sections E and F cite a few databases from some of these other vendors. To know more, read the "Sources of Information" and "For Further Information" paragraphs below.

Sources of Information

The information presented in Sections E and F was obtained primarily from direct examination of the online databases. If a database is available from more than one vendor, it is possible that its content and format vary from one vendor's version to another's.

Additionally, vendor catalogs were used to verify which services make available which databases. The catalogs are quite useful lists, especially for the new or infrequent user of online databases. Use the vendor phone numbers or addresses to inquire about obtaining catalogs. (This vendor information is in Appendix III.) The catalogs used were:

Database Catalog 1990. McLean, VA: BRS Information Technologies, 1990. (800) 289-4277.

Dialog Database Catalog 1990. Palo Alto, CA: Dialog Information Services, 1990. (800) 334-2564.

Users Guide. Columbus, OH: CompuServe Information Service, 1988. (800) 848-8199.

Limitations

The field of online databases is an ever-changing one; therefore, please keep in mind the following limitations as you use Sections E and F.

1. If there is more than one database listed for a question, it is possible that each database might answer different aspects of that question. For example, if a question seeks information about balance-sheet data for a company, one database might provide more columns or different years of data than does another database. For some questions, it may be necessary to examine several of the databases listed, if all aspects of the question need to be covered.

2. Over time the type of information in a database can change, as publishers and vendors add or delete features. Some databases go out of existence. New ones appear. The information contained in this book is current as of the time of writing.

3. Although the emphasis in Sections E and F is on databases that provide information about business activity in the U.S., online vendors do sell access to many databases that cover the international business community.

4. Some special services of the chosen vendors have been excluded. For example, we have not included the online banking, shopping, and investment-portfolio management services that might be available from the same vendor that sells access to online databases.

5. More and more databases are becoming available in CD-ROM (Compact Disk, Read-Only Memory). This permits having the CD-ROM version of a database stored in a personal computer, thus eliminating the need to connect a computer with the phone lines to an online vendor. Section F indicates which of the databases mentioned are also available in CD-ROM from the database publisher or vendor; however, there has not been included those business databases available exclusively in CD-ROM format.

6. The databases mentioned do not include those available only by purchasing or leasing them on computer disks or computer tapes.

For Further Information

To use the online databases listed here, a subscription to a database service and the proper computer hardware and software are needed.

To obtain a subscription to the database services mentioned, contact the vendor, using the address or phone number given in Appendix III. For the After Dark and BRS services, contact BRS Information Technologies. For the CompuServe service, contact CompuServe Information Service. For the Dialog and Knowledge Index services, contact Dialog Information Services.

Once a subscription has been obtained, you can use a computer to actually look for information in a database. Many people use a personal computer for this activity. The contact between your computer and the online vendor's computer is made over telephone lines, so in addition to the computer itself, a modem and access to a telephone line are required. The modem is a device that is able to translate between computerized communications and telephone communications. Computer software will also be necessary to tell the computer how to use the modem. The software might be built into the modem itself or could be separate. If help is needed with the computer, the modem, or the communications software, seek out a colleague who already uses online databases, ask for help at a local computer store, or read one of the many books that explain how to use a personal computer for communicating with online databases.

Some people go to database-searching services as an alternative to using their own computers to contact online databases. These database services usually will charge a fee. Many public and college libraries have these services. Such a service might exist in your own firm's library or information center. Some cities also have information brokers from whom such services can be purchased.

Format

Each question in Section E highlights one or more features of the databases that have been profiled in Section F. The questions have been categorized by field and subject area. Some questions have been entered in multiple categories as applicable.

To provide the reader with further information about each database, an item entry number (for example, F-1) follows each database title. The item entry number refers to the database descriptions in Section F. After locating a question and deciding which database is of interest, turn to Section F for additional information. See Appendix III for addresses and telephone numbers of database publishers and vendors.

Data Sources

<u>*WHERE SHOULD I GO TO FIND...*</u>   <u>*TRY*</u>

| Accounting/Financial Analysis |

Accounting Standards

summaries of reports from the Financial
Accounting Standards Bureau (FASB)
and Government Accounting Standards
Board (GASB)?

TAX NOTES TODAY [F-127]

Company Financial Statistics

financial ratios for a company?

D & B—DUN'S FINANCIAL RECORDS
PLUS [F-39]
DISCLOSURE [F-44]
MEDIA GENERAL [F-86]
S & P ONLINE [F-121]
VALUE LINE DATABASE II [F-137]

comparisons of a company's financial
ratios with those of its industry?

D & B—DUN'S FINANCIAL RECORDS
PLUS [F-39]
INVESTEXT [F-72]

balance-sheet statistics for an individual
company—either for a few months or a
few years?

DISCLOSURE [F-44]
MEDIA GENERAL [F-86]
MOODY'S CORPORATE PROFILES
[F-91]
STANDARD & POOR'S CORPORATE
DESCRIPTIONS ONLINE [F-122]
VALUE LINE DATABASE II [F-137]

changes in the ratings of a corporation's
debt?

INVESTOR'S DAILY [F-73]

Industry Profiles

financial data on specific industries?

INDUSTRY DATA SOURCES [F-65]

Tax Accounting

the full text of sections from the Internal
Revenue Code or Treasury Regulations
that cover tax accounting?

RIA FEDERAL TAX COORDINATOR
2D [F-120]

WHERE SHOULD I GO TO FIND...	*TRY*

Tax Accounting

explanations of federal codes and regulations that affect tax accounting, including the computation of inventories and allocation of income?   RIA FEDERAL TAX COORDINATOR 2D [F-120]

Banking and Finance

Bank Management and Marketing

case studies of successful marketing plans used in the bank and finance industry?   FINIS [F-60]

management news about financial-service institutions, covering advertising, compensation, facilities planning, marketing, personnel development, pricing, sales, and training?   FINIS [F-60]

Currencies of the World

foreign exchange rates—current and historical?   ISSUE PRICING HISTORY [F-76]
NEWS-A-TRON MARKET REPORTS [F-96]
PRICING STATISTICS [F-108]

Federal Reserve Board

reports on Federal Reserve Board activity, including analyses of economic, political, and other factors that might affect its decisions on interest rates?   FEDWATCH [F-56]

Financial Industry News

the full text of articles about the financial industry that have appeared in recent issues of financial newspapers?   AMERICAN BANKER [F-4]
AMERICAN BANKER NEWS [F-5]
BOND BUYER [F-11]
FINANCIAL TIMES FULL TEXT [F-58]

WHERE SHOULD I GO TO FIND...	*TRY*

Financial Industry News

speeches on banking and finance delivered by business and government leaders?	AMERICAN BANKER [F-4] AMERICAN BANKER NEWS [F-5]
news on almost any aspect of finance, especially with an international emphasis?	FINANCIAL TIMES ABSTRACTS [F-57] FINANCIAL TIMES FULL TEXT [F-58]

Financial Institution News

news about a bank, brokerage house, thrift institution, or other member of the financial-services industry?	AMERICAN BANKER [F-4] AMERICAN BANKER NEWS [F-5] BOND BUYER [F-11] FINIS [F-60]
new-position notices for executives in banking and finance?	AMERICAN BANKER [F-4] AMERICAN BANKER NEWS [F-5]

Financial Institutions and Services: Listings and Profiles

listings of financial institutions, with descriptive information?	AMERICAN BANKER [F-4]
listings of financial institutions according to amount of their assets?	FINIS [F-60]

Information Sources

an index to banking and finance statistics published by federal executive, judicial, and legislative agencies, offices, and other units?	ASI [F-7]
an index to articles and case studies about the banking and finance industry?	FINIS [F-60]

Mergers and Acquisitions

merger notices in the banking and finance industry?	AMERICAN BANKER [F-4] AMERICAN BANKER NEWS [F-5]

WHERE SHOULD I GO TO FIND...	*TRY*

Regulations

| regulations and rulings that affect banking, bonds, credit, and finance? | AMERICAN BANKER [F-4]
AMERICAN BANKER NEWS [F-5]
BOND BUYER [F-11] |

Business Careers

Company Listings

a listing of addresses and telephone numbers of employment agencies?	D & B—DUN'S ELECTRONIC YELLOW PAGES [F-38]
the typical number of employees in a business, by type of product or service?	TRINET COMPANY DATABASE [F-134] TRINET U.S. BUSINESSES [F-135]
a listing of companies according to geographic location?	CORPORATE AFFILIATIONS [F-35] D & B—DUN'S ELECTRONIC YELLOW PAGES [F-38] D & B—DUN'S FINANCIAL RECORDS PLUS [F-39] D & B—DUN'S MARKET IDENTIFIERS [F-40] D & B—MILLION DOLLAR DIRECTORY [F-42] DISCLOSURE [F-44] INSIDER TRADING MONITOR [F-68] MEDIA GENERAL [F-86] PTS ANNUAL REPORTS ABSTRACTS [F-111] STANDARD & POOR'S REGISTER—CORPORATE [F-125] THOMAS REGISTER ONLINE [129] TRINET COMPANY DATABASE [F-134] TRINET U.S. BUSINESSES [F-135]
a company's address, telephone number, a description of its products and services, and names of its directors and officers?	CORPORATE AFFILIATIONS [F-35] D & B—DUN'S ELECTRONIC YELLOW PAGES [F-38] D & B—DUN'S FINANCIAL RECORDS PLUS [F-39] D & B—DUN'S MARKET IDENTIFIERS [F-40] D & B—MILLION DOLLAR DIRECTORY [F-42]

WHERE SHOULD I GO TO FIND...	*TRY*

Company Listings

a company's address, telephone number, a description of its products and services, and names of its directors and officers?

DISCLOSURE [F-44]
MOODY'S CORPORATE PROFILES [F-91]
PTS ANNUAL REPORTS ABSTRACTS [F-111]
S & P ONLINE [F-121]
STANDARD & POOR'S CORPORATE DESCRIPTIONS ONLINE [F-122]
STANDARD & POOR'S REGISTER—CORPORATE [F-125]
THOMAS REGISTER ONLINE [129]
TRINET COMPANY DATABASE [F-134]
TRINET U.S. BUSINESSES [F-135]

Information Sources

an index to articles that give suggestions about job interviews, career changes, writing résumés, and so on?

ABI/INFORM [F-1]
BUSINESS PERIODICALS INDEX [F-16]
MAGAZINE ASAP [F-81]
MAGAZINE INDEX [F-82]
NATIONAL NEWSPAPER INDEX [F-94]
NEWSEARCH [F-97]

an index to articles on the psychological aspects of succeeding in one's career?

PSYCINFO [F-109]

an index to employment and labor statistics published by federal executive, judicial, and legislative agencies, offices, and other units?

ASI [F-7]

Résumés

résumés of job seekers, reporting their availability, occupational interests and skills, salary expectations, and willingness to relocate?

CAREER PLACEMENT REGISTRY [F-20]

listings of software that assist in the planning, writing, and printing of résumés?

BUSINESS SOFTWARE DATABASE [F-17]
COMPUTER ASAP [F-32]
COMPUTER DATABASE [F-33]

WHERE SHOULD I GO TO FIND...	*TRY*

Wage Statistics

| average hourly-earnings data for several recent years in a specified industry? | ECONBASE [F-50] |

Business Law

Decisions

| an index to labor relations decisions made by federal and state courts and administrative bodies, including decisions related to collective bargaining, fair-employment practices, health, safety, and wages? | LABORLAW [F-78] |

Incorporating

| incorporating requirements and costs in each state, including pros and cons of incorporating and how to qualify for foreign incorporation? | BUSINESS INCORPORATING GUIDE [F-15] |

Information Sources

| indexes to legal developments reported by bar journals, law reviews, and business periodicals concerning such business-law topics as acquisitions, mergers, securities, taxation, and others? | ABI/INFORM [F-1] BUSINESS DATELINE [F-13] BUSINESS PERIODICALS INDEX [F-16] LEGAL RESOURCE INDEX [F-79] PTS PROMT [F-117] TRADE & INDUSTRY ASAP [F-130] TRADE & INDUSTRY INDEX [F-131] |

Legislation and Regulations

| legislative documents, federal-agency publications, and court opinions on tax law? | TAX NOTES TODAY [F-127] |

| summaries of current tax bills and the full text of major tax bills under consideration by Congress? | TAX NOTES TODAY [F-127] |

WHERE SHOULD I GO TO FIND . . .   *TRY*

Legislation and Regulations

the full text of news about developments in federal and state tax legislation, court cases, and related matters?	CCH TAX DAY—FEDERAL [F-22] CCH TAX DAY—STATE [F-23] TAX NOTES TODAY [F-127]
the opinions of expert witnesses, often representing major corporations, on proposed or passed U.S. legislation affecting business?	CIS [F-26]
an index to publications of congressional committees, including reports on hearings and background information gathered to support legislative decisions?	CIS [F-26]
notices of regulations and proposed regulations announced by federal agencies?	AMERICAN BANKER [F-4] AMERICAN BANKER NEWS [F-5] BOND BUYER [F-11] FEDERAL REGISTER ABSTRACTS [F-55] PTS NEWSLETTER DATABASE [F-116]
the full text of sections from the Internal Revenue Code or Treasury Regulations that cover a tax issue, problem, or question?	RIA FEDERAL TAX COORDINATOR 2D [F-120]
commentary on recent developments in federal taxation, including new Internal Revenue rules, statements, and proposed regulations?	RIA FEDERAL TAX COORDINATOR 2D [F-120]
explanations of federal codes and regulations that affect a specific tax issue, problem, or question, plus suggestions on when, why, and how to apply the codes and regulations to the tax problem?	RIA FEDERAL TAX COORDINATOR 2D [F-120]

State Securities

decisions, fees, laws, policies, regulations, and other information for dealing in state securities, including the text of the Uniform Securities Act?	CCH BLUE SKY LAW REPORTER [F-21]

WHERE SHOULD I GO TO FIND...	*TRY*

State Securities

the name of each state's securities administrator? — CCH BLUE SKY LAW REPORTER [F-21]

Business Organizations, Trade Associations, and Unions

Association News

news releases issued by trade associations? — NEWSWIRE ASAP [F-100]
PR NEWSWIRE [F-107]

Associations and Organizations: Listings and Profiles

a listing of business, government, labor, professional, and other membership associations, federations, and societies, with a description of their activities, membership, and publications? — ENCYCLOPEDIA OF ASSOCIATIONS [F-52]

a listing of associations, societies, and other such groups according to area code, ZIP code, annual budget size, or membership size? — ENCYCLOPEDIA OF ASSOCIATIONS [F-52]

Business Resources

Assistance to Businesses

federal laboratory facilities, such as labs that handle fluidics, food irradiation, plumbing, or polymers, that are available to the business community? — FEDERAL APPLIED TECHNOLOGY DATABASE [F-54]

a listing of companies and other organizations where I am likely to find an expert on a product or process? — FAIRBASE [F-53]

Exhibitions

opportunities to exhibit products at conferences, trade shows, and other meetings, including dates and locations? — FAIRBASE [F-53]

WHERE SHOULD I GO TO FIND...	*TRY*

Incorporating

incorporating requirements and costs in each state, including pros and cons of incorporating and how to qualify for foreign incorporation?

BUSINESS INCORPORATING GUIDE [F-15]

Suppliers

a list of suppliers that offer industrial products or services?

THOMAS NEW INDUSTRIAL PRODUCTS [F-128]
THOMAS REGISTER ONLINE [F-129]

Travel

commercial airline flights available for a particular day and time, how to make flight reservations, fare information, and room rates for hotels/motels?

OFFICIAL AIRLINE GUIDE [F-103]

Computers and Information Processing

Computer and Electronics Ventures

companies or researchers working on new technologies, especially in computing, electronics, and engineering?

COMPENDEX*PLUS [F-31]
INSPEC [F-69]

Computer Hardware and Software

descriptions of software available for business?

BUSINESS SOFTWARE DATABASE [F-17]
COMPUTER ASAP [F-32]
COMPUTER DATABASE [F-33]

a listing of business software available in a particular price range?

BUSINESS SOFTWARE DATABASE [F-17]

evaluations of computer hardware and software?

COMPUTER ASAP [F-32]
COMPUTER DATABASE [F-33]

company information and a contact person for the producer of a business software package?

BUSINESS SOFTWARE DATABASE [F-17]

WHERE SHOULD I GO TO FIND...	*TRY*

Computer Hardware and Software

business software that is appropriate for a particular micro- or mini-computing operating system and/or type of computer?   BUSINESS SOFTWARE DATABASE [F-17]

Consumers and Consumerism

Computers and Software

descriptions and prices of software for consumer applications?   BUSINESS SOFTWARE DATABASE [F-17]
CONSUMER REPORTS [F-34]

evaluations of computer hardware and software?   COMPUTER ASAP [F-32]
COMPUTER DATABASE [F-33]

Consumer Assistance

descriptions of consumer-assistance organizations?   ENCYCLOPEDIA OF ASSOCIATIONS [F-52]

Cost of Living

cost-of-living data for various cities in the U.S., including income and consumer price information?   ECONBASE [F-50]

indexes to periodical articles about cost of living in the U.S.?   ABI/INFORM [F-1]
NATIONAL NEWSPAPER INDEX [F-94]
NEWSPAPER ABSTRACTS [F-99]

Product Evaluations

product evaluations and recommendations?   CONSUMER REPORTS [F-34]

products that have such qualities as being safe, easy to clean, easy to install, energy efficient, vibration free, or other requirements?   THOMAS NEW INDUSTRIAL PRODUCTS [F-128]

| *WHERE SHOULD I GO TO FIND...* | *TRY* |

Vendor Products and Services

the name, address, and telephone number of a trade name's manufacturer?

THOMAS REGISTER ONLINE [F-129]

the name, address, and telephone number of companies that provide a specified product or service?

THOMAS REGISTER ONLINE [F-129]

| **Corporate Operations, Officials, and Profiles** |

Company/Industry News

news about individual companies and industries?

ABI/INFORM [F-1]
BUSINESS DATELINE [F-13]
BUSINESS PERIODICALS INDEX [F-16]
FINANCIAL TIMES ABSTRACTS [F-57]
FINANCIAL TIMES FULL TEXT [F-58]
HARVARD BUSINESS REVIEW [F-62]
INVESTOR'S DAILY [F-73]
MANAGEMENT CONTENTS [F-83]
MCGRAW-HILL PUBLICATIONS ONLINE [F-85]
MOODY'S CORPORATE NEWS—INTERNATIONAL [F-89]
MOODY'S CORPORATE NEWS—U.S. [F-90]
PTS F & S INDEX [F-112]
PTS MARKETING & ADVERTISING REFERENCE SERVICE [F-114]
PTS PROMT [F-117]
STANDARD & POOR'S NEWS ONLINE [F-123]
TRADE & INDUSTRY ASAP [F-130]
TRADE & INDUSTRY INDEX [F-131]

news about regional and local companies?

BUSINESS DATELINE [F-13]
PTS PROMT [F-117]
TRADE & INDUSTRY ASAP [F-130]
TRADE & INDUSTRY INDEX [F-131]

<u>*WHERE SHOULD I GO TO FIND*...</u>   <u>*TRY*</u>

Company/Industry News

intelligence reports about an individual
company?

CORPORATE AND INDUSTRY
RESEARCH REPORTS [F-36]
FINDEX DIRECTORY OF MARKET
RESEARCH [F-59]
INVESTEXT [F-72]
MOODY'S CORPORATE PROFILES
[F-91]
PTS PROMT [F-117]

newsletter articles about a company's
activities?

PTS NEWSLETTER DATABASE [F-116]

contract awards, intelligence reports, and
other news about aerospace and defense
companies?

DMS CONTRACT AWARDS [F-47]
DMS CONTRACTORS [F-48]
DMS MARKET INTELLIGENCE
REPORTS [F-49]
JANE'S DEFENSE & AEROSPACE
NEWS/ANALYSIS [F-77]
PTS AEROSPACE/DEFENSE MARKETS
& TECHNOLOGY [F-110]

latest marketing plans, products, and
other news about high-technology
companies?

COMPUTER ASAP [F-32]
COMPUTER DATABASE [F-33]

new business ventures, recent product
advances, and other news about
companies involved in agriculture,
biological, and medical research?

AGRIBUSINESS U.S.A. [F-2]
BIOBUSINESS [F-10]

news releases from companies, in full
text, including the name and phone
number of a contact person at the
company?

BUSINESS WIRE [F-18]
NEWSWIRE ASAP [F-100]
PR NEWSWIRE [F-107]

news about foreign and international
companies from sources that emphasize
non-U.S. news?

FINANCIAL TIMES ABSTRACTS
[F-57]
FINANCIAL TIMES FULL TEXT
[F-58]
INFOMAT INTERNATIONAL
BUSINESS [F-66]
MOODY'S CORPORATE
NEWS—INTERNATIONAL [F-89]

Company Listings and Comprehensive Profiles

a listing of companies according to
geographic location?

CORPORATE AFFILIATIONS [F-35]
D & B—DUN'S ELECTRONIC
YELLOW PAGES [F-38]
D & B—DUN'S FINANCIAL RECORDS
PLUS [F-39]
D & B—DUN'S MARKET
IDENTIFIERS [F-40]
D & B—MILLION DOLLAR
DIRECTORY [F-42]
DISCLOSURE [F-44]
INSIDER TRADING MONITOR [F-68]
MEDIA GENERAL [F-86]
STANDARD & POOR'S
REGISTER—CORPORATE [F-125]
THOMAS REGISTER ONLINE [F-129]
TRINET COMPANY DATABASE
[F-134]
TRINET U.S. BUSINESSES [F-135]

a company's address, telephone number,
a description of its products and services,
and names of its directors and officers?

CORPORATE AFFILIATIONS [F-35]
D & B—DUN'S ELECTRONIC
YELLOW PAGES [F-38]
D & B—DUN'S FINANCIAL RECORDS
PLUS [F-39]
D & B—DUN'S MARKET
IDENTIFIERS [F-40]
D & B—MILLION DOLLAR
DIRECTORY [F-42]
DISCLOSURE [F-44]
MOODY'S CORPORATE PROFILES
[F-91]
PTS ANNUAL REPORTS ABSTRACTS
[F-111]
S & P ONLINE [F-121]
STANDARD & POOR'S CORPORATE
DESCRIPTIONS ONLINE [F-122]
STANDARD & POOR'S
REGISTER—CORPORATE [F-125]
THOMAS REGISTER ONLINE [129]
TRINET COMPANY DATABASE
[F-134]
TRINET U.S. BUSINESSES [F-135]

WHERE SHOULD I GO TO FIND…	*TRY*

Company Listings and Comprehensive Profiles

a foreign company's address, telephone number, and a brief description of its major product or service?	D & B—INTERNATIONAL DUN'S MARKET IDENTIFIERS [F-41]
the *Fortune* or *Forbes* code for a company?	DISCLOSURE [F-44]
a company's parent, ultimate parent, or subsidiaries?	CORPORATE AFFILIATIONS [F-35] D & B—DUN'S MARKET IDENTIFIERS [F-40] D & B—MILLION DOLLAR DIRECTORY [F-42] STANDARD & POOR'S CORPORATE DESCRIPTIONS ONLINE [F-122] THOMAS REGISTER ONLINE [F-129]
"management's discussion" taken from a company's annual report?	DISCLOSURE [F-44] PTS ANNUAL REPORTS ABSTRACTS [F-111] PTS PROMT [F-117] STANDARD & POOR'S CORPORATE DESCRIPTIONS ONLINE [F-122]

Corporate Officials

biographical data about a company official?	STANDARD & POOR'S REGISTER—BIOGRAPHICAL [F-124]
articles about a person associated with a business or industry?	ABI/INFORM [F-1] AGRIBUSINESS U.S.A. [F-2] BIOBUSINESS [F-10] BUSINESS DATELINE [F-13] BUSINESS PERIODICALS INDEX [F-16] COMPUTER ASAP [F-32] COMPUTER DATABASE [F-33] INVESTOR'S DAILY [F-73] MANAGEMENT CONTENTS [F-83] NEWSWIRE ASAP [F-100] TRADE & INDUSTRY ASAP [F-130] TRADE & INDUSTRY INDEX [F-131]

WHERE SHOULD I GO TO FIND...	*TRY*

Corporate Officials

names of directors or officers of a company?	CORPORATE AFFILIATIONS [F-35] D & B—DUN'S MARKET IDENTIFIERS [F-40] D & B—MILLION DOLLAR DIRECTORY [F-42] DISCLOSURE [F-44] STANDARD & POOR'S CORPORATE DESCRIPTIONS ONLINE [F-122] STANDARD & POOR'S REGISTER—BIOGRAPHICAL [F-124] STANDARD & POOR'S REGISTER—CORPORATE [F-125]

Financial Profiles

changes in the ratings of a corporation's debt?	INVESTOR'S DAILY [F-73]
balance-sheet statistics for an individual company—either for a few months or a few years?	DISCLOSURE [F-44] MEDIA GENERAL [F-86] MOODY'S CORPORATE PROFILES [F-91] STANDARD & POOR'S CORPORATE DESCRIPTIONS ONLINE [F-122] VALUE LINE DATABASE II [F-137]
financial ratios for a company?	D & B—DUN'S FINANCIAL RECORDS PLUS [F-39] DISCLOSURE [F-44] MEDIA GENERAL [F-86] S & P ONLINE [F-121] VALUE LINE DATABASE II [F-137]
SEC 8K, 10K, 10Q, 20F, and corporate annual reports, and other data on individual companies?	DISCLOSURE [F-44] MEDIA GENERAL [F-86] MOODY'S CORPORATE PROFILES [F-91] PTS ANNUAL REPORTS ABSTRACTS [F-111] STANDARD & POOR'S CORPORATE DESCRIPTIONS ONLINE [F-122]

<u>*WHERE SHOULD I GO TO FIND...*</u>	<u>*TRY*</u>

Financial Profiles

the share of market held by a company?   ABI/INFORM [F-1]
BUSINESS DATELINE [F-13]
INVESTEXT [F-72]
PTS PROMT [F-117]
TRADE & INDUSTRY ASAP [F-130]
TRADE & INDUSTRY INDEX [F-131]
TRINET U.S. BUSINESSES [F-135]

Mergers and Acquisitions

merger or acquisitions documents filed   M & A FILINGS [F-80]
by a company, including data on the
value of the deal, the organization
managing the merger, and the source of
funds?

news on mergers and acquisition   INFOMAT INTERNATIONAL
transactions?   BUSINESS [F-66]
MOODY'S CORPORATE
NEWS—INTERNATIONAL [F-89]
MOODY'S CORPORATE NEWS—U.S.
[F-90]
PTS PROMT [F-117]
STANDARD & POOR'S NEWS ONLINE
[F-123]

Stockholders

insider, institutional, and 5-percent   DISCLOSURE SPECTRUM
shareholders of a company?   OWNERSHIP [F-45]

Trade Names

what product or service is sold under a   THOMAS REGISTER ONLINE [F-129]
given trade name?

if a trade name currently is being used?   PTS NEW PRODUCT ANNOUNCE-
MENTS [F-115]
THOMAS NEW INDUSTRIAL
PRODUCTS [F-128]
THOMAS REGISTER ONLINE [F-129]

WHERE SHOULD I GO TO FIND...	*TRY*

Vendor Products and Services

products and services of a competitor?	PTS F & S INDEX [F-112] PTS MARKETING & ADVERTISING REFERENCE SERVICE [F-114] PTS NEW PRODUCT ANNOUNCE-MENTS [F-115] PTS NEWSLETTER DATABASE [F-116] PTS PROMT [F-117] THOMAS NEW INDUSTRIAL PRODUCTS [F-128] THOMAS REGISTER ONLINE [F-129] TRADE & INDUSTRY ASAP [F-130] TRADE & INDUSTRY INDEX [F-131]
a listing of companies that provide a specified category of product or service?	CORPORATE AFFILIATIONS [F-35] D & B—DUN'S ELECTRONIC YELLOW PAGES [F-38] D & B—DUN'S FINANCIAL RECORDS PLUS [F-39] D & B—DUN'S MARKET IDENTIFIERS [F-40] D & B—MILLION DOLLAR DIRECTORY [F-42] DISCLOSURE [F-44] MEDIA GENERAL [F-86] MOODY'S CORPORATE PROFILES [F-91] PTS F & S INDEX [F-112] PTS NEW PRODUCT ANNOUNCE-MENTS [F-115] PTS PROMT [F-117] STANDARD & POOR'S CORPORATE DESCRIPTIONS ONLINE [F-122] STANDARD & POOR'S REGISTER—CORPORATE [F-125] THOMAS REGISTER ONLINE [F-129] TRADE & INDUSTRY ASAP [F-130] TRADE & INDUSTRY INDEX [F-131] TRINET COMPANY DATABASE [F-134] TRINET U.S. BUSINESSES [F-135]
the product lines of an individual company, with data on sales and share of market for each line?	TRINET U.S. BUSINESSES [F-135]

WHERE SHOULD I GO TO FIND...	*TRY*

Demographics

Information Sources

an index to demographic statistics published by an executive, judicial, or legislative agency, office, commission, committee, or other unit of the federal government?

ASI [F-7]

Occupational Statistics

the number of people in different occupations in a city, county, metropolitan area, or state?

D & B—DONNELLEY DEMOGRAPHICS [F-37]

Population Statistics

name and addresses of local and federal offices that supply census data?

CENDATA [F-24]

the number of businesses, employees, or people in a city, county, state, metropolitan area, ZIP code, Arbitron, or Nielsen area?

BUSINESS DEMOGRAPHICS REPORTS [F-14]
D & B—DONNELLEY DEMOGRAPHICS [F-37]

the number of people in an Arbitron area, county, metropolitan area, Nielsen area, state, or ZIP code, including types of jobs, housing, and average income?

D & B—DONNELLEY DEMOGRAPHICS [F-37]
NEIGHBORHOOD DEMOGRAPHIC REPORTS [F-95]
SUPERSITE [F-126]

selected U.S. Bureau of the Census current and projected population, income, and other data for states, counties, and municipalities?

CENDATA [F-24]

Wage Statistics

average-hourly-earnings data for several recent years in an industry?

ECONBASE [F-50]

payroll data for business and government employers, by county?

CENDATA [F-24]

| *WHERE SHOULD I GO TO FIND...* | *TRY* |

Economic Analyses

Cost of Living

cost of living data for various cities in the U.S., including income and consumer price information?

ECONBASE [F-50]

Federal Reserve Board

reports on Federal Reserve Board activity, including analyses of economic, political, and other factors that might affect its decisions on interest rates?

FEDWATCH [F-56]

Forecasts

economic forecast data for various products and industries for the 1990s?

PTS FORECASTS [F-113]

forecasts of earnings, sales, or stock prices of individual companies?

I/B/E/S [F-64]
INVESTEXT [F-72]
VALUE LINE DATABASE II [F-137]

economic growth forecasts for individual industries?

INDUSTRY DATA SOURCES [F-65]

national and industrial forecasts made by the federal government?

ASI [F-7]
ECONBASE [F-50]

Historical Trend Data

ten to twenty years of annual data for various products and industries, covering expenditures, exports, imports, profits, sales, and other statistics?

PTS U.S. TIME SERIES [F-118]

a daily summary of an industry's stock activity, indicating its five-year earnings per share compared with other industries and its stock-price performance compared with that of other industries for the past year?

INVESTOR'S DAILY [F-73]

| *WHERE SHOULD I GO TO FIND...* | *TRY* |

Historical Trend Data

| financial, labor-force, production, shipment, and sales data for an industry, ranging from several years to several decades? | ECONBASE [F-50] |

| daily market analyses, summarizing the current or expected effects of political and economic events on the cash, currency, equity, futures index, and options markets? | MMS INTERNATIONAL [F-88] |

| analyses of Gross National Product, employment, flow of funds, employment, and other economic data regularly released by the federal government? | MMS INTERNATIONAL [F-88] |

| stock-market indicators, consumer price indexes, inflation data, and other national statistics displayed as time series? | ECONBASE [F-50] |

| recent economic indicators such as prime rate, outstanding consumer installment credit, new-home mortgage rates, and money supply? | CENDATA [F-24] |

Information Sources

| an index to articles containing economic analyses? | ABI/INFORM [F-1] BUSINESS PERIODICALS INDEX [F-16] ECONOMIC LITERATURE INDEX [F-51] HARVARD BUSINESS REVIEW [F-62] NATIONAL NEWSPAPER INDEX [F-94] NEWSEARCH [F-97] PTS PROMT [F-117] TRADE & INDUSTRY ASAP [F-130] TRADE & INDUSTRY INDEX [F-131] |

Wage Statistics

| average-hourly-earnings data for several recent years in an industry? | ECONBASE [F-50] |

WHERE SHOULD I GO TO FIND...   *TRY*

Wage Statistics

payroll data for business and government   CENDATA [F-24]
employers, by county?

| **General Business Reference Sources and General Facts** |

Newsletters

the full text of articles in business   MCGRAW-HILL PUBLICATIONS
newsletters?   ONLINE [F-85]
     PTS NEWSLETTER DATABASE [F-116]

Newspapers and Newswires

the full text of stories from major   ASSOCIATED PRESS NEWS
newswires?   HIGHLIGHTS [F-8]
     NEWSGRID [F-98]
     UPI NEWS [F-136]

an index to articles found in major   CHICAGO TRIBUNE [F-25]
newspapers and newswires?   FINANCIAL TIMES ABSTRACTS
     [F-57]
     NATIONAL NEWSPAPER INDEX
     [F-94]
     NEWSEARCH [F-97]
     NEWSPAPER ABSTRACTS [F-99]
     NEWSWIRE ASAP [F-100]
     TRADE & INDUSTRY INDEX [F-131]

an index to articles published in the *Wall*   NATIONAL NEWSPAPER INDEX
Street Journal?   [F-94]
     NEWSEARCH [F-97]
     NEWSPAPER ABSTRACTS [F-99]
     TRADE & INDUSTRY INDEX [F-131]

an index to articles published in the *New*   NATIONAL NEWSPAPER INDEX
York Times?   [F-94]
     NEWSEARCH [F-97]
     NEWSPAPER ABSTRACTS [F-99]
     TRADE & INDUSTRY INDEX [F-131]

the full text of articles found in the   AMERICAN BANKER [F-4]
American Banker?   AMERICAN BANKER NEWS [F-5]

WHERE SHOULD I GO TO FIND...	*TRY*

Newspapers and Newswires

the full text of articles found in the *Chicago Tribune*?

CHICAGO TRIBUNE [F-25]

the full text of articles found in the *Financial Times*?

FINANCIAL TIMES FULL TEXT [F-58]

Periodicals

the identification and location of periodical articles on a business topic?

ABI/INFORM [F-1]
BUSINESS DATELINE [F-13]
BUSINESS PERIODICALS INDEX [F-16]
HARVARD BUSINESS REVIEW [F-62]
INFOMAT INTERNATIONAL BUSINESS [F-66]
MAGAZINE ASAP [F-81]
MAGAZINE INDEX [F-82]
MANAGEMENT CONTENTS [F-83]
NATIONAL NEWSPAPER INDEX [F-94]
NEWSEARCH [F-97]
PTS F & S INDEX [F-112]
PTS PROMT [F-117]
TRADE & INDUSTRY ASAP [F-130]
TRADE & INDUSTRY INDEX [F-131]

the full text of magazine and journal articles on a business topic?

BUSINESS DATELINE [F-13]
FINANCIAL TIMES FULL TEXT [F-58]
HARVARD BUSINESS REVIEW [F-62]
MAGAZINE ASAP [F-81]
MCGRAW-HILL PUBLICATIONS ONLINE [F-85]
TRADE & INDUSTRY ASAP [F-130]

Statistics

an index to statistics published by the U.S. government?

ASI [F-7]

industry statistics (such as expenditures, income, and prices) published by U.S. government agencies?

AGRIBUSINESS U.S.A. [F-2]
INDUSTRY DATA SOURCES [F-65]

Guide to Federal, State, and Local Governments

Federal Government Procurement

the announcements for goods and services contracts from U.S. government agencies?

COMMERCE BUSINESS DAILY [F-28]

reports of aerospace and defense-industry transactions with the armed services and U.S. government agencies?

DMS CONTRACT AWARDS [F-47]
JANE'S DEFENSE & AEROSPACE NEWS/ANALYSIS [F-77]
PTS AEROSPACE/DEFENSE MARKETS & TECHNOLOGY [F-110]

reports of research and development conducted under grants from the U.S. government?

NTIS [F-102]

Federal Government Product Development

new inventions, materials, equipment, processes, and software developed by the U.S. government and available for exclusive licensing to businesses, including whom to contact for more information?

FEDERAL APPLIED TECHNOLOGY DATABASE [F-54]

Government News Releases

news releases, in full text, from federal, state, and city government agencies?

NEWSWIRE ASAP [F-100]
PR NEWSWIRE [F-107]

Legislation and Regulations

the opinions of expert witnesses, often representing major corporations, on proposed or passed U.S. legislation?

CIS [F-26]

notices of regulations and proposed regulations announced by federal agencies?

AMERICAN BANKER [F-4]
AMERICAN BANKER NEWS [F-5]
BOND BUYER [F-11]
FEDERAL REGISTER ABSTRACTS [F-55]
PTS NEWSLETTER DATABASE [F-116]

<u>*WHERE SHOULD I GO TO FIND...*</u>   *TRY*

State and Local Governments

payroll data for state and local   CENDATA [F-24]
governments?

Insurance

Associations and Organizations

a listing of insurance associations,   ENCYCLOPEDIA OF ASSOCIATIONS
organizations, and societies, with   [F-52]
a description of their activities,
membership, and publications?

Company Listings and Comprehensive Profiles

financial and operating data for a life,   BESTLINK ONLINE DATABASE [F-9]
health, property, or casualty insurance
company, along with an A. M. Best
rating?

an insurance company's address,   CORPORATE AFFILIATIONS [F-35]
telephone number, and names of its   D & B—DUN'S ELECTRONIC
directors and officers?   YELLOW PAGES [F-38]
                                            D & B—DUN'S FINANCIAL RECORDS
                                            PLUS [F-39]
                                            D & B—DUN'S MARKET
                                            IDENTIFIERS [F-40]
                                            D & B—MILLION DOLLAR
                                            DIRECTORY [F-42]
                                            STANDARD & POOR'S
                                            REGISTER—CORPORATE [F-125]

directories of agencies, agents, brokers,   INSURANCE PERIODICALS INDEX
or consultants in the insurance industry?   [F-71]

Information Sources

news stories and journal articles about   ABI/INFORM [F-1]
the insurance industry, including   BUSINESS DATELINE [F-13]
consumer issues, legal matters, products   BUSINESS PERIODICALS INDEX
and services, and other topics?   [F-16]
                                            BUSINESS WIRE [F-18]
                                            ECONOMIC LITERATURE INDEX
                                            [F-51]

WHERE SHOULD I GO TO FIND...   *TRY*

Information Sources

news stories and journal articles about the insurance industry, including consumer issues, legal matters, products and services, and other topics?

INSURANCE PERIODICALS INDEX [F-71]
MANAGEMENT CONTENTS [F-83]
PTS PROMT [F-117]
TRADE & INDUSTRY ASAP [F-130]
TRADE & INDUSTRY INDEX [F-131]
TRINET COMPANY DATABASE [F-134]
TRINET U. S. BUSINESSES [F-135]

Insurance Claims

the procedures to follow when filing an insurance claim?

INSURANCE CONSUMER INFORMATION SERVICE [F-70]

Regulations

insurance-securities regulations of the individual states?

CCH BLUE SKY LAW REPORTER [F-21]

the name of the insurance commissioner for each state?

CCH BLUE SKY LAW REPORTER [F-21]

notices of federal regulations and proposed regulations that may affect the insurance industry?

FEDERAL REGISTER ABSTRACTS [F-55]

Shopping for Insurance

how to shop for automobile, homeowner, landlord, or rental insurance?

INSURANCE CONSUMER INFORMATION SERVICE [F-70]

International Business Transactions

Associations and Organizations: Listings and Profiles

a listing of international and non-U.S. business, government, labor, professional, and other membership associations, federations, and societies, with a description of their activities, membership, and publications?

ENCYCLOPEDIA OF ASSOCIATIONS [F-52]

<u>WHERE SHOULD I GO TO FIND...</u>	*TRY*

Company/Industry News

news about international activities of U.S. and foreign companies and industries?

ABI/INFORM [F-1]
BUSINESS PERIODICALS INDEX [F-16]
FINANCIAL TIMES ABSTRACTS [F-57]
FINANCIAL TIMES FULL TEXT [F-58]
HARVARD BUSINESS REVIEW [F-62]
INFOMAT INTERNATIONAL BUSINESS [F-66]
MANAGEMENT CONTENTS [F-83]
MCGRAW-HILL PUBLICATIONS ONLINE [F-85]
MOODY'S CORPORATE NEWS—INTERNATIONAL [F-89]
PTS F & S INDEX [F-112]
PTS PROMT [F-117]
TRADE & INDUSTRY ASAP [F-130]
TRADE & INDUSTRY INDEX [F-131]

newsletter articles about international markets and trade?

PTS NEWSLETTER DATABASE [F-116]

Company Listings and Profiles

excerpts from the annual report of a U.S. company concerning its international activities?

PTS ANNUAL REPORTS ABSTRACTS [F-111]

a foreign company's address, telephone number, and a brief description of its major product or service?

D & B—INTERNATIONAL DUN'S MARKET IDENTIFIERS [F-41]

intelligence reports on a foreign company, as well as intelligence reports on U.S. companies with international dealings?

INVESTEXT [F-72]

Currencies of the World

foreign exchange rates—current and historical?

ISSUE PRICING HISTORY [F-76]
NEWS-A-TRON MARKET REPORTS [F-96]
PRICING STATISTICS [F-108]

WHERE SHOULD I GO TO FIND...	*TRY*

Currencies of the World

the full text of sections from the Internal Revenue Code or Treasury Regulations that deal with foreign currency transactions?	RIA FEDERAL TAX COORDINATOR 2D [F-120]
explanations of federal codes and regulations that affect foreign currency transactions, and suggestions on when, why, and how to apply the codes and regulations?	RIA FEDERAL TAX COORDINATOR 2D [F-120]

Exports and Imports

forecasts of export and import activity for various U.S. products and industries for the 1990s?	PTS FORECASTS [F-113]
ten to twenty years of annual export and import data for different products and industries?	PTS U. S. TIME SERIES [F-118]

Patents, Trademarks, and Trade Names

a listing of patents issued outside the U.S.?	INPADOC/FAMILY AND LEGAL STATUS [F-67] WORLD PATENTS INDEX [F-138]

Tax Treaties

a listing of income-tax treaties between the U.S. and other nations, including descriptions and explanations?	RIA FEDERAL TAX COORDINATOR 2D [F-120]

Trade Shows, Exhibitions, and Conventions

worldwide listings of trade shows, conferences, and other meetings where new products are exhibited?	FAIRBASE [F-53]

Travel

commercial airline flights available for a particular day and time, how to make flight reservations, fare information, and room rates for hotels/motels?	OFFICIAL AIRLINE GUIDE [F-103]

| *WHERE SHOULD I GO TO FIND...* | *TRY* |

Investments

Company Financial Profiles and Stock Data

financial ratios for a company?	D & B—DUN'S FINANCIAL RECORDS PLUS [F-39] DISCLOSURE [F-44] MEDIA GENERAL [F-86] S & P ONLINE [F-121] VALUE LINE DATABASE II [F-137]
a comparison of financial data between a company and others in its industry?	D & B—DUN'S FINANCIAL RECORDS PLUS [F-39] MEDIA GENERAL [F-86]
the share of market held by a company?	ABI/INFORM [F-1] BUSINESS DATELINE [F-13] INVESTEXT [F-72] PTS PROMT [F-117] TRADE & INDUSTRY ASAP [F-130] TRADE & INDUSTRY INDEX [F-131] TRINET U. S. BUSINESSES [F-135]
balance-sheet statistics for an individual company—either for a few months or a few years?	DISCLOSURE [F-44] MEDIA GENERAL [F-86] MOODY'S CORPORATE PROFILES [F-91] STANDARD & POOR'S CORPORATE DESCRIPTIONS ONLINE [F-122] VALUE LINE DATABASE II [F-137]
SEC 8K, 10K, 10Q, 20F, and corporate annual reports, and other data on individual companies?	DISCLOSURE [F-44] MEDIA GENERAL [F-86] MOODY'S CORPORATE PROFILES [F-91] PTS ANNUAL REPORTS ABSTRACTS [F-111] STANDARD & POOR'S CORPORATE DESCRIPTIONS ONLINE [F-122]
a history of daily-price and volume-stock data for a company?	ISSUE PRICING HISTORY [F-76] MEDIA GENERAL [F-86] MULTIPLE ISSUES [F-92] PRICING STATISTICS [F-108]

WHERE SHOULD I GO TO FIND...	*TRY*

Company Financial Profiles and Stock Data

forecasts of earnings, sales, or stock prices for individual companies?	I/B/E/S [F-64] INVESTEXT [F-72] VALUE LINE DATABASE II [F-137]
intelligence reports on an individual company?	CORPORATE AND INDUSTRY RESEARCH REPORTS [F-36] FINDEX DIRECTORY OF MARKET RESEARCH [F-59] INVESTEXT [F-72] MOODY'S CORPORATE PROFILES [F-91] PTS PROMT [F-117]
financial and operating information from a company's annual report?	DISCLOSURE [F-44] MEDIA GENERAL [F-86] MOODY'S CORPORATE PROFILES [F-91] PTS ANNUAL REPORTS ABSTRACTS [F-111] PTS PROMT [F-117] STANDARD & POOR'S CORPORATE DESCRIPTIONS ONLINE [F-122]

Industry Profiles

financial ratios for an industry?	INVESTEXT [F-72] MEDIA GENERAL [F-86]
industry statistics: assets, expenditures, income, market share, and prices?	INDUSTRY DATA SOURCES [F-65]
stock-price data for an industry, including various moving averages?	MEDIA GENERAL [F-86]
a daily summary of an industry's activity, indicating its five-year earnings per share compared with other industries and its stock-price performance compared with that of other industries for the past year?	INVESTOR'S DAILY [F-73]
financial analysis reports on the health industry?	HEALTH INDUSTRY RESEARCH REPORTS [F-63]

| *WHERE SHOULD I GO TO FIND...* | *TRY* |

Industry Profiles

market research reports on an industry, product, or individual company?

ARTHUR D. LITTLE/ONLINE [F-6]
CORPORATE AND INDUSTRY RESEARCH REPORTS [F-36]
FINDEX DIRECTORY OF MARKET RESEARCH [F-59]
INDUSTRY DATA SOURCES [F-65]

developments in the pharmaceuticals and cosmetics industry?

PNI [F-106]

developments in the banking and finance industry?

AMERICAN BANKER [F-4]
AMERICAN BANKER NEWS [F-5]

news about computer and other high-technology firms?

COMPUTER ASAP [F-32]
COMPUTER DATABASE [F-33]

news about the agricultural industry?

AGRIBUSINESS U. S. A. [F-2]
AGRICOLA [F-3]
BIOBUSINESS [F-10]
CAB ABSTRACTS [F-19]

news about aerospace and defense companies?

DMS CONTRACT AWARDS [F-47]
DMS CONTRACTORS [F-48]
DMS MARKET INTELLIGENCE REPORTS [F-49]
JANE'S DEFENSE & AEROSPACE NEWS/ANALYSIS [F-77]
PTS AEROSPACE/DEFENSE MARKETS & TECHNOLOGY [F-110]

Insider Trading

information about the securities transactions of company insiders?

INSIDER TRADING MONITOR [F-68]

institutional, insider, and five-percent shareholders of a company?

DISCLOSURE SPECTRUM OWNERSHIP [F-45]

Investment Instruments and Indicators

a listing of financial indicators available for specific stock exchanges, industry groups, and investment issues, giving the ticker symbol for each indicator?

MICROQUOTE INDEXES [F-87]

WHERE SHOULD I GO TO FIND...	*TRY*
Investment Instruments and Indicators	
bonds, commodities, stocks, and other investments offered by a company or other issuer?	NAME/SYMBOL LOOKUP [F-93]
names of the exchanges that trade a particular commodity?	COMMODITIES LIST [F-29] COMMODITIES PRICING [F-30]
no-load mutual funds that match the investor's investment objectives, purchase requirements, and redemption preferences?	NO-LOAD MUTUAL FUND DIRECTORY [F-101]
the profile of a bond, stock, or other security, giving its exchange and other data such as earnings per share, dividend rate, yield, 52-week high/low, Moody's Quality Rating, and Standard & Poor's Quality Rating?	ISSUE EXAMINATION [F-75]
a directory of the Standard & Poor's 500 stocks?	S & P ONLINE [F-121]
a listing of stocks favored by Standard & Poor's analysts?	S & P ONLINE [F-121]
Investment Performance	
strike prices and expiration dates of puts and calls for a stock option or index?	OPTIONS PROFILE [F-104]
corporate bonds available, giving yield, price, recent quality rating, and ticker symbol for each bond?	BONDS LISTING [F-12]
developments in the government bond industry, including announcements of current and proposed bond sales?	BOND BUYER [F-11]
dividends, splits, and interest paid over a specified range of time for a particular stock, bond, mutual fund, or option?	DIVIDENDS, SPLITS, INTEREST [F-46]

WHERE SHOULD I GO TO FIND...	*TRY*
Investment Performance	
the price history for a particular commodity, including the open, high, low, settlement, volume, and open-interest data for each day during a specified period?	COMMODITIES PRICING [F-30]
a history of daily-price and volume-stock data for a company?	ISSUE PRICING HISTORY [F-76] MEDIA GENERAL [F-86] MULTIPLE ISSUES [F-92] PRICING STATISTICS [F-108]
price-trend series and statistical analyses for a stock, bond, market indicator, mutual fund, or option?	ISSUE PRICING HISTORY [F-76] MULTIPLE ISSUES [F-92] PRICING STATISTICS [F-108]
stock-price data for an industry, including various moving averages?	MEDIA GENERAL [F-86]
for selected common stocks on the AMEX, NYSE, and NASDAQ-OTC exchanges, their five-year rankings of earnings growth per share and their daily relative price change for the past 12 months compared with stock of other selected companies?	INVESTOR'S DAILY [F-73]
current U.S. and selected foreign prime-interest rates?	INVESTOR'S DAILY [F-73]
current U.S. and foreign money-interest rates, including discount rate, federal funds, Treasury bills, bankers' acceptances, certificates of deposit, and Eurodollars?	INVESTOR'S DAILY [F-73]
daily quotations for U.S. stocks, commodities, futures, options, mutual funds, and other investments?	INVESTOR'S DAILY [F-73] QUICK QUOTE [F-119]
daily quotations on the foreign markets?	INVESTOR'S DAILY [F-73]
daily or hourly average performances of the AMEX, NYSE, NASDAQ, Dow Jones, and other stock-market indexes?	INVESTOR'S DAILY [F-73] NEWSGRID [F-98]

WHERE SHOULD I GO TO FIND...	*TRY*
Investment Performance	
current (within minutes) stock and stock option prices?	DIALOG QUOTES AND TRADING [F-43] QUICK QUOTE [F-119]
daily foreign-exchange rates?	NEWS-A-TRON MARKET REPORTS [F-96] QUICK QUOTE [F-119]
daily prices on metals, petroleum products, and grains from commodity exchanges?	NEWS-A-TRON MARKET REPORTS [F-96]
historical data on foreign-exchange rates for a specified period?	ISSUE PRICING HISTORY [F-76] PRICING STATISTICS [F-108]
daily stock-market leaders, with summaries of performance statistics?	INVESTOR'S DAILY [F-73] MARKET HIGHLIGHTS [F-84]
State Securities	
decisions, fees, laws, policies, regulations, and other information for dealing in state securities, including the text of the Uniform Securities Act?	CCH BLUE SKY LAW REPORTER [F-21]
the name of each state's securities administrator?	CCH BLUE SKY LAW REPORTER [F-21]
Stockholders and Officers	
institutional, insider, and five-percent shareholders of a company?	DISCLOSURE SPECTRUM OWNERSHIP [F-45]
who, as a company insider, has bought, sold, or given company stock?	INSIDER TRADING MONITOR [F-68]
biographical information on the executives and directors of a company?	STANDARD & POOR'S REGISTER—BIOGRAPHICAL [F-124]
Ticker Symbols	
the meaning of ticker symbols that are representative of individual bonds, stocks, and commodities?	BONDS LISTING [F-12] BUSINESS DATELINE [F-13] BUSINESS WIRE [F-18]

WHERE SHOULD I GO TO FIND...	*TRY*

Ticker Symbols

the meaning of ticker symbols that are representative of individual bonds, stocks, and commodities?	COMMODITIES LIST [F-29] CORPORATE AFFILIATIONS [F-35] CORPORATE AND INDUSTRY RE-SEARCH REPORTS [F-36] D & B MILLION DOLLAR DIREC-TORY [F-42] DISCLOSURE [F-44] DISCLOSURE SPECTRUM OWNER-SHIP [F-45] INSIDER TRADING MONITOR [F-68] MEDIA GENERAL [F-86] MOODY'S CORPORATE PROFILES [F-91] NAME/SYMBOL LOOKUP [F-93] PR NEWSWIRE [F-107] PTS F & S INDEX [F-112] PTS MARKETING & ADVERTISING REFERENCE SERVICE [F-114] PTS NEW PRODUCT ANNOUNCE-MENTS [F-115] PTS PROMT [F-117] STANDARD & POOR'S CORPORATE DESCRIPTIONS ONLINE [F-122] STANDARD & POOR'S NEWS ONLINE [F-123] VALUE LINE DATABASE II [F-137]

Management

Information Sources

the identification and location of articles on management topics in magazines, journals, and newspapers?	ABI/INFORM [F-1] BUSINESS DATELINE [F-13] BUSINESS PERIODICALS INDEX [F-16] HARVARD BUSINESS REVIEW [F-62] MAGAZINE ASAP [F-81] MAGAZINE INDEX [F-82] MANAGEMENT CONTENTS [F-83] NATIONAL NEWSPAPER INDEX [F-94] NEWSEARCH [F-97] PTS PROMT [F-117]

WHERE SHOULD I GO TO FIND...	*TRY*

Marketing

Information Sources

the identification and location of articles on advertising and marketing topics in magazines and journals?

PTS MARKETING & ADVERTISING REFERENCE SERVICE [F-114]

Intelligence Gathering: U.S. Companies

intelligence reports about an individual company?

CORPORATE AND INDUSTRY RESEARCH REPORTS [F-36]
FINDEX DIRECTORY OF MARKET RESEARCH [F-59]
INVESTEXT [F-72]
MOODY'S CORPORATE PROFILES [F-91]
PTS PROMT [F-117]

Marketing Data

statistics on a type of product or service in an industry, including costs, profits, sales, and exports?

PTS FORECASTS [F-113]
PTS PROMT [F-117]
PTS U. S. TIME SERIES [F-118]

market-research reports for major industries?

FINDEX DIRECTORY OF MARKET RESEARCH [F-59]
INDUSTRY DATA SOURCES [F-65]

the share of market held by a company?

ABI/INFORM [F-1]
BUSINESS DATELINE [F-13]
INVESTEXT [F-72]
PTS PROMT [F-117]
TRADE & INDUSTRY ASAP [F-130]
TRADE & INDUSTRY INDEX [F-131]
TRINET U. S. BUSINESSES [F-135]

the market or sales territory of a company—at least indicating whether it is national or international?

D & B—DUN'S MARKET IDENTI-FIERS [F-40]
STANDARD & POOR'S REGISTER—CORPORATE [F-125]

WHERE SHOULD I GO TO FIND...	*TRY*

Marketing Data

number of businesses, employees, or people in a city, county, state, metropolitan area, ZIP code, Arbitron, or Nielsen area?	BUSINESS DEMOGRAPHICS REPORTS [F-14] D & B—DONNELLEY DEMOGRAPHICS [F-37]
population characteristics in an Arbitron area, census tract, county, metropolitan area, Nielsen area, state, or ZIP code, including types of jobs, housing, and income?	D & B—DONNELLEY DEMOGRAPHICS [F-37] NEIGHBORHOOD DEMOGRAPHIC REPORTS [F-95] SUPERSITE [F-126]

Marketing Management

case studies of successful marketing plans used in the banking and finance industry?	FINIS [F-60]
articles on the management of advertising and marketing firms?	MANAGEMENT CONTENTS [F-83]

Marketing of Products and Services

articles on the marketing of financial services?	AMERICAN BANKER [F-4] AMERICAN BANKER NEWS [F-5]
articles on the marketing of pharmaceuticals and cosmetics?	PNI [F-106]
opportunities to exhibit products at conferences, trade shows, and other meetings?	FAIRBASE [F-53]
information on the marketing of defense industry products, including identification of competitors and their major products or development programs?	DMS CONTRACT AWARDS [F-47] DMS CONTRACTORS [F-48] DMS MARKET INTELLIGENCE REPORTS [F-49] JANE'S DEFENSE & AEROSPACE NEWS/ANALYSIS [F-77] PTS AEROSPACE/DEFENSE MARKETS [F-110]
marketing innovations and methods in the banking and finance industry?	FINIS [F-60]

WHERE SHOULD I GO TO FIND...	*TRY*

Marketing Services

| mailing labels for companies in a particular industry or geographic area? | D & B—DUN'S ELECTRONIC YELLOW PAGES [F-38]
D & B—DUN'S MARKET IDENTIFIERS [F-40]
MEDIA GENERAL [F-86]
THOMAS NEW INDUSTRIAL PRODUCTS [F-128]
THOMAS REGISTER ONLINE [F-129]
TRINET COMPANY DATABASE [F-134]
TRINET U. S. BUSINESSES [F-135] |

Products and Services

| a listing of companies in an area code, city, metropolitan area, state, or ZIP code that provide a particular product or service? | CORPORATE AFFILIATIONS [F-35]
D & B—DUN'S ELECTRONIC YELLOW PAGES [F-38]
D & B—DUN'S FINANCIAL RECORDS PLUS [F-39]
D & B—DUN'S MARKET IDENTIFIERS [F-40]
D & B—MILLION DOLLAR DIRECTORY [F-42]
DISCLOSURE [F-44]
MEDIA GENERAL [F-86]
MOODY'S CORPORATE PROFILES [F-91]
STANDARD & POOR'S CORPORATE DESCRIPTIONS ONLINE [F-122]
STANDARD & POOR'S REGISTER—CORPORATE [F-125]
THOMAS NEW INDUSTRIAL PRODUCTS [F-128]
THOMAS REGISTER ONLINE [F-129]
TRINET COMPANY DATABASE [F-134]
TRINET U. S. BUSINESSES [F-135] |
| the advertising slogan used for a product or service? | PTS MARKETING & ADVERTISING REFERENCE SERVICE [F-114] |

WHERE SHOULD I GO TO FIND...	*TRY*

Products and Services

the products and services endorsed by a specific celebrity?	PTS MARKETING & ADVERTISING REFERENCE SERVICE [F-114]
a listing of advertising agencies that have had experience with a specific product or service?	PTS MARKETING & ADVERTISING REFERENCE SERVICE [F-114]

New Products and Services: Invention, Development, and Protection

Biomedical Ventures

companies involved in the development of new biological and medical products?	BIOBUSINESS [F-10]

Computer and Electronics Ventures

companies or researchers working on new technologies, especially in computing, electronics, and engineering?	COMPENDEX*PLUS [F-31] INSPEC [F-69]

Government Contracts and Products

new inventions, materials, equipment, processes, and software developed by the U.S. government and available for exclusive licensing to businesses, and whom to contact for more information?	FEDERAL APPLIED TECHNOLOGY DATABASE [F-54]
research and development results from work done under contract with the U.S. government?	NTIS [F-102]
announcements of contract, procurement, and research needs of U.S. government agencies?	COMMERCE BUSINESS DAILY [F-28]

New-Product Descriptions

new-product descriptions and their manufacturers' names?	BUSINESS WIRE [F-18] NEWSWIRE ASAP [F-100] PR NEWSWIRE [F-107]

WHERE SHOULD I GO TO FIND...	*TRY*

New-Product Descriptions

new-product descriptions and their man-ufacturers' names?

PTS NEW PRODUCT ANNOUNCE-MENTS [F-115]
THOMAS NEW INDUSTRIAL PROD-UCTS [F-128]

new-product announcements?

PTS NEW PRODUCT ANNOUNCE-MENTS [F-115]
PTS NEWSLETTER DATABASE [F-116]
PTS PROMT [F-117]

a listing of new products that match such needs as easy to install, safe to use, vibration-free, wear-resistant, energy effi-cient, or other requirements?

THOMAS NEW INDUSTRIAL PROD-UCTS [F-128]

Patents, Trademarks, and Trade Names

a listing of U.S. and/or international patents organized by industry and type of patent?

CLAIMS [F-27]
INPADOC/FAMILY AND LEGAL STA-TUS [F-67]
PATDATA [F-105]
WORLD PATENTS INDEX [F-138]

if a trade name currently is being used?

PTS NW PRODUCT ANNOUNCE-MENTS [F-115]
THOMAS NEW INDUSTRIAL PROD-UCTS [F-128]
THOMAS REGISTER ONLINE [F-129]

if a trademark currently is being used?

D & B—DUN'S ELECTRONIC YEL-LOW PAGES [F-38]
TRADEMARKSCAN—FEDERAL [F-132]
TRADEMARKSCAN—STATE [F-133]

Trade Shows, Exhibitions, and Conventions

worldwide listings of trade shows, con-ferences, and other meetings where new products are exhibited?

FAIRBASE [F-53]

WHERE SHOULD I GO TO FIND...	*TRY*

Personnel Administration

Associations and Organizations

| a listing of labor unions, associations, and federations with their addresses, telephone numbers, and other information? | ENCYCLOPEDIA OF ASSOCIATIONS [F-52] |

Company Listings

| a listing of addresses and telephone numbers of employment agencies? | D & B—DUN'S ELECTRONIC YELLOW PAGES [F-38] |
| the typical number of employees in a business, by type of product or service? | TRINET COMPANY DATABASE [F-134] TRINET U. S. BUSINESSES [F-135] |

Decisions

| an index to labor-relations decisions made by federal and state courts and administrative bodies, including decisions related to collective bargaining, fair employment practices, health, safety, and wages? | LABORLAW [F-78] |

Financial-Services Industry

| an index to articles and case studies that cover personnel compensation, development, and training in the financial-services industry? | FINIS [F-60] |

General News

| an index to articles about developments in personnel administration? | ABI/INFORM [F-1] BUSINESS PERIODICALS INDEX [F-16] MAGAZINE ASAP [F-81] MAGAZINE INDEX [F-82] MANAGEMENT CONTENTS [F-83] NATIONAL NEWSPAPER INDEX [F-94] NEWSEARCH [F-97] |

WHERE SHOULD I GO TO FIND...	*TRY*

General News

an index to articles, research reports, and other documents on the psychological aspects of personnel administration?

PSYCINFO [F-109]

Legislation and Regulations

an index of reports of the U.S. Congress, including the history and rationale for federal labor legislation?

CIS [F-26]

announcements of federal regulations and proposed regulations that could affect collective bargaining, job classifications, employee health and safety, employee rights, and other issues?

FEDERAL REGISTER ABSTRACTS [F-55]

the full text of sections from the Internal Revenue Code or Treasury Regulations that cover employee compensation, fringe benefits, and retirements plans?

RIA FEDERAL TAX COORDINATOR 2D [F-120]

explanations of federal codes and regulations that affect employee compensation, fringe benefits, and retirement plans?

RIA FEDERAL TAX COORDINATOR 2D [F-120]

Résumés

résumés of job seekers, reporting their availability, occupational interests and skills, salary expectations, and willingness to relocate?

CAREER PLACEMENT REGISTRY [F-20]

Software

descriptions and/or evaluations of software that assist with personnel-records management?

BUSINESS SOFTWARE DATABASE [F-17]
COMPUTER ASAP [F-32]
COMPUTER DATABASE [F-33]

Statistics

historical, current, and forecasted labor statistics (including hours worked, labor-force level, wages) that have been published by the U.S. government?

ASI [F-7]
ECONBASE [F-50]

WHERE SHOULD I GO TO FIND...	*TRY*

Statistics

| historical, current, and forecasted statistics on expenditures for employee benefits, by industry? | INDUSTRY DATA SOURCES [F-65]
PTS FORECASTS [F-113]
PTS U. S. TIME SERIES [F-118] |

| Real Estate |

Associations and Organizations

| a listing of professional organizations of real-estate appraisers, brokers, consultants, executives, and others in the field? | ENCYCLOPEDIA OF ASSOCIATIONS [F-52] |

Company Listings

| a real-estate company's address, telephone number, and names of its directors and officers? | CORPORATE AFFILIATIONS [F-35]
D & B—DUN'S ELECTRONIC YELLOW PAGES [F-38]
D & B—DUN'S FINANCIAL RECORDS PLUS [F-39]
D & B—DUN'S MARKET IDENTIFIERS [F-40]
D & B—MILLION DOLLAR DIRECTORY [F-42]
STANDARD & POOR'S REGISTER—CORPORATE [F-125]
TRINET COMPANY DATABASE [F-134]
TRINET U. S. BUSINESSES [F-135] |

Industry Profiles

| market-research reports on the real-estate industry or an individual real-estate firm? | ARTHUR D. LITTLE/ONLINE [F-6]
CORPORATE AND INDUSTRY RESEARCH REPORTS [F-36]
FINDEX DIRECTORY OF MARKET RESEARCH [F-59]
INDUSTRY DATA SOURCES [F-65] |
| historical and forecast data covering employees, firms, profits, sales, and other areas of the real-estate industry? | PTS FORECASTS [F-113]
PTS U. S. TIME SERIES [F-118] |

WHERE SHOULD I GO TO FIND...	*TRY*

Information Sources

| an index to news stories or journal articles on the real-estate industry, including consumer issues, legal matters, products and services? | ABI/INFORM [F-1]
BUSINESS DATELINE [F-13]
BUSINESS PERIODICALS INDEX [F-16]
BUSINESS WIRE [F-18]
ECONOMIC LITERATURE INDEX [F-51]
MANAGEMENT CONTENTS [F-83]
PTS PROMT [F-117]
TRADE & INDUSTRY ASAP [F-130]
TRADE & INDUSTRY INDEX [F-131] |
| an index to real estate statistics published by federal executive, judicial, and legislative agencies, offices, and other units? | ASI [F-7] |

Taxation

Decisions

| the full text of federal judicial decisions on tax matters? | TAX NOTES TODAY [F-127] |
| references to U.S. Tax Court and other judicial decisions on tax matters? | RIA FEDERAL TAX COORDINATOR 2D [F-120] |

General News

| the full text of tax news about developments in federal and state legislation, court cases, and related matters? | CCH TAX DAY—FEDERAL [F-22]
CCH TAX DAY—STATE [F-23]
TAX NOTES TODAY [F-127] |

Legislation and Regulations

| the full text of sections from the Internal Revenue Code or Treasury Regulations that cover a tax issue, problem, or question? | RIA FEDERAL TAX COORDINATOR 2D [F-120] |
| commentary on recent developments in federal taxation, including new Internal Revenue rules, statements, and proposed regulations? | RIA FEDERAL TAX COORDINATOR 2D [F-120] |

WHERE SHOULD I GO TO FIND...	*TRY*
Legislation and Regulations	
explanations of federal codes and regulations that affect a specific tax issue, problem, or question, and suggestions on when, why, and how to apply the codes and regulations to that problem?	RIA FEDERAL TAX COORDINATOR 2D [F-120]
the full text of taxpayer-information booklets issued by the Internal Revenue Service?	TAX NOTES TODAY [F-127]
tips on filing personal income taxes, including information about amending returns, capital gains, record keeping, and rental losses?	H & R BLOCK [F-61]
news on changes in personal income tax regulations and a listing of filing dates from the Internal Revenue Service calendar?	H & R BLOCK [F-61]
legislative documents, federal agency publications, and court opinions on tax law?	TAX NOTES TODAY [F-127]
summaries of all current tax bills and the full text of major tax bills under consideration by Congress?	TAX NOTES TODAY [F-127]
full text of news articles on the status of federal and state tax laws, policies, and regulations?	TAX NOTES TODAY [F-127]
a listing of income tax treaties between the U.S. and other nations, including descriptions and explanations?	RIA FEDERAL TAX COORDINATOR 2D [F-120]

SECTION
F

Descriptive Profiles of Online Databases

The authors have made a diligent effort to provide correct information about the names of the products and vendors cited in this book. The following product and vendor names are servicemarks, trademarks, or registered trademarks.

ABI/UNIFORM
AEROSPACE/DEFENSE MARKETS & TECHNOLOGY
AGRIBUSINESS U. S. A.
ANNUAL REPORTS ABSTRACTS
BESTLINK
BIOBUSINESS
BUSINESS DATELINE
BUSINESS SOFTWARE DATABASE
BUSINESS WIRE
CANSIM
CENDATA
CLAIMS
COMPENDEX
CompuServe
COMPUTER ASAP
COMPUTER DATABASE
CUSIP
D & B—DUN'S FINANCIAL RECORDS PLUS
D & B—DUN'S MARKET IDENTIFIERS
D & B—INTERNATIONAL DUN'S MARKET IDENTIFIERS
D & B—MILLION DOLLAR DIRECTORY
Dialog

DISCLOSURE
DISCLOSURE ONLINE
DMS MARKET INTELLIGENCE REPORTS
Dow Jones
DOW JONES ENHANCED CURRENT QUOTES
DOW JONES FUTURES AND INDEX QUOTES
DOW JONES HISTORICAL QUOTES
Dow Jones News/Retrieval
DOW JONES NEWS/RETRIEVAL WORLD REPORT
DOW JONES PROFESSIONAL INVESTOR REPORT
DOW JONES QUICKSEARCH
DOW JONES REAL-TIME QUOTES
DOW JONES TEXT-SEARCH SERVICES
DOW JONES TRACKING SERVICE
D-U-N-S
DUN'S FINANCIAL RECORDS
F & S INDEX
H & R BLOCK
HISTORICAL DOW JONES AVERAGES
INDUSTRY DATA SOURCES
INVESTEXT
IQUEST
JAPAN ECONOMIC DAILY
Knowledge Index
LEGAL RESOURCE INDEX
LEXIS
LEXPAT
MAGAZINE ASAP
MAGAZINE INDEX
MANAGEMENT CONTENTS
MARKETING & ADVERTISING REFERENCE SERVICE
MICROQUOTE
MOODY'S
NATIONAL NEWSPAPER INDEX
NEW PRODUCT ANNOUNCEMENTS
NEWSEARCH
NEWSGRID
NewsNet
NEWSWIRE ASAP
NEXIS
OFFICIAL AIRLINE GUIDE
PNI

PROMT
PTS NEWSLETTER DATABASE
QUICK QUOTE
STANDARD & POOR'S ONLINE
SUPERSITE
THOMAS NEW INDUSTRIAL PRODUCTS
THOMAS REGISTER ONLINE
TRADE & INDUSTRY ASAP
TRADE & INDUSTRY INDEX
TRADEMARKSCAN
VALUE LINE DATABASE II
WALL $TREET WEEK
WORDS OF WALL STREET
ZACKS CORPORATE EARNINGS ESTIMATOR

Information Contained in Section F

This section presents descriptions of the online databases cited in Section E. See the introduction to Section E for information about what a database is and what is needed to start looking for information in a database.

The databases in this section appear in alphabetical order, by database name. If a database is known by several names, the name given by the publisher of the database has been used.

For each database there has been reported:

- an item entry number (for example, F-1)
- the database name, in upper-case letters
- coverage dates, if the database is an index or full-text database
- the database publisher
- the online vendor(s) that sell access to the database
- each vendor's file name or number for the database. This is the name or number to use when contacting the database
- a CD-ROM vendor for the database, if it is also available in Compact Disk Read-Only Memory format
- brief description of the database's contents

Types of Databases Described

Most of the databases in this section and in Section E are available from three online vendors of business databases, namely, BRS Information Technologies, CompuServe Information Service, and Dialog Information Services. See the introduction to Section E for more information about the online vendors.

There are basically four types of online databases: directories, full-text databases, indexes, and statistical databases. Some databases are hybrids of two or more of these types.

A directory database, like the ENCYCLOPEDIA OF ASSOCIATIONS, is often a list of organizations or firms. You will find information like the address, telephone number, and description of the organization. Some directory databases, instead of listing organizations, provide lists of commodities, contract awards, stock transactions, and other catalogs of information.

A full-text database, like TAX NOTES TODAY, contains the full texts, not merely the summaries, of articles, news stories, reports, or other documents. This type of database sometimes contains a subject index to its material.

An index database, like ABI/INFORM, is a subject index to magazine and journal articles, and, sometimes, books and reports. The index includes a reference to where the article or book was published. Often there is an abstract (summary) of the article or book.

A statistical database, like DISCLOSURE, contains numerical data about companies, industries, products, services, or other items. Some of these databases also include narrative descriptions of the company or industry.

What Should I Know About the Database Descriptions?

Database Versions. The description of an online database refers to its fullest version. If a database is available from more than one vendor, each vendor might have a different version of the database. For example, an index database might include abstracts or summaries of its articles in one version but not in another.

Access Points. The descriptions sometimes list "special access points" for the databases. An access point is a way to obtain a particular piece of information. It is what is customarily meant by saying "Look under" when you use a database or a book. For example, consider a directory database that lists the address, telephone number, and president of each organization in its collection. Access to such a database could be the names of companies, the states in which they are located, and the names of their officers. You could ask for a list of all companies with the word "fastener" in their names or all the companies in a certain area code or ZIP code. You could ask for the name of the company for whom a particular individual works.

The access points are something that make databases quite different from books. Even if a book directory provides a way to look up a company's name, you probably would have to know the first word in the company's name. In a database directory, you often can look up a company by using any word in the company's name. So it is very common for online databases to provide many access points to the information they hold.

The descriptions in this section sometimes indicate access points considered special; that is, more unusual or useful than customary. Many databases allow access by a company's name. This is not special. Only a relatively few permit looking for a list of companies by using Standard Industrial Classification (SIC) codes. This is special. For some databases we will select examples of the database's most special access points. There probably will be many other access points in addition to the ones listed here.

Some of the names of the access points have been shortened or abbreviated. Here is a list of our access-point abbreviations:

Abbreviations	*Access Points*
area codes	telephone area codes
CUSIP numbers	Committee on Uniform Securites Identification Procedures numbers
D-U-N-S numbers	unique numbers assigned to business locations by Dun & Bradstreet
SIC codes	Standard Industrial Classification codes

Directory Information. Some descriptions include a phrase like "contains directory information." This means that the database gives for businesses or other organizations information like addresses, names of officers, and telephone numbers.

File Names and Numbers. Each vendor assigns a file name or number to each of its databases. When your computer is communicating with the vendor's computer, use the file name or number to ask for the database that is wanted. There is more than one name or number for some databases. This often happens for large databases that are indexes to articles. A vendor might assign one name or number to the most recent portion and another name or number to the older portions. When there is more than one file name or number, we have listed only the name or number that refers to the whole database or to the most recent segment of the database. See vendor catalogs for more information on how they have divided some databases into files.

CD-ROM Databases. It has been indicated if an online database also is available in CD-ROM (Compact Disk Read-Only Memory) format from its online publisher or vendor. However, our description of the database comes from our examination of the online version. A CD-ROM version of a database might differ from the online version. For example, a CD-ROM version of a database might not cover the entire range of years covered by the online version. For more information, contact the CD-ROM publishers. Their addresses and telephone numbers are in Appendix III.

Sources of Information

The information presented in Sections E and F was obtained primarily from direct examination of the online databases. If a database is available from more than one vendor, it is possible that its content and format vary from one vendor's version to another.

Additionally, vendor catalogs were used to verify which services make available which databases. The catalogs are quite useful lists, especially for the new or infrequent user of online databases. Use the vendor telephone numbers or addresses to inquire about obtaining catalogs. (This vendor information is in Appendix III.) The catalogs used were:

Database Catalog 1990. McLean, VA: BRS Information Technologies, 1990. (800) 289-4277.

Dialog Database Catalog 1990. Palo Alto, CA: Dialog Information Services, 1990. (800) 334-2564.

Users Guide. Columbus, OH: CompuServe Information Service, 1988. (800) 848-8199.

For Further Information

For more information about the databases listed, contact the database publishers and vendors. Their addresses and telephone numbers are in Appendix III. For more information about the authors' choices of databases for this book, please read the introductory material in Section E.

Contact the database vendors cited herein about databases not listed in this book. The number of available databases is so extensive that it was not possible to cite all of them in this edition. An expanded offering will appear in future editions. Albeit limitations have been set on the number of databases selected for description, Appendix I is included to inform the reader about additional databases; the descriptions in Appendix I, however, are abbreviated. Many of those databases will receive more extensive coverage in Sections E and F of the next edition of this book.

Database Descriptions

[F-1] ABI/INFORM. 1971–present. Published by UMI/Data Courier. Available online from After Dark (file INFO), BRS Search Service (file INFO), Dialog (file 15), and Knowledge Index (file BUSI1). Available in CD-ROM from University Microfilms International.

An index to articles published in more than 800 business periodicals. Covers a wide variety of business topics as well as some specific companies and products. Includes abstracts. A special access point is D-U-N-S numbers.

[F-2] AGRIBUSINESS U. S. A. 1985–present. Published by Pioneer Hi-Bred International. Available online from Dialog (file 581) and Knowledge Index (file AGRI2). Available in CD-ROM from Dialog.

Agricultural news, products, statistical data, and company profiles are indexed or are in full text from over 300 periodicals and government publications. Includes reports from the U.S. Department of Agriculture. Some abstracts. Special access points include trade names, D-U-N-S numbers, and SIC codes.

[F-3] AGRICOLA. 1970–present. Published by the U.S. Department of Agriculture, National Agricultural Library. Available online from After Dark (file CAIN), BRS Search Service (file CAIN), Dialog (file 10), and Knowledge Index (file AGRI1).

An index to articles and books on all aspects of agriculture, including the business of agriculture. Some abstracts. A special access point is the National Agricultural Library's call numbers.

[F-4] AMERICAN BANKER. 1981–present. Published by American Banker. Available online from Dialog (file 625).

Contains the full text of articles published in this financial newspaper. Online articles often appear within 24 hours after their print publication.

[F-5] AMERICAN BANKER NEWS. Published by American Banker. Available online from Dialog (file BANKNEWS).

Contains the full text of articles from some of the most recent issues of the financial newspaper *American Banker.* Online articles often appear within 24 hours after their print publication. Has menus, with major categories like "Today's News," "Previous Days' News," "Washington Monday," "Executive Changes," "Speeches and Texts," and "Opinion and Analysis."

[F-6] ARTHUR D. LITTLE/ONLINE. Published by Arthur D. Little. Available online from Dialog (file 192).

Market research reports from Arthur D. Little on industries, products, and services. Most of the reports arc in full text. Contains abstracts.

[F-7] ASI. Published by Congressional Information Service. 1973–present. Available online from Dialog (file 102).

Indexes statistical data published by U.S. executive, judicial, and legislative branches and their boards, committees, councils, commissions, and offices. Includes abstracts. Special access points include report numbers and Superintendent of Documents Classification numbers.

[F-8] ASSOCIATED PRESS NEWS HIGHLIGHTS. Published by the Associated Press. Available online from CompuServe (file APV).

The Associated Press's hourly full-text news reports, including those on business topics. Dow Jones Industrial Average is reported every half hour.

[F-9] BESTLINK ONLINE DATABASE. Published by A. M. Best. Available online from A. M. Best.

Financial and operating data on life/health and property/casualty insurance companies. Major data sources are each company's quarterly and annual statements to the National Association of Insurance Commissioners. When available for a company, Best's ratings are indicated.

[F-10] BIOBUSINESS. 1985–present. Published by BIOSIS. Available online from BRS Search Service (file BBUS) and Dialog (file 285).

An index to articles about business matters associated with biological and medical research. Contains some abstracts.

[F-11] BOND BUYER. 1981–present. Published by American Banker. Available online from Dialog (file 626).

Contains the full text of articles from two newspapers, the *Bond Buyer* and *Credit*

Markets. Covers fixed-income, municipal-bond, and tax-exempt markets. Online articles often appear within 24 hours after their publication.

[F-12] BONDS LISTING. Published by CompuServe. Available online from CompuServe (file BONDS).

Reports yield, price, recent quality rating, CUSIP number, and ticker symbol for bonds issued by a corporation.

[F-13] BUSINESS DATELINE. 1985–present. Published by UMI/Data Courier. Available online from BRS Search Service (file BDLN) and Dialog (file 635).

Full text of articles from over 180 regional business periodicals, including at least 10 daily newspapers. Covers regional business activities, executives, and products. Special access points include D-U-N-S numbers, SIC codes, and ticker symbols.

[F-14] BUSINESS DEMOGRAPHICS REPORTS. Published by Market Statistics. Available online from CompuServe (file BUSDEM).

The number of employees arranged by broad SIC codes, and the number of retail businesses arranged by SIC codes 52 through 59, in a geographic area. Special access points include counties, metropolitan areas, states, ZIP codes, Arbitron television-market areas, and Nielsen television-market areas.

[F-15] BUSINESS INCORPORATING GUIDE. Published by Corporate Agents. Available online from CompuServe (file INC).

Lists state costs and requirements for incorporating a business. Comments on the pros and cons of incorporating. Contains excerpts from Delaware incorporation law. The publisher accepts on-line applications for incorporating a business.

[F-16] BUSINESS PERIODICALS INDEX. 1982–present. Published by H. W. Wilson. Available online from Wilsonline (file BPI). Available in CD-ROM from H. W. Wilson.

An index to articles published in approximately 300 business periodicals. Covers a wide variety of business topics as well as specific companies and products.

[F-17] BUSINESS SOFTWARE DATABASE. Published by Information Sources. Available online from After Dark (file BSOF), BRS Search Service (file BSOF), Dialog (file 256), and Knowledge Index (file COMP6).

A directory that contains product descriptions of micro- and minicomputer software for business applications. Nonevaluative. Lists prices, the type of computer and operating systems appropriate to the software, contact person, and intended users (such as consumers, small businesses, all industries). Special access points include price range and operating system.

[F-18] BUSINESS WIRE. Published by Business Wire. Available online from CompuServe (file TBW) and Dialog (file 610).

The full text of press releases from corporations and other organizations. A special access point is the ticker symbol.

[F-19] CAB ABSTRACTS. 1972–present. Published by CAB International. Available online from After Dark (file CABA), BRS Search Service (file CABA), Dialog (file 50), and Knowledge Index (AGRI3).

An index to articles, books, and other documents on all aspects of agriculture, including the business of agriculture. Contains abstracts.

[F-20] CAREER PLACEMENT REGISTRY. Published by Career Placement Registry. Available online from Dialog (file 162).

Contains the full text of the résumés of several thousand job seekers in a variety of fields. Each résumé has the same structure, including standard experience and background information, date available, geographic preferences, highest salary, occupational preferences, and willingness to relocate.

[F-21] CCH BLUE SKY LAW REPORTER. Published by Commerce Clearing House. Available online from Mead Data Central.

Full text of blue-sky securities laws, regulations, case-law rulings, and other decisions from the individual states; newsletter articles on blue-sky legal matters; Commerce Clearing House's commentary on blue-sky laws and regulations; policy statements published by various securities associations; and the Uniform Securities Act.

[F-22] CCH TAX DAY—FEDERAL. 1985–present. Published by Commerce Clearing House. Available online from Mead Data Central.

The full text of news developments about taxes in the executive, judicial, and legislative branches of the federal government.

[F-23] CCH TAX DAY—STATE. 1985–present. Published by Commerce Clearing House. Available online from Mead Data Central.

The full text of news developments about taxes in the individual states.

[F-24] CENDATA. Published by the U.S. Department of Commerce. Bureau of the Census. Available online from CompuServe (file CENDATA) and Dialog (file 580).

Business and population data. Includes current and some projected figures. Business information covers the U.S. by county and industry group, reporting the number of business establishments, employees, and payroll figures. Population information is for the U.S., states, and localities. Also reports recent updates on such indicators as money supply, mortgage rates, and the prime rate. A special access point is the SIC code.

[F-25] CHICAGO TRIBUNE. 1988–present. Published by the Chicago Tribune. Available online from Dialog (file 632).

The full text of news stories published in this newspaper, a major source of Midwest and national business news. Some statistical tables from the business section of the paper are not available in the database. A special access point is the ability to restrict a search to specific editions of the paper.

[F-26] CIS. Published by Congressional Information Service. 1970–present. Available online from Dialog (file 101).

Indexes the working papers of committees of the U.S. Congress. Covers legislative history of individual laws, statistics, and other data provided by testimonies during committee hearings. Abstracts. Special access points include names of witnesses and the companies or organizations for whom they work.

[F-27] CLAIMS. Published by IFI/Plenum Data. 1950–present. Available online from Dialog (files 340–341).

An index of U.S. patents issued since 1950, giving the text of the claim, the assignee(s), inventor(s), patent number(s), and in-depth indexing terms/codes for each patent listed. Covers aeronautical, agricultural, chemical, civil engineering, electrical, mechanical, nuclear, and other categories. Abstracts. Special access points include U.S. and international patent classification codes and patent numbers, *Chemical Abstracts* Service registry numbers, and names of companies assigned the patents.

[F-28] COMMERCE BUSINESS DAILY. 1982–present. Published by the U.S. Department of Commerce. Available online from Dialog (file 195).

The full text of announcements of contracts, procurements, and requests for the product, research, and service needs of U.S. government agencies. Also includes information about government surplus sales.

[F-29] COMMODITIES LIST. Published by CompuServe. Available online from CompuServe (file CSYMBOL).

A directory of commodities traded on major exchanges, arranged by categories, including fiber, food, grains, metals, and petroleum. Also reports currency prices. Identifies ticker symbols.

[F-30] COMMODITIES PRICING. Published by MJK Commodity Data Services. Available online from CompuServe (file CPRICE).

History of commodity prices from major exchanges for specified ranges of days, weeks, or months. Covers categories such as fiber, food, grains, metals, and petroleum. Also reports currency prices. Gives open, high, low, settlement, volume, and open-interest data.

[F-31] COMPENDEX*PLUS. 1969–present. Published by Engineering Information. Available online from BRS Search Service (file COMP), Dialog (file 8), and Knowledge Index (file ENGI1).

An index to engineering applications and research articles, books, papers, and reports. Abstracts. A special access point is the names of companies doing the work.

[F-32] COMPUTER ASAP. 1983–present. Published by Information Access. Available online from Dialog (file 675).

The full text of articles on computers, electronics, and telecommunications from over 130 business and technical periodicals. Covers hardware and software evaluations.

[F-33] COMPUTER DATABASE. 1983–present. Published by Information Access. Available online from After Dark (file CMPT), BRS Search Service (file CMPT), CompuServe (file COMPDB), and Dialog (file 275).

An index to articles on computers, electronics, and telecommunications from more than 130 business and technical periodicals. Contains abstracts and the full text of some articles. Covers hardware and software evaluations. Daily updates first appear in the NEWSEARCH database [F-97]. Special access points include operating systems and SIC codes.

[F-34] CONSUMER REPORTS. 1982–present. Published by Consumers Union of U.S. Available online from CompuServe (file CONSUMER), Dialog (file 646), and Knowledge Index (REFR6).

An index to and the full text of articles from *Consumer Reports* magazine. Evaluates, rates, and recommends products, financial services, and movies. Advises on family and personal budget and on health matters.

[F-35] CORPORATE AFFILIATIONS. Published by National Register Publishing. Available online from Dialog (file 513).

Provides a corporate family directory for a company, listing its parent company, distribution centers, divisions, plants, subsidiaries, and so forth. Directory information, including names of directors and officers. Brief financial information (net worth, liabilities, sales, and total assets) for parent companies. Covers private and public companies. Special access points include area codes, SIC codes, ticker symbols, and ZIP codes.

[F-36] CORPORATE AND INDUSTRY RESEARCH REPORTS (CIRR). Published by JA Micropublishing. Available online from After Dark (file CIRR) and BRS Search Service (file CIRR).

An index to intelligence reports on companies and industries. Some abstracts. Reports drawn from analyses by securities firms. The reports are stored on microfiche. Special access points include SIC codes and ticker symbols.

[F-37] D & B—DONNELLEY DEMOGRAPHICS. Published by Donnelley Marketing Information Services. Available online from Dialog (file 575).

1980 census data, with estimates for the current year plus five-year projections. Figures available for the U.S., cities, counties, metropolitan areas, states, ZIP codes, A. C. Nielsen, Arbitron, and Selling Areas Marketing areas. Data cover population by age, education, income, marital status, race, sex, and travel time to work. Also reports family and housing characteristics, number of business establishments by industry, types of occupations, and employment status.

[F-38] D & B—DUN'S ELECTRONIC YELLOW PAGES. Published by Dun's Marketing Services. Available online from Dialog (file 515).

Directory information for millions of private and public companies and professionals. Special access points include area codes, D-U-N-S numbers, SIC codes, and ZIP codes.

[F-39] D & B—DUN'S FINANCIAL RECORDS PLUS. Published by Dun's Marketing Services. Available online from Dialog (file 519).

Directory and financial information on private and public companies. Data on assets, liabilities, profits, ratios, and sales for the given company and for its industry. Narrative on company history and operation. Special access points include area codes, D-U-N-S numbers, SIC codes, and ZIP codes. Permits searching for companies that fall within numerical ranges of financial criteria.

[F-40] D & B—DUN'S MARKET IDENTIFIERS. Published by Dun's Marketing Services. Available online from Dialog (file 516).

Directory information for private and public companies, including names of officers and some sales data. Special access points include area codes, D-U-N-S numbers, SIC codes, sales territories, and ZIP codes.

[F-41] D & B—INTERNATIONAL DUN'S MARKET IDENTIFIERS. Published by Dun's Marketing Services. Available online from Dialog (file 518).

Directory information on private and public U.S. and foreign companies. Some sales data expressed in both foreign and U.S. currency. Special access points include D-U-N-S numbers and SIC codes.

[F-42] D & B—MILLION DOLLAR DIRECTORY. Published by Dun's Marketing Services. Available online from Dialog (file 517).

Directory information for private and public companies, including names of directors and officers. Some sales data. Special access points include area codes, D-U-N-S numbers, SIC codes, ticker symbols, and ZIP codes.

[F-43] DIALOG QUOTES AND TRADING. Published by Trade*Plus. Available online from Dialog (file QUOTES).

Current stock and stock-option prices on major U.S. exchanges. Delayed at least 20 minutes.

[F-44] DISCLOSURE. Published by Disclosure. Available online from After Dark (file DSCL) BRS Search Service (file DSCL), CompuServe (file DISCLOSURE), and Dialog (file 100). Available in CD-ROM from Disclosure.

Financial data and directory information on over 12,000 public companies. Sources include 8K, 10K, 10Q, and 20F reports as well as annual reports. Extensive data for each company, such as annual and quarterly balance sheets; five-year financial summary; ratio analysis covering about 30 ratios; dividends; earnings; share figures; a listing of directors and officers; subsidiaries; narrative from president's letter and "management discussion"; address; telephone number; ticker symbol; and CUSIP, D-U-N-S, *Forbes, Fortune,* and SIC numbers. Many special access points. Permits searching for companies that match specified numerical ranges of financial criteria.

[F-45] DISCLOSURE SPECTRUM OWNERSHIP. Published by Disclosure. Available online from After Dark (file OWNR), BRS Search Service (file OWNR), and Dialog (file 540). Available in CD-ROM from Disclosure.

A stock-ownership directory for about 5,000 public companies. Lists and gives number of shares of institutional, five-percent, and insider stockholders. Also reports total market value of shares held by each of the three groups. Special access points include CUSIP numbers, SIC codes, and ticker symbols.

[F-46] DIVIDENDS, SPLITS, INTEREST. Published by CompuServe. Available online from CompuServe (file DIVIDENDS).

Dividend-rate data, with the ex-dividend, payment, and record data for dividends, interest, and splits for bonds, mutual funds, options, and stocks. A special access point is the option to request data for a range of dates.

[F-47] DMS CONTRACT AWARDS. Published by Jane's Information Group. Available online from Dialog (file 588).

A directory of nonclassified contracts (especially those in aerospace and defense) of more than $25,000 awarded by U.S. government agencies to companies. Provides the amount and length of each contract and the name of the company and its product or program. Abstracts. Special access points include D-U-N-S numbers and ZIP codes, as well as the ability to create tabular reports that compare contract award totals between specific companies and for specific years.

[F-48] DMS CONTRACTORS. Published by Jane's Information Group. Available online from Dialog (file 984).

A directory of worldwide prime and sub-contractors for aerospace/defense product and weapon programs. Access to the database requires prior approval from the publisher.

[F-49] DMS MARKET INTELLIGENCE REPORTS. Published by Jane's Information Group. Available online from Dialog (file 988).

Intelligence reports on weapons and other aerospace/defense products and programs under development by U.S. and international companies. Provides a narrative as well as such data as funding amounts, price range, production forecasts, and units in service and planned. Access to the database requires prior approval from the publisher.

[F-50] ECONBASE: TIME SERIES AND FORECASTS. Published by WEFA Group. Available online from Dialog (file 565).

Time series of economic data in tables arranged by year, quarter, or month. Covers such items as expenditures, production, sales, and wages in various industries; personal-consumption expenditures and personal income; consumer price indexes, interest rates, and stock-market indicators. Tables may list only several recent years or extend back 20 or more years. Some include two years of forecast data. A special access point is the ability to call up only tables that include forecast data.

[F-51] ECONOMIC LITERATURE INDEX. 1969–present. Published by the American Economic Association. Available online from Dialog (file 139) and Knowledge Index (file ECON1).

An index to articles in consumer economics; economic growth; general economics; monetary and fiscal theory; quantitative economic methods; and urban, regional, national, and international economics. Covers about 300 economics journals. Includes some abstracts.

[F-52] ENCYCLOPEDIA OF ASSOCIATIONS. Published by Gale Research. Available online from Dialog (file 114).

A directory of more than 92,000 associations, giving a descriptive profile of many of them. Covers local, regional, national, and international associations. The associations are in areas that include business, commerce, education, government, health, labor, medicine, public affairs, science, technology, and trade. Includes professional societies, trade organizations, federations of organizations, and many other types. An annual budget level is given for about 40 percent of the associations. Special access points include area codes, size of budgets or memberships, and ZIP codes.

[F-53] FAIRBASE. Published by FAIRBASE Database. Available online from After Dark (file FAIR) and BRS Search Service (file FAIR).

An international directory of planned and past conferences, conventions, exhibitions, expositions, trade fairs, trade shows, and other such meetings of interest to business and industry. Indicates date, location, and organizers of the meeting, and, sometimes, the number of visitors expected and the amount of space available for exhibitors.

[F-54] FEDERAL APPLIED TECHNOLOGY DATABASE. Published by the U.S. Department of Commerce. National Technical Information Service. Available online from BRS Search Service (file FATD).

An index to patents held by U.S. government agencies and new products and processes developed by these agencies. Also indicates the availability of chemical and engineering laboratory facilities for temporary use. Contains abstracts. Special access points include contact persons at agencies available to assist in licensing or obtaining more information.

[F-55] FEDERAL REGISTER ABSTRACTS. 1977–present. Published by National Standards Association. Available online from After Dark (file FREG), BRS Search Service (file FREG), and Dialog (file 136).

A index to regulations, proposed regulations, meetings, notices, and other federal regulatory matters covered in the daily *Federal Register*. Includes abstracts.

[F-56] FEDWATCH. Published by MMS International. Available online from CompuServe (file FW).

Weekly analysis and forecasts of Federal Reserve Board activity and on economic, political, social, and other news that might affect the Board's decisions on interest rates.

[F-57] FINANCIAL TIMES ABSTRACTS. 1982–present. Published by Financial Times Business Information. Available online from Dialog (file 560).

Indexes articles about companies that have appeared in the *Financial Times* newspaper. Abstracts. The whole text given for short articles. A special access point is product codes.

[F-58] FINANCIAL TIMES FULL TEXT. 1986–present. Published by Financial Times Business Information. Available online from Dialog (file 622).

Contains the full text of articles appearing in the *Financial Times* newspaper. Covers almost any topic in business, including information on specific companies, as well as government regulations, industry information, labor and management issues, and world trade. International in scope. No abstracts, but lead paragraph in each article is available for searching and display.

[F-59] FINDEX DIRECTORY OF MARKET RESEARCH. 1972–present. Published by Cambridge Information Group Directories. Available online from Dialog (file 196).

A directory of market-research reports on industries, products, and individual firms prepared by market- and investment-research companies. Includes abstracts. Provides report prices and publishers' telephone numbers.

[F-60] FINIS: FINANCIAL INDUSTRY INFORMATION SERVICE. 1982– present. Published by the Bank Marketing Association. Available online from After Dark (file FINI), BRS Search Service (file FINI), and Dialog (file 268).

An index to articles from over 200 periodicals and to case studies gathered by the publisher. Emphasizes marketing articles on banks, thrift institutions, and other elements of the financial services industry. Contains abstracts. A special access point is the amount of assets of individual financial institutions.

[F-61] H & R BLOCK. Published by H & R Block. Available online from CompuServe (file HRB).

The full text of tips and news on income-tax regulations. Includes important filing dates from the Internal Revenue Service calendar.

[F-62] HARVARD BUSINESS REVIEW. 1971–present. Published by Harvard Business Review. Available online from After Dark (file HBRO), BRS (file HBRO), Dialog (file 122), and Knowledge Index (file BUSI3).

The full text of articles since 1976, from this periodical. The articles also have abstracts and are indexed by subject. Only abstracts and indexing is available for 1971–1975 articles.

[F-63] HEALTH INDUSTRY RESEARCH REPORTS (HIRR). Published by JA Micropublishing. Available online from After Dark (file HIRR) and BRS Search Service (file HIRR).

An index to intelligence reports on health-care companies and in-depth studies of the industry. Abstracts. Reports provided by investment and securities firms and by periodicals in the health profession.

[F-64] I/B/E/S (INSTITUTIONAL BROKERS' ESTIMATE SYSTEM). Published by Lynch, Jones & Ryan. Available online from CompuServe (file IBES).

Reports earnings estimates for individual companies. The reported estimate for a given company is the average of estimates made by leading analysts.

[F-65] INDUSTRY DATA SOURCES. Published by Information Access. 1979–present. Available online from Dialog (file 189).

An index to reports on financial, marketing, and statistical data for 65 industries. Typical data cover economic forecasts; industry profits, earnings, and growth; manufacturing-plant sites and closings; market-research reports; and market share. Abstracts. Includes address and telephone number of the producer of each report. A special access point is the SIC code.

[F-66] INFOMAT INTERNATIONAL BUSINESS. 1984–present. Published by Infomat. Available online from Dialog (file 583).

An index to articles on companies, markets, and products outside the U.S. Covers more than 425 journals and newspapers, with emphasis on European publications. Abstracts.

[F-67] INPADOC/FAMILY AND LEGAL STATUS. 1968–present. Published by International Patent Documentation Center. Available online from Dialog (file 345).

An index of patents issued by about 50 nations, including the U.S. It reports assignee(s), inventor(s), and patent number(s) for each issuing nation. Covers all technologies. Special access points include individual nation patent numbers, international patent classification codes, and companies assigned the patents.

[F-68] INSIDER TRADING MONITOR. Published by Invest/Net. Available online from Dialog (file 549).

A listing of stock transactions by corporate insiders (directors, officers, and major shareholders of a company). Gives insider's name, company name, position, number and date of transaction, and share price at time of transaction. Special access points include area codes, CUSIP numbers, ZIP codes, filing dates, insiders' names, transaction types (sale, purchase, gift), SIC codes, and ticker symbols.

[F-69] INSPEC. 1969–present. Published by Institution of Electrical Engineers. Available online from After Dark (file INSZ), BRS Search Service (file INSZ), Dialog (file 13), and Knowledge Index (file COMP1).

An index to articles and papers on research and applications in computers, electronics, information technology, and physics. Includes abstracts. Special access points include names of the companies doing the work.

[F-70] INSURANCE CONSUMER INFORMATION SERVICE. Published by the Independent Insurance Agents of America. Available online from CompuServe (file INS).

A full-text database explaining the procedure involved with filing an insurance claim and giving advice on how to shop for insurance. Covers automobile, homeowner's, landlord, and renter's insurance.

[F-71] INSURANCE PERIODICALS INDEX. 1983–present. Published by NILS Publishing. Available online from Dialog (file 169).

An index to articles in about 45 insurance periodicals. Provides abstracts. A special access point is the ability to search for directory information in these periodicals, such as directories of agencies, agents, annuities, brokers, consultants, policyholder-owned facilities, and software products.

[F-72] INVESTEXT. Published by Technical Data International. 1982–present. Available online from Dialog (file 545).

Provides the full text of financial intelligence reports on companies and industries. Prepared by Wall Street, regional, and foreign security analysts and industry experts. A special access point is the SIC code.

[F-73] INVESTOR'S DAILY. 1986–present. Published by JA Micropublishing. Available online from After Dark (file IVDA) and BRS Search Service (file IVDA).

An index to articles and features appearing in the newspaper with the same title. Contains some abstracts. Emphasis on financial analyses of companies and on the stock markets.

[F-74] IQUEST. Published by CompuServe. Available online from CompuServe (file IQUEST).

This is not a database but a "gateway" to databases. As a gateway, it provides CompuServe users with access to many of the databases available from other online services, such as the BRS Search Service and Dialog.

[F-75] ISSUE EXAMINATION. Published by CompuServe. Available online from CompuServe (file EXAMINE).

Provides the profile of a bond, stock, or other security issue, including such data as the exchange that trades the issue, dividend rate, earnings per share, yield, 52-week high/low, and the Moody's Quality and Standard & Poor's Quality ratings.

[F-76] ISSUE PRICING HISTORY. Published by Interactive Data Services. Available online from CompuServe (file PRICES).

Historical pricing data by day, week, or month for bonds, stocks, foreign-exchange rates, market indexes, mutual funds, and options. Gives volumes and close/average, high/ask, and low/bid prices. Special access points include the starting date and the length of the period to be examined.

[F-77] JANE'S DEFENSE & AEROSPACE NEWS/ANALYSIS. 1982–present. Published by Jane's Information Group. Available online from Dialog (file 587).

The full text of articles from at least ten defense and aerospace periodicals. Covers budgeting, contract awards, marketing, new products, new technologies, and requests for proposals, in the defense and aerospace industry.

[F-78] LABORLAW. Published by the Bureau of National Affairs. Available online from Dialog (file 243).

An index to decisions made by federal and state courts and administrative bodies on labor relations and other issues, such as health, safety, and wages. Contains abstracts. A special access point is the Bureau of National Affairs' citation number.

[F-79] LEGAL RESOURCE INDEX. 1980–present. Published by Information Access. Available online from After Dark (file LAWS), BRS Search Service (file LAWS), Dialog (file 150), and Knowledge Index (file LEGA1).

An index to over 750 legal periodicals, including bar-association journals, law reviews, and legal newspapers. Also, selective indexing of legal articles from more than a thousand general publications. Daily updates first appear in the NEWSEARCH database [F-97]. Special access points include case and statute citations and SIC codes.

[F-80] M & A FILINGS. Published by Charles E. Simon. 1985–present. Available online from Dialog (file 548).

An index to merger and acquisition documents filed by companies with the Securities and Exchange Commission. Abstracts. Indicates if the transaction is a completion of a merger transaction, a tender offer, a response to a tender offer, a buy-out deal, a stock-purchase agreement, an option agreement, or other negotiated arrangement. Special access points include CUSIP numbers, SIC codes, ticker symbols, and the names of the organizations managing and providing information about the deal.

[F-81] MAGAZINE ASAP. 1983–present. Published by Information Access. Available online from BRS Search Service (file MSAP) and Dialog (file 647).

The full text of articles from about 60 general-interest and business magazines.

[F-82] MAGAZINE INDEX. 1959–present. Published by Information Access. Available online from After Dark (file MAGS), BRS Search Service (file MAGS), Dialog (file 47), and Knowledge Index (file MAGA1).

An index to articles from about 300 general-interest and business magazines.

[F-83] MANAGEMENT CONTENTS. 1974–present. Published by Information Access. Available online from After Dark (MGMT), BRS Search Service (file MGMT), and Dialog (file 75).

An index to articles in over 120 management periodicals. Emphasizes management topics in accounting, advertising, banking, finance, marketing, personnel, and general management. Contains abstracts. Daily updates first appear in the NEWSEARCH database [F-97]. A special access point is the D-U-N-S number.

[F-84] MARKET HIGHLIGHTS. Published by CompuServe. Available online from CompuServe (file MARKET).

Listings of the most active stocks in various categories on the last full day of trading on the American, New York, and over-the-counter stock exchanges. Categories include largest loss, largest gain, highest volume, largest percent gain and loss, and new six-month low.

[F-85] MCGRAW-HILL PUBLICATIONS ONLINE. 1985–present. Published by McGraw-Hill Publications Online. Available online from Dialog (file 624).

The full text of articles from about 30 McGraw-Hill business periodicals, such as *Business Week, Electric Utility Week,* and *Securities Week.*

[F-86] MEDIA GENERAL. Published by Media General Financial Services. Available online from Dialog (file 546).

Stock analysis and financial intelligence by company and industry. Extensive data covers daily and weekly stock price and volume statistics for a company, annual financial ratios, balance sheet data for the past several years, and a comparison of financial data between a company and its industry. Special access points include cities, SIC codes, states, ticker symbols, ZIP codes, and the ability to search for companies that fall within a specified range of financial criteria.

[F-87] MICROQUOTE INDEXES. Published by CompuServe. Available online from CompuServe (file INDICATORS).

A comprehensive list of financial indicators covering bonds, exchange rates, stock-exchange volumes, and many other areas. Gives a brief description as well as the CUSIP number and ticker symbol of each indicator.

[F-88] MMS INTERNATIONAL. Published by MMS International. Available online from CompuServe (file MMS).

Daily analysis of factors now affecting or expected to affect the various investment markets.

[F-89] MOODY'S CORPORATE NEWS—INTERNATIONAL. Published by Moody's Investors Service. Available online from Dialog (file 557).

News about companies in approximately 100 countries. A news report may be narrative or statistical. Moody's culls the information from sources like annual reports, news releases, newswires, and periodicals.

[F-90] MOODY'S CORPORATE NEWS—U.S. Published by Moody's Investors Service. Available online from Dialog (file 556).

News about public U.S. companies gathered from annual reports, news releases, newswires, and periodicals. A news report may be narrative or statistical. Special access points include D-U-N-S numbers and SIC codes.

[F-91] MOODY'S CORPORATE PROFILES. Published by Moody's Investors Service. Available online from Dialog (file 555).

Directory and financial information on thousands of public companies, including address, telephone number, balance-sheet data, and price/earnings ratio. Some companies have a brief narrative evaluation by Moody's. Special access points include D-U-N-S numbers, SIC codes, and ticker symbols.

[F-92] MULTIPLE ISSUES. Published by Interactive Data Services. Available online from CompuServe (file QSHEET).

Historical pricing data on a given day for one or more bonds, market indexes, mutual funds, stocks, and options. Gives volumes and the close/average, high/ask, and low/bid prices.

[F-93] NAME/SYMBOL LOOKUP. Published by CompuServe. Available online from CompuServe (file LOOKUP).

Lists bonds, commodities, stocks, and other investment instruments available from a company. Special access points include CUSIP numbers, SIC codes, and ticker symbols.

[F-94] NATIONAL NEWSPAPER INDEX. 1979–present. Published by Information Access. Available online from After Dark (file NOOZ), BRS Search Service (file NOOZ), Dialog (file 111), and Knowledge Index (file NEWS2). Available in CD-ROM from Information Access.

Indexes five major national newspapers and three newswires: *Christian Science Monitor, Los Angeles Times,* the *New York Times,* the *Wall Street Journal,* the *Washington Post,* Kyodo's Japan Economic Newswire, PR Newswire, and Reuters Financial Report. Indexing of the first three is comprehensive; the others are covered selectively. Daily updates first appear in the NEWSEARCH database [F-97]. A special access point is the SIC code.

[F-95] NEIGHBORHOOD DEMOGRAPHIC REPORTS. Published by CACI. Available online from CompuServe (file NEIGHBOR).

Demographics by ZIP code providing such data as population, average income, number of households, types of occupations, and housing.

[F-96] NEWS-A-TRON MARKET REPORTS. Published by News-a-tron. Available online from CompuServe (file NAT).

Provides daily prices on grains, metals, and petroleum products from the commodity markets. Also lists daily rates for foreign currencies.

[F-97] NEWSEARCH. Published by Information Access. Available online from After Dark (file DALY), BRS Search Service (file DALY), Dialog (file 211), and Knowledge Index (file NEWS1).

Contains daily updates to other Information Access databases: COMPUTER DATABASE [F-33], LEGAL RESOURCE INDEX [F-79], MANAGEMENT CONTENTS [F-83], NATIONAL NEWSPAPER INDEX [F-94], NEWSWIRE ASAP [F-100], and TRADE & INDUSTRY INDEX [F-131]. A very up-to-date index to newspapers, magazines, and other periodicals. References from the *New York Times* and the *Wall Street Journal* usually appear within 48 hours after publication.

[F-98] NEWSGRID. Published by Comtex Scientific. Available online from CompuServe (file NEWSGRID).

U.S. and world business headlines and full-text stories. Current indicators, sometimes within an hour, from major stock exchanges and other markets.

[F-99] NEWSPAPER ABSTRACTS. 1984–present. Published by University Microfilms International. Available online from Dialog (file 603). Available in CD-ROM from University Microfilms International.

An index to articles from about 20 newspapers, including *American Banker,* the *New York Times,* and the *Wall Street Journal.* Brief Abstracts.

[F-100] NEWSWIRE ASAP. Published by Information Access. 1985–present. Available online from Dialog (file 649).

Full text of stories from three major newswires: Kyodo's Japan Economic Newswire, PR Newswire, and Reuters Financial Report. Daily updates also appear in the NEWSEARCH database [F-97]. A special access point is the SIC code.

[F-101] NO-LOAD MUTUAL FUND DIRECTORY. Published by the No-Load Mutual Fund Association. Available online from CompuServe (file NOLOAD).

Listings of the assets, investment objectives, purchase requirements, redemption options, and other features of individual mutual funds. Covers equity, fixed income, growth, money market, municipal bond, and tax-exempt funds. A special access point is the ability to find funds that match the investor's investment objectives.

[F-102] NTIS. 1964–present. Published by the U.S. Department of Commerce. National Technical Information Service. Available online from After Dark (file NTIS), BRS Search Service (file NTIS), Dialog (file 6), and Knowledge Index (file GOVE2). Available in CD-ROM from Dialog.

An index to progress and final reports of research and development done under grants or contracts with the federal government. Contains abstracts.

[F-103] OFFICIAL AIRLINE GUIDE. Published by Official Airline Guides. Available online from CompuServe (file OAG) and Dialog (file OAG).

Lists worldwide commercial airline schedules and fare information. Also gives hotels and motels, with locations and room rates.

[F-104] OPTIONS PROFILE. Published by CompuServe. Available online from CompuServe (file OPRICE).

For an index or stock option on a major exchange on a specified date, provides a table of exercise prices and expiration dates for puts and calls.

[F-105] PATDATA. 1971–present. Published by the U.S. Department of Commerce. Office of Patents and Trademarks. Available online from After Dark (file PATS) and BRS Search Service (file PATS).

An index to U.S. patents issued since 1971 for chemical, electrical, and mechanical inventions. Abstracts describe the inventions. Lists inventors, patent assignees, and patent dates. Special access points include U.S. and international patent classification codes, patent numbers, and companies assigned the patents.

[F-106] PNI: PHARMACEUTICAL NEWS INDEX. 1974–present. Published by UMI/Data Courier. Available online from BRS Search Service (file PNII) and Dialog (file 42).

An index to more than 20 periodicals that cover pharmaceuticals, cosmetics, and medical devices. Includes news on acquisitions and mergers, drug approvals and recalls, research, and other health-related issues.

[F-107] PR NEWSWIRE. 1987–present. Published by PR Newswire. Available online from Dialog (file 613).

The full text of news releases from companies, public relations agencies, and other news sources. A special access point is the ticker symbol.

[F-108] PRICING STATISTICS. Published by Interactive Data Services. Available online from CompuServe (file PRISTATS).

Historical pricing data for bonds, foreign-exchange rates, market indexes, mutual funds, options, and stocks. Gives volumes and close/average, high/ask, and low/bid prices for the selected periods. Also calculates percentage change, average, standard deviation, high, and low for the period.

[F-109] PSYCINFO. 1967–present. Published by the American Psychological Association. Available online from After Dark (file PSYC), BRS Search Service (file PSYC), Dialog (file 11), and Knowledge Index (file PSYC1).

A major index to worldwide articles, dissertations, and other documents in psychology and related fields. Provides abstracts.

[F-110] PTS AEROSPACE/DEFENSE MARKETS & TECHNOLOGY. 1982–present. Published by Predicasts. Available online from Dialog (file 80).

An index to articles about 75 aerospace and defense periodicals. Contains abstracts, some with statistical tables. A special access point is the modified SIC code.

[F-111] PTS ANNUAL REPORTS ABSTRACTS. Published by Predicasts. Available online from Dialog (file 17).

Public company information gathered from in-house annual reports. Narrative excerpts and tables of statistics on such items as company performance, corporate structure, marketing strategy, and outlook for the company.

[F-112] PTS F & S INDEX. 1972–present. Published by Predicasts. Available online from BRS Search Service (file PTSI) and Dialog (file 18).

An index to articles on almost any business topic from over 2,400 periodicals. Special access points include CUSIP numbers, D-U-N-S numbers, modified SIC codes, ticker symbols.

[F-113] PTS FORECASTS. 1970–present. Published by Predicasts. Available online from Dialog (file 81).

Statistical tables from periodical articles and other publications. Covers U.S. industry, product, and service data such as consumption, expenditures, exports, imports, price indexes, and sales. Tables list data for current and/or past years and then projections for at least one year into the future. A special access point is the modified SIC code.

[F-114] PTS MARKETING & ADVERTISING REFERENCE SERVICE. 1984–present. Published by Predicasts. Available online from Dialog (file 570).

An index to articles on advertising from about 75 periodicals and other sources. Includes abstracts. Special access points include advertising slogans, agency spokespersons' names, CUSIP numbers, D-U-N-S numbers, modified SIC codes, and ticker symbols.

[F-115] PTS NEW PRODUCT ANNOUNCEMENTS. 1985–present. Published by Predicasts. Available online from Dialog (file 621).

Announcements of new products in full-text news-release style. Directory-type information for the announcing companies. Special access points include CUSIP numbers, D-U-N-S numbers, modified SIC codes, and ticker symbols.

[F-116] PTS NEWSLETTER DATABASE. 1988–present. Published by Predicasts. Available online from Dialog (file 636).

The full text of articles appearing in over 170 business and industry newsletters. Emphasis is on industry analysis, new products and technologies, company activities, and government regulations and programs. Provides directory information about the newsletter's publisher plus subscription prices and frequencies. Special access points include industry categories.

[F-117] PTS PROMT. 1972–present. Published by Predicasts. Available online from BRS Search Service (file PTSP) and Dialog (file 16).

A major index to business articles from over 1,200 periodicals, as well as to information from annual reports, news releases, and other sources. Provides abstracts that sometimes are in the form of statistical tables. Wide variety of topics, with an emphasis on product and company information. If the reader wants to make a choice among PTS databases, this is the most comprehensive. It duplicates information found in some of the other PTS databases listed and also incorporates a couple of now-defunct PTS databases. "PROMT" stands for Predicasts Overview of Markets and Technology. Special access points include CUSIP numbers, D-U-N-S numbers, modified SIC codes, and ticker symbols.

[F-118] PTS U. S. TIME SERIES. Published by Predicasts. Available online from Dialog (file 82).

Statistical tables on many areas of business with an emphasis on product and industry trends. Typical table contains 10 to 20 years of statistics on any one factor, such as consumption, expenditures, exports, imports, price, production, or sales. A special access point is the modified SIC code.

[F-119] QUICK QUOTE. Published by CompuServe. Available online from CompuServe (file QQUOTE).

Today's current prices on major U.S. exchanges, delayed at least 20 minutes for stocks and stock options, and 24 hours for exchange rates and mutual funds. Provides time of the quote, current volume, and high/ask, low/bid, and current prices.

[F-120] RIA FEDERAL TAX COORDINATOR 2D. Published by Research Institute of America. Available online from Mead Data Central.

The full text of sections from the Internal Revenue Code and Treasury Regulations, plus the publisher's explanations, cautions, illustrations, observations, and recommendations. Coverage includes individual and corporate income tax, excise tax, estate tax, gift tax, tax accounting, deductions, retirement plans, tax treaties, Tax Court rules, and other tax-related information.

[F-121] S & P ONLINE. Published by Standard & Poor's. Available online from CompuServe (file S&P).

Public-company profiles, including such data as dividends, earnings, ratios, sales, and stock-price performance. Includes a directory of the S & P 500 stocks, as well as listings of stocks favored by S & P analysts.

[F-122] STANDARD & POOR'S CORPORATE DESCRIPTIONS ONLINE. Published by Standard & Poor's. Available online from Dialog (file 133) and Knowledge Index (file CORP3). Available in CD-ROM from Dialog.

Types of information include detailed directory, strategic business, and financial information on public companies. Some of the information covers balance-sheet data, bond descriptions, corporate-background narrative, names of officers and directors, stock data, and subsidiaries. Special access points include CUSIP numbers, SIC codes, and ticker symbols. Permits searching for companies with financial data that fall within specified ranges.

[F-123] STANDARD & POOR'S NEWS ONLINE. 1979–present. Published by Standard & Poor's. Available online from Dialog (file 132).

Daily business and financial news stories about public companies. Stories may contain full text or tabular financial data. Special access points include SIC codes and ticker symbols.

[F-124] STANDARD & POOR'S REGISTER—BIOGRAPHICAL. Published by Standard & Poor's. Available online from Dialog (file 526), and Knowledge Index (file CORP5). Available in CD-ROM from Dialog.

Biographical information on officers and directors of private and public companies, including birth date, colleges attended, current position, and home and company addresses. Special access points include colleges attended, place and year of birth, and ZIP codes.

[F-125] STANDARD & POOR'S REGISTER—CORPORATE. Published by Standard & Poor's. Available online from Dialog (file 527) and Knowledge Index (file CORP6). Available in CD-ROM from Dialog.

Directory information on more than 40,000 private and public companies. Lists officers and directors. Narrative description of market territory, products, and services. Some sales data. Special access points include area codes, CUSIP numbers, market territories, SIC codes, and ZIP codes.

[F-126] SUPERSITE. Published by CACI. Available online from CompuServe (file SUPERSITE).

Demographic data, such as population, average income, number of households, types of occupations, and housing. Target areas include Arbitron TV market areas, census tracts, counties, metropolitan areas, Nielsen market areas, states, and ZIP codes.

[F-127] TAX NOTES TODAY. 1986–present. Published by Tax Analysts. Available online from Dialog (file 650).

The full text and/or summaries of tax information taken from news stories and commentary, federal bills, federal court and selected state court opinions, Internal Revenue Service publications, state budget and tax actions, tax-accounting news, and other documents.

[F-128] THOMAS NEW INDUSTRIAL PRODUCTS. Published by Thomas Online. Available online from Dialog (file 536).

For recently introduced products and technologies, provides name and telephone number of manufacturer, product specifications, trade names, model numbers, and SIC codes. Special access points include area codes, model numbers, SIC codes, ZIP codes, and attribute codes (such as LGT, "light weight"; CON "easy to install"; SAF, "safe").

[F-129] THOMAS REGISTER ONLINE. Published by Thomas Online. Available online from Dialog (file 535).

Lists the manufacturers of a given product, providing directory information on each of the companies. Also lists all the products made by each manufacturer. Special access points include area codes, product trade names, and ZIP codes.

[F-130] TRADE & INDUSTRY ASAP. 1983–present. Published by Information Access Company. Available online from BRS Search Service (file TSAP) and Dialog (file 648).

The full text of articles and indexing on almost any trade or industry from over 125 business periodicals. Some emphasis on regional and trade publications. A special access point is the SIC code.

[F-131] TRADE & INDUSTRY INDEX. 1981–present. Published by Information Access. Available online from Dialog (file 148).

An index to articles on almost any trade or industry from over 600 periodicals, including the *Wall Street Journal,* the *New York Times,* and other local, national, and regional business publications. Contains some abstracts and some articles in full text. Daily updates first appear in the NEWSEARCH database [F-97]. A special access point is the SIC code.

[F-132] TRADEMARKSCAN—FEDERAL. Published by Thomson & Thomson. Available online from Dialog (file 226).

Contains registered and pending trademarks from the U.S. Department of commerce, Office of Patents and Trademarks. Includes text and/or design (which might require special software for viewing), original and current owners, and whether active or inactive. A special access point is the ability to search with standard spelling for a trademark that uses unconventional spelling.

[F-133] TRADEMARKSCAN—STATE. Published by Thomson & Thomson. Available online from Dialog (file 246).

Reports trademarks registered with the 50 states and Puerto Rico. Includes text, state of registration, and owner. A special access point is the ability to search with standard spelling for a trademark that uses unconventional spelling.

[F-134] TRINET COMPANY DATABASE. Published by Trinet. Available online from Dialog (file 532).

Directory information about private and public companies. Indicates number of locations, employment, and sales data for each company. Special access points include area codes, SIC codes, and ZIP codes.

[F-135] TRINET U. S. BUSINESSES. Published by Trinet. Available online from Dialog (file 531).

Directory information about private and public company locations. Indicates number of employees, sales, and share of market for each location. Special access points include area codes, SIC codes, and ZIP codes. Permits searching for companies that fall within a specified market-share range.

[F-136] UPI NEWS. 1983–present. Published by United Press International. Available online from Dialog (file 261) and Knowledge Index (file NEWS3).

The full text of stories from this newswire. Stories appear in the database about two days after being on the newswire.

[F-137] VALUE LINE DATABASE II. Published by Value Line. Available online from CompuServe (file VLINE).

Balance sheets, financial ratios, and stock-price projections for individual companies. A special access point is the ticker symbol.

[F-138] WORLD PATENTS INDEX. 1963–present. Published by Derwent Publications. Available online from Dialog (file 351).

An index to patents issued by approximately 30 nations including the U.S. Lists assignee(s), inventor(s), and patent number(s) for each issuing nation. Covers general, chemical, electrical, and mechanical inventions. Abstracts. Special access points include individual nation patent numbers, international patent-classification codes, and companies assigned the patents.

Directory of Selected Business and Trade Organizations

Information Contained in Section G

Listed in this section are selected business and trade organizations that have information that may be of value to some members of the business community. Many of them have names like association, institute, or society. Some have a membership that consists of individuals (for example, accountants, insurance agents, or managers) who share a common business or trade interest. Other organizations are groups of companies or even groups of other organizations. There also are organizations that do not actually have members but which offer services to some area of the business community.

This list is small in relation to the thousands of organizations that exist in the U.S. and the rest of the world. The organizations included will give an idea of the kinds of organizations that serve the business community.

For each organization there has been reported

- the organization's name
- an address
- a telephone number
- a brief example of the organization's activities, data collected, or services available

and, when available from our sources, as much of the following as possible:

- the organization's fax number
- the name of at least one of its publications, which, unless stated otherwise, is a periodical.

For some of the organizations listed, it may be necessary to be a member to take advantage of certain publications or services.

Sources of Information

The descriptive information about each organization listed below comes from publications issued by the organization.

For Further Information

Additional information about each organization may be obtained from publications of that organization, directories, chambers of commerce, and by contacting the organization. The offices of the executive director or information officer can inform you of the specific kinds of information or services that are available.

Professional Societies

These organizations have a membership of individuals who work in or who are otherwise interested in a specific profession. Such societies often have functions such as holding meetings and publishing materials that provide continuing education to their profession; establishing a code of ethics for the profession; organizing conventions, establishing local chapters, and publishing periodicals that encourage communication among members.

American Accounting Association

5717 Bessie Drive
Sarasota, FL 34233
(813) 921-7747

Serves educators, practitioners, and students of accounting, and has the purpose of improving education, practice, research, and standards in accounting. Accountants in the business community can use the association to make contacts with college and university accounting educators. New accounting faculty members can use the association's New Faculty Consortium for help in teaching and research. The association has a strong international component and publishes international accounting directories. It is an advocate for and produces research on the uses of accounting for internal management. Publishes the *Accounting Review*.

American Bankers Association

1120 Connecticut Avenue, NW
Washington, DC 20036
(800) 872-7747

For bankers, including those specializing in bank cards, bank investments, commercial lending, installment lending, marketing, operations, and trusts. Helps improve financial services through activities such as taking positions on federal legislative and regulatory actions, performing and encouraging research, and maintaining education and training programs. Its American Institute of Banking offers courses, seminars, training programs, diplomas, and certification in various areas of banking. Its Bank Marketing Association operates an information center that serves bank-marketing members. The center provides answers, assistance, and an on-line database for members needing information related to financial-services marketing. The American Bankers Association's library makes available research and information services to members. The association collects and publishes data on the demographics and marketing of financial services, compensation programs for bank employees, operations (check processing, data processing, telecommunications, retail and wholesale operations) from a national survey of banks, comparative information by bank size on credit operations of banks, and other banking intelligence. Its *ABA Banking Journal* annually includes the "Bank Operations Buyers Guide" to help bankers find sources of operations equipment and "Guide to Services" to help locate sources of services, such as consultants, information, investment, and training.

American Institute of Certified Public Accountants

1211 Avenue of the Americas
New York, NY 10036
(212) 575-3888 Fax (212) 575-3846

The professional association for accounting. Issues accounting and auditing guides and standards for members of the accounting profession. Advises the Financial Accounting Standards Board on the promulgation of accounting principles. Administers a quality-review program for its members and for accounting firms. Members of the institute have access to its Technical Information Division for help with accounting, auditing, and financial reporting questions. Members also have mail and telephone access to the institute's library of accounting materials. The institute's board of examiners prepares and grades the national CPA examination. Publishes *Journal of Accountancy*.

American Management Association

135 W. 50th Street
New York, NY 10020
(212) 586-8100 (800) 262-6969

For management personnel at all levels. It seeks to increase the managerial knowledge of its membership. Its Center for Management Development administers thousands of job-training and career-development courses. These are for employees at all levels of a business and cover such areas as finance, general and administrative services, manufacturing, marketing, packaging, and purchasing. The association regularly conducts surveys of management issues and practices through interviews, questionnaires, and visits to organizations. Survey results are sent regularly to members as part of the *AMA Survey Reports* program. Members have exclusive use of the association's Management Information Service, whose management research specialists are available to gather background information on questions dealing with management problems. Members also have exclusive borrowing privileges at the association's Library, which handles letter, in-person, and telephone requests. Among the library resources are thousands of examples of company documents, such as employee handbooks, job descriptions, and organizational charts. Firms and other organizations can hold membership in the association. A special Growing

Company Membership is available for smaller organizations. The association has a publishing division and its own bookstores in three of its centers across the country. Publishes the *AMA Management Handbook*, and its periodicals include *Management Review, Supervisory Management*, and *Personnel*.

American Marketing Association
250 S. Wacker Drive
Chicago, IL 60606
(312) 648-0536 Fax (312) 993-7542

A society of marketing professionals who have interests that include advertising, consumer behavior, education for marketing, industrial marketing, organizational culture, planning and strategy, production management, and sales management. Members have book-borrowing privileges and access to an online reference service at the association's Marguerite Kent Library/Information Center. The center also contains a Software Review Center that lends demonstration marketing disks. Meetings of the association include the annual week-long School of Sales Management and an annual symposium on health-care marketing. Publishes *Journal of Marketing* and *Journal of Marketing Research*.

American Society for Industrial Security
1655 N. Fort Myer Drive, Suite 1200
Arlington, VA 22209
(703) 522-5800 Fax (703) 243-4954

For professionals in the security industry. Administers the Certified Protection Professional credentials program. Sponsors three week-long courses on assets protection. The Society's O. P. Norton Information Resource Center can be used by members for security-related research. Resource Center services include on-line reference services and mail-loans of books. Each of the society's 29 committees and councils provides referral services to members seeking security problem-solving assistance. The committees and councils cover security matters in such areas as banking and finance, coupons, insurance, retailing, telecommunications, and terrorism. Publishes a handbook of guidelines on security investigations and a listing of U.S. and international security-industry market studies on equipment, personnel, and technology. Publishes *Security Management*.

American Society for Personnel Administration
606 N. Washington Street
Alexandria, VA 22314
(703) 548-3440

For practitioners in personnel administration, human-resource management, and industrial relations. Has 425 local chapters. Members have telephone access to the association's Technical Services Department for the answering of technical questions. There are volunteer experts on call to provide advice to members on matters such as equal-employment opportunity and occupational-health-and-safety issues. The association's Library on human-resource management materials is available to members, as is ASPA*Net, which provides on-line access to association publications and reference materials. The association participates in collecting data on human resources professionals' salaries. Members have access to a Government Affairs office, which provides information on the status of legislation related to human resources issues. Publishes *Personnel Administrator*.

American Society of CLU & ChFC
270 Bryn Mawr Avenue
Bryn Mawr, PA 19010
(215) 526-2500 Fax (215) 527-4010

Provides continuing education and develops ethical guidelines for the life-insurance underwriter industry. Administers granting of two professional designations; CLU (Chartered Life Underwriter) and ChFC (Chartered Financial Consultant). Provides periodic teleconferences and, through its institute, a series of five-day seminars for its members. Publishes *Journal of the American Society of CLU & ChFC*.

American Society of Transportation and Logistics
P. O. Box 33095
Louisville, KY 40232
(502) 451-8150

Disseminates information on technical developments, legal issues, and trends to aid the training and continuing education of professionals in transportation, traffic, logistics, and physical-distribution management. Administers a Certificate in Transportation and Logistics program. Publishes *Transportation Journal*.

Association for Systems Management
24587 Bagley Road
Cleveland, OH 44138
(216) 243-6900

An organization for information-resource managers, systems analysts, end-user counselors, management-information systems directors, and other information-systems professionals. Offers two- to five-day courses on basic and advanced systems analysis, computer-assisted software engineering, desktop publishing, hands-on expert systems, and systems project management. Publishes *Journal of Systems Management*.

Association of Records Managers and Administrators
4200 Somerset Drive, Suite 215
Prairie Village, KS 66208
(913) 341-3808 Fax (913) 341-3742

Provides continuing education and professional growth to members who work in fields such as archives management, filing systems, forms management, office automation, retention scheduling, and reprography. Administers the home study course "An Introduction to Records and Information Management." Produces a guide to records management for small businesses. Publishes guidelines and standards on developing and operating a records-retention program, job descriptions, records-center operations, and related concerns. Publishes *Records Management Quarterly*.

Data Processing Management Association
505 Busse Highway
Park Ridge, IL 60068
(312) 825-8124

A professional society for application engineers, data-processing managers and operations staff, lawyers, operations researchers, programmers, and other information-management professionals. Its purpose is to develop effective programs for the self-improvement of its members through various educational tools, including handbooks, audiocassettes, conferences, and seminars. Administers a Certificate in Data Processing program. Has developed model computer-crime legislation. Publishes *Information Executive*.

Independent Insurance Agents of America
127 S. Peyton Street
Alexandria, VA 22314
(800) 221-7917

The professional society for independent insurance agents. Its on-line information network gives members access to motor-vehicle reports, insurance-association directories, and other information. Advertising guides, workshops, and kits are available to help members tie in their individual advertising programs with the organization's marketing efforts. Publishes *Independent Agent*.

Institute of Industrial Engineers
P. O. Box 6150
Norcross, GA 30091
(404) 449-0460 Fax (404) 263-8532

Society for the industrial engineering profession. Concerned with productivity and quality improvement in business and industry. A source of information on innovation in this field. For example, the institute's Society for Integrated Manufacturing and Society for Health Systems provide technical information to members facing problems in these areas. There are 20 other specialized divisions, or interest groups, within the institute. Makes available microcomputer software for economic analysis, production control, work measurement, plant layout, and other enterprises. Its Accreditation Board for Engineering and Technology evaluates college and university industrial-engineering programs. Publishes *Industrial Engineering*.

Institute of Internal Auditors
249 Maitland Avenue
Altamonte Springs, FL 32701
(407) 830-7600

Professional society for internal auditors. Its activities include production of educational products for continuing education of its members, facilitating industrial and government relations with the internal-auditing profession, holding national and international conferences, and contributing to the development of professional standards. Publishes the *Professional Internal Auditing Standards*. Supports research activity for internal auditing through its foundation. Administers a certification program for internal auditors. Publishes *Internal Auditor*.

International Personnel Management Association
1617 Duke Street
Alexandria, VA 22314
(703) 549-7100

Professional society for personnel managers in county, federal, municipal, state, and other governmental bodies. Operates a Test Rental Service through which it supplies communities with written tests that can be used in selection and promotion decisions for clerical, fire, and police positions. Also provides assistance in learning about the legal requirements of employment testing. Publishes various reports on personnel management, including a review of state and local laws related to drug testing in the workplace and an analysis of legal decisions and state laws covering AIDS in the workplace. Publishes *Public Personnel Management*.

National Association of Accountants
P. O. Box 433
Montvale, NJ 07645
(800) 356-7611

Professional society of accountants holding such positions as accountant, chief financial officer, budget analyst, controller, cost analyst, financial vice president, treasurer, and any other position responsible for processing financial information to be used by management in business and public service. Administers the Certified Management Accountant certification program and other continuing education programs. Services to members include those provided by the association's technical staff, who answer technical inquiries, and the NAA Library. Publishes *Management Accounting*.

National Association of Realtors
430 N. Michigan Avenue
Chicago, IL 60611
(800) 874-6500

Professional society of individuals in the real-estate industry that is dedicated to increasing the knowledge, productivity, and skills of its members. Its structure includes nine affiliated councils, institutes, and societies for such groups as appraisers, counselors, international members, land brokers, managers, and women. Collects and publishes directory information on real-estate computer software, real-estate instructors, state associations, local real-estate board officers, realtors arranged by local board affiliation, real-estate appraisers, and other members of the field. Collects and publishes data on industrial and office real-estate market activity, profiles of real-estate firms and brokerage operations, existing- and new-home sales and prices, housing affordability, profiles of homebuyers, and foreign investment in U.S. real estate. Its real-estate library provides reference and loan services to members and a fee-based reference service for nonmembers. Publishes *Real Estate Today*.

National Tax Association, Tax Institute of America
5310 E. Main Street
Columbus, OH 43213
(614) 864-1221

Society with a broad membership, including accountants, business and government tax administrators, and tax lawyers. Its educational program covers federal, international, local, and state government taxation concerns. Encourages discussion and study in its eight divisions, which include Federal Taxation and Finance, Local Nonproperty Taxation, Public Utility and Transportation Taxation, and State Sales and Use Taxation. Cosponsors an annual week-long workshop for state and business administrators on the valuation of public-utility and railroad property. Publishes *National Tax Journal*.

Planning Forum
P. O. Box 70
5500 College Corner Pike
Oxford, OH 45056
(513) 523-4185 Fax (513) 523-7539

Professional society for executives and others involved in planning and strategic management. Members include academicians, board directors, chief executive officers, consulting-firm directors, and line-and-staff executives. Publishes *Planning Review*, which includes an annual "Political and Economic Forecast Chart." The chart rates each nation on risk for financial transfers to, direct investments in, and exporting goods to the nation. Historical and projected data on growth and inflation are provided, as are ratings on the forecast for political turmoil and probable regime-holding power in each country during the next two to five years.

Society of Manufacturing Engineers
P. O. Box 930
One SME Drive
Dearborn, MI 48121
(313) 271-1500 Fax (313) 271-2861

A society of manufacturing professionals who may belong to one of the society's associations or groups: Association for Finishing Processes, Computer and Automated Systems Association, Composites Group, Electronics Manufacturing Group, Machine Vision Association, North American Manufacturing Research Institution, and Robotics International. Offers hundreds of educational courses, workshops, clinics, and conferences every year, covering manufacturing innovations such as artificial intelligence, composites, machine controls, and product design. Its Manufacturing Engineering Certification Institute administers two professional certificates, namely, the "Certified Manufacturing Engineer" and the "Certified Manufacturing Technologist." Publishes *Journal of Manufacturing Systems*. Its active publishing program produces materials on selecting manufacturing software, troubleshooting manufacturing processes, U.S. manufacturers' ratings of foreign-built machine tools, and related concerns of the field.

United States Association for Small Business and Entrepreneurship
University of Wisconsin, Madison
905 University Avenue
Madison, WI 53706
(608) 263-2221

Professional society for those in education, government, and industry who serve the small-business community. The association is an affiliate of the International Council for Small Business. Produces annual surveys, conferences (including some associated with the international council), and publications that report on entrepreneurship and small-business practices and management. Its Minority Business Division specializes in developing skills for black, Hispanic, and women entrepreneurs. Publishes *Entrepreneurship: Theory and Practice*.

Other Organizations

Listed below are other organizations. Unlike professional societies, these other organizations typically do not have large memberships of individuals. Membership may be limited to companies or even other organizations. What distinguishes these organizations is that their missions of service, research, publishing, and education are primarily delivered to member organizations and/or the public instead of individuals. Some of the services and information disseminated by them is meant for specialized areas of the business community. Again, much is available to the general public.

Some of these organizations serve business and industry by providing dispute-resolution programs. Some are research groups that study and publish reports on various problems associated with business. Others of the organizations listed below do extensive publishing, which allows them to provide books and periodicals on topics related to the organization's mission. There also are organizations with strong education programs that present clinics, seminars, workshops, and other resources to increase the skills of individuals in business and industry. Some of the organizations listed here have missions that combine several of these activities.

American Arbitration Association
140 W. 51st Street
New York, NY 10020
(212) 484-4000

An organization of firms, associations, and individuals interested in the arbitration process for the resolution of disputes. Provides dispute-resolution services to business executives, communities, consumers, employees, governments, trade associations, unions, and other parties. It administers some 40,000 disputes annually. Its Election Department provides impartial administration of elections of many types, and it will assist in drafting ballots, implementing the election itself, and certifying results. Its Eastman Arbitration Library provides reference and research assistance to members. Publishes the *Arbitration Journal* and *Arbitration Times*.

American Enterprise Institute for Public Policy Research
1150 Seventeenth Street, NW
Washington, DC 20036
(202) 862-5800

Sponsors research and education in areas such as economic policy, fiscal policy, government regulations, health policy, international issues, legislative analysis, and political and social processes. Has published over 2,000 titles. Typical of the information disseminated by the institute are studies on international business services (accounting, advertising, law); an analysis of America's trade deficit; a comparison of trade associations in the U.S. and Japan; future structure of the housing-finance system; personal resources for retirement; and effects of tax policy on farm exports. Publishes *Public Opinion*.

Bank Administration Institute
60 Gould Center
Rolling Meadows, IL 60008
(312) 228-6200

An association of community banks, money-center banks, and other financial institutions. It is a source of professional development and improvement of bank performance in human resources, accounting, marketing, and technology. Consists of commissions on Accounting and Finance, Audit, Corporate Services and Technology, Human Resources, Retail Financial Services, Security, Tax, Washington Liaison, and others. Provides a video training program for tellers, a testing instrument to measure employee attitudes, and computer software for analyzing bank costs. Its School for Bank Administration provides courses of study in operations, community-bank management, and audit and financial management for bankers. Publishes handbooks and guides on subjects including asset quality control, cost analysis, customer service, disaster recovery, financial-information systems, internal audits, mergers, record retention, and selecting software. Collects and publishes annual data on electronic fund transfers and a directory of retail delivery-system suppliers. Publishes *Bank Administration*.

Brookings Institution

1775 Massachusetts Avenue, NW
Washington, DC 20036
(202) 797-6000

A research organization that collects data on U.S. domestic and foreign policy issues. Its research, education, and publication responsibilities are fulfilled through various programs: Economic Studies, Foreign Policy Studies, and Governmental Studies; its Center for Public Policy Education and Social Science Computation Center; and its Publication Program. Its Center for Public Policy Education has held seminars for corporate executives, including sessions on business conditions in Europe and in Japan and a six-day course on understanding the operations of the federal government. The institution publishes data and other information on such matters as composition of the U.S. external deficit, consequences of mergers and takeovers, debt ratios for heavily indebted countries, economic and social forces affecting women in the workforce, exchange value of the dollar, inflation rates, the investment climate in China, projected income and assets of the elderly, regional U.S. differences in wages and personal income growth, state and local use of sales-tax income, and the U.S. savings-and-loan crisis. It funds its research from grants received from corporations, private foundations, government, individuals, and its own endowment income. Publishes *Brookings Review*.

Conference Board

845 Third Avenue
New York, NY 10022
(212) 759-0900

A research and education organization that seeks to assist business leaders in decision making. Receives financial support from more than 3,600 businesses, known as associates, from all over the world. Executives of associate firms have access to the board's business library and to its information service, which responds to requests for information and publications. The board collects data and performs analyses in five areas: consumer research (market trends, consumer income and expenditures), corporate relations (organizational behavior, business ethics, corporate contributions to society, corporate image), economic environment (national and international economic trends), human resources (personnel benefits, compensation, training), and management (organizational structure, management techniques). Collects and publishes monthly data on the leading economic indicators, its Conference Board diffusion index, business executives' forecasts for the economy, key determinants of profit margins, help-wanted advertising indexes, consumer expectations for the economy, business-cycle indicators, and other intelligence. It regularly reports on the expenditures for new plants and equipment in the manufacturing and investor-owned utility industries. Publishes *Across the Board*.

Eno Foundation for Transportation
Box 2055
Westport, CT 06880
(203) 227-4852

Conducts and commissions research, disseminates information, and supports education in the design, operation, planning, and regulation of transportation. Publishes *Transportation Quarterly* and a series of reports on its research findings. For example, findings cover the solutions to parking and traffic problems at hospitals and special events, methods and issues in intermodal transportation of freight, the effects of airline deregulation, and trends in commuting patterns. *Transportation in America* is an annual publication that provides and analyzes statistical descriptions of transportation in the U.S.

Financial Analysts Federation
P. O. Box 3726
Charlottesville, VA 22903
(804) 977-8977 Fax (804) 977-1103

Consists of more than 50 financial analysts societies in the U.S. and Canada. Each member group is a professional society for those professionals in investment administration, portfolio management, or security analysis. Affiliated with the Institute of Chartered Financial Analysts, which awards the professional designation of "Chartered Financial Analyst." The institute's Research Foundation publishes analyses covering such matters as Canadian stocks and bonds from 1950 to 1987, the effect of interest-rate changes on pension-fund liabilities, and strategies for selecting excellent stock investments. For investment practitioners working in international markets, the federation has established the International Society of Financial Analysts, which provides continuing education and cooperative programs with investment organizations outside the U.S. Publishes *Financial Analysts Journal*.

Investment Company Institute
1600 M Street, NW
Washington, DC 20036
(202) 293-7700

A trade association of mutual-fund companies, their investment advisors and underwriters, unit investment trusts, and closed-end funds. Provides information and support for its members and their clients regarding advertising, legislation, regulation, research, statistics, and other matters dealing with mutual funds. Has a Speaker Referral Service to identify mutual-fund executives to address groups. Collects and publishes directory information on mutual funds. Publishes *Trends in Mutual Fund Activity*, which provides monthly data on sales, exchanges, redemptions, assets, and holdings of funds, and the annual *Mutual Fund Fact Book*, which includes data on sales, assets, performance, and other facts and figures for the industry.

National Association of Credit Management
520 Eighth Avenue
New York, NY 10018
(212) 947-5070

Federation of local credit-management organizations in the U.S. with an international branch in Europe. Members of the local affiliates are credit and finance executives in financial institutions, manufacturing, wholesaling, and service organizations. Compiles and publishes an annual handbook of credit and commercial law. Sells standard forms that comply with federal and state laws for such transactions as credit applications, financial statements, and trade acceptances. Publishes *C&M*.

National Council of Savings Institutions
1101 Fifteenth Street, NW
Washington, DC 20005
(202) 857-3100

An organization of savings institutions. Its purpose is to help savings-and-loan executives keep their industry competitive by appropriately affecting U.S. government policy toward the industry. It seeks to influence the Federal Deposit Insurance Corporation, Federal Reserve Board, and Securities and Exchange Commission. Toward this end, the council makes recommendations on pending legislation, establishes task forces, and files lawsuits. The council provides continuing education to executives of its members by holding conferences such as the Consumer Compliance Workshop, Government Affairs Roundtable, National Human Resources Conference, National Mortgage Conference, and National Operations Conference and Exhibit. It publishes a monthly analysis of savings-and-loans stocks and an annual savings institutions fact book that includes data on balance sheets, income statements, market shares, mortgage flows, and other facts. Publishes *Bottomline*.

RAND Corporation
P. O. Box 2138
1700 Main Street
Santa Monica, CA 90406
(213) 393-0411

Research organization that focuses on planning and policy in domestic and foreign affairs. Sources of funding for its research include local, state, and U.S. governments, private foundations, and its own funds. Annually publishes hundreds of books, notes, papers, and reports on a wide variety of topics. Recent studies have gathered data and other information about the cable-television market, aircraft-cost estimates, dental-utilization patterns, government regulations on toxic substances, improving automobile safety, multiple damages in antitrust cases, office innovation, price caps on telecommunications services, and many materials dealing with U.S. defense policy and the defense industry. Publishes *Selected RAND Abstracts*.

Tax Foundation
One Thomas Circle, NW
Washington, DC 20005
(202) 822-9050

Research and education organization that monitors government tax and fiscal policies. Publishes *Tax Features*, which analyzes federal tax policies and federal, state, and local fiscal activities. Also publishes *Facts and Figures on Government Finance*, which provides statistics on federal, state, and local tax and spending activity. Its public-finance researchers and library staff are available to executives, tax analysts, economists, and other specialists of member organizations via an information hotline.

United States League of Savings Institutions
111 E. Wacker Drive
Chicago, IL 60601
(312) 644-3100

A trade organization of savings institutions. It develops products, services, and forecasts to assist the day-to-day operations and planning of the institutions. Develops and publishes monthly forecasts on interest rates, inflation, and federal economic policy. Produces a biennial home-buyers survey and an annual savers survey that report geographic, demographic, and other trends. Collects operations statistics from about 2,000 savings institutions and lending data from about 1,000 institutions. Publishes about a dozen periodicals dealing with the thrift industry. It is associated with Savings Leagues in individual states. Sponsors many meetings, such as the Mergers and Acquisitions Clinic, National Consumer Lending Conference, and the Real Estate Consumer Lending Compliance Clinic. Publishes *Savings Institutions*, which has monthly columns on appraisal, investment management, the money market, real-estate finance, and retail funds.

H

Directory of Selected Federal Departments and Agencies

Information Contained in Section H

Departments and agencies of the federal government are rich sources of information. This section provides a selection of such offices. Many of the listings below consist of specific offices found within large agencies or departments. An example is the Office of Business Liaison, which is listed under the Department of Commerce. Other entries name an entire agency, like the Commodity Futures Trading Commission, especially if all the activities of the agency would be of interest to the business community. Some of the offices are in familiar cabinet departments, while others are components of agencies that are unknown to many Americans. A few of the lesser-known agencies are only indirect members of the federal government and might be called quasi-governmental agencies. In any case, each of these offices provides information and/or services to the business community.

This list is selective. It gives an idea of the kinds of information and services available from the federal government. Keep in mind that a complex institution like the federal government is constantly changing and that some of the offices listed here might alter the nature of their services from time to time. Also, offices go out of existence, and new ones are formed. See the paragraph "For Further Information," below.

For each office there has been included:

- the agency or department's name
- for some entries, the name of a specific office (or administration, program, service, or other component of the agency or department)
- an address
- a telephone number
- for some entries, how many local offices the agency or department has across the U.S.
- a brief example of the office's activities, data collected, or services available

425

Sources of Information

This information has been culled from many publications supplied by individual offices of the federal government. Two general sources also have been used:

> *United States Government Manual, 1989/90*. Washington, DC: Office of the Federal Register, National Archives and Records Administration, 1989.
>
> *Statistical Abstract of the United States 1989*. Washington, DC: U.S. Department of Commerce, 1989.

For Further Information

For an office listed here, you can use the telephone number or address provided to get more information about it. One of the sources, the *United States Government Manual, 1989/90*, will tell you more about the office, too, and perhaps list its regional outlets. Your local telephone directory might provide a federal-information telephone number for your area, through which you would be able to find more about a federal office without contacting Washington, DC. Many public and college libraries, also, have the means to help you obtain information about a federal office. There are city, county, municipal, and state offices that provide information and services to the business community. The public library, the chamber of commerce, and your colleagues are other sources.

Commodity Futures Trading Commission
2033 K. Street, NW
Washington, DC 20581
(202) 254-8630

Regulates futures trading on major U.S. exchanges, public brokerage houses, and individuals associated with the sales of futures contracts. Collects and publishes data, such as monthly commodity-markets reports covering puts and calls, concentration ratios, long and short positions, number of traders, and open interest.

Congress of the U.S., Government Printing Office
North Capitol and H Streets, NW
Washington, DC 20401
(202) 275-2701

Administers printing, binding, and distribution orders placed by the Congress and federal agencies for their publications. It does some of the printing and binding itself and contracts the rest of its orders, about 80 percent, to commercial suppliers of printing and binding. Its Printing Procurement Offices (in Washington DC, and 13 other cities) handle inquiries from firms wishing to do business with the Government Printing Office. For prospective suppliers, publishes a manual of contract provisions and terms, and a guide for doing business with the office.

Congress of the U. S., Office of Technology Assessment

600 Pennsylvania Avenue, SE
Washington, DC 20510
(202) 224-9241

A planning body that helps Congress be aware of the impact of the country's policies on the application of new technology. In the process of fulfilling this responsibility, it does research in such areas as communication and information technologies, employment, the environment, foods, health, international commerce, and transportation. Data available from the published reports of this research cover items such as bond issues, financial performance, land use, and management practices in airport administration; costs, length of stay, age and sex distribution for patients in intensive-care units; U.S. waterborne foreign-trade liner service, shipyard orders by nation, and the changing size of maritime fleets by nation; financial statistics for biotechnology companies and projected delivery dates of new technologies over the next decade for human therapeutic products.

Consumer Product Safety Commission

5401 Westbard Avenue
Bethesda, MD 20816
(301) 492-6580
There are five regional and satellite offices.

Regulates the safety of consumer products by establishing and encouraging the development of product standards, banning unsafe products, and requiring manufacturers to report and correct safety defects. Has a hotline (800-638-2772) for reporting potentially hazardous products and for getting information about recalled products. Publishes many booklets on how to use products safely. Issues a retailer's guide, which outlines the businessperson's legal responsibilities in handling products covered by the Consumer Products Safety Act, Federal Hazardous Substances Act, Flammable Fabrics Act, and Poison Prevention Packaging Act. Its National Electronic Injury Surveillance System collects and produces data on injuries associated with various consumer products. The data indicate the number of injuries caused by various categories of product and these injuries are arranged by the age and sex of injured consumers and the average severity of injuries.

Department of Agriculture, Agricultural Marketing Service

P. O. Box 96456
Washington, DC 20090
(202) 447-8999

Creates grade standards for more than 300 agricultural products. Regulates such activity as fair-trading practices in the marketing of fruits and vegetables; truth in seed labeling and advertising; inspections of certain egg-processing facilities; and maintenance of stable prices and supplies in milk, fruit, vegetable, and other markets. Collects and publishes data on demand, location, movement, prices, quality, and supply of agricultural products in specific geographic areas. Collects and publishes names of important contact people in various federal agencies involved in managing food-quality assurance programs.

Department of Agriculture, Agricultural Research Service
Beltsville, MD 20705
(301) 344-2264
There are eight area offices.

Conducts basic and applied agricultural research, usually in cooperation with universities, other federal agencies, or private organizations. Publishes quarterly data on the Consumer Price Index for about 50 categories of products, services, and consumer expenses. Publishes quarterly cost of food data, by type of family, age and sex of consumers, and type of food budget.

Department of Agriculture, Economic Research Service
Washington, DC 20005
(202) 786-1504

Performs research on the marketing and production of agricultural goods, on foreign agriculture and trade, and on the performance of the U.S. agricultural industry. Collects and publishes many statistics. This includes periodic outlook reports on aquaculture, cotton and wool, dairy, feed, livestock and poultry, tobacco, and other agricultural commodities. Also issues, generally on a monthly schedule, forecasts on farm income and food prices, and annual reports on U.S. exports and imports, giving units and dollar value of each commodity, by nation.

Department of Agriculture, Farmers Home Administration
Fourteenth Street and Independence Avenue, SW
Washington, DC 20250
(202) 447-4323
There are 2,200 local county and district offices.

Makes loans available to those who might not be able to get credit elsewhere. The loans cover such activity as operation of family-sized farms; establishment, by young people, of businesses in rural America; recovery of farmers and ranchers from natural disasters; puchasing housing in rural communities; and establishment or improvement of business enterprises in rural communities run by public, private, or coopertave associations. Collects and publishes monthly data, by state, on the number of loan applications received, bankruptcies, and foreclosures.

Department of Agriculture, Federal Crop Insurance Corporation
Fourteenth Street and Independence Avenue, SW
Washington, DC 20250
(202) 447-6795
There are 25 field offices.

Insures some crop losses due to such events as adverse weather conditions and plant disease. There are limitations, such as losses cause by neglect and low prices. The corporation delegates some of its sales and services to private insurance companies.

Department of Agriculture, National Agricultural Statistics Service
Washington, DC 20005
(202) 786-1504
There are 44 regional offices.

Compiles and publishes statistics on agricultural commodities and products, covering price, production, supply, and other data. Its regional offices collect and disseminate local agricultural data. Crop reports estimate the acreage to be planted each year and forecasts yields. Livestock and poultry reports estimate the number of animals on farms. Dairy reports give data on cows and milk products. Price reports tabulate prices received by farmers. Publishes a directory of state statisticians who can provide state or county agricultural data and product specialists who can help the farmer obtain data on a specific product.

Department of Agriculture, Rural Electrical Administration
Fourteenth Street and Independence Avenue, SW
Washington, DC 20250
(202) 382-1255

Provides loans and assists in seeking loans from other organizations for rural electric and telephone utilities. Collects and publishes data that list former borrowers from the administration, giving amount of loan paid, interest paid, and date paid in full. Lists companies that are current borrowers, giving loan, operating, and other financial data. Provides average operating expenses by size of electric utility system and average residential electric bills, by state.

Department of Commerce, Bureau of the Census
Washington, DC 20233
(301) 763-4040
There are 12 regional offices.

Collects and publishes a large variety of census data. Its regional offices have some data not readily located in the bureau's published reports. Depending on the information needed, data may be available for the whole nation and for various areas, such as states, counties, cities, or villages. Complete data for the housing and population census appear every ten years, while economic census reports are published every five years. Housing data cover such matters as structural characteristics, equipment and plumbing facilities, fuel and financial characteristics, occupancy, rent, owner costs, prices asked and received, space utilization, and mortgage characteristics of housing units. Economic census data are available for the agricultural, construction, manufacturing, retail-trade, service, transportation, and wholesale-trade industries. Reports also cover businesses owned by minorities and women. Economic data include such items as number of business establishments, number of employees, types of businesses, expenses, inventory, payroll, and sales. Economic data published by the bureau also describes monthly import and export activity of the U.S., by commodity and nation.

Department of Commerce, Bureau of Economic Analysis
Fourteenth Street and Constitution Avenue, NW
Washington, DC 20230
(202) 523-0777

Publishes data that analyzes business and economic activities in the U.S. This includes monthly national data on personal income, disposition of income, exports and imports by type of good, banking and credit, retail sales, employment, and manufacturing by type of industry. Provides monthly graphs of national cyclical economic processes over the past 25 years, covering costs, employment, income, prices, production, and other data, and tabular historical data over the past 35 years for various national economic indicators. Publishes composite balance sheet and other data by nation and industry for nations having direct investments in the U.S. Publishes composite balance sheet and other data by nation and industry for U.S. direct investments in other nations.

Department of Commerce, Economic Development Administration
Fourteenth Street and Constitution Avenue, NW
Washington, DC 20230
(202) 377-5113
There are 51 regional offices.

Provides loan guarantees, planning grants, public works grants, technical assistance, and other services that might help economically distressed areas solve their commercial and industrial problems. Some of this aid is available to public and private nonprofit organizations, industrial and commercial firms, and businesses owned by Native Americans. Contracts with various organizations for technical assistance reports, available to the public, on such matters as how to develop and maintain an industrial park, the feasibility of certain business ventures in specific geographic areas (for example, lactic-acid production in McHenry County, North Dakota), and the assessment of specific industries.

Department of Commerce, International Trade Administration
Fourteenth Street and Constitution Avenue, NW
Washington, DC 20230
(202) 377-3808
There are 48 district offices.

Provides marketing assistance to U.S. businesses involved in international trade. Publishes a series of competitive assessments that are statistical and narrative forecasts, by industry, of worldwide competitors to the U.S. Produces statistical surveys of the market potential for specific U.S. products in specific nations abroad. Publishes many guides and handbooks that advise U.S. firms on doing business outside the U.S. Has Export Development Offices throughout the world that aid U.S. exporters by providing facilities for exhibitions of products and meetings with foreign business people. Operates a clearinghouse for U.S. suppliers and export trading companies. It will help suppliers of products and exporters get in contact with each other. Its district offices provide counseling services to help U.S. firms evaluate potential export markets.

Department of Commerce, Minority Business Development Agency

Fourteenth Street and Constitution Avenue, NW
Washington, DC 20230
(202) 377-1936
There are 10 district or regional offices and about 100 Minority Business Development Centers.

The Minority Business Development Centers provide managerial, marketing, and technical assistance as well as counseling and referral to minority businesses and to minority entrepreneurs planning to start businesses. Assistance is available for acquisition analysis, advertising, budgeting, compilation of financial statements, construction-bid preparation, cost accounting, long-range planning, office management, tax planning, writing loan proposals, and other business-management concerns. The agency also awards grants to state and local agencies, business-development organizations, and trade associations to help them assist minority-owned businesses.

Department of Commerce, National Technical Information Service

5285 Port Royal Road
Springfield, VA 22161
(703) 487-4600

This is the major publisher of research, development, and engineering reports about projects funded by U.S. government agencies and some projects administered by foreign organizations. It provides a bimonthly index of these reports. The service sells computer software and computerized data files that have been created by various federal offices, and it publishes annual directories of these materials. It also provides licensing of federally owned patents.

Department of Commerce, Office of Business Liaison

Fourteenth Street and Constitution Avenue, NW
Washington, DC 20230
(202) 377-3176

Responsible for managing communications between the business community and all offices of the Department of Commerce. The office's Business Assistance Program answers telephone questions on government policies, programs, and services for the business community, or provides the name of the federal office that can answer the question.

Department of Commerce, Office of Small and Disadvantaged Business Utilization
Fourteenth Street and Constitution Avenue, NW
Washington, DC 20230
(202) 377-5614

Helps small or disadvantaged businesses obtain a fair share of the Department of Commerce's procurement contracts. There are similar offices in other departments of the federal government. This particular office solicits capability statements from qualified businesses, and then the statements are used to create lists of potential suppliers for the department. The department publishes a handbook covering such matters as a list of products and services the department buys, a directory of its procurement offices, how to get on its solicitation mailing lists and commodity index file, and how to submit unsolicited proposals.

Department of Commerce, Patent and Trademark Office
Washington, DC 20231
(703) 557-3341

This is the office with which to file patent applications and trademark registrations. It maintains a selected list of patent attorneys and agents and sells copies of patent descriptions. Sixty-two Patent Depository libraries throughout the country are available for patent searching. Publishes annual indexes of patents and trademarks. Publishes weekly lists of patents granted and trademarks registered.

Department of Defense
The Pentagon
Washington, DC 20301
(202) 545-6700

A major buyer of products and services from businesses. Businesses can file Solicitation Mailing List and Bidder's Mailing List application forms with the individual defense activities of interest. Department publications advise on how to do business with the military, list department contract and procurement administrators, and identify small-business specialists in each state.

Department of Justice, Antitrust Division
Tenth Street and Pennsylvania Avenue, NW
Washington, DC 20530
(202) 633-2421
There are seven field offices.

Enforces federal antitrust laws that cover almost every business and industry. Its staff of attorneys and paralegals handle mail and telephone complaints from business people and consumers regarding possible obstructions of free enterprise. Provides a business review service for businesses that need the division's advice on whether proposed activities might violate antitrust regulations. Publishes Department of Justice guidelines on matters such as joint ventures and mergers.

Department of Labor, Bureau of Labor Statistics
200 Constitution Avenue, NW
Washington, DC 20210
(202) 523-1327
There are eight regional offices.

Collects, analyzes, and publishes comprehensive statistics about the labor economics of the U.S., including consumer expenditures, consumer prices, earnings, economic projections, employee benefits, employment, labor utilization, level of education of the workforce, occupational health and safety, productivity, unemployment, and wages. Most of these data are available both in national compilations and by U.S. geographical region. Some of the data is available on microcomputer disks. The bureau also collects employment, price, unemployment, and wage data for other nations. It maintains a public file of collective-bargaining agreements.

Department of Labor, Employment and Training Administration, Federal Unemployment Insurance Service
200 Constitution Avenue, NW
Washington, DC 20210
(202) 535-0600

Reviews state unemployment-insurance practices and provides national guidance for development of state unemployment-insurance programs. Collects and publishes data that identify areas of high unemployment (and thus possible eligibility for special consideration in the awarding of certain federal contracts), that compare state unemployment-insurance laws, and that tally state unemployment claims filed and claims receiving benefits.

Department of Labor, Employment Standards Administration
200 Constitution Avenue, NW
Washington, DC 20210
(202) 523-7503
There are ten regional offices.

Administers laws and regulations covering employment standards through its four components: Office of Federal Contract Compliance Programs; Office of Management, Administration, and Planning; Office of Workers' Compensation; and the Wage and Hour Division. Collects and publishes listings of the features of each state's workers' compensation program, as well as state program data, such as program cash balance and income, amount of benefits paid, claims filed, and total workforce.

Department of Labor, Occupational Safety and Health Administration
200 Constitution Avenue, NW
Washington, DC 20210
(202) 523-8017
There are 10 regional and 72 area offices.

Issues regulations and conducts inspections to prevent and reduce health and safety hazards in the workplace. Develops health and safety standards in four areas: general industry, agriculture, construction, and the maritime industries. Provides free consultation assistance to employers on occupational health-and-safety matters. Area office personnel are available for speeches and technical advice. OSHA offers basic and advanced courses in health and safety and also disseminates publications that suggest how businesses can monitor health and safety programs, what to expect from OSHA inspections, and how an employee can obtain access to employer exposure and medical records. Collects and publishes data on health and safety cases, such as data on occupational fatalities in some industries.

Department of Labor, Office of Labor Management Standards
200 Constitution Avenue, NW
Washington, DC 20210
(202) 523-7320
There are 13 area offices.

Administers statutes that affect about 50,000 unions. The statutes cover union administrative procedures, financial transactions, and workers' rights. Collects and publishes listings of labor organizations (including their assets, directory information, and number of member unions) and directories of labor relations consultants.

Department of Transportation, Federal Highway Administration
400 Seventh Street, SW
Washington, DC 20590
(202) 366-0630
There are ten regional offices.

Administers financial-assistance programs to states for highway construction, improvement, and safety. Collects and publishes data on monthly gasoline consumption by state; motor vehicle miles traveled by type of road and geographic area; for the entire country, how traffic is distributed by hour, day of week, and season. Occasionally publishes state gasoline-tax rates and receipts, number of state motor-vehicle registrations; and distribution of motor-vehicle trips in the U.S. according to purpose of the trip and type of motor vehicle.

Department of Transportation, Urban Mass Transportation Administration
400 Seventh Street, SW
Washington, DC 20590
(202) 426-4043

Assists state and local governments in meeting urban mass-transit needs and encourages the involvement of private firms in providing urban mass-transportation services. Administers a grants program, and as part of the grantees' reporting process the administration collects data on mass transit. It publishes financial, operation, and performance data for mass-transit systems by mode of transportation and by size of the system. It publishes these data also for individual transit systems, covering such matters as accidents, age of equipment, energy consumption, miles traveled, performance indicators, and services supplied.

Department of the Treasury, Internal Revenue Service
1111 Constitution Avenue, NW
Washington, DC 20224
(202) 566-5000
There are 7 regional and 64 district offices.

In addition to administering Internal Revenue statutes, the service collects and publishes extensive tax data. These include annual compilations of individual income-tax returns covering such items as sources of income; number and type of exemptions taken; annual compilations of corporate income-tax returns that list, by industry, assets, credits taken, depreciation deductions, distributions to shareholders, income, and other statistics; annual compilations of partnership income-tax returns; and a 1957–1984 compilation of proprietorship income-tax returns.

Department of the Treasury, Office of the Comptroller of the Currency
409 L'Énfant Plaza, SW
Washington, DC 22019
(202) 447-1800

Administers about 4,600 national and District of Columbia banks. Collects and publishes quarterly data on assets, capital accounts, and liabilities. Tallies for each state the deposits, leases, and loans generated by the national banks.

Department of the Treasury, Office of Thrift Supervision
1700 G Street, NW
Washington, DC 20552
(202) 906-6000
There are 12 regional offices.

The Financial Institutions Reform, Recovery, and Enforcement Act of 1989 assigns regulatory and oversight responsibility for thrift institutions to this office. The OTS collects and publishes such data as lending activity, average mortgage interest rates, mortgage foreclosures, balance sheet data, and other statistics on thrift institutions. For information on the thrifts concerning deposit insurance, consult the Federal Deposit Insurance Corporation, Savings Association Insurance Fund.

Environmental Protection Agency
401 M Street, SW
Washington, DC 20460
(202) 382-2090
There are ten regional offices.

Monitors, enforces, and sets standards to prevent and control pollution. Supports antipollution research by both public and private groups. Collects and publishes health assessments on various pollutants, reporting for each environmental sources, emission sources, environmental levels, effects on humans and other life, and toxicity levels. Provides listings of typical-pollutant-release data for many specific industry sources, such as automobile body incineration, baking bread, dry cleaning, graphic arts material, and roofing.

Export-Import Bank of the United States
811 Vermont Avenue, NW
Washington, DC 20571
(202) 566-8990

Also known as Eximbank. Provides loans and loan guarantees to foreign buyers of U.S. exports. Administers an export-credit insurance program. These activities help American exporters remain competitive in the world market. One of its programs focuses on support for the exports of small U.S. businesses. Publishes annual data on dollars loaned, guaranteed, or put into export insurance, all arranged by target nations. Releases listings of each of its loans and loan guarantees, indicating the name of the foreign supplier, the loan amount, and the interest rate.

Farm Credit Administration
1501 Farm Credit Drive
McLean, VA 22102
(703) 883-4000

Regulates the federal land banks and other credit associations and cooperatives that make loans to farmers, rural homeowners, farm-related businesses, and commercial fishermen. Collects and publishes data, by state or district, such as loan volume, earnings, and property acquired by loan liquidation. Publishes national data on the characteristics of typical borrowers from its banks and associations, including age, loan balance, and debt-to-asset ratio of borrower.

Federal Deposit Insurance Corporation
550 Seventeenth Street, NW
Washington, DC 20429
(202) 393-8400
There are 14 regional offices.

Insures individual deposits up to $100,000 in nationally chartered banks and thrift institutions and in state-chartered banks. As provided by the Financial

Institutions Reform, Recovery, and Enforcement Act of 1989, the FDIC encompasses the Savings Association Insurance Fund for thrift institutions and the Bank Insurance Fund for banks. The FDIC collects and publishes annual data on the assets, income, and liabilities of its financial institutions along with other information on these banks and thrifts.

Federal Mediation and Conciliation Service
2100 K Street, NW
Washington, DC 20427
(202) 653-5290
There are two regional offices.

Provides arbitrators and mediators to help resolve labor-management disputes in any industry (except airline and rail industries) significantly affecting interstate commerce. Also administers a preventive-mediation program. Operates a grant program that funds the activities of labor-management committees set up at the worksite, industry, or national levels. Publishes some case studies of successful cases handled by the service. Collects and publishes data on arbitrators' typical fees and average days per case, including a breakdown of arbitration into five stages of activity.

Federal Reserve System, Board of Governors
Twentieth and C Streets, NW
Washington, DC 20551
(202) 452-3000
There are 12 regional Federal Reserve Banks.

Regulates the commercial-banking system and makes national policy on credit conditions and monetary supply. Collects and publishes monthly data on national money figures such as reserves and borrowings of depository institutions, Federal Reserve Bank interest rates, tallies of commercial-bank loans and securities, assets and liabilities of the commercial-banking industry, commercial paper and bankers dollar acceptances outstanding, tallies of new security issues (corporate and government), total nonfarm business expenditures on new plant and equipment, and total outstanding consumer installment credit.

Federal Trade Commission
Pennsylvania Avenue at Sixth Street, NW
Washington, DC 20580
(202) 326-2222
There are ten regional offices.

Promotes fair business competition by such activities as enforcing the Fair Credit Reporting Act, the Federal Trade Commission Franchise and Business Opportunities Rule, the Federal Trade Commission Mail Order Rule, and the Truth in Lending Act and by investigating credit advertising and marketing practices that may be unfairly restricting business competition. Enforces the Hart-Scott-Rodino Antitrust Improvements Act, under which certain companies planning mergers must first notify the commission. Consumers and businesses can register complaints with the commission about deceptive advertising and marketing practices and about laws and regulations they feel are hindering business activity. Produces manuals for businesses, and its regional offices sponsor conferences for small businesses on how to comply with the laws and regulations it enforces. Collects and publishes data on the relationship between competition and business practices in specific industries.

General Accounting Office
441 G Street, NW
Washington, DC 20548
(202) 275-2812
There are 15 regional offices.

Provides assistance to the U.S. Congress in carrying out various legislative responsibilities. This includes audit authority over federal agencies and their contractors. It specifies the accounting principles and standards to be followed by federal agencies. Its Office of the General Council issues decisions of the U.S. comptroller general on claims of bidders or contractors concerning dealings with federal agencies. Maintains the Congressional Information Sources Inventories database, which is available to the public in paper format. The database is an index to annual and other regularly occurring reports that federal offices are required by law to produce. Statistics in such reports cover a wide variety of items, including employee-owned firms receiving federal loan guarantees, federal pension plans, motor-vehicle fuel consumption, oil and gas leasing and exploration, and state and local taxes. The office also collects and publishes listings of state auditor offices, giving directory information and data on each office's funding sources and staff.

General Services Administration, Business Service Center Program
General Services Building
Eighteenth and F Streets, NW
Washington, DC 20405
(202) 566-1201
There are ten regional Business Service Centers.

Provides listings of procurement offices for doing business with various federal agencies. The regional Business Service Centers provide advice on how to sell to the federal government, including how to get on bidders' mailing lists and how to obtain government specifications and standards. Publishes a guide to doing business with the federal government.

General Services Administration, Federal Information Centers Program
General Services Building
Eighteenth and F Streets, NW
Washington, DC 20405
(202) 472-1082
There are 47 regional Federal Information Centers.

By phoning or writing the nearest Federal Information Center, one can obtain information about federal agencies, programs, and information resources. The center's staff either directly answers questions or refers people to an appropriate expert. Especially useful for those who need information but do not know where to look for it.

Interstate Commerce Commission

Twelfth Street and Constitution Avenue, NW
Washington, DC 20423
(202) 275-7119

Regulates surface interstate transportation. This covers certification of carriers, quality of service, mergers and rates of such companies as bus lines, railroads, truckers, and water carriers. Collects and publishes data on the status of interstate commerce. For example, trips per year by type of railroad car, container and trailer loadings onto railroad cars per year, and annual earnings for some individual railroads and motor carriers. Publishes listings of the fees it charges for its interstate-carrier operation certificates.

National Credit Union Administration

1776 G Street, NW
Washington, DC 20456
(202) 357-1100
There are six regional offices.

Grants charters, insures, and supervises federal credit unions. Collects and publishes annual balance-sheet and operating ratios for its Central Liquidation Facility. Provides annual data on federal credit unions as a group, covering assets, loans outstanding, losses, and other figures. Publishes a directory of National Credit Unions.

National Labor Relations Board

1717 Pennsylvania Avenue, NW
Washington, DC 20570
(202) 632-4950
There are 52 field offices.

Administers laws that prohibit unfair labor practices by employers and unions. It takes action only upon written request to the board. It oversees elections that decide if a labor organization is to represent a collective-bargaining unit in a business having operations that substantially affect interstate commerce. This is determined through published listings of minimum standards for types of businesses, often in terms of annual dollar volume. The board publishes the results of collective-bargaining elections, giving number of votes for and against a union and the number of employees eligible to vote. The data cover both single-union and multiple-union elections.

National Mediation Board
1425 K Street, NW
Washington, DC 20572
(202) 523-5920

Assists in the resolution of labor-management disputes in the airline and rail industries. Collects and publishes information about these disputes. For example, listings of arbitrators, neutrals, and referees appointed to the disputes; which unions represent which categories of workers in these two industries; and the number of cases closed by the board according to categories of employees involved.

Securities and Exchange Commission
450 Fifth Street, NW
Washington, DC 20549
(202) 272-2650
There are nine regional offices.

Regulates securities markets and investment companies. Maintains registration information required from companies that make public offerings of securities. Represents the interests of public investors in companies facing reorganization proceedings. Collects and makes available to the public periodically updated data on public companies, including such information as narrative description of the company, balance sheet, income statement, listings of properties, plants, and subsidiaries, and names and salaries of officers and directors. Publishes monthly data on individual securities trades by insiders, giving amount and price of securities traded. For small businesses, provides a handbook of forms and regulations for filing data with the commission.

Small Business Administration
Imperial Building
1441 L Street, NW
Washington, DC 20416
(800) 268-5855
There are 118 regional offices.

The Small Business Administration (SBA) has many programs to encourage and support small-business development. Its Procurement Automated Source System (PASS) is a computerized service that matches small businesses with the procurement needs of federal agencies. When a small business registers with PASS, it describes its capabilities and products. It then will appear on vendor lists of government agencies that use PASS to find sources of services and products. The SBA's Office of Advocacy collects and publishes information about state and local activities, such as information-assistance programs to small businesses, legislative updates, state business-development programs, state procurement-assistance programs, local loan programs. This office also staffs the toll-free telephone number listed above to refer callers to the proper sources of information. The SBA loan program provides general business loans and special loans, the latter being for disaster assistance, energy conservation, pollution control, short-term financing for small-construction firms, and other exceptions to ordinary financing needs. The SBA arranges with privately operated small-business investment companies to make venture or risk investments in small businesses. The SBA Business Development Program offers, or arranges, counseling, courses, publications, and training through its Small Business Institutes on college campuses, Small Business Development Centers, and other sources. The SBA Office of International Trade administers the Export Information System. This system provides data on nations and products to help small-business owners decide if there is a market in other nations for their products and, if so, what competition they can expect.

U.S. International Development Cooperation Agency, Overseas Private Investment Corporation
1615 M Street, NW
Washington, DC 20527
(202) 457-7010

Helps U.S. companies invest in developing countries by indicating opportunities and providing financial assistance. The financial assistance consists of political-risk insurance, loans, and loan guarantees. It publishes listings of companies it has assisted, including the target nations, a description of the investment projects, and brief financing data.

U.S. International Trade Commission
500 E Street, NW
Washington, DC 20436
(202) 523-0161

Conducts investigations concerning imports sold in the U.S. at less than fair value and unfair practices used in importing goods into the U.S. A group of workers, a business, or an industry can petition the commission for such an investigation. Collects and publishes export and import data for selected industries. Publishes tariff schedules by product, giving rates of duty on each. Publishes the status and results of its investigation.

Selected Sources of Information Used to Compile Section H

1982 Census of Agriculture. Washington, DC: U.S. Department of Commerce, Bureau of the Census, 1984.

1982 Census of Construction Industries. Washington, DC: U.S. Department of Commerce, Bureau of the Census, 1985.

1982 Census of Manufacturers. Washington, DC: U.S. Department of Commerce, Bureau of the Census, 1985.

1982 Census of Retail Trade. Washington, DC: U.S. Department of Commerce, Bureau of the Census, 1984–1985.

1982 Census of Service Industries. Washington, DC: U.S. Department of Commerce, Bureau of the Census, 1984–1985.

1982 Census of Transportation. Washington, DC: U.S. Department of Commerce, Bureau of the Census, 1985.

1982 Census of Wholesale Trade. Washington, DC: U.S. Department of Commerce, 1984–1985.

1982 Survey of Minority-Owned Business Enterprises. Washington, DC: U.S. Department of Commerce, Bureau of the Census, 1979–1980.

1986 Urban Mass Transportation Administration Grants Assistance Programs Statistical Summaries. Washington, DC: U.S. Department of Transportation, Urban Mass Transportation Administration, 1987.

Airport System Development. Washington, DC: Congress of the U.S., Office of Technology Assessment, 1984.

All About OSHA. Washington, DC: U.S. Department of Labor, Occupational Safety and Health Administration, 1985.

Analysis of National and Regional Travel Trends 1986. U. S. Department of Transportation. Federal Highway Administration, 1986.

Annual Report. Washington, DC: Farm Credit Administration, 1981.

Antitrust Division Manual. Washington, DC: U.S. Department of Justice, Antitrust Division, 1987.

An Assessment of Maritime Trade and Technology. Washington, DC: Congress of the U.S. Office of Technology Assessment, 1983.

Basic Facts about Patents. Washington, DC: U.S. Department of Commerce, Patent and Trademark Office, 1988.

Basic Facts about Trademarks. Washington, DC: U.S. Department of Commerce, Patent and Trademark Office, 1988.

Business Conditions Digest. Washington, DC: U.S. Department of Commerce, Bureau of Economic Analysis, December 1988.

CBC'S Guide for Retailers. Washington, DC: Consumer Product Safety Commission, 1986.

Central Liquidity Facility 1987 Annual Report. Washington, DC: National Credit Union Administration, 1988.

Commitments of Traders in Commodities Futures of February 1988. Washington, DC: Commodity Futures Trading Commission, 1988.

Commitments of Traders in Commodities Options for August 1988. Washington, DC: Commodity Futures Trading Commission, 1988.

A Competitive Assessment of the U.S. Ethylene Industry. Washington, DC: U.S. Department of Commerce, International Trade Administration, 1986.

Compilation of Air Pollutant Emission Factors, Vol. 1. Washington, DC: Environmental Protection Agency, Office of Air Quality, 1985.

Contact Facilities Service Directory. Washington, DC: U.S. Department of Commerce, International Trade Administration, 1984.

CPI Detailed Report, December 1988. Washington, DC: U.S. Department of Labor, Bureau of Labor Statistics, 1988.

Directory of Computer Software/1988. Washington, DC: U.S. Department of Commerce, National Technical Information Service, 1988.

Directory of Computerized Data Files, 1988. Washington, DC: U.S. Department of Commerce, National Technical Information Service, 1988.

Directory of State Audit Organizations, 1985. Washington, DC: General Accounting Office, 1985.

Doing Business with the Federal Government. Washington, DC: General Services Administration, 1986.

ESA Orientation Booklet. Washington, DC: U.S. Department of Labor, Employment Standards Administration, 1987.

An Examination of Declining UI Claims During the 1980s. Draft Final Report. Washington, DC: U.S. Department of Labor Employment and Training Administration, Federal Unemployment Insurance Service, 1988.

Export Development Offices and Facilities. Washington, DC: U.S. Department of Commerce, International Trade Administration, 1984.

Export-Import Bank of the United States. 1987 Annual Report. Washington, DC: Export-Import Bank of the U.S., 1988.

Export Information System (XIS) User Manual. Washington, DC: Small Business Administration, 1988.

Export Trading Company Guidebook. Washington, DC: U.S. Department of Commerce, International Trade Administration, 1987.

Exporter's Guide to Federal Resources for Small Businesses. Washington, DC: Small Business Administration, 1988.

Family Economics Review. Washington, DC: U.S. Department of Agriculture, Agricultural Research Service, February 1989.

Farm and Housing Activity Report. Washington, DC: U.S. Department of Agriculture, Farmers Home Administration, December 1986.

Federal Buying Directory. Washington, DC: General Services Administration, 1985.

Federal Mediation and Conciliation Service. Thirty-ninth Annual Report. Fiscal Year 1986. Washington, DC: Federal Mediation and Conciliation Service, 1987.

Federal Reserve Bulletin. Washington, DC: Federal Reserve System, Board of Governors, March 1989 and February 1989.

Fees for Various Licensing and Related Services of the Interstate Commerce Commission. Washington, DC: Interstate Commerce Commission, 1988.

Fiftieth Annual Report. National Mediation Board. Washington, DC: National Mediation Board, 1984.

Foreign Agricultural Trade of the United States, Calendar Year 1986. Washington, DC: U.S. Department of Agriculture, Economic Research Service, 1987.

Foreign Direct Investment in the United States. Washington, DC: U.S. Department of Commerce, Bureau of Economic Analysis, 1987.

GAO: Responsibilities & Services to Congress. Washington, DC: General Accounting Office, 1985.

GAO: Working for the People. Washington, DC: General Accounting Office, 1986.

A General Description of the Corporation Source Book. Washington, DC: U.S. Department of the Treasury, Internal Revenue Service, 1986.

Government Reports Announcements and Index. Washington, DC: U.S. Department of Commerce, National Technical Information Service, 1 January, 1988.

Government-Wide Food Quality Assurance Program Interagency Functional Directory. Washington, DC: U.S. Department of Agriculture, Agricultural Marketing Service, 1984.

GPO: Contract Terms. Washington, DC: Congress of the U.S. Government Printing Office, 1987.

GPO: How to Do Business with the United States Government Printing Office. Washington, DC: Congress of the U.S. Government Printing Office, 1986.

A Guide to Basic Law and Procedures under the National Labor Relations Act. Washington, DC: National Labor Relations Board, 1987.

A Guide to the Federal Trade Commission. Washington, DC: Federal Trade Commission, 1987.

Health Assessment for Acrylonitrile, Final Report. Washington, DC: Environmental Protection Agency, Office of Health and Environmental Assessment, 1983.

How to Sell to the United States Department of Commerce. Washington, DC: U.S. Department of Commerce, 1988.

Industrial Parks: A Step by Step Guide. Washington, DC: U.S. Department of Commerce, Economic Development Administration, 1988.

Information Contacts. Washington, DC: U.S. Department of Agriculture, 1988.

Intensive Care Units (ICUs): Clinical Outcomes, Costs, and Decisionmaking. Washington, DC: Congress of the U.S., Office of Technology Assessment, 1984.

Interstate Commerce Commission Reports, Vol. 1, 2nd Session. Washington, DC: Interstate Commerce Commission, 1986.

MDBA Minority Business Development Centers. Washington, DC: U.S. Department of Commerce, Minority Business Development Agency, 1983.

Monthly Labor Review. Washington, DC: U.S. Department of Labor, Bureau of Labor Statistics, January 1989.

N. L. R. B. Election Report. Washington, DC: National Labor Relations Board, February 1987.

National Urban Mass Transportation Administration Statistics, 1985. Section 15 Annual Report. Washington, DC: U.S. Department of Transportation, Urban Mass Transportation Administration, 1987.

NEISS*Needs Your Help. Washington, DC: Consumer Product Safety Commission, 1987.

New Developments in Biotechnology: Ownership of Human Tissues and Cells. Washington, DC: Congress of the U.S., Office of Technology Assessment, 1987.

Official Summary of Security Transactions and Holdings. Washington, DC: Securities and Exchange Commission, November–December 1988.

Overseas Private Investment Corporation 1986 Annual Report. Washington, DC: U.S. International Development Cooperation Agency, Overseas Private Investment Corporation, 1987.

Producer Price Indexes Data for January 1989. Washington, DC: U.S. Department of Labor, Bureau of Labor Statistics, 1989.

Public Roads. Washington, DC: U.S. Department of Transportation, Federal Highway Administration, September 1988 and December 1988.

Publications of the U.S. Department of Labor. Washington, DC: U.S. Department of Labor, 1985.

Quarterly Journal. Washington, DC: U.S. Department of the Treasury, Office of the Comptroller of the Currency, December 1986.

Railroad TOFC/COFC Monitoring Study. Washington, DC: Interstate Commerce Commission, 1985.

Reports. Washington, DC: U.S. Department of Agriculture, Economic Research Service, Winter 1988–1989.

Requirements for Recurring Reports to Congress. Washington, DC: General Accounting Office, 1982.

SEC Monthly Statistical Review. Washington, DC: Securities and Exchange Commission, January 1989.

Selling to the Military. Washington, DC: U.S. Department of Defense, 1987.

The Small Business Answer Desk Directory. Washington, DC: Small Business Administration, 1986.

Small Business Informational Package. Washington, DC: Securities and Exchange Commission, 1988.

Small Business Specialists. Washington, DC: U.S. Department of Defense, 1986.

Source Book of Sole Proprietorship Returns 1957–1984. Washington, DC: U.S. Department of the Treasury, Internal Revenue Service, 1986.

State Workers' Compensation: Administration Profiles. Washington, DC: U.S. Department of Labor, Employment Standards Administration, 1987.

The States and Small Businesses: Programs and Activities. Washington, DC: Small Business Administration, 1986.

Statistical Abstract of the United States 1989. Washington, DC: U.S. Department of Commerce, 1989.

Statistical Report, Rural Electric Borrowers. Washington, DC: U.S. Department of Agriculture, Rural Electrical Administration, 1987.

Statistics on Banking 1985. Washington, DC: Federal Deposit Insurance Corporation, 1986.

Summary Description of Recent Studies and Publication. Washington, DC: U. S. Department of Commerce, Economic Development Administration, 1987.

Survey of Current Business. Washington, DC: U.S. Department of Commerce, Bureau of Economic Analysis, December 1988.

Tariff Schedules of the United States Annotated (1984). Washington, DC: U.S. International Trade Commission, 1983.

The U.S. Automobile Industry: Monthly Report on Selected Economic Indicators. Washington, DC: U.S. International Trade Commission, September, 1987.

U.S. Direct Investment Abroad. Washington, DC; U.S. Department of Commerce, Bureau of Economic Analysis, 1987.

U.S. Exports, Schedule E. Commodity by Country. Washington, DC: U.S. Department of Commerce, Bureau of the Census, October 1981.

U.S. General Imports, Schedule A. Commodity by Country. Washington, DC: U.S. Department of Commerce, Bureau of the Census, October 1981.

U.S. Government Printing Office 1985 Annual Report. Washington, DC: Congress of the U.S., Government Printing Office, 1986.

United States Government Manual, 1988/89. Washington, DC: Office of the Federal Register, National Archives and Records Administration, 1988.

United States International Trade Commission. Washington, DC: U.S. International Trade Commission, 1988.

User's Guide for NCUA's Financial Performance Report F-P-R. Washington, DC: National Credit Union Administration, 1987.

What Every Investor Should Know. Washington, DC: Securities and Exchange Commission, 1986.

You Can Do It! Washington, DC: General Services Administration, Office of Small and Disadvantaged Business Utilization, 1985.

Your Business and the SBA. Washington, DC: Small Business Administrator, 1987.

I

Additional Online Databases

Information Contained in Appendix I

This appendix lists supplementary online databases available from vendors other than those used as the primary sources in Sections E and F. Sections E and F describe databases available primarily from three major vendors of business databases: BRS Information Technologies, CompuServe Information Service, and Dialog Information Services.

A few of the databases in this appendix also are mentioned in Sections E and F, when, for example, a database is available both from Dialog and from one of the vendors listed below. However, most of the databases listed in this appendix are not described elsewhere in this book. There are plans to add many of these databases to Sections E and F in the next edition of the *Business Information Desk Reference*, thereby giving them more extensive coverage.

The listings below do not completely cover all the important sources. There are yet other vendors that the authors have not had time to include. They will also be considered for the next edition.

The online vendors included in this appendix are:

Data-Star
Dow Jones News/Retrieval
DRI/McGraw Hill
Mead Data Central
NewsNet
Orbit Search Service

What Should I Know About the Database Descriptions?

The descriptions in this appendix are very brief, usually just the name of the database and a concise phrase about its contents. Listed is a selection of business-related online databases from each vendor. Many of these vendors also offer other types of databases.

Sources of Information

The listings below were derived from vendor catalogs. The catalog name appears along with each vendor's databases.

For Further Information

If more information is needed, contact the vendor. The addresses and telephone numbers of these vendors are in Appendix III.

Database Descriptions

Vendor: Data-Star

Source of Information: *Services, Databases, Technical Catalogue.* London: Data-Star, 1990.

DATABASE	CONTENT
ABI/INFORM	Index to articles on a wide variety of business topics
AMERICAN BANKER	Full text of articles from the *American Banker* newspaper
BIOBUSINESS	Business aspects of biological and medical research
BUSINESS	Listings of worldwide contacts for marketing opportunities
BUSINESS/PROFESSIONAL SOFTWARE	Descriptions of software packages
CHEMICAL BUSINESS NEWSBASE	Summaries of chemical-industry news from annual reports, periodicals, press releases, and other sources
CHEMICAL INDUSTRY NOTES	Information that includes facilities, pricing, and sales in the chemical industry
CHEMICAL PLANTS WORLDWIDE	Directory of chemical-plant locations
CHEMICAL PRODUCTION AND TRADE STATISTICS	Worldwide production, import, and export data for chemicals
CHEMICAL SAFETY NEWSBASE	An index to documents on health and safety matters for the chemical industry

DATABASE	*CONTENT*
COMPENDEX	An index to engineering applications and research articles
COMPUTER DATABASE	Hardware and software evaluations
COUNTRY REPORT SERVICE	Analysis of the economies of 85 nations
DEVELOPMENT BUSINESS SCAN-A-BID DATABASE	Notices of third-world development projects
DIOGENES	Regulation of drugs, including information from unpublished sources and newsletters
DOW JONES NEWS SERVICE	News gathered from the Dow Jones News Wire Service and other sources
ENGINEERING & INDUSTRIAL SOFTWARE DIRECTORY	Directory of engineering and manufacturing software packages
FAIRBASE	Trade conventions, expositions, and fairs
FINANCIAL TIMES ABSTRACTS INFORMATION	An index to articles about European companies from the *Financial Times*
FINANCIAL TIMES BUSINESS REPORTS	News and analysis of new technologies, communications, and the financial markets
FOREIGN TRADE AND ECON ABSTRACTS	An index to articles on worldwide economic and trade developments
FROST & SULLIVAN MARKET RESEARCH REPORTS	Summaries of intelligence reports available from Frost & Sullivan
HARVARD BUSINESS REVIEW/ONLINE	Full text of *Harvard Business Review* articles
ICC STOCKBROKER RESEARCH	Full-text analyses of companies and industries, especially those in the U.K.
INDUSTRY DATA SOURCES	Financial, marketing, and statistical data for 65 industries

DATABASE	CONTENT
INSPEC	An index to articles about computers, electronics, information technology, and physics
INVESTEXT	Full text of intelligence reports on companies and industries
KYODO NEWS SERVICE	News of Japanese business activity
MANAGEMENT CONTENTS	An index to articles on a wide variety of management topics
MATERIALS BUSINESS FILE	Developments in metals, ceramics, and other materials
NTIS	Cites in-progress and final reports of U.S. government–sponsored research
P/E NEWS	Petroleum and energy news
PREDICASTS	Ten Predicasts databases covering statistics and other information on companies, industries, and products
TRADSTAT	Import and export data for 19 nations
VOLKSWAGEN	An index to articles about the automobile and transportation industries

Vendor: *Dow Jones News/Retrieval*

Source of Information: *Dow Jones News/Retrieval User's Guide*. Princeton, NJ: Dow Jones & Company, 1989.

DATABASE	CONTENT
BUSINESS AND FINANCE REPORT	Summaries of business news from the *Wall Street Journal* and other sources
CAPITAL MARKETS AND FINANCIAL FUTURES REPORT	Worldwide market activity
CORPORATE OWNERSHIP WATCH	Stock transactions of corporate insiders
DISCLOSURE DATABASE	Financial profiles of thousands of companies

DATABASE	*CONTENT*
DOW JONES ENHANCED CURRENT QUOTES	Current stock prices (delayed at least 15 minutes) from the American, Midwest, New York, Pacific, and Over-the-Counter exchanges
DOW JONES FUTURES AND INDEX QUOTES	Current quotes (delayed up to 30 minutes) and historical quotes on 80 commodities and futures
DOW JONES HISTORICAL QUOTES	Daily stock data for one year from major exchanges
DOW JONES NEWS	Full text of business news from *Barron's*, the *Wall Street Journal*, and other sources
DOW JONES NEWS/RETRIEVAL WORLD REPORT	Business and general news gathered from newswires and other sources
DOW JONES PROFESSIONAL INVESTOR REPORT	Newswire for stock-market stories
DOW JONES QUICKSEARCH	Permits simultaneous searching for company information in eight Dow Jones databases
DOW JONES REAL-TIME QUOTES	Current stock prices from major exchanges, displayed without the usual 15 minute delay. Requires special arrangements to be made with the online vendor.
DOW JONES TEXT-SEARCH SERVICES: BARRON'S	Full text of *Barron's* articles, 1987 to present
DOW JONES TEXT-SEARCH SERVICES: BUSINESS DATELINE	Full text of selected business articles from local and regional magazines and newspapers
DOW JONES TEXT-SEARCH SERVICES: BUSINESS LIBRARY	Full text of selected articles from *Forbes, Fortune,* and other major business publications
DOW JONES TEXT-SEARCH SERVICES: DOW JONES NEWS ARCHIVE	Summaries of selected articles from *Barron's*, the *Wall Street Journal*, and other sources, 1979 to present

DATABASE	*CONTENT*
DOW JONES TEXT-SEARCH SERVICES: THE WALL STREET JOURNAL	Full text of the *Wall Street Journal* articles, 1984 to present
DOW JONES TEXT-SEARCH SERVICES: THE WASHINGTON POST	Full text of selected articles from the *Washington Post*, 1984 to present
DOW JONES TRACKING SERVICE	News and financial information about companies
DUN'S FINANCIAL RECORDS	Profiles and financial reports on hundreds of thousands of companies
HISTORICAL DOW JONES AVERAGES	Daily Dow Jones averages since 1982
INNOVEST TECHNICAL ANALYSIS REPORTS	Stock-price forecasts
INVESTEXT	Full text of financial intelligence reports on companies and industries
JAPAN ECONOMIC DAILY	Worldwide and Japanese business news from Kyodo News International
MEDIA GENERAL FINANCIAL SERVICES	Price and volume data for stocks on the American, New York, and Over-the-Counter exchanges
MMS WEEKLY MARKET ANALYSIS	Currency, debt, and equity market analyses
NEWS/RETRIEVAL SYMBOLS DIRECTORY	Symbols for bonds (corporate, foreign, U.S.), mutual funds, stocks, stock options, U.S. Treasury notes
OFFICIAL AIRLINE GUIDES ELECTRONIC EDITION TRAVEL SERVICE	Worldwide commercial-airline schedules
STANDARD & POOR'S ONLINE	Financial profiles of thousands of companies
TRADELINE	Fifteen years of stock prices
WALL $TREET WEEK TRANSCRIPTS	Full text of "Wall $treet Week" transcripts

DATABASE	*CONTENT*
WORDS OF WALL STREET	Definitions of investment terms
ZACKS CORPORATE EARNINGS ESTIMATOR	Forecasts of company earnings-per-share data

Vendor: DRI/McGraw-Hill

Source of Information: *DRI Data Catalog*. New York: McGraw-Hill, 1989.

DATABASE	*CONTENT*
ASSOCIATION OF INTERNATIONAL BOND DEALERS	Eurobond yields and prices
AUTOMOTIVE NEWS	Data on the international automobile market
BUDGETRACK	Data on U.S. Department of Defense and National Aeronautics and Space Administration budgets
CANADIAN CONSTRUCTION	Canadian commercial and residential building data
CANSIM MINI BASE	Indicators of the Canadian economy
CBD PLUS	U.S. government contract awards and procurements, including data from *Commerce Business Daily*
COMPUSTAT	U.S. company financial statements
CONFERENCE BOARD	U.S. economic forecasts and historical economic data
DEFENSE-NET	Abstracts of articles on international defense issues
DODGE CONSTRUCTION ANALYSIS SYSTEM	U.S. construction-starts data
DODGE DRI BUILDING STOCK FORECAST	Square footage and other data on U.S. buildings
DODGE DRI CONSTRUCTION MARKET FORECAST	Forecasts of construction activity in the U.S.

DATABASE	*CONTENT*
DODGE DRI REAL ESTATE ANALYSIS AND PLANNING FORECAST	Forecasts of supply and demand for building space in various U.S. metropolitan areas
DRI AGRICULTURE	U.S. and international agricultural data
DRI AGRICULTURE FORECAST	Price and other U.S. agricultural statistical forecasts
DRI ASIAN FORECAST	Economic forecasts for Asian nations
DRI AUSTRALIA	Australian economic statistics
DRI BUSINESS FIXED INVESTMENT FORECAST	Forecasts for equipment and structures
DRI CANADIAN ENERGY FORECAST	Forecasts of supply and demand for energy in Canada
DRI CANADIAN PRIMARY SOURCE	Canadian economic statistics
DRI CANADIAN QUARTERLY MODEL FORECAST	Quarterly forecast data for the Canadian economy
DRI CANADIAN QUARTERLY MODEL HISTORY	Quarterly data on the state of the Canadian economy
DRI CANADIAN REGIONAL FORECAST	Economic forecast data for Canadian regions
DRI CFS COST AND INDUSTRY	U.S. industry price and wage indicators
DRI CHEMICAL	Data on the U.S. chemical industry
DRI CHEMICAL FORECAST	Forecast data for U.S. chemical products
DRI COAL FORECAST	Forecast data on the U.S. coal industry
DRI COMMODITIES	Price and contract data for commodities traded on major world markets
DRI CONSUMER MARKETS FORECAST	Forecasts of U.S. consumer income and spending
DRI COUNTY FORECAST	County demographic and economic forecasts

DATABASE	*CONTENT*
DRI CURRENT ECONOMIC INDICATORS	Economic indicators for about 35 nations
DRI DEFENSE ECONOMICS	Data on defense-industry costs and spending in U.S.
DRI DEVELOPING COUNTRIES	Economic data for about 20 developing nations
DRI ENERGY	Data on U.S. and worldwide energy consumption, exploration, inventories, prices, and sales
DRI ESTIMARKET SYSTEM	Forecast data for various U.S. industries
DRI EUROPE	Economic indicators for about 15 European nations
DRI EUROPEAN ENERGY FORECAST	Forecast data on European supply and demand for energy
DRI EUROPEAN FORECAST	Economic forecasts for European nations
DRI EUROPEAN OIL SPOT MARKET FORECAST	Forecast of European spot oil prices
DRI EUROPEAN SECTORAL	Economic data for France, Germany, Italy, and the U.K.
DRI EUROPEAN SECTORAL MODEL FORECAST	Forecasts of industrial activity in France, Germany, Italy, and the U.K.
DRI EUROPEAN TRUCK FORECAST	Forecasts of the truck market in Europe
DRI EXTERNAL DEBT	External debt data of developing nations
DRI FEDERAL CONTRACT ANNOUNCEMENTS	Text of U.S. federal government contract announcements
DRI FEDERAL CONTRACT AWARDS	For U.S. federal contracts awarded, details on awardee companies and their research and development
DRI FINANCIAL AND CREDIT STATISTICS	U.S. and international foreign-exchange money-market rates

<u>*DATABASE*</u>	<u>*CONTENT*</u>
DRI FINANCIAL MARKET INDICES	Major U.S. and international market indexes
DRI FREIGHT TRANSPORTATION FORECAST	Forecasts on rail and truck traffic patterns in the U.S.
DRI GDP BY INDUSTRY FORECAST	Gross product and compensation forecasts by U.S. industry
DRI GENERAL AVIATION FORECAST	Forecast data for the U.S. and international general-aviation industry
DRI HEALTH CARE COST FORECASTING	Operating-cost projections and other data for U.S. health-care facilities
DRI HOUSING FORECAST	Forecasts for existing and new home markets in the U.S.
DRI INTERNATIONAL AUTO	Data on the international automobile industry
DRI INTERNATIONAL COST FORECASTING	Forecasts of price and wage data for Brazil, Canada, France, Germany, Japan, South Korea, Taiwan, and the U.K.
DRI INTERNATIONAL ENERGY	Data on international consumption, exports, imports, and production of energy
DRI INTERNATIONAL PASSENGER CAR FORECAST	Forecasts of auto supply and demand in 29 nations
DRI INTERNATIONAL TRUCK	Data on the international truck industry
DRI ITIS DETAILED MONTHLY TRADE MONITOR	Export and import data, by commodity, between nine industrial nations and their trading partners
DRI ITIS TRADE SERIES C	Trade data on member nations of the Organization for Economic Cooperation and Development
DRI JAPANESE FORECAST	Economic forecasts for Japan's economy
DRI J. D. POWER LIGHT VEHICLE FORECAST	Forecasts for the U.S. light-truck industry

DATABASE	*CONTENT*
DRI J. D. POWER OEM AUTO SUPPLIER FORECAST	Forecasts for the North American automobile and light-truck industries
DRI LATIN AMERICAN FORECAST	Economic forecasts for Latin America
DRI LONG-TERM INDUSTRY FORECAST	Forecast data for U.S. industries
DRI METROPOLITAN AREA FORECAST	Demographic and economic forecasts for Metropolitan Statistical Areas
DRI METROPOLITAN AREA INDUSTRY FORECAST	Industrial forecasts for Metropolitan Statistical Areas
DRI MIDDLE EAST AND AFRICAN FORECAST	Economic forecasts for Middle Eastern and African nations
DRI NATURAL GAS FORECAST	Data on gas supply and demand in the U.S.
DRI NATURAL GAS PIPELINE	Data on U.S. gas-pipeline companies
DRI NATURAL GAS SPOT PRICES	U.S. spot-price quotes for natural gas
DRI NEWS SERVICE	News releases concerning U.S. economic indicators
DRI NORTH AMERICAN COMMERCIAL TRUCK FORECAST	Forecast of supply and demand for trucks
DRI NPDC CENSUS	U.S. census data
DRI NPDC COUNTY BUSINESS PATTERNS	U.S. employment statistics by county
DRI PLANT & EQUIPMENT EXPENDITURES FORECAST	Forecasts for plant and equipment spending by U.S. industries
DRI PLATT'S OIL PRICES	Worldwide spot and posted oil prices
DRI QUARTERLY INDUSTRY FORECAST	Quarterly industry forecasts, including U.S. exports, imports, prices, and shipments
DRI REGIONAL INDUSTRY FORECAST	U.S. regional and state industry employment and output forecasts

DATABASE	*CONTENT*
DRI REGIONAL MODEL FORECAST	U.S. regional and state economic forecasts
DRI REGIONAL MODEL HISTORY	Regional and state economic data
DRI STEEL	U.S. iron- and steel-production data
DRI STEEL FORECAST	Forecasts of steel consumption and production for the U.S.
DRI TBS WORLD SEA TRADE FORECAST	Worldwide forecasts of cargo movements
DRI TRANSPORTATION	Data on the U.S. and Canadian transportation industry
DRI TRANSPORTATION COST FORECASTING	Forecasts of costs for inland waterway, rail, and truck transportation in the U.S.
DRI TRANSPORTATION DETAIL	Inventory and use data for freight, motor-carrier, rail, and waterborne transportation industries
DRI U.S. ANNUAL MODEL FORECAST	Forecasts of U.S. economic conditions
DRI U.S. CENTRAL	U.S. demographic and economic data
DRI U.S. COST FORECASTING	Wage and price forecasts
DRI U.S. COUNTY	Demographic and economic data by U.S. county
DRI U.S. EQUITY AND DEBT SECURITIES	Daily prices for U.S. and Canadian stocks, bonds, and options
DRI U.S. LONG-TERM ENERGY FORECAST	Forecasts of U.S. long-term supply and demand for energy
DRI U.S. PRICES	Consumer Price and Producer Price Indexes
DRI U.S. QUARTERLY MODEL FORECAST	Quarterly forecasts of the state of the U.S. economy
DRI U.S. QUARTERLY MODEL HISTORY	Historical quarterly U.S. economic indicators

DATABASE	*CONTENT*
DRI U.S. REGIONAL	Regional demographic and economic data
DRI U.S. SHORT-TERM ENERGY FORECAST	Forecasts of U.S. short-term supply and demand for energy
DRI UTILITY COST FORECASTING	Economic forecasts for the electric and gas industries in the U.S.
DRI WORLD FORECAST	Forecast of economic and social data for about 50 nations
DRI WORLD OIL FORECAST	Worldwide forecasts of supply and demand for oil
DRI WORLD TRADE FORECAST	Forecasts of exports and imports for nations in the Organization for Economic Cooperation and Development
FINANCIAL POST INVESTMENT	Balance-sheet statistics for Canadian companies
FORECAST ASSOCIATES ON-LINE	Analysis of the aerospace and defense markets
HANDY-WHITMAN INDEX	Plant construction cost indexes for U.S. utility companies
I/B/E/S	Estimates of earnings for U.S. and Canadian companies, from the Institutional Brokers' Estimate System
IMF DIRECTION OF TRADE	International Monetary Fund values of exports and imports, by nation
IMF INTERNATIONAL FINANCIAL STATISTICS	International Monetary Fund's economic and monetary data for about 175 nations
MERRILL LYNCH BOND PRICING	Daily prices on U.S. and corporate bond prices
METALS WEEK	Price data for metals from U.S. and London exchanges
MORGAN STANLEY CAPITAL INTERNATIONAL INDICES	Worldwide data on stocks, by industry

DATABASE	*CONTENT*
NIKKEI CORPORATE FINANCIALS	Balance-sheet statistics for Japanese companies
NIKKEI MACRO ECONOMIC STATISTICS	Demographic and economic data on Japan's economy
OECD MAIN ECONOMIC INDICATORS	Economic indicators for the nations in the Organization for Economic Cooperation and Development
OECD NATIONAL ACCOUNTS	National income data for nations in the Organization for Economic Cooperation and Development
PLATT'S CHEMICAL PRICES	U.S. and international petrochemical prices
RANDOM LENGTHS	Prices for U.S. and Canadian wood products
RISI FOREST PRODUCTS	Data on the U.S., Canadian, and Japanese lumber industry
RISI PULP AND PAPER	Data on the international pulp-and-paper industry
SECURITIES INDUSTRY	Balance-sheet data for firms in the securities industry
STANDARD & POOR'S INDUSTRY FINANCIAL	Balance-sheet data and stock-price indexes, by U.S. industry
SUPERSITE	Current and projected demographics, including housing, income, and occupation data
TRINET COMPANY	Directory information about U.S. companies
TRINET ESTABLISHMENT	Directory information about U.S. companies and each of their locations

Vendor: Mead Data Central

Source of Information: *LEXIS NEXIS Library Contents and Alphabetical List.* Dayton, OH: Mead Data Central, 1988.

Because of the vast number of databases available through Mead Data Central (MDC), the listing below identifies only database "libraries." An MDC database library is a collection of databases in a particular category. Neither the listing of libraries nor their descriptions is exhaustive. Each library listed here contains full-text databases.

DATABASE LIBRARY	*CONTENT*
LEXIS Bureau of National Affairs, Inc., Library	*BNA International Trade Daily, BNA Tax Updates, Daily Labor Report, Daily Tax Report, Federal Contracts Report*
LEXIS Commerce Clearinghouse Library	*CCH State Tax Review, CCH State Tax Week, CCH Tax Day—Federal and State*
LEXIS Corporate Law Library	State case law affecting corporations
LEXIS Federal Banking Library	*BNA Banking Daily, Federal Reserve Bulletin*
LEXIS Federal Bankruptcy Library	Cases of bankruptcy courts
LEXIS Federal Labor Library	Federal-labor case law
LEXIS Federal Patent, Trademark & Copyright Library	Intellectual property decisions from Claims Court, Court of Appeals, Commissioner of Patent & Trademarks, and other sources
LEXIS Federal Securities Library	*SEC News Digest*, 10-Q and 10-K filings, SEC administrative decisions
LEXIS Federal Tax Library	Federal tax case law and regulations, IRS Code and publications, public tax laws and proposed statutes, state tax case law, tax treaties, Research Institute of America's *Federal Tax Coordinator 2d* and a collection of its *Tax Alert* newsletters
LEXIS Federal Trade Regulation Library	*Federal Trade Commission Reports, ABA Antitrust Law Journal*
LEXIS Financial Information Service Company Library	Company and industry research reports, SEC company filings
LEXIS General Federal Library	U.S. Supreme Court, Court of Appeals, Court of Claims, and District Court cases. *Code of Federal Regulations*. Rules of procedure of the U.S. Tax Court

<u>*DATABASE LIBRARY*</u>	<u>*CONTENT*</u>
LEXIS Insurance Law Library	State-insurance case law and attorney-general opinions
LEXIS International Trade Library	Customs Court cases and International Trade Commission decisions
LEXIS Public Utilities Law Library	State case and administrative law on utilities
LEXIS State Employment Law Library	State and federal employment case law
LEXIS State Tax Library	State case and administrative tax law
LEXIS States Library	Cases on all areas of law from individual states, including Courts of Appeal and Supreme Courts
NAARS Accounting Information Library	Annual reports of corporations
NEXIS Advertising and Public Relations Library	Magazines and other publications concerning advertising and public relations
NEXIS Government and Political News Library	*Banking Expansion Reporter, Issues in Bank Regulation*
NEXIS Information Bank Library	The *New York Times*, since June 1980
NEXIS LEXPAT United States Patent and Trademark Office Library	U.S. chemical, electrical, and mechanical patents since 1975
NEXIS Library—ASAP II Files	Magazines, including *Business America, Sales & Marketing Management*
NEXIS Library—Business Dateline	Local and regional business publications
NEXIS Library—Business Files	Business magazines, newspapers, and wire services
NEXIS Library—Finance Files	Magazines and other publications covering finance and investing
NEXIS Library—Magazine Files	Local and national magazines, including *ADWEEK, Business Week, Forbes, Fortune, Harvard Business Review, Nation's Business,* and many others

DATABASE LIBRARY	CONTENT
NEXIS Library—Newsletters Files	*BNA's Banking Report, FEDWATCH, Survey of Current Business*, and many others
NEXIS Library—Newspaper Files	*American Banker*, the *New York Times*, the *Washington Post*, and many local business newspapers
NEXIS Library—Trade/Technology Files	Magazines and other publications covering specific trades or technologies
NEXIS Library—Wires Files	News from the Associated Press, Reuter Business Report, and United Press International wires

Vendor: NewsNet

Source of Information: "News on NewsNet." *NewsNet Action Letter*. Bryn Mawr, PA: NewsNet, June 1988.

This is a small selection from NewsNet's collection of over 300 newsletters and other databases, almost all of which are related to business and industry. Each item in this listing is a full-text database.

DATABASE	CONTENT
AMERICAN BANKER FULL TEXT	The full text of articles from this newspaper
BANKING REGULATOR	Reports about federal regulations on the banking industry
BIOTECHNOLOGY INVESTMENT OPPORTUNITIES	Analysis of investment opportunities in new biomedical technologies
CCH TAX DAY: FEDERAL	News about federal tax developments
CCH TAX DAY: STATE	News about state tax developments
CD COMPUTING NEWS	New CD-ROM products and markets
CONSUMER CREDIT LETTER	Federal laws and other developments in consumer credit
CREDIT UNION REGULATOR	Federal regulations covering credit unions

DATABASE	*CONTENT*
DEFENSE DAILY	U.S. and international developments in defense policies
DEFENSE R & D UPDATE	Research and development in the defense industry
FEDERAL RESEARCH REPORT	Availability of federal funding for research
JIJI PRESS TICKER SERVICE	The full text of stories from this newswire
OUTLOOK ON AT&T	News and analysis of AT&T
OUTLOOK ON IBM	News and analysis of IBM
PACS & LOBBIES	Activities of political action committees and lobbyists
PR NEWSWIRE	The full text of stories from this newswire
PRIVATIZATION	Information on contracting government services to be performed by the private sector
REUTER NEWS REPORTS	The full text of stories from this newswire
SDI INTELLIGENCE REPORT	Strategic Defense Initiative research and development
SOLID WASTE REPORT	Laws, regulations, and news about the management of solid waste
SPACE BUSINESS NEWS	Commercial-space-industry news
TAX NOTES TODAY	Legislative and judicial developments and news concerning state and federal taxes
TOXIC MATERIALS	Regulations and other news for carriers of toxic materials
UPI BUSINESS & FINANCIAL WIRE	The full text of stories from this newswire

DATABASE	*CONTENT*
VIDEO MARKETING NEWSLETTER	Analysis of the home-video industry
XINHUA ENGLISH LANGUAGE NEWS SERVICE	The full text of stories from this newswire

Vendor: *Orbit Search Service*

Source of Information: *Databases at a Glance.* McLean, VA: Orbit Search Service, 1990.

DATABASE	*CONTENT*
ABI/INFORM	Index to articles on a wide variety of business topics
ACCOUNTANTS	Accounting information from the American Institute of Certified Public Accountants
APILIT	An index to articles on petroleum
APIPAT	An index to petroleum patents
AQUALINE	An index to articles on water: analysis, pollutants, quality, use
BIOTECHNOLOGY ABSTRACTS	Cites articles and other documents in biotechnology
CHEMICAL INDUSTRY NOTES	Information including facilities, pricing, and sales, in the chemical industry
CHINAPATS	Index to patent applications from the People's Republic of China
CLAIMS	Index to U.S. patents issued since 1950
COMPENDEX*PLUS	An index to engineering applications and research articles
DIRECTORY OF AMERICAN RESEARCH AND TECHNOLOGY	A listing of nongovernment industrial research and development centers

<u>DATABASE</u>	<u>CONTENT</u>
ELECTRIC POWER INDUSTRY ABSTRACTS	Indexes articles about electric power
FEDERAL REGISTER ABSTRACTS	An index to the federal regulations cited in the *Federal Register*
FOREST	Indexes the literature of the wood products industry
HEALTH AND SAFETY EXECUTIVE	An index to articles about occupational health and safety
ICONDA	Indexes articles on building construction
INPADOC/INPANEW	An index to patents issued by about 50 nations
INSPEC	An index to articles about computers, electronics, information technology, and physics
IPABASE	An index to articles about the petroleum industry
JAPIO	Indexes Japanese patents
LABORDOC	Cites documents dealing with industrial labor relations
LITALERT	Lists patent-infringement suits
NATIONAL INSTITUTE FOR OCCUPATIONAL SAFETY AND HEALTH	Indexes articles on occupational health and safety
NTIS	Cites in-progress and final reports of U.S. government–sponsored research
PETROLEUM/ENERGY BUSINESS NEWS	An index to petroleum-industry news
PNI	An index to pharmaceutical-industry news

DATABASE	*CONTENT*
RAPRA ABSTRACTS	An index to articles about the rubber and plastics industries
RAPRA TRADE NAMES	Trademarks and tradenames
SAFETY SCIENCE ABSTRACTS	An index to articles about industrial safety
STANDARDS SEARCH	Automotive-engineering standards
TULSA	An index to articles about natural-gas exploration
WORLD PATENTS INDEX	An index to patents of about 30 nations
WORLD SURFACE COATINGS ABSTRACTS	Indexes articles about the paint and surface-coatings industries

Directory of Publishers

Bob Adams, Inc.
260 Center Street
Holbrook, MA 02343
(617) 767-8100
(800) USA-JOBS

Addison-Wesley Publishing Co.
1 Jacob Way
Reading, MA 01867
(617) 944-3700
(800) 447-2226

ADP Brokerage Information
Services Group
East Park Drive
Mt. Laurel, NJ 08054
(609) 778-3493

American Institute of Small Business
Suite 201
7515 Wayzata Blvd.
Minneapolis, MN 55426
(612) 545-7001
(800) 328-2906

American Management Association
135 West 50th Street
New York, NY 10020
(212) 586-8100
(800) 262-6969

American Marketing Association,
New York Chapter, Inc.
310 Madison Avenue
New York, NY 10017
(212) 687-3280

Asher-Gallant Press
201 Montrose Road
Westbury, NY 11590
(516) 333-7440

AT&T
Toll-Free 800 Directories
Room 02-4M02
55 Corporate Place
Bridgewater, NJ 08807
(800) 426-8686, Ext. 222

Avon Books
105 Madison Avenue
New York, NY 10016
(212) 481-5600
(800) 654-5888

Barron's Educational Series, Inc.
250 Wireless Boulevard
Hauppauge, NY 11788
(516) 434-3311
(800) 645-3476
(800) 257-5729 (in New York)

Matthew Bender & Co.
11 Penn Plaza
New York, NY 10001
(212) 967-7707
(800) 821-2232

A. M. Best Company
Ambest Road
Oldwick, NJ 08858
(201) 439-2200

Basil Blackwell, Inc.
3 Cambridge Center
Cambridge, MA 02142
(617) 225-0430
(800) 638-3030

Clark Boardman Co.
Trade Activities Division
435 Hudson Street
New York, NY 10014
(212) 929-7500
(800) 221-9428

R. R. Bowker Co.
Order Dept.
P.O. Box 31
New Providence, NJ 07974
(800) 521-8110
(800) 537-8416 (in Canada)

Brodart Company
500 Arch Street
Williamsport, PA 17705
(717) 326-2461
(800) 233- 8467

Bureau of National Affairs, Inc.
1231 25th Street, NW
Washington, DC 20037
(202) 452-4200

Burwell Enterprises
Suite 214
3724 F.M. 1960 West
Houston, TX 77068
(713) 537-9051

Business Research Publications, Inc.
817 Broadway
New York, NY 10003
(212) 673- 4700
(800) 622-7237

Business Research Services, Inc.
Suite 202
2 East 22nd Street
Lombard, IL 60148
(708) 495-8787
(800) 325-8720

Buyers Laboratory, Inc.
20 Railroad Ave.
Hackensack, NJ 07601
(201) 488-0404

CACI, Inc.
3040 Williams Drive
Fairfax, VA 22031
(703) 698-4600
(800) 292-2224

Cambridge Information Group
   Directories, Inc.
7200 Wisconsin Avenue
Bethesda, MD 20814
(301) 961-6750
(800) 227-3052

Chamber of Commerce of the U.S.
1615 H Street, NW
Washington, DC 20062
(202) 659-6000
(800) 638-6582 (subscriptions)
(800) 352-1450 (subscriptions in MD)

College Placement Council, Inc.
62 Highland Avenue
Bethlehem, PA 18017
(215) 868-1421

Columbia Books, Inc.
Suite 207
1350 New York Avenue, NW
Washington, DC 20005
(202) 737-3777

Commerce Clearing House, Inc.
4025 West Peterson Avenue
Chicago, IL 60646
(312) 583-8500

Compu-Mark U.S.
Suite 400
7201 Wisconsin Avenue
Washington, DC 20814
(202) 737-7900
(800) 421-7881

Computer Directions Advisors Investment
   Technologies, Inc.
1355 Piccard Drive
Rockville, MD 20850
(301) 975-9600

Congressional Information Service, Inc.
4520 East-West Highway
Bethesda, MD 20814
(301) 654-1550
(800) 638-8380

Congressional Quarterly, Inc.
1414 22nd Street, NW
Washington, DC 20037
(202) 887-8500

Congressional Staff Directory, Ltd.
P. O. Box 62
Mt. Vernon, VA 22121
(703) 765-3400

Consultant News
Templeton Road
Fitzwilliam, NH 03447
(603) 585-2200
(603) 585-6544

Consumers Union of U.S., Inc.
256 Washington Street
Mt. Vernon, NY 10553
(914) 667-9400

Corporate Technology Information Services, Inc.
1 Market Street
P. O. Box 81281
Wellesley Hills, MA 02181
(617) 237-2001
(800) 843-8036

The Council of State Governments
Iron Works Pike
P. O. Box 11910
Lexington, KY 40578
(606) 252-2291

Croner Publications, Inc.
211-03 Jamaica Avenue
Queens Village, NY 11428
(718) 464-0866
(718) 465-6171

Cuadra-Elsevier
52 Vanderbilt Avenue
New York, NY 10017
(212) 370-5520

Dalton Communications, Inc.
1123 Broadway
New York, NY 10010
(212) 675-0531

Datapro Research Corporation
1805 Underwood Boulevard
Delran, NJ 08075
(609) 764-0100
(800) 328-2776

Marcel Dekker, Inc.
270 Madison Avenue
New York, NY 10016
(212) 696-9000
(800) 228-1160

Dial-A-Fax Directories Corp.
1761 West Hillsboro Boulevard
Deerfield Beach, FL 33442
(305) 421-2101
FAX (305) 421-2040

Dow Jones & Co., Inc.
200 Liberty Street
New York, NY 10281
(212) 416-2000

Dow Jones-Irwin, Inc.
SEE Richard D. Irwin, Inc.

Dun & Bradstreet Business Credit Services
Re: *Dun & Bradstreet Reference Book*
Dun's Core Business Services
1 Diamond Hill Road
Murray Hill, NJ 07974
(201) 665-5703

Dun & Bradstreet Business Credit Services
Re: *Industry Norms & Key Business Ratios*
Dun's Analytical Services
1 Diamond Hill Road
Murray Hill, NJ 07974
(201) 665-5224
(800) 223-0141

Dun's Marketing Services
3 Century Drive
Parisippany, NJ 07054
(201) 455-0900
(800) 526-0651

The Economist Newspaper Ltd.
25 St. James Street
London SW1A 1HG,
England
(800) 525-0643 (U.S. subscriptions)

Europa Publications Limited
[Distributed by] Unipub
4611-F Assembly Drive
Lanham, MD 20706
(301) 459-7666
(800) 274-4888

Facts On File Publications, Inc.
460 Park Avenue South
New York, NY 10016
(212) 683-2244
(800) 322-8755

Financial Accounting Standards Board
401 Merritt 7
P. O. Box 5116
Norwalk, CT 06856
(203) 847-0700

Financial Information, Inc.
398 West Camino Gardens Boulevard
Boca Raton, FL 33432
(407) 394-3404

Forbes, Inc.
60 Fifth Avenue
New York, NY 10011
(212) 620-2200

The Foundation Center
79 Fifth Avenue
New York, NY 10003
(212) 620-4230
(800) 424-9836

Free Press
Book Order Dept.
Front & Brown Streets
Riverside, NJ 08370
(609) 461-6500
(800) 257-5755

FT Publications, Inc.
14 East 60th Street
New York, NY 10022
(212) 752-4500

Gale Research Co., Inc.
Dept. 77748
Detroit, MI 48277
(313) 961-2242
(800) 347-4253

Garland Publishing Co.
136 Madison Avenue
New York, NY 10016
(212) 686-7492

Glencoe Publishing Co.
Front & Brown Streets
Riverside, NJ 08075
(609) 461-6500
(800) 257-5755

Gravity Publishing
6324 Heather Ridge
Oakland, CA 94611
(415) 339-3774

Greenwood Press, Inc.
88 Post Road West
P. O. Box 5007
Westport, CT 06881
(203) 226-3571

Harcourt Brace Jovanovich, Publishers
1250 Sixth Avenue
San Diego, CA 92101
(619) 699-6335
(800) 543-1918

Harper & Row, Publishers
10 East 53 Street
New York, NY 10022
(212) 207-7000
(800) 242-7737

Information Access Company
11 Davis Drive
Belmont, CA 94002
(800) 227-8431

Information Industry Association
Suite 800
555 New Jersey Avenue, NW
Washington, DC 20001
(202) 639-8262

Institute for Business Planning, Inc.
200 Old Tappan Road
Old Tappan, NJ 07675
(201) 767-5059

Institutional Investor, Inc.
488 Madison Avenue
New York, NY 10022
(212) 303-3300

International Currency Analysis, Inc.
7239 Avenue, N
Brooklyn, NY 11234
(718) 531-3685

International Monetary Fund
Publication Services
700 19th Street
Washington, DC 20431
(202) 623-7430

Investor's Daily, Inc.
1941 Armacost Avenue
Los Angeles, CA 90025
(213) 207-1832
(800) 831-2525

Richard D. Irwin, Inc.
1818 Ridge Road
Homewood, IL 60430
(708) 798-6000
(800) 323-4560

Journal of Commerce
110 Wall Street
New York, NY 10005
(212) 425-1616

Libraries Unlimited, Inc.
P. O. Box 3988
Englewood, CO 80155
(303) 770-1220
(800) 237-6124

Macmillan Publishing Co.
Book Order Dept.
Front & Brown Streets
Riverside, NJ 08370
(609) 461-6500

Manufacturers' Agents National Association
23016 Mill Creek Rd.
Laguna Hills, CA 92654
(714) 859-4040

Marquis Who's Who
Macmillan Directory Division
3002 Glenview Road
Wilmette, IL 60091
(708) 441-2387
(800) 621-9669

McGraw-Hill Co., Inc.
1221 Avenue of the Americas
New York, NY 10020
(212) 512-2000

Minerva Books
137 West 14th Street
New York, NY 10011
(212) 929-2833
(800) 345-5946

MLR Publishing Co.
229 South 18th Street
Philadelphia, PA 19103
(215) 875-2330

Moody's Investors Service
99 Church Street
New York, NY 10007
(212) 553-0300

Robert Morris Associates
Order Dept.
P. O. Box 8500, S-1140
Philadelphia, PA 19178
(215) 665-2850

National Ad Search, Inc.
P. O. Box 2028
Milwaukee, WI 53201
(414) 351-1398

National Register Publishing Co.
3004 Glenview Road
Wilmette, IL 60091
(708) 256-6067
(800) 323-6772

National Standards Association
Suite 601
7200 Wisconsin Avenue
Bethesda, MD 20814
(301) 961-6700
(800) 227-3052

National Technical Information Service
U.S. Department of Commerce
5285 Port Royal Road
Springfield, VA 22161
(703) 487-4600

National Textbook Company
4255 West Touhy Avenue
Lincolnwood, IL 60646
(708) 679-5500
(800) 323-4900

Newspaper Enterprise Association
(Pharos Books)
200 Park Avenue
New York, NY 10166
(212) 692-3700

New York Times, Inc.
229 West 43rd Street
New York, NY 10036
(212) 556-1234
(800) 631-2500

Nolo Press
950 Parker Street
Berkeley, CA 94710
(415) 549-1976
(800) 992-6656
(800) 445-6656 (in CA)

North American Publishing Co.
401 North Broad Street
Philadelphia, PA 19108
(215) 238-5300

Oceana Publications, Inc.
75 Main Street
Dobbs Ferry, NY 10522
(914) 693-1733

Oryx Press
4041 North Central Avenue, Suite 700
Phoenix, AZ 85012
(602) 265-2651
(800) 279-6790

Oxbridge Communications, Inc.
Suite 301
150 Fifth Avenue
New York, NY 10011
(212) 741-0231

Performance Dynamics, Inc.
(defunct)

Peterson's Guides, Inc.
P. O. Box 2123
Princeton, NJ 08543
(609) 243-9111
(800) 338-3282

The Pierian Press
P. O. Box 1808
Ann Arbor, MI 48106
(313) 434-5530
(800) 678-2435

Predicasts, Inc.
11001 Cedar Avenue
Cleveland, OH 44106
(216) 795-3000 (in Ohio)
(800) 321-6388

Prentice-Hall, Inc.
  East of the Mississippi River
    Order Dept.
    200 Old Tappan Road
    Old Tappan, NJ 07675
    (800) 223-1360
  West of the Mississippi River
    Order Dept.
    4700 South 5400 West
    Salt Lake City, UT 84118
    (800) 225-7162

Prentice-Hall Information Services
240 Frisch Court
Paramus, NJ 07652
(800) 562-0245
(800) 872-6386

Probus Publishing Co.
Suite 305
118 North Clinton
Chicago, IL 60606
(312) 346-7985
(800) 426-1520

Public Affairs Information Service, Inc.
521 West 43rd Street
New York, NY 10036
(212) 736-4161
(800) 288-7247

Quorum Books
Greenwood Press, Inc.
88 Post Road West
Westport, CT 06881
(203) 226-3571

Rand McNally & Co.
P. O. Box 7600
Chicago, Il 60680
(312) 673-9100
(800) 323-4070

Research Institute of America
90 Fifth Avenue
New York, NY 10011
(212) 645-4800
(800) 431-9025

St. James Press, Inc.
233 East Ontario
Chicago, IL 60611
(312) 787-5800
(800) 345-0392

St. Martin's Press, Inc.
175 Fifth Avenue
New York, NY 10010
(212) 674-5151
(800) 221-7945

Sales & Marketing Management Magazine
Bill Communications, Inc.
633 Third Avenue
New York, NY 10017
(212) 986-4800

Howard W. Sams & Co., Inc.
4300 West 62nd Street
Indianapolis, IN 46268
(317) 298-5400
(800) 428-7267

Scarecrow Press, Inc.
52 Liberty Street
P. O. Box 4167
Metuchen, NJ 08840
(201) 548-8600
(800) 537-7107

Simon & Schuster, Inc.
1230 Avenue of the Americas
New York, NY 10020
(212) 698-7000
(800) 223-2336

South-Western Publishing Co.
5101 Madison Road
Cincinnati, OH 45227
(513) 271-8811
(800) 543-0487

Stamats Communications, Inc.
427 Sixth Avenue, SE
Cedar Rapids, IA 52406
(319) 364-6032
(800) 553-8878

Standard & Poor's Corporation
25 Broadway
New York, NY 10004
(212) 208-8000

Standard Rate and Data Service, Inc.
3004 Glenview Road
Wilmette, IL 60091
(708) 256-6067
(800) 323-4601

The Stockton Press
15 East 26th Street
New York, NY 10010
(212) 481-1332
(800) 221-2123

TAB Books, Inc.
P. O. Box 40
Blue Ridge Summit, PA 17214
(717) 794-2191
(800) 233-1128

Ten Speed Press
P. O. Box 7123
Berkeley, CA 94707
(415) 845-8414
(800) 841-2665

Thomas International Publishing Co.
One Penn Plaza
250 West 34th Street
New York, NY 10119
(212) 290-7343

Thomas Publishing Co.
One Penn Plaza
New York, NY 10001
(212) 695-0500

Time, Inc.
Time & Life Building
1271 Avenue of the Americas
New York, NY 10020
(212) 586-1212

The Trademark Register
Suite 1297
National Press Building
Washington, DC 20045
(202) 662-1233
(800) 888-8062

Unique Publishing Co.
Suite D
1825 Clinton Avenue
Alameda, CA 94501
(415) 865-1987

United Nations
Publishing Division
Room DC2-0853
New York, NY 10017
(212) 963-1234

University of California Press
2120 Berkeley Way
Berkeley, CA 94720
(415) 642-4361
(800) 822-6657

U.S. Government Printing Office
Superintendent of Documents
Washington, DC 20402
(202) 783-3238

U.S. Office of Consumer Affairs
Consumer Information Center
Pueblo, CO 81009
(719) 948-3334

Value Line, Inc.
711 Third Avenue
New York, NY 10017
(212) 687-3965

Van Nostrand Reinhold Co.
7625 Empire Drive
Florence, KY 41042
(606) 525-6600

Venture Economics, Inc.
Suite 700
75 2nd Avenue
Needham, MA 02194
(617) 449-2100

Vickers Stock Research Corp.
226 New York Avenue
Huntington, NY 11743
(516) 423-7710
(800) 645-5043

Walker and Company
720 Fifth Avenue
New York, NY 10019
(212) 265-3632
(800) 289-25537

Wall Street Transcript Corporation
99 Wall Street
New York, NY 10005
(212) 747-9500

Warner Books, Inc.
Book Distribution Service
666 Fifth Avenue
New York, NY 10103
(212) 484-2900
(800) 726-0600

Warren, Gorham & Lamont, Inc.
210 South Street
Boston, MA 02111
(800) 922-0066 (central number)
(800) 950-1217 (order dept.)

Washington Researchers Publishing
2612 P Street, NW
Washington, DC 20007
(202) 333-3533

West Publishing Company
50 West Kellogg Blvd.
P. O. Box 64833
St. Paul, MN 55164
(612) 228-2973
(800) 328-2209

What to Buy, Inc.
350 Theodore Fremd Avenue
Rye, NY 10580
(914) 921-0085
(800) 247-2185

John Wiley & Sons, Inc.
605 Third Avenue
New York, NY 10158
(212) 850-6418

W. H. Wilson Co.
950 University Avenue
Bronx, NY 10452
(212) 588-8400
(800) 367-6770

Ziff-Davis Publishing Co.
20 Brace Road
Cherry Hills, NJ 08034
(609) 795-7012
(800) 932-0017

III

Directory of Online Database Publishers and Vendors

After Dark/BRS Information Technologies
Maxwell Online
8000 Westpark Drive
McLean, VA 22102
(800) 289-4277

A. M. Best
Ambest Road
Oldwick, NJ 08858
(201) 439-2200

American Banker
1 State Street Plaza
New York, NY 10004
(800) 356-4763

American Economic Association
P. O. Box 7320, Oakland Station
Pittsburgh, PA 15213
(412) 268-3869

American Psychological Association
1200 17th Street, NW
Washington, DC 20036
(800) 336-4980

Arthur D. Little
25 Acorn Park
Cambridge, MA 02140
(617) 864-5770

Associated Press
50 Rockefeller Plaza
New York, NY 10020
(212) 621-1585

Bank Marketing Association
309 West Washington Street
Chicago, IL 60606
(312) 782-1442

BIOSIS
2100 Arch Street
Philadelphia, PA 19103
(800) 523-4806

BRS Search Service/BRS Information
Technologies
Maxwell Online
8000 Westpark Drive
McLean, VA 22102
(800) 289-4277

Bureau of National Affairs
1231 25th Street, NW
Washington, DC 20037
(202) 452-4200

Business Wire
1185 Avenue of the Americas, 3rd Floor
New York, NY 10036
(800) 221-2462

CAB International
Wallingford, Oxon OX10 8DE
United Kingdom
(0491) 32111

CACI
3040 Williams Drive
Fairfax, VA 22031
(800) 292-2224

Cambridge Information Group Directories, Inc.
7200 Wisconsin Avenue
Bethesda, MD 20814
(800) 638-8094

Career Placement Registry
302 Swann Avenue
Alexandria, VA 22301
(703) 683-1085

Charles E. Simon
Suite 500
1333 H Street, NW
Washington, DC 20005
(202) 289-5300

Chicago Tribune
435 North Michigan Avenue
Chicago, IL 60611
(312) 222-3232

Commerce Clearing House
4025 West Peterson Avenue
Chicago, IL 60646
(312) 583-8500

CompuServe
P. O. Box 20212
Columbus, OH 43220
(800) 848-8199

Comtex Scientific
P. O. Box 4838
911 Hope Street
Stamford, CT 06907
(203) 358-0007

Congressional Information Service
Suite 800
4520 East-West Highway
Bethesda, MD 20814
(800) 638-8380

Consumers Union of U.S., Inc.
256 Washington Street
Mount Vernon, NY 10553
(914) 667-9400

Corporate Agents
P. O. Box 1281
1013 Centre Road
Wilmington, DE 19899
(800) 441-4303

Data-Star
Suite 110
485 Devon Park Drive
Wayne, PA 19087
(800) 221-7754

Derwent Publications
6845 Elm Street
McLean, VA 22101
(703) 790-0400

Dialog/Dialog Information Services
3460 Hillview Avenue
Palo Alto, CA 94304
(800) 334-2564

Disclosure
5161 River Road
Bethesda, MD 20816
(301) 951-1300

Donnelley Marketing Information Services
P. O. Box 10250
70 Seaview Avenue
Stamford, CT 06904
(203) 353-7474

Dow Jones News/Retrieval
P. O. Box 300
Princeton, NJ 08543
(609) 452-1511

DRI/McGraw-Hill
24 Hartwell Avenue
Lexington, MA 02173
(617) 863-5100

Dun's Marketing Service
3 Sylvan Way
Parsippany, NJ 07054
(800) 223-1026

Engineering Information
345 East 47th Street
New York, NY 10017
(800) 221-1044

FAIRBASE Database
P. O. Box 91 04 46
D-3000 Hannover
West Germany
+49(511) 44330

Financial Times Business Information
126 Jermyn Street
2nd Floor
London SW1Y 4UJ
England
01-825-2323

Gale Research
835 Penobscot Building
Detroit, MI 48226
(800) 347-4253

H & R Block
c/o CompuServe
P. O. Box 20212
Columbus, OH 43220
(800) 848-8199

H. W. Wilson
950 University Avenue
Bronx, NY 10452
(800) 367-6770

Harvard Business Review
c/o John Wiley & Sons, Inc.
605 Third Avenue
New York, NY 10158
(212) 850-6331

IFI/Plenum Data
302 Swann Avenue
Alexandria, VA 22301
(800) 368-3093

Independent Insurance Agents of America
127 South Peyton Street
Alexandria, VA 22314
(800) 221-7917

Infomat
c/o Predicasts
11001 Cedar Avenue
Cleveland, OH 44106
(800) 321-6388

Information Access
362 Lakeside Drive
Foster City, CA 94404
(800) 227-8431

Information Sources
1173 Colusa Avenue
Berkeley, CA 94707
(415) 525-6220

Institution of Electrical Engineers
IEEE Service Center
P. O. Box 1331
445 Hoes Lane
Piscataway, NJ 08855
(201) 562-5549

Interactive Data Services
22 Cortlandt Street
New York, NY 10007
(212) 306-6500

International Patent Documentation Center
Moellwaldplatz 4
Vienna
Austria
0222-658784

Invest/Net
99 NW 183rd Street
North Miami, FL 33169
(305) 652-1721

JA Micropublishing
Box 218
271 Main Street
Eastchester, NY 10707
(800) 227-2477

Jane's Information Group
P. O. Box 1436
Suite 300
1340 Braddock Place
Alexandria, VA 22313
(800) 544-3678

Knowledge Index/Dialog Information Services
3460 Hillview Avenue
Palo Alto, CA 94304
(800) 334-2564

Lynch, Jones & Ryan
345 Hudson Street
New York, NY 10014
(212) 243-3137

Market Statistics
633 Third Avenue
New York, NY 10017
(212) 986-4800

McGraw-Hill Publications Online
1221 Avenue of the Americas
48th Floor
New York, NY 10020
(212) 512-2911

Mead Data Central
P. O. Box 933
Dayton, OH 45401
(800) 227-4908

Media General Financial Services
301 Grace Street
Richmond, VA 23219
(804) 649-6587

MJK Commodity Data Services
Suite 11
122 Saratoga Avenue
Santa Clara, CA 95051
(408) 247-5102

MMS International
30 Broad Street
New York, NY 10004
(800) 227-7304

Moody's Investors Service
99 Church Street
New York, NY 10007
(800) 342-5647

National Register Publishing
3004 Glenview Road
Wilmette, IL 60091
(800) 323-6772

National Standards Association
1200 Quince Orchard Boulevard
Gaithersburg, MD 20878
(800) 638-8094 (not in Maryland)
(301) 590-2300 (in Maryland)

News-a-tron
1 Peabody Street
Salem, MA 01970
(617) 744-4744

NewsNet
945 Haverford Road
Bryn Mawr, PA 19010
(800) 345-1301

NILS Publishing
21625 Prairie Street
Chatsworth, CA 91311
(818) 998-8830

No-Load Mutual Fund Association
Suite 2204
11 Penn Plaza
New York, NY 10001
(212) 563-4540

Official Airline Guides
2000 Clearwater Drive
Oak Brook, IL 60521
(800) 323-4000

Orbit Search Service
8000 Westpark Drive
McLean, VA 22102
(800) 456-7248

Pioneer Hi-Bred International
400 Locust Street
Des Moines, IA 50309
(515) 245-3500

Predicasts
11001 Cedar Avenue
Cleveland, OH 44106
(800) 321-6388

PR Newswire
150 East 58th Street
31st Floor
New York, NY 10155
(800) 832-5522

Research Institute of America
90 Fifth Avenue
New York, NY 10011
(800) 431-9025

Standard & Poor's/Electronic Services
25 Broadway
New York, NY 10004
(212) 208-8622

Tax Analysts
6830 North Fairfax Drive
Arlington, VA 22213
(800) 336-0439

Technical Data International
11 Farnsworth Street
Boston, MA 02210
(800) 662-7878

Thomas Online
1 Penn Plaza
New York, NY 10119
(212) 290-7291

Thomson & Thomson
500 Victory Road
North Quincy, MA 02171
(617) 479-1600

Trade*Plus
480 South California Avenue
Palo Alto, CA 94306
(415) 324-4554

Trinet
9 Campus Drive
Parsippany, NJ 07054
(800) 874-6381

U.S. Department of Agriculture
National Agricultural Library
Information Systems Division
Beltsville, MD 20705
(301) 344-4248

U.S. Department of Commerce
Fourteenth Street and Constitution Avenue, NW
Washington, DC 20230
(202) 377-2000

U.S. Department of Commerce
Bureau of the Census
Fourteenth Street and Constitution Avenue, NW
Washington, DC 20230
(202) 377-2000

U.S. Department of Commerce
National Technical Information Service
5285 Port Royal Road
Springfield, VA 22161
(703) 487-4600

U.S. Department of Commerce
Office of Patents and Trademarks
2021 Jefferson Davis Highway
Arlington, VA 20231
(703) 557-3341

UMI/Data Courier
620 South Third Street
Louisville, KY 40202
(800) 626-2823

United Press International
220 East 42nd Street
New York, NY 10017
(212) 850-8600

University Microfilms International
300 North Zeeb Road
Ann Arbor, MI 48106
(800) 521-3044

Value Line, Inc.
711 Third Avenue
New York, NY 10017
(800) 634-3583

WEFA Group
150 Monument Road
Bala Cynwyd, PA 19004
(800) 322-9332

Wilsonline/H. W. Wilson
950 University Avenue
Bronx, NY 10452
(800) 367-6770

INDEX

Numbers following the entries refer to page numbers, not to item numbers in the sections.